SRA

REAL SCIENCE

William C. Kyle, Jr.   **Joseph H. Rubinstein**   **Carolyn J. Vega**

A Division of The McGraw·Hill Companies

Columbus, Ohio

Authors

William C. Kyle, Jr.
E. Desmond Lee Family
   Professor of Science Education
University of Missouri – St. Louis
St. Louis, Missouri

Joseph H. Rubinstein
Professor of Education
Coker College
Hartsville, South Carolina

Carolyn J. Vega
Classroom Teacher
Nye Elementary
San Diego Unified School District
San Diego, California

PHOTO CREDITS
Cover Photo: © Dave Schiefelbein/Tony Stone Images

SRA/McGraw-Hill

A Division of The **McGraw·Hill** *Companies*

Send all inquiries to:
SRA/McGraw-Hill
8787 Orion Place
Columbus OH 43240-4027

Printed in the United States of America.

ISBN 0-02-683807-9

   5 6 7 8 9 RRW 05 04 03

Content Consultants

Reviewers

UNIT A

Life Science

Earth Science

UNIT
C

Physical Science

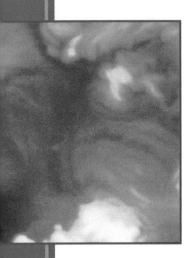
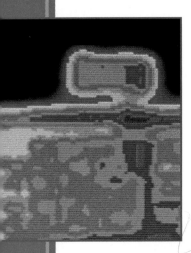

UNIT D

Health Science

Science Process Skills

Understanding and using scientific process skills is a very important part of learning in science. Successful scientists use these skills in their work. These skills help them with research and discovering new things.

Using these skills will help you to discover more about the world around you. You will have many opportunities to use these skills as you do each activity in the book. As you read, think about how you already use some of these skills every day. Did you have any idea that you were such a scientist?

OBSERVING

Use any of the five senses (seeing, hearing, tasting, smelling, or touching) to learn about objects or events that happen around you.

> **Looking** at objects with the help of a microscope is one way to observe.

COMMUNICATING

Express thoughts, ideas, and information to others. Several methods of communication are used in science—speaking, writing, drawing graphs or charts, making models or diagrams, using numbers, and even body language.

> **Making a graph** to show the rate of growth of a plant over time is communicating.

CLASSIFYING

Organize or sort objects, events, and things that happen around you into categories or groups. The classified objects should all be alike in some way.

> **Sorting** students in the room into groups according to hair color is classifying.

USING NUMBERS

Use math skills to help understand and study the world around you. These skills include ordering, counting, adding, subtracting, multiplying, and dividing.

> **Comparing** the temperatures of different locations around your home is using numbers.

MEASURING

Use standard measures of time, distance, length, area, mass, volume, and temperature to compare objects or events. Measuring also includes estimating and using standard measurement tools to find reasonable answers.

> **Using a meterstick** to find out how far you can jump is measuring.

CONSTRUCTING MODELS

Draw pictures or build models to help tell about thoughts or ideas or to show how things happen.

> **Drawing** the various undersea formations on the ocean floor is constructing a model.

INFERRING

Use observations and what you already know to reach a conclusion about why something happened. Inferring is an attempt to explain a set of observations. Inferring is not the same as guessing because you must observe something before you can make an inference.

> Imagine you put a lettuce leaf in your pet turtle's aquarium. If the lettuce is gone the next day, then you can **infer** that the turtle ate the lettuce.

PREDICTING

Use earlier observations and inferences to forecast the outcome of an event or experiment. A prediction is something that you expect to happen in the future.

Stating how long it will take for an ice cube to melt if it is placed in sunlight is **predicting.**

INTERPRETING DATA

Identify patterns or explain the meaning of information that has been collected from observations or experiments. Interpreting data is an important step in drawing conclusions.

You interpret data when you **study** daily weather tables and **conclude** that cities along the coast receive more rainfall than cities in the desert.

IDENTIFYING AND CONTROLLING VARIABLES

Identify anything that may change the results of an experiment. Change one variable to see how it affects what you are studying. Controlling variables is an important skill in designing investigations.

You can **control** the amount of light plant leaves receive. Covering some of the leaves on a plant with foil allows you to compare how plant leaves react to light.

HYPOTHESIZING

Make a statement that gives a possible explanation of how or why something happens. A hypothesis helps a scientist design an investigation. A hypothesis also helps a scientist identify what data to collect.

Saying that bean seeds germinate faster in warm areas than cold areas is a hypothesis. You can **test** this hypothesis by germinating bean seeds at room temperature and in the refrigerator.

DEFINING OPERATIONALLY

An operational definition tells what is observed and how it functions.

Saying the skull is a bone that surrounds the brain and is connected to the backbone is an operational definition.

DESIGNING INVESTIGATIONS

Plan investigations to gather data that will support or not support a hypothesis. The design of the investigation determines which variable will be changed, how it will be changed, and the conditions under which the investigation will be carried out

You can **design an investigation** to determine how sunlight affects plants. Place one plant in the sunlight and an identical plant in a closet. This will allow you to control the variable of sunlight.

EXPERIMENTING

Carry out the investigation you designed to get information about relationships between objects, events, and things around you.

Experimenting pulls together all of the other process skills.

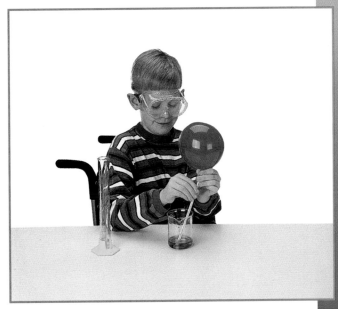

UNIT A

Life Science

Classification

We like to know how to organize things. When you visit a music store, you look for the section with your type of music in it. Then, you look for your favorite artist or group. In the library, you know what sections have the types of books you like to read. In these places, similar items are grouped together, or classified.

We can classify living things too. In fact, for over 2000 years, scientists and philosophers have attempted to organize groups of living things. One early system grouped all living things as plants or animals. Over the years, scientists have discovered that there are other living things and that more categories are needed.

Hundreds of groups of living things are classified every year. Some of these living things have only one cell! Many are found deep in the ocean. Others cannot be seen without a microscope. How organisms look and what they do in an environment are just some of the ways scientists classify new living things.

The Big IDEA

There is more than one system of classification of living things.

CHAPTER SCIENCE INVESTIGATION

Classify living things. Find out how in your *Activity Journal.*

Kingdoms of Life

Find Out

- How to classify things
- What monera, protista, and fungi are

Vocabulary

genus
species
kingdom
phylum (*pl.* **phyla**)
monera
protista
fungi

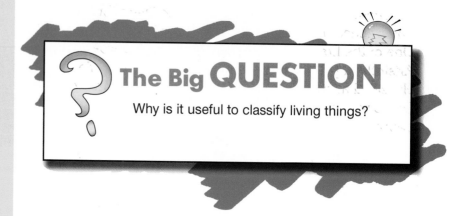

The Big QUESTION

Why is it useful to classify living things?

*I*f you found a living thing, would you know what to call it? How would you tell other people about it? There are many millions of living things on Earth. How would you keep track of all living things?

Ways to Classify Living Things

There is an amazing diversity of life on Earth. Keeping track of things is easier if we group them. There are many ways to group living things. We could group living things by where they live; we could label all organisms as water, air, or land organisms. We might group living things by what they eat; we could label all organisms as food producers or food consumers. We might also classify living things by their features and characteristics.

Field guides and keys often group living things by how they look. If we found a living thing, such as a flowering plant, we could use a field guide or a key to identify it. A field guide is a book with descriptions of commonly found organisms. It usually has illustrations or photographs of them. Some field guides have maps showing where to find different varieties of similar organisms. Field guides also list common and scientific names for organisms.

Keys are another way to tell one organism from another. Keys list questions about common features and characteristics usually found in a group of organisms. The questions help the user tell one organism from another. Field guides and keys are good for identifying common things, such as flowers, birds, and seashells.

There are many ways of classifying living things. The science of classifying living things is taxonomy. One of the first people to practice taxonomy was Aristotle, a philosopher in ancient Greece. Aristotle classified all living things as either plants or animals. Plants were trees, shrubs, or herbs. Animals were flyers, swimmers, or walkers. Do you think birds, bees, and butterflies belong in the same group? Aristotle did.

Eventually, Aristotle's system of classification was outdated. His system considered only an organism's form. Form is what the organism looks like. We now know that organisms have internal structures that perform different functions. Form and function are often used to place organism groups in a classification system.

Carolus Linnaeus, a Swedish scientist, created a naming system called binomial nomenclature (nō′ mən klā chur) that classifies organisms with a two-part scientific name. This system is still in use today. The first name, the **genus,** indicates a general category to which an organism belongs. The second name, the **species,** describes the specific group to which the organism is related.

When scientists talk about living things, they use the scientific names. Each organism has only one scientific name. That helps everyone understand exactly which living thing is being discussed. For example, a tomato is called by many different names in different languages, but it has only one scientific name.

One taxonomy system is the five-kingdom classification system. In it, all living things are assigned to one of five groups, called kingdoms. A **kingdom** is the most general category. The species is the most specific category.

Taxonomy systems and names can change. Sometimes new organisms are discovered. Other times names change when organisms are reclassified as a result of discovering new information about them.

North American bluejay

Honeybee

Skeleton butterfly

Look at the illustration on this page. All of the organisms listed on the top line are animals. They all belong to Kingdom Animalia. The second line illustrates a subset of the kingdom, the **phylum.** Animals with backbones belong to the phylum Chordata. Because the leaf beetle does not have a backbone, it is left out. In the next subset, there are only mammals. Mammals belong in the class Mammalia. Because the sunfish is not a mammal, it is left out. The next subset is the order. Animals that eat only meat belong to the order Carnivora. Because humans eat plants and meat, they are left out.

Now, look at the line with three bears. This is the family subset. Ursidae is the family name for bear. The next subset shows that not all bears belong to the same genus. Brown and polar bears belong to the genus *Ursus.* The spectacled bear is a member of the genus *Tremarctos.* Because it is a different genus, the spectacled bear is left out.

Finally, we see one animal on the species line. The polar bear has a different habitat from the brown bear. Because the polar bear is a different species, it is left out. The complete scientific name of the brown bear is made up of its genus and species names, *Ursus arctos.*

The five-kingdom classification system separates plants, animals, fungi, protista, and monera. Plants are the subject of Lesson 2. Animals are the subject of Lesson 3. First, let's find out more about the other three kingdoms.

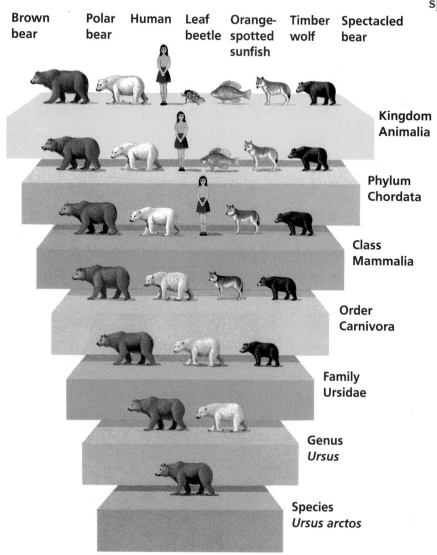

Brown bear   Polar bear   Human   Leaf beetle   Orange-spotted sunfish   Timber wolf   Spectacled bear

Kingdom Animalia

Phylum Chordata

Class Mammalia

Order Carnivora

Family Ursidae

Genus *Ursus*

Species *Ursus arctos*

Organisms That Are Neither Plants nor Animals

Early scientists thought of living things as only plants or animals. We know that there are millions of organisms that don't fit into either of these categories. What about bacteria and plankton and mushrooms? How would you categorize them? These organisms are neither plants nor animals. They belong respectively to the monera, protista, and fungi kingdoms.

Kingdom Monera

Monera are blue-green algae and bacteria. They are the only organisms made of cells that have no nucleus and no organelles. Even without these cell structures, monera carry out the same basic life processes as other cells and organisms. They reproduce, grow, and break down food to provide energy in the process of respiration.

Cyanophytes (sī an′ ō fīts) are blue-green algae. Blue-green algae are water organisms. Most live in the ocean. Some grow in freshwater ponds. Like plants, blue-green algae make their own food through photosynthesis. In some older classification systems, cyanophytes were classified in a phylum in the plant kingdom. However, because blue-green algae cells have no nuclei or other cell structures, they are usually classified as monera.

Bacteria live everywhere. They live in milk, in the air we breathe, and on all surfaces, including our skin. Bacteria can survive in all kinds of places. Many bacteria grow very well at temperatures close to that of the human body, 37 °C. Some types of bacteria can live at temperatures below 0 °C. Others can survive temperatures near 100 °C. Most bacteria need oxygen. Some can live without oxygen. In fact, some bacteria die in the presence of oxygen.

Most bacteria are decomposers. They get their energy by breaking down, or decomposing, dead materials. These bacteria return minerals and other nutrients to the soil where they are available to other organisms.

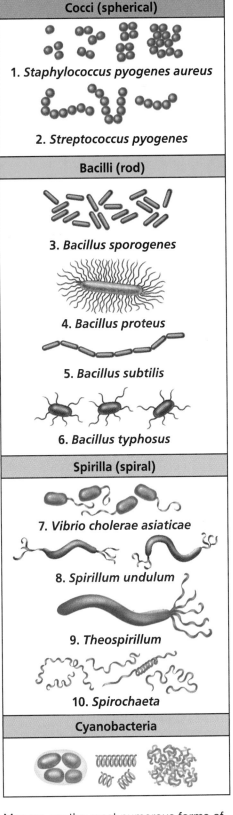

Cocci (spherical)

1. *Staphylococcus pyogenes aureus*

2. *Streptococcus pyogenes*

Bacilli (rod)

3. *Bacillus sporogenes*

4. *Bacillus proteus*

5. *Bacillus subtilis*

6. *Bacillus typhosus*

Spirilla (spiral)

7. *Vibrio cholerae asiaticae*

8. *Spirillum undulum*

9. *Theospirillum*

10. *Spirochaeta*

Cyanobacteria

Monera are the most numerous forms of life on Earth.

Kingdom Protista

Like bacteria, **protista** are single-celled organisms. However, protista have nuclei and other structures, called organelles, in their cytoplasm. For this reason, protista are in their own kingdom. There are 15 different phyla of protista. Some protista make food by photosynthesis. Other protista consume living or dead organisms for food. Protista grow and reproduce in moist environments all over Earth.

Plantlike Protista

In addition to nuclei and organelles, some protista have characteristics similar to plants. These are plantlike protista. All plantlike protista have chlorophyll, as plants do. In fact, plantlike protista provide most of Earth's supply of oxygen.

Plantlike protista are different from plants too. Some plantlike protista, such as euglena and dinoflagellates, have structures that enable them to move. Colorful, immovable shells surround others, such as diatoms. You probably use the shells of diatoms every day. When diatoms die, their hard, glasslike shells remain and form a rough, powdery substance. This substance is often an ingredient in toothpaste.

Plantlike protista are also an important part of plankton, or microscopic organisms that live in oceans and lakes. Plankton is an important source of food for whales and other water animals.

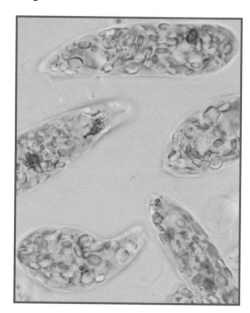

Euglena

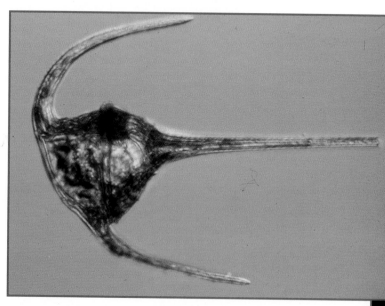

Dinoflagellate

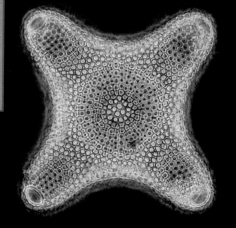

Diatom

Animal-like Protista

Protozoa (prō′ tō zō′ ə) are protista with characteristics similar to animals. Ciliates, flagellates, amoebas, slime molds, and sporozoa are all different protozoa. Protozoa consume plant or animal tissues for food. Scientists once classified protozoa as part of the animal kingdom. Their name, *protozoa,* means "first animals." Scientists classify protozoa by how they move.

Some protozoa have hairlike structures called cilia, sticking out of their cells. The rapid beating of these structures moves the organisms. They also sweep floating food particles into the organisms. Paramecia are good examples of these protozoa. Their beating cilia often look like whirling oars. Paramecia are frequently found in freshwater ponds.

Other animal-like protista move by forming "false feet," or pseudopods. Slime molds and amoebas move themselves over a surface by extending a pseudopod and then pulling the rest of the cell after it. Slime molds are moist, flat blobs that seem to ooze over dead trees and plants. Food is consumed when the pseudopod surrounds the bacteria, fungi, or decayed particles in soil. Slime molds reproduce by producing spores.

Sporozoa (spōr′ ə zō′ ə), like plants, do not move. Like animals, they consume food for energy. Sporozoa also reproduce by forming spores. Many of these protozoa cause disease in humans and other organisms. Malaria is a disease caused by a spore-forming protozoan.

Amoebas surround a particle of food or another organism with a pseudopod. The cell membrane forms a sack around the food, and this sack moves inside the cell. The food is then digested inside the amoeba.

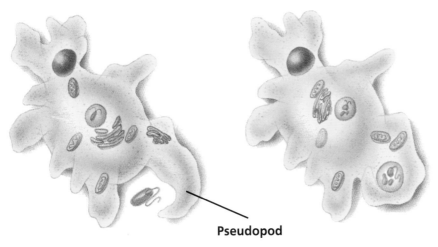

Pseudopod

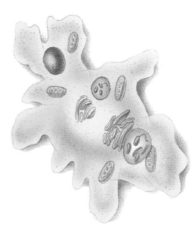

Kingdom Fungi

Fungi (fun′ jī) are plantlike organisms that lack chlorophyll. They chemically break down other organic matter and absorb it as food. Fungi range in size from one-celled organisms to organisms with many similar cells. About 50,000 species of fungi have been identified.

Fungi cells are tubelike. They form thin, winding branches of hyphae (hī′ fā). Hyphae are made of many similar cells with pores between them. The illustration on this page shows how the cells in fungus hyphae are connected. This allows the cytoplasm to flow back and forth between the cells. A mushroom has both aboveground and underground structures of hyphae. The cap and stalk are tightly packed hyphae. The mycelium (mī sē′ lē əm) is an underground mesh of hyphae.

Fungi consume food by secreting chemicals from the hyphae onto it. The food source is broken down into nutrients by the chemicals, and the hyphae absorb the nutrients.

Fungi are made of hyphae, formed of many cells with pores between them. Hyphae make up a mycelium.

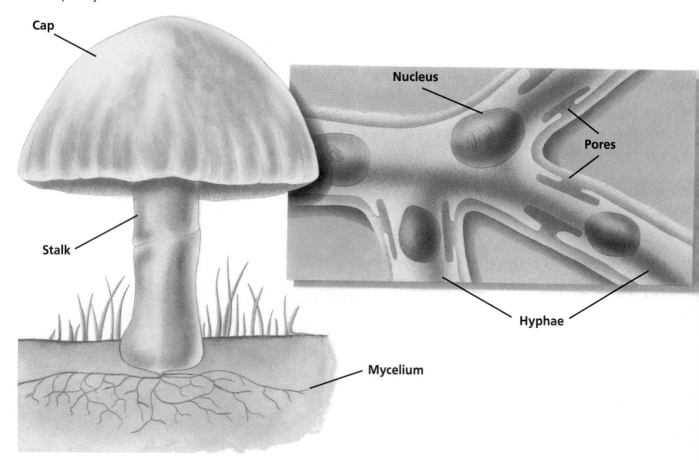

Cap

Stalk

Mycelium

Nucleus

Pores

Hyphae

Like bacteria, many fungi fill the role of decomposers in an ecosystem. Fungi that decompose dead organisms are beneficial to our environment. Like decomposing bacteria, fungi break down materials into reusable nutrients. Unfortunately, fungi also decompose materials like cloth, paper, and rubber. Fungi also grow on living organisms. Some fungi even grow on humans. In humans, some fungi cause disease or an infection like athlete's foot.

Fungi are food sources for humans too. Imagine a mushroom. Are you thinking about how it tastes on a pizza? Maybe you were thinking of mushrooms used in salads, soups, or other food dishes. It is true that humans raise some mushrooms as food crops. However, many mushrooms are poisonous.

Did you know that the first antibiotic to be discovered was produced by a fungus? In 1928, Dr. Alexander Fleming noticed that bacteria would not grow where a certain fungus was present. Dr. Fleming named the new antibiotic "penicillin" after the type of fungus from which it was created. Doctors still use penicillin to treat many bacterial infections.

Humans use some fungi as food.

 CHECKPOINT

1. What is a kingdom?
2. What are monera, protista, and fungi?
   Why is it useful to classify living things?

ACTIVITY
Observing Fungi

WHAT YOU NEED

prepared
slides of fungi
hyphae

mushroom

microscope

hand lens

Activity
Journal

WHAT TO DO

1. Examine a mushroom. Draw a picture of your mushroom.
2. Select the appropriate tool to examine the underside of the mushroom cap. Record your observations.

3. **Observe** a prepared slide of fungi hyphae under the microscope. **Sketch** what you see.

CONCLUSIONS

1. What did the underside of the cap of the mushroom look like?
2. What did the mushroom hyphae look like under the microscope?
3. Were the cells of the hyphae similar?

ASKING NEW QUESTIONS

1. How do your sketches compare to the illustration on page A10?
2. How are different mushrooms similar?
3. What other questions about fungi do you have?

SCIENTIFIC METHODS SELF CHECK

✔ Did I **observe** the mushroom, its parts, and the prepared slide?

✔ Did I **record** my observations?

The Plant Kingdom

Find Out

- About internal plant transportation structures
- How long different plants live
- What different ways plants reproduce

Vocabulary

xylem
phloem
gymnosperms
angiosperm
cotyledons
monocot
dicot

The Big QUESTION

How are plants classified?

*P*lants live almost everywhere on Earth. They live in water, on land, in sunshine, and in shade. We use them for our clothes, our tools, and our toys. But most important of all, plants are food. Without plants there would be no life on Earth.

Plants and Their Structures

Plant structures and characteristics help us classify the huge variety of organisms in the plant kingdom. Plants are multicellular organisms. Their cells contain a nucleus, cell membrane, cell wall, and cytoplasm. Most plants use carbon dioxide gas, water, and energy from sunlight to make their own food in the process of photosynthesis. Most plant cells contain pigment organelles. The pigments allow the plant cells to absorb light. Plant cells that contain the green pigment chlorophyll (klôr′ ə fil) appear green.

Where plants live, on water or on land, affects how plants get nutrients. Leaves, stems, and roots can be used to identify and classify plants.

Other ways to classify plants include their life spans and reproduction cycles. Some plants live for a year or less. Other plants, such as trees and bushes, live for many years. In fact, the oldest living things on Earth are trees. One bristlecone pine tree is estimated to be over 4600 years old. Some plants reproduce without seeds. Most plants reproduce with seeds. Some seed-producing plants produce flowers, others do not.

Like all organisms, plants need food to survive. They produce their own food, but individual groups of plants have different ways of getting nutrients to their different parts.

Vascular plants have a system of tubes that transport food, water, and other materials throughout the plant. The vascular system is a set of tubelike tissues that move water and other nutrients through the plant. Vascular plants can be very tall. In fact, the largest organisms on Earth are sequoia (sə kwoi′ ə) trees. These trees can be over 110 m tall. All seed-producing plants and ferns are also vascular plants.

How many plant products can you identify?

Plant stems and roots contain vascular tissues. There are two different types of vascular tissues in plants. **Xylem** (zī′ ləm) is tissue that carries water and nutrients up from the roots of the plant. Xylem cell walls are thick. They help support the plant. **Phloem** (flō′ əm) tissues transport water, nutrients, and waste materials throughout the plant. Xylem tissues only carry materials up. Phloem tissues carry materials both up and down. These tissues provide a way for all parts of the plant to get the substances they need to grow and survive.

There are two kinds of stems. Herbaceous (hûr bā′ shəs) stems are green and soft. Plants such as tulips and tomatoes are herbaceous.

Woody stems are rigid and hard. Trees and bushes have woody stems. Xylem and phloem in woody stems grow in rings. Each year, a circle of xylem tissue, or growth tissue, is added. One way to tell the age of a tree is to count its rings.

Nonvascular plants make and use food by the same processes that vascular plants do. However, nonvascular plants do not have xylem and phloem tissues to transport water, dissolved nutrients, or food throughout the plants. Nonvascular plants cannot move food long distances and don't grow very large. They seldom grow more than 20 cm tall. They usually live in moist areas.

Mosses are examples of nonvascular plants. Some mosses have conducting cells through which food moves. However, these food-conducting cells don't form large conducting tubes. They are not true vascular tissues.

Nonvascular plants are small. The moss here is a large group of tiny individual moss plants.

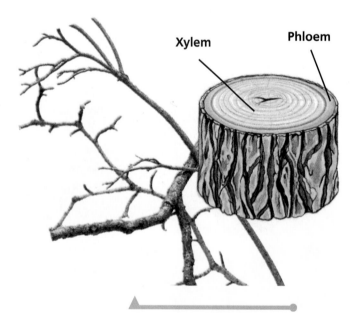

Xylem   Phloem

Vascular plants can grow very tall. Plants with a lot of xylem tissues have rigid stems. Old xylem tissues become the wood of a tree.

A16

Plant Life Spans

Some plants live longer than others do. Some live less than a year. Some live many years. Some have leaves that fall off each year, but they grow leaves again the next year. We can classify plants by their life spans.

Annuals are plants that complete their life cycle in one year or less. These plants grow from a seed, produce flowers, create new seeds, and die all in one growing season. Petunias, impatiens, and sunflowers are annuals. Can you name other annual plants that grow in a garden?

Plants that have a two-year life cycle are biennials. (The Latin prefix *bi* means "two.") Biennials grow roots, stems, and leaves during the first growing year. When winter comes, the stems and leaves die, but the roots stay alive. During the second year, biennials grow new stems and leaves as well as flowers and seeds. Once a biennial plant produces seeds, the plant dies. Celery is a common biennial.

Plants that live for more than two growing seasons are perennials. Perennials live from one growing season to another. Most woody plants, like trees and bushes, are perennials.

In areas that have cool autumns and cold winters, some perennials go through a period of dormancy. The leaves fall from the branches in autumn. These perennials have bare stems and branches throughout winter. Plants that lose their leaves this way are called deciduous (dē sid′ jū əs). Deciduous plants are usually trees and bushes. In spring, when warmer days return, the deciduous plants develop new leaves and renew their growth cycle.

Some perennials stay green all year. Evergreens, like pine trees, fir trees, and juniper bushes, lose their leaves gradually throughout the year. They always appear to have leaves on their stems.

Plants can be annuals, biennials, or perennials, like those seen in this home garden.

Plant Life Cycles

All plants have life cycles. The life cycle of a plant includes its life span and its way of producing more plants like itself. Whether a plant is an annual, biennial, or perennial, its life cycle includes some method of reproduction. Some plants reproduce by making spores. Some plants reproduce by making cones with seeds. Most plants reproduce by flowering and making seeds.

Plants from Spores

Mosses and ferns are two kinds of plants that produce spores. Producing spores involves the joining of male and female sex cells, or gametes. As shown in the diagram below, the moss plant's gametes form in the tops of leaflike structures. When gametes from the male plant join with gametes on the female plant, fertilization takes place. A long, thin stalk then develops from the tip of the female plant. A capsule forms at the top of this stalk. Spores form inside the capsule. When the capsule bursts, the spores come out. If the spores land on a moist surface, they may develop into a new moss plant.

The Life Cycle of a Moss

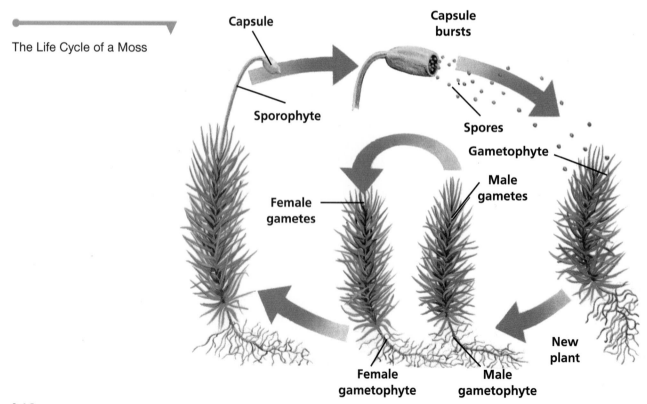

Capsule

Capsule bursts

Sporophyte

Spores

Gametophyte

Male gametes

Female gametes

Female gametophyte

Male gametophyte

New plant

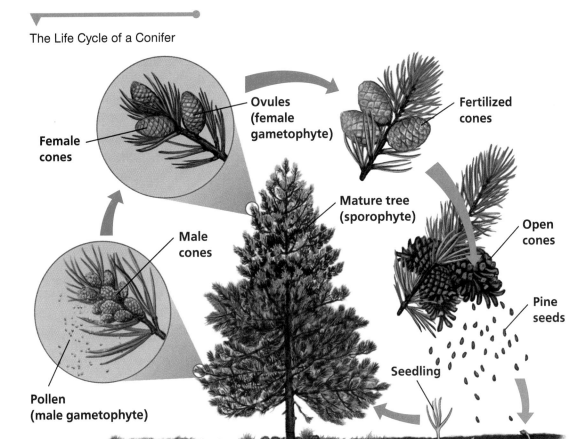

The Life Cycle of a Conifer

Female cones

Ovules (female gametophyte)

Fertilized cones

Male cones

Mature tree (sporophyte)

Open cones

Pine seeds

Pollen (male gametophyte)

Seedling

Seeds from Cones

Gymnosperms (jim′ nō spurmz) are seed-bearing plants. Gymnosperms do not produce flowers or fruits. Most gymnosperms produce their seeds on the woody scales of the female cones.

The illustration above shows the life cycle of a typical gymnosperm, the pine tree. The female cones at the top of the tree have a spiral of woody scales on a short stem. There are female gametes on each scale. Male cones are smaller and less woody than the female cones. Male cones grow at the tips of lower pine branches in spring.

A male pinecone can produce millions of pollen grains. Pollen grains, carried by the wind, may land on a female cone. If pollen grains land on a female cone, fertilization may take place and a new conifer seed will develop. During the fall and winter, female cones fall off the pine trees. When scales open, the seeds fall out. Some pine trees need fire to open their scales. Animals or the wind scatter other pine seeds. If a seed lands where the conditions are right for germination, a new pine tree will grow.

Flowering Plants

Flowering plants are the largest group of plants. A plant that produces flowers is an **angiosperm** (an′ jē ō spûrm). There are about 230,000 known species of angiosperms. We can classify flowering plants by the parts of their flowers and their seeds.

Flower parts include sepals, petals, stamens, and pistils. Sepals are leaflike parts of a flower that protect the flower when it is a young bud. Petals are also leaflike and usually have bright colors. The petals surround the pistils and stamens. Some flowers have both pistils and stamens. Other flowers have one or the other but not both. Not all angiosperms have bright petals. For example, grasses and some deciduous trees and shrubs do not have bright, showy petals even though they are angiosperms.

Look at the illustration of a flower on this page. The pistil at the center of the flower is the female reproductive organ. The pistil has a stigma and an ovary, which contains the female gametes. Stamens surround the stigma and are the male reproductive organs of a flower. Stamens are filaments topped by small anthers, which contain the male gametes.

Pollination occurs when pollen from the anthers comes in contact with the stigma and moves down

If a pollen grain lands on a stigma, a pollen tube grows down through the style into the ovary.

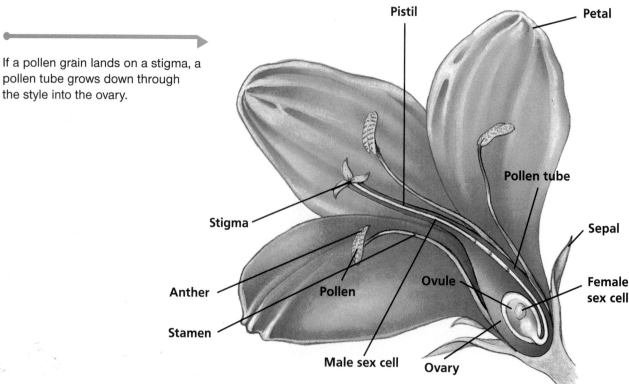

Pistil · Petal · Pollen tube · Sepal · Female sex cell · Ovule · Ovary · Male sex cell · Pollen · Anther · Stamen · Stigma

the pollen tube. When the male and female gametes join in the ovule, fertilization takes place and an embryo forms. As the embryo grows, the outer layers of the ovule become tough layers that form a seed coat. The seed coat protects the embryo after it is released into the environment. The seed contains the embryo, stored food, and the seed coat. The ovary that surrounds a seed or seeds gets larger and develops into a fruit. A fruit is a ripened ovary of a flower and contains one or more seeds, like an apple.

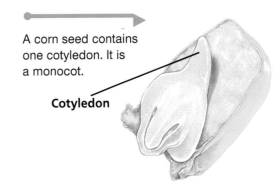
A corn seed contains one cotyledon. It is a monocot.

Cotyledon

Cotyledons (cot′ ə lē dəns) are the parts of the plant seed that provide nutrients to the growing embryo. In **monocot** seeds, there is one cotyledon. In **dicot** seeds, there are two cotyledons. *Monocot* is short for *monocotyledon,* and *dicot* is short for *dicotyledon.* Remember that an embryo is a developing organism in the early stages of growth. An embryo needs the stored nutrients in the cotyledons to support its life functions when it germinates.

Cotyledons

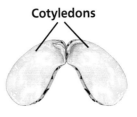

A bean seed contains two cotyledons. It is a dicot.

Cross-pollination occurs when pollen comes from another flower. Most flowering plants have characteristics that encourage cross-pollination. These characteristics include bright colors, sugary nectar, and sweet odors. Hummingbirds, bees, and moths are attracted to different flowers by their colors, nectar, and smells. For example, as a bee visits a flower, some pollen grains stick to its legs and body. These pollen grains then stick to the next flower it visits, and the next one, and so on. Thus, the flowers become cross-pollinated. Pollen can also move from plant to plant or tree to tree as the wind blows. People can also pollinate flowers. Some gardeners collect and distribute pollen using the dry tip of a paintbrush on the plants in their gardens. By doing so, the gardeners can grow plants with specific characteristics.

CHECKPOINT

1. What are vascular tissues?
2. What are different plants' life spans?
3. In what ways do plants reproduce?

 How are plants classified?

ACTIVITY
Observing Plant Parts

Find Out

Do this activity to learn about characteristics of different flowers.

Process Skills

Observing
Communicating

WHAT YOU NEED

lily: flower, stem, and leaves

gladiolus: flower, stem, and leaves

geranium: flower, stem, and leaves

hand lens

microscope

surgical mask (for allergic students)

dropper

water

Activity Journal

eight glass slides and coverslips

WHAT TO DO

1. Examine each plant with its stem and leaves. Record the name, color and number of petals for each flower.

2. Each group member should pick one plant to work with for the rest of the activity.

3. Examine the structures inside the petals of the flower of your plant with the hand lens. Find the structures, called stamens, that have yellow pollen grains on top. How many stamens are in your flower? Record this number.

4. The pollen grains can be shaken or rubbed off the stamens. Shake a few pollen grains onto a clean glass slide. Add a drop of water and a coverslip. Observe the grains under the low power setting of the microscope. Observe the pollen grains from your group. Sketch the appearance of these grains.

 Safety! *Be careful with glass slides and coverslips.*

5. Find the structure inside the petals of your flower that has a sticky area on top. This structure is called the pistil. Shake a few of the pollen grains from a stamen onto the structure. Do they stick? How many pistils are in your flower? Record this number.

6. Have your teacher open a pistil. Remove the contents of the pistil and place one of the pieces, called an ovule, on a clean glass slide. Add a drop of water and a coverslip. Observe the ovule under the low power setting of the microscope. Observe the ovules from the flowers of each of your group members. Sketch the appearance of these ovules.

CONCLUSIONS

1. Were the pollen grains from all the flowers in your group the same under the microscope? Describe the similarities and differences.

2. Were the ovules from the pistils from all the flowers in your group the same under the microscope? Describe the similarities and differences.

3. Record whether the flowers in your group contained both stamens and pistils.

ASKING NEW QUESTIONS

1. With your group, discuss ways that pollen from the stamen can be transferred to the pistil.

2. Can you find conditions under which the pollen grains will germinate outside of the flower?

SCIENTIFIC METHODS SELF CHECK

✔ Did I **observe** all parts of my flower?

✔ Did I **record** my observations?

✔ Did I **communicate** my observations with my group?

The Animal Kingdom

Find Out

- What animals are
- What different groups of invertebrates are
- What the difference is between cold-blooded and warm-blooded vertebrates

Vocabulary

vertebrates
invertebrates
arthropod
amphibians
birds
mammals

The Big QUESTION

How can animals be classified?

Where can you go when you want to see many different animals? Perhaps you'd go to a safari park or an aquarium. You could also go to the zoo. Zoo is short for zoological (zō′ ō loj′ ik əl) *garden. Zoology* (zō ol′ ə jē) *is the study of animals.*

What Is an Animal?

All animals are multicellular organisms. Their cells have a membrane but do not have a cell wall like plant cells do. Animals do not produce their own food; they must obtain it. Animals get energy from food.

As with single-celled organisms and plants, animals may be classified according to their similarities. One way scientists classify animals is to look at their physical characteristics as well as how they develop and what chemicals they have in their bodies.

The presence or absence of a backbone is the first characteristic scientists use to classify animals. Animals with backbones are **vertebrates.** Animals without backbones are **invertebrates.**

Most sponges are found in salt water and vary in size from 1 cm to more than 2 m. At left is a barrel sponge.

Finger sponge

Invertebrates

There are over a dozen phyla of invertebrates. Animals like insects, spiders, and shrimp are arthropods. Octopuses and snails are mollusks. Sponges and different kinds of worms have their own phyla. These are only a few of the phyla of animals without backbones.

Scientists believe that sponges were the first animals to exist in multicellular form. Most sponges, like the ones shown here, live in salt water. Sponges have no organ systems and no true tissues. Many have no definite shape and live attached to one spot. A sponge has two layers of cells with a jellylike substance between the layers. The cells are specialized to perform different tasks. Flagella, which are whiplike structures sticking out of the cells, direct currents of water through the sponge.

Cavity of a Worm

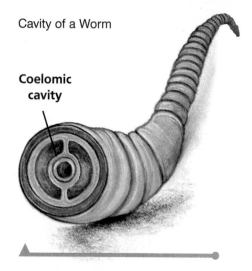

Coelomic cavity

A coelom (sē′ ləm) is a fluid-filled space in which organs develop. Scientists hypothesize that segmented worms were the first organisms to develop a coelom.

The type of shell helps us to identify mollusks.

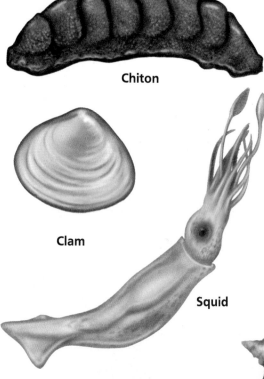

Chiton

Clam

Squid

Snail

There are three phyla of worms. One phylum is the segmented worms. The other two are flatworms and roundworms.

Both flatworms and roundworms have heads, tails, and nervous and digestive systems. The flatworm has one digestive-system opening, whereas the roundworm has two. Most flatworms and roundworms are parasites. A parasite lives inside another organism and obtains food from it. Although parasitic worms do not usually kill their hosts, they do cause disease.

Earthworms are segmented worms. They have well-developed body systems, including nervous, digestive, and circulatory systems. The earthworm has a closed circulatory system. In a closed circulatory system, the blood is contained in vessels and transported throughout the body. Through the rings, or segments, of the earthworm is a cavity, or coelom (sē′ ləm). A coelom is a fluid-filled space in which organs develop. Scientists hypothesize that segmented worms were the first organisms to develop a coelom.

Mollusks are soft-bodied animals that live on land or in freshwater or salt water. Most mollusks have a head with eyes and sensory cells that receive stimuli from their environment.

Some mollusks, like snails, move with the use of a muscular foot. This foot releases a trail of slime upon which the animal moves. Some mollusks have a radula, a tonguelike organ with rows of teeth used for scraping and tearing food.

Shells help classify mollusks. Shells act as a shield and prevent the mollusks' bodies from drying out. Some mollusks, such as slugs, have no shells. Snails have one shell. Bivalves, such as clams and oysters, have two shells with a hinge. Squids have an internal shell.

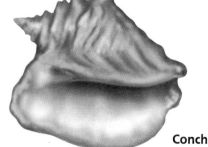

Conch

Scallop

An **arthropod** is an animal with a segmented body and an exoskeleton, or skeleton on the outside of the body. They also have appendages, or structures, such as antennae and legs, attached to the body. You are probably familiar with many different types of arthropods. After all, there are over 850,000 known species of them. Some scientists estimate there may be as many as 2,000,000 species that are not yet identified.

Scientists believe that arthropods were the first group of animals to live on land and the first to have jointed appendages such as legs, claws, wings, or antennae. Most arthropods have well-developed sensory, nervous, and digestive systems. They also have muscles. Insects are the largest class of arthropods and live almost everywhere on Earth. Bugs, beetles, ants, bees, wasps, flies, fleas, grasshoppers, butterflies, and dragonflies are all insects. Other arthropods are crustaceans (krus tā′ shənz), such as crabs, shrimp, and lobsters, and arachnids (ə rak′ nids), such as spiders, scorpions, and ticks.

Like the shell of a mollusk, the exoskeleton of an arthropod protects its soft body and prevents it from drying out. The exoskeleton of an arthropod doesn't grow as the animal grows. From time to time, the arthropod sheds its exoskeleton and forms a new one. This is called molting. After molting has occurred, the new exoskeleton takes a while to harden. During this time, the animal isn't well protected. Molting occurs several times during an arthropod's lifetime.

Ladybug

Millipede

Black and yellow argipoe spider

Ghost crab

Shrimp

A27

Vertebrates

Animals with backbones are vertebrates and belong to one phylum. Each group of vertebrates—fish, amphibians, reptiles, birds, and mammals—has specific characteristics.

All vertebrates have an internal skeleton with a spine and spinal cord. This skeleton is inside the body. It supports and protects the internal organs of the body. It also provides the structure upon which muscles are attached.

One way vertebrates can be classified is by the way they control their body temperatures. The body temperature of a cold-blooded animal, like a frog, changes with the surrounding temperature. On a cold day, a frog will be cold. On a warm day, it will be warm. It will be the same temperature as its surroundings.

Other vertebrates maintain a constant internal temperature. The body temperature of warm-blooded animals stays about the same even if the temperature of their surroundings changes. Warm-blooded animals, such as dogs and cats, may shiver or move about more actively in the cold. In the heat, they pant. Because of these activities, warm-blooded animals require more food for their size than cold-blooded animals do.

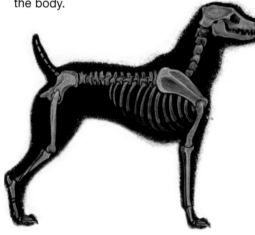

The internal skeleton of vertebrates increases mobility and protection and supports the body.

Frogs rely on heat from the environment for their internal temperature.

Warm-blooded animals, such as humans, produce their own body heat.

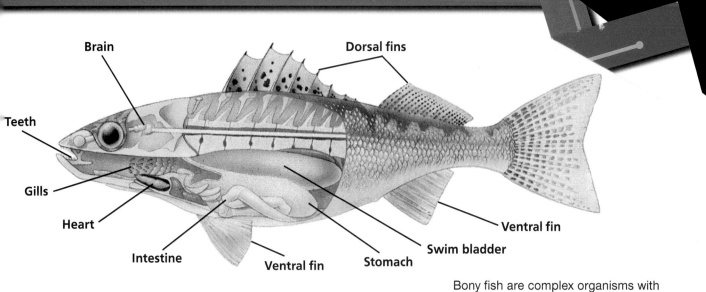

Brain

Dorsal fins

Teeth

Gills

Heart

Intestine

Ventral fin

Stomach

Swim bladder

Ventral fin

Bony fish are complex organisms with well-developed body systems.

Cold-Blooded Vertebrates: Fish, Amphibians, and Reptiles

Fish are cold-blooded animals that live in water. Fish have a two-chambered heart, jaws, teeth, and paired fins. Scientists classify fish into three classes: jawless fish, cartilage fish, and bony fish.

Jawless fish have a round mouth, a tubelike body, single fins, no scales, and a skeleton made of cartilage. Cartilage is a tough, flexible tissue that is not as hard as bone. The lamprey eel is one example of a jawless fish.

Cartilage fish have a skeleton made of cartilage, but they also have jaws and paired fins. Some examples are sharks and rays.

Bony fish, such as goldfish, tuna, and trout, have scales, well-developed sense organs, fins, and skeletons made of bone.

Scientists think that the first **amphibians** (am fib′ ē əns) appeared on Earth 360 million years ago. Amphibians spend part of their lives in water and part on land. Amphibians lay eggs in water. Most newborn amphibians look completely different from the adult organisms. As the young amphibian grows, its body changes. Eventually, it reaches maturity and has the body of an adult.

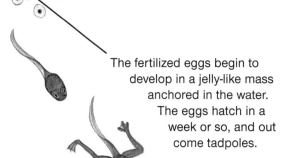

A frog is an example of an amphibian that undergoes metamorphosis.

The fertilized eggs begin to develop in a jelly-like mass anchored in the water. The eggs hatch in a week or so, and out come tadpoles.

The tadpole develops a long tail and gills so that it can move, take in oxygen, and get rid of wastes in the water.

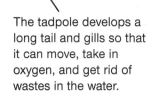

This alligator is hatching from its egg.

Salamanders, frogs, and toads are amphibians. Amphibians are cold-blooded. Amphibians also have gills and lungs. They have three-chambered hearts, strong muscles, and bones for support and movement. Some amphibians have poison glands, a feature that protects them from other land animals.

Reptiles, scientists believe, were the first animals able to live on land from birth to death without returning to the water to reproduce. Many reptiles, including the sea turtle, lay fertilized eggs that have tough, leatherlike coverings. Other reptiles, such as rattlesnakes, give birth to their young. All reptiles breathe and most have three-chambered hearts. Reptiles have thick, dry, waterproof skin covered with scales. Snake skeletons show evidence that, at one time, snake ancestors had four legs like other reptiles. Pythons and boa constrictors still have hip bones in their skeletons. As a reptile grows, it sheds its skin by molting. Turtles, alligators, lizards, and snakes are reptiles.

Warm-Blooded Vertebrates: Birds and Mammals

Warm-blooded animals make up two classes of vertebrates: birds and mammals. Both have well-developed internal organ systems and hair or feathers. Warm-blooded animals use these systems to maintain a constant body temperature no matter how hot or cold the environment is.

Birds are vertebrates that have wings, a beak, two legs, and a body covering of feathers. Birds were the first warm-blooded vertebrates to have insulated body coverings. Birds also have hollow bones and lay hard-shelled eggs.

Most, but not all, birds fly. Adult birds have soft, fluffy feathers next to their skin that help keep them warm. Birds also have outer feathers, which are strong, light, and airtight. Birds groom their feathers to keep them from being soaked and matted by rain or other water. This keeps the feathers light, which enables the birds to fly.

See how a contour feather is adapted for flight. A shaft runs up the center of each feather. The vane on each side of the shaft is made up of many tiny branches that interlock, forming an airtight structure.

Bird eggs are different from reptile eggs. Reptile eggs have leathery shells, while bird eggs have hard shells. Bird eggs usually need to be incubated until they hatch.

Mammals are warm-blooded vertebrates that have hair and feed milk to their young. The hair protects the skin. Most mammals have oil and sweat glands in their skin as well as scent glands that allow similar mammals to recognize them. Their mammary glands produce milk, which feeds their young. All mammals have specialized teeth and well-developed body systems.

We can classify mammals by how their young are born. There are three different kinds of mammals: monotremes, marsupials, and placentals. Monotremes are egg-laying mammals, such as the duck-billed platypus, and hatch their young from eggs.

Marsupials are pouched mammals that give birth to underdeveloped young. Young marsupials have no hair and sometimes have no eyes. The tiny marsupials crawl into the pouch of the female to develop further. Kangaroos and opossums are marsupials.

Most mammals are placental (plə sen′ təl) mammals. Placental mammals develop their young inside the body of the female. When born, placental mammals are well-developed and have completely functioning body systems. Humans, dogs, bears, whales, tigers, and elephants are placental mammals.

The duck-billed platypus is a good example of a monotreme.

The opossum is the only North American marsupial.

The Bengal tiger is a carnivorous mammal.

CHECKPOINT

1. What is an animal?
2. What are four different phyla of invertebrates?
3. What is the difference between cold-blooded and warm-blooded vertebrates?

? How can animals be classified?

ACTIVITY
Comparing Bones

Find Out
Do this activity to see how bird bones are similar to and different from mammal bones.

Process Skills
Observing
Communicating
Inferring
Classifying
Measuring

WHAT YOU NEED

whole bird bone

cross section of a bird bone

whole mammal bone

cross section of mammal bone

hand lens

balance

rubber gloves

Activity Journal

WHAT TO DO

1. Observe your four pieces of bone. Compare the bones of the bird and the mammal with the hand lens.

   Safety! *Wear rubber gloves when handling bones. Wash your hands with soap and water after handling bones.*

2. Sketch and label the cross sections of the bird bone and the mammal bone. Note any similarities in the two types of bone.

3. Select the appropriate tool to weigh the whole bones. Compare the shape and texture of the whole bones. Infer which is stronger. Identify which one is more dense.

4. Sketch and label each whole bone. List the similarities and the differences between them.

CONCLUSIONS

1. What similarities between the two types of bones did you observe?
2. Which type of bone is more dense?
3. What other differences between the two types of bones did you observe?

ASKING NEW QUESTIONS

1. What advantage do solid bones have?
2. What advantage do hollow bones have?

SCIENTIFIC METHODS SELF CHECK

✔ Did I **observe** the density of the bones?

✔ Did I **record** my observations?

✔ Did I **compare** the shape, weight, and texture of the bones?

✔ What evidence did I use to **infer** the strength of the bones?

Review

Reviewing Vocabulary and Concepts

Write the letter of the answer that best completes each sentence.

1. When classifying plants and animals, the most general category is the ___.

   a. order   b. species

   c. kingdom   d. phylum

2. The only organisms made of cells that have no organelles in them are ___.

   a. protista   b. monera

   c. fungi   d. gymnosperms

3. Tissue that carries water and nutrients up from the roots of plants and becomes the wood of trees is ___.

   a. phloem   b. cotyledon

   c. monocot   d. xylem

4. An invertebrate is an animal that ___.

   a. has a skeleton   b. causes disease

   c. has no backbone   d. lays eggs in water

5. A vertebrate that has hollow bones and lays hard-shelled eggs is a ___.

   a. bird   b. mammal

   c. mollusk   d. reptile

Match the definition on the left with the correct term.

6. a plant that produces flowers   a. dicot

7. a seed that has two parts that provide nutrients   b. mammal

8. an animal with a skeleton outside its segmented body   c. angiosperm

9. an animal that can live both on land and in water   d. arthropod

10. a warm-blooded animal that feeds milk to its young   e. amphibian

Understanding What You Learned

1. Animals with backbones belong to Kingdom Animalia and the phylum Chordata. Would a horse belong to this kingdom and phylum? Would a starfish? Why?

2. Why aren't fungi, such as mushrooms, classified as plants?

3. What kinds of plants have vascular tissues?

4. How are annual and biennial plants alike? How are they different?

5. Ants, bees, spiders, and lobsters are all arthropods. What do these animals have in common?

Applying What You Learned

1. Why would a field guide be useful when visiting a nature preserve or a park?

2. Explain how bacteria and fungi can be helpful to someone with a garden.

3. Explain how the bright colors and sweet odors of many flowers help the plant species survive.

4. Suppose your friend wanted a pet frog. What advice would you give him or her about leaving the frog outside?

 5. How can living things be classified?

For Your **Portfolio**

Think about all you've learned about how plants and animals are classified. Then, choose a familiar plant or animal and make as detailed a drawing of it as possible. Label all the structural characteristics that might be used to classify the plant or animal. To accompany your drawing, write a paragraph describing any characteristics about the plant or animal you chose.

Communities and Ecosystems

Yellowstone National Park covers parts of Idaho, Montana, and Wyoming. It has dry mountaintops, pine forests, deciduous forests, grasslands, and lakes. In 1988, firestorms swept through the park, destroying great areas of forest. Although the fire changed the park's ecosystems, it did not destroy them.

The hollow, burned trees now supply homes for insects that eat deadwood and the woodpeckers that eat them. Woodpeckers provide food for carnivorous animals, such as mountain lions and hawks or other birds. If there are fewer trees, more sunlight reaches the forest floor, providing conditions that are more favorable for ground plants. More plants provide more food for herbivores, such as mule deer and elk. Yellowstone National Park is a good example of the diversity and flexibility of Earth's ecosystems.

The Big IDEA

Many communities make up Earth's ecosystems.

CHAPTER SCIENCE INVESTIGATION

Gather weather data from around the world. Find out how in your *Activity Journal.*

Communities

Find Out

- What populations are and how they are measured
- How communities change over time
- What equilibrium in an ecosystem is

Vocabulary

habitat
community
population
biodiversity
succession
carrying capacity

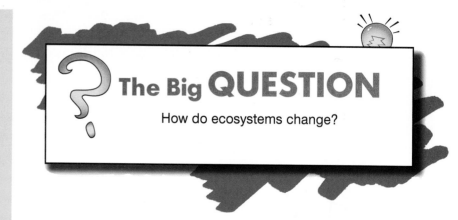

The Big QUESTION

How do ecosystems change?

*E*lephants live in one ecosystem. California poppies live in another. Bamboo is found in yet another ecosystem. Each organism has different needs for its survival. It can be found where those needs can be met. Groups of the same kind of organism are often found living close to each other. What kinds of organisms live in your environment?

How Many Live There?

Ecology is the study of the interactions between the living organisms and nonliving parts of the environment. The mix of living and nonliving parts creates a **habitat.** Different species live in different habitats. A species adapts to the factors in a particular environment. However, a species is not the only one living in its habitat.

There is a green seaweed that lives in shallow ocean tidepools. The tidepool is the green seaweed's habitat. Other organisms share the tidepool habitat too. Plants, small crabs, mollusks, starfish, and anemones, as well as diatoms, algae, and other protists, also live in the tidepool habitat. When organisms share the same habitat, they form a **community.**

A **population** is all the organisms of the same species that live in an area. All oak trees in a front yard, all humans in the world, and all bats in a cave make up different populations.

When organisms are large and there aren't too many of them, such as oak trees in a front yard, scientists can easily count them by looking at them. However, counting the numbers of individuals in a population isn't always easy. Suppose a bat moves in and out of a cave, and a scientist is trying to figure out the cave's bat population. A bat may be counted twice—once on the way out of the cave and again on its way back in. A fast-moving bat may escape the scientist's notice altogether.

A tidepool habitat is home to many populations.

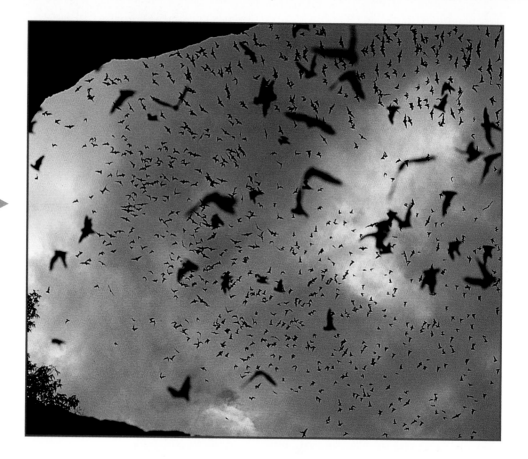

Videotaping the bats at Carlsbad Caverns helped scientists calculate population density.

Scientists who study populations have developed ways to ensure that variables, such as rapid movement or even small size, don't prevent them from obtaining an accurate count. One way is videotaping. Scientists wanted to estimate the population of Mexican free-tail bats in Carlsbad Caverns, New Mexico. They videotaped the bats at dusk as they flew out of the cave. The scientists used a computer program to count the number of bats in each frame of the videotape. Another way to estimate a large population, such as the human population on Earth, is by sampling.

Biodiversity and Ecosystems

The variety of species of plants and animals that live in the same environment is **biodiversity.** The more species in an ecosystem, the more biodiversity it has. An ecosystem might have many populations, each occupying its own habitat. The ecosystem on a farm might include a barn, a field, a pond, a stream, and a small forest. Barn owls and barn swallows live in barns and fields. Mice and grass live in fields. Cattails grow at the edge of ponds, and mosquitoes grow in pond waters. Each population has a particular role, or function, in its community. The role or function of an organism in a community is its niche.

Whether an organism is a producer of food or a consumer of food determines its niche in its community. The barn owl's niche is eating small animals in the barn and field. The barn swallow eats small insects. The mosquito has the niche of feeding off of warm-blooded animals in the community. The cattail's niche is to produce food from nutrients in the pond and provide materials for nests. Mice eat grass, help disperse grass seeds, and provide food for animals that eat mice.

Populations may share habitats, but only one population occupies a niche.

How Does an Ecosystem Change?

Populations in a community sometimes completely replace each other over time. If a farm is abandoned, wild grass, shrubs, and field mice eventually replace the crops and livestock. When beavers dam a stream and a pond forms, the grass and shrubs on the stream bank disappear. Frogs, algae, and cattails appear. The process of plant and animal populations replacing others over time is **succession** (suk sesh′ ən).

Why does succession happen? The climate, soil, and nutrients available in an area determine the types of organisms that can survive there. If even *one* of these factors changes, the community will change. If a wet habitat suddenly became dry, most of the plants would die because they were adapted to a wet climate. If a pond formed in a field, the grass could not survive in the water, but algae could.

Natural disasters such as the eruption of Mount Saint Helens can destroy an ecosystem.

Primary Succession

Volcanic eruptions and other natural events such as earthquakes, floods, fires, and droughts can destroy an ecosystem. For instance, after the eruption of Mount Saint Helens in 1980, there were no living things where the volcano burst out. No soil was visible. The ground was a mix of volcanic rock and ash.

The process of communities forming in barren areas is a special type of succession. Primary succession is the formation of a community in an area where no previous organisms existed. Primary succession starts with soil being formed. This type of succession usually takes centuries to occur.

The first organism to grow in a completely barren area is a pioneer species. Bacteria, algae, or lichens are often the pioneer species in primary succession. They start to break down rock into soil. As more soil forms, more species can grow.

During the second stage, moss plants might grow and eventually crowd out the lichens. Insects begin to live in this ecosystem. Decaying and dead matter build up as soil that contains nutrients.

Lichens are often pioneer species in succession.

Mosses can appear during the second stage of succession.

Complex plants might begin to grow in the area, putting the ecosystem in a third stage of succession. Plants might attract additional insect species and other small animals. These animals have short life spans. As their bodies decay, the soil improves.

Shrub growth might indicate a fourth stage of community development. Shrubs grow in the improved soil. Fruiting shrubs attract larger animals like deer and opossums. Predator species like foxes are also present in a fourth-stage community.

Eventually, if other conditions are right, small trees will grow, starting a fifth stage. More animals, especially birds, are present in the community. The biodiversity of the community has increased.

The last stage of succession is the mature-tree stage. The mature species vary. Mature forests may be pine, maple, or oak, depending on other factors in the community. The mature-tree stage is a diverse array of animal and plant communities. They interact to support ongoing life in the entire community. This creates a stable environment. The community also becomes stable. The stable community formed at the end of succession is called a climax community.

When conditions are right, trees may develop in an ecosystem, starting a fifth stage of succession.

In a third stage of succession, complex plants like grasses will begin to grow.

Shrubs are good indicators of a fourth stage of succession.

Secondary Succession

Secondary succession is the process that occurs when an existing community is disturbed and new growth occurs. This process is usually faster than primary succession. In Yellowstone National Park, grasses and small plants began growing the spring following the fire. Trees and bushes began growing, too. The animal populations took a few years to return to their original numbers.

Human activity is often the cause of changes in an ecosystem that start the process of secondary succession. Activities such as logging, ranching, and farming change the communities of an area.

The illustrations on these pages show the pattern of secondary succession for an abandoned cornfield. The first *community* to appear after a disturbance is the pioneer community. Eventually, as years pass and there are no further disturbances, a stable community of deciduous trees, squirrels, birds, and other animals occurs.

During the first year, a pioneer community of crabgrass, insects, and mice invade a field where corn is no longer planted.

In the second and third years after the field is abandoned, tall grass and small plants grow among the crabgrass. The crabgrass can't live in the shade of tall grass and begins to die out. Mice, rabbits, insects, and seed-eating birds are common.

The hot dry fields of grass are perfect environments for pine seeds to sprout. As pine trees thrive and get bigger, grass can no longer grow in the shade they cast.

A pine forest has replaced the field. Because pine seeds need full sun to germinate, the number of new pine seedlings drops, but the seeds of deciduous trees such as maple, hickory, or oak are able to grow in the shade.

Thirty to 70 years after the farm field was abandoned, a deciduous forest has replaced the other communities.

Equilibrium

When a stable community exists, the same species live in an area for a long period of time. The plants and animals in the community are well-suited to the soil, climate, and nutrients available in this environment. A community becomes stable at the environment's **carrying capacity.** The carrying capacity is the number of individuals and populations that can live in an environment.

Every environment has a limit to the number of individuals that can live there. Usually, populations do not reach their maximum size because of these limiting factors. Limiting factors are resources, such as food, light, and water, that the population needs to grow. As the population approaches its carrying capacity, individuals compete with each other for these scarce resources, and eventually, the size of the population stabilizes. Equilibrium occurs at the carrying capacity of the environment.

CHECKPOINT

1. What are populations and how are they measured?

2. How do communities change over time?

3. What factors influence equilibrium in an ecosystem?

 How do ecosystems change?

A45

ACTIVITY
Counting Populations

Find Out

Do this activity to learn how to count the number of individuals living in an area.

Process Skills

Measuring
Using Numbers
Communicating
Interpreting Data

WHAT YOU NEED

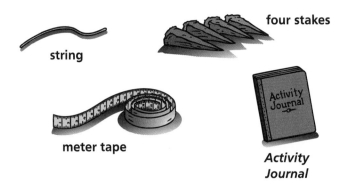

string

four stakes

meter tape

Activity Journal

WHAT TO DO

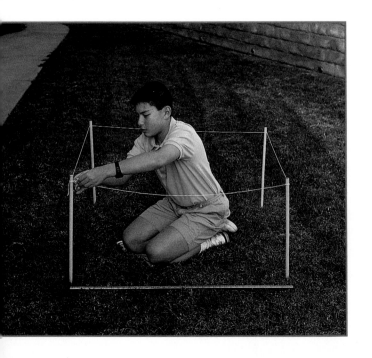

1. Work with three other students in your classroom. Go to the area your teacher has assigned. Randomly select a starting point.

2. Use the meter tape to measure a square that is 1 m on each side. Place a stake at each corner of the square and tie a string around the stakes.

3. Draw a square and divide it into four equal sections. Diagram any physical features such as rocks, trees, or pavement that happen to be in your plot.

4. Divide the plot into four 50 cm square sections. Lay the meter tape along one side and a piece of string across the plot 50 cm from the outside edge. Place the second string across the first, 50 cm from the edge perpendicular to the previous outside edge.

5. **Count** the number of each type of plant in the first 50 cm square section. **Record** the number. Using a different symbol for each plant, map the plants on the diagram. If any animals are present, **count** those as well.

6. Repeat Step 5 until you have counted and mapped all four sections.

7. **Total** the number of each kind of plant and animal counted in your plot.

8. Share your data with the other groups. **Record** the data from all groups. Note the number of groups you have.

9. **Total** the number of each type of organism. Divide that number by the number of groups. The result for each type is the average number per 1-m square in the areas your class sampled. **Record** the averages for each type of organism.

CONCLUSIONS

1. How were the organisms distributed in your plot? Was this different from the plots your classmates studied?

2. Did you see evidence of animals, without actually seeing them? If so, what was the evidence?

ASKING NEW QUESTIONS

1. What are some factors that might make the number of plants or animals change if you sampled the same area next month?

2. Why is the class average a better estimate of the number of plants or animals in an area than just one plot?

SCIENTIFIC METHODS SELF CHECK

✔ Did I accurately **measure** my plot?

✔ Did I accurately **count** the number and kind of each plant or animal?

✔ Did I **record** my data and **communicate** it to my classmates?

✔ Did I **interpret** my **data** to create an average population density for the area I examined?

Biomes

Find Out

- What affects climate
- About six land biomes and one marine biome

Vocabulary

climate
latitude
abiotic
biotic
biomes

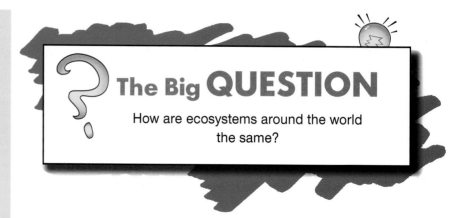

The Big QUESTION

How are ecosystems around the world the same?

*E*arth is a place of great diversity and beauty. Walk outside and look around. What kinds of plants and animals live where you do? Are there maple trees and squirrels? Could you see a moose and pine trees in your neighborhood? How about a cactus and a rattlesnake? Would you find all of these plants and animals in the same environment?

Environmental Climate

Do you live in an area where the weather is very different in the winter and summer? If you do, you can probably predict that it will snow in winter and be hot in summer. You know about how soon it will be warm enough to take the first swim of the year and when to expect the first snow. If you live around mountains, you know the weather high in the mountains is different from that in valleys, plains, or nearby deserts. Some environments have the same weather most of the time, like the desert, where little rain falls during the year.

Where a region is on Earth helps to determine its **climate.** Climate is the typical weather pattern in a place over a long period, including its precipitation, temperature, and seasonal patterns. Features like mountains, wind currents, and bodies of water interact to influence the weather and eventually the climate of a particular place. In fact, there are many places on Earth that have similar climates.

You already know something about the climate where you live on Earth. The United States is so large, it has several different climates. For example, the Pacific Northwest, the Midwest, and the Northeast all have four seasons, with mild summers and cold winters. They get precipitation all year long. The Southeast and the southern coast of California have hot summers and mild winters. The Southeast gets precipitation all year, but southern California has dry summers. Even the mountain regions in the United States have different climates. The climate in the mountains depends on how high the mountains are.

Masai Mara, Kenya. The factors present in the African grassland contribute to its unique and stable characteristics.

World Climates

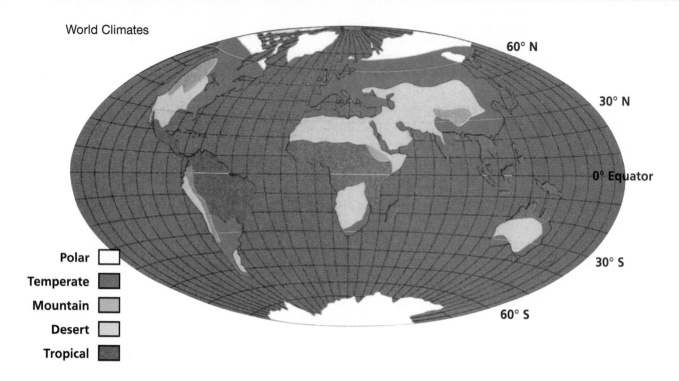

60° N

30° N

0° Equator

30° S

60° S

Polar
Temperate
Mountain
Desert
Tropical

Mountain ranges affect climate, often creating areas on one side of the range with more-than-adequate precipitation and areas on the opposite side with a dry climate.

Look at the map showing Earth's major climates. Notice that most of the continental 48 states are between the 30°N and 50°N lines, and Alaska is at or above the 60°N line on the map. **Latitude** (la′ ti tōōd) is the distance north or south of the equator. The average temperature falls as you move away from the equator to higher latitudes.

Temperature is only one way of determining climate; precipitation is another. Features such as mountains and oceans affect precipitation. Mountains affect precipitation by stopping clouds that are carrying moisture. The clouds release their moisture as rain on one side of a mountain, and the other side remains fairly dry. Next to an ocean or large lake, air blowing inland is moist from the evaporated water. Because of this, coastal areas typically have more humidity than inland areas. Rain isn't the only form of precipitation. What types of precipitation form in the area where you live—rain, snow, hail, sleet, dew, or fog?

Precipitation, like temperature, is related to latitude. Areas near the equator generally receive heavy rainfall all year long. Because warm air can hold more moisture, these locations have not only rain, but also humid conditions. As you move away from the equator, the climate generally becomes drier.

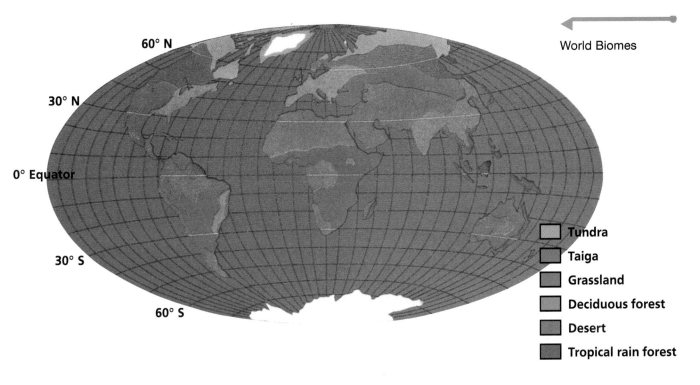

60° N

30° N

0° Equator

30° S

60° S

Tundra

Taiga

Grassland

Deciduous forest

Desert

Tropical rain forest

Climate is one of several **abiotic,** or nonliving, factors that affect the environment of a region. Soil minerals, recurring natural disasters, and the amount of sunlight a region gets are other abiotic factors that affect the environment.

Biomes

When climates stay the same over a long period, the **biotic,** or living, parts of the ecosystem tend to become stable. Stable climatic conditions determine the types of organisms that live there. However, two different types of organisms living in two similar biomes can have similar roles. For example, predator species like a bear and a wolf can live in the taiga and tundra biomes and have similar roles.

Biomes are stable communities of plants and animals in particular geographic areas with a distinct climate. Scientists have classified biomes into six land biomes and one marine biome. The six land biomes are desert, tundra, taiga, grassland, temperate deciduous forest, and tropical rain forest. Compare the world biomes map above with the world climates map shown on the opposite page. Can you see a relationship between climate and biome type?

Grassland

Location: mid-latitudes, interiors of continents

Typical Plants: bluestem grass, buffalo grass, grama grass, sagebrush, rabbit brush, antelope brush, cottonwood trees, willow trees

Typical Animals: lions, moles, prairie dogs, ground squirrels, badgers, gophers, zebras, bison, deer, coyotes, wildebeests, prairie chickens, jackrabbits, hawks

Grassland is a land biome with annual precipitation of nearly 75 cm. Temperatures in the grasslands range from –45 °C in the winter to 50 °C in the summer. Rain falls irregularly in the grasslands. Grasses are the dominant plants, but the winds blow constantly. Prairies in North America, steppes in Europe and Asia, pampas in South America, and velds and savannas in Africa are grassland biomes. Most of the world's wheat, corn, and soybeans are grown in the grassland biome.

Tundra

Location: northern latitudes

Typical Plants: lichens, liverworts, mosses, grasses, sedges, small shrubs, small flowering plants

Typical Animals: lemmings, snowshoe hares, wolves, caribou, arctic foxes, musk oxen, ptarmigans, geese, mosquitoes

Tundra is a land biome with annual precipitation of nearly 20 cm. Temperatures in the tundra range from –60 °C in the winter to 15 °C in the summer. Tundra is the treeless area found in the far northern parts of the world and on the tops of very high mountains. Most of the ground is frozen. During the short summer, the soil thaws through just the top few centimeters. Permafrost is a layer of earth that remains frozen all year. Because of permafrost, no deep-root plants can grow.

Taiga
Location: northern latitudes, south of tundra
Typical Plants: lichens, peat mosses, grasses, sedges, conifers, spruce, lodgepole pines, hemlock, willows, aspens
Typical Animals: deer, moose, elk, bears, wolves, mice, snowshoe hares, migrating birds

Taiga (tī′ gə) is a land biome with annual precipitation of nearly 50 cm. Taiga temperatures range from –35 °C in winter to 20 °C in summer. Conifer trees are the dominant species. Taiga is found in northern regions, south of the tundra. The permafrost thaws in summer, creating standing water. Many lakes and streams are found in taiga.

Desert is a land biome that receives less than 25 cm of rain per year. Some deserts have warm to hot temperatures all year long. In other deserts, such as the dry side of a mountain range, temperatures range from –40 °C in the winter to 45 °C in the summer. In all deserts, the daytime temperatures are much higher than the nighttime temperatures. Cacti are the dominant plants. Euphorbias and some trees are also desert plants. Desert animals are also adapted to these daily temperature extremes. Many animals are active only at night, when the temperature is cooler.

Desert
Location: near 30° N and 30° S latitudes, Africa, Asia, Australia, western North and South America
Typical Plants: cacti, creosote bushes, ocotillo, palo verde, rabbit brush, sagebrush, euphorbias
Typical Animals: kangaroo rats, peccaries, dromedaries, jackrabbits, badgers, elf owls, cactus wrens, roadrunners, gila monsters, rattlesnakes, collared lizards, scorpions

Temperate Deciduous Forest

Location: mid-latitudes of northeastern and southeastern U.S., Europe, parts of Japan, Australia

Typical Plants: mosses, ferns, small flowering plants, shrubs, maples, oaks, walnuts, hickories

Typical Animals: bears, owls, migrating birds, deer, mice, foxes, weasels, rabbits, raccoons, opossums, squirrels

The temperate deciduous forest is a land biome with annual precipitation of nearly 100 cm. Temperatures in this biome range from –30 °C in the winter to 40 °C in the summer. Deciduous trees are the dominant species. This biome has four distinct seasons each year: spring, summer, autumn, and winter. The soil is very rich in nutrients, and abundant plant life grows. The varied types of plants allow many types of consumers to grow in these forests.

Tropical Rain Forest

Location: near the equator, Africa, Asia, South America

Typical Plants: palm trees, tree ferns, vines, bromeliads, balsa trees, mahogany trees, orchids

Typical Animals: panthers, pythons, insects, spiders, tree frogs, monkeys, birds, sloths

The tropical rain forest is a land biome with annual precipitation of 250 cm. Temperature in the tropical rain forest stays around 25 °C all year long. Vines and broadleaf trees are the dominant species. With little variation in temperature, there are no temperature-related seasons. The growing season is all year long. More kinds of plants grow in this biome than in any other. Rainfall does come in seasons in the tropical rain forest. There is a "rainy" season and a "dry" season. However, the dry season isn't like the desert. A rain forest could get as much as 10 cm of rain in a dry season. That's as much as a desert gets all year.

Marine
Location: oceans around the world
Typical Plants: plankton, red algae, green algae, seaweed
Typical Animals: crustaceans, arthropods, mollusks, starfish, anemones, coral, tuna, perch, dolphins, whales

The marine biome is a saltwater biome that consists of all the world's oceans. It covers about three–fourths of Earth's surface. Compared with land biomes, scientific study of the marine biome has only recently begun. Light, salt content, temperature, and water pressure are all important abiotic factors for life in the ocean.

The area where sunlight reaches only extends about 100 m below the surface of the water. Some plants live below 100 m in thermal vents and make their food by the process of chemosynthesis. Animals can live at lower depths than the plants do. Some bacteria can even live on the ocean bottom. We still know very little about the marine biome.

CHECKPOINT

1. What affects climate?
2. How do we categorize the six land biomes and one marine biome?

 How are ecosystems around the world the same?

ACTIVITY
Modeling a Biome

Find Out
Do this activity to see what's in a biome by making a model.

Process Skills
Constructing Models
Communicating
Classifying
Inferring

WHAT YOU NEED

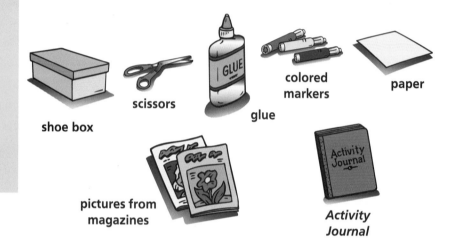

shoe box

scissors

glue

colored markers

paper

pictures from magazines

Activity Journal

WHAT TO DO

1. Make a model of a biome using the shoe box as the basis for your diorama. Choose one of the seven biomes from this lesson to model.

2. Illustrate the type of climate conditions found in your biome as the background for your diorama. Cut out pictures of plants and animals that would be found in your biome from the magazines. If you wish, you may draw your own pictures.

3. Communicate the information about your biome by writing a paragraph. Include factors such as climate and major plants and animals. Imagine an organism that would be successful in this biome.

4. **Write** a description of the features that help the organism survive in this biome. Include the factors of the biome the organism would thrive on. **Illustrate** your paragraph with your organism.

CONCLUSIONS

1. What factors led you to include certain plants or animals?
2. Explain how the kind of plants in your biome determine the kind of animals.

ASKING NEW QUESTIONS

1. If the climate changed in your biome, what would happen to the plants and animals that live there?
2. How could a species of animal inhabit more than one biome?

SCIENTIFIC METHODS SELF CHECK

✔ Did I **make a model** of a biome?

✔ Did I **identify** the types of climate, plants, and animals that would live in that biome?

✔ Did I **infer** what features my imaginary organism would need to survive?

✔ Did I **communicate** information about the specific biome in my model?

Energy Transfer in Ecosystems

Find Out

- Where energy in the ecosystem comes from
- How materials in ecosystems are recycled
- How humans interact with their environments

Vocabulary

producers
consumers
food web
water cycle
carbon cycle
nitrogen cycle

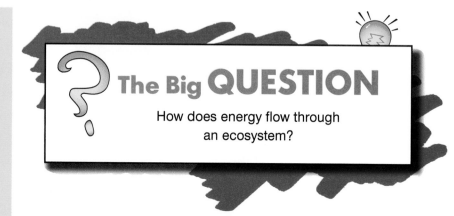

The Big QUESTION

How does energy flow through an ecosystem?

*O*n a typical day, you expend a lot of energy doing many things. Rushing to school, studying math, playing soccer, sitting and watching television, and even growing take energy. If you were an automobile, your energy would come from gasoline. If you were a lightbulb, you would need electrical energy. Where does the energy that living things use come from?

Energy in Ecosystems

Ecosystems and habitats on our planet depend on energy just as automobiles and lightbulbs do. Plants need energy to make food. Animals need energy to capture their prey, to reproduce, and to raise their young. The energy that you and all other living things need to grow and survive comes from the sun. Sunlight provides the energy that makes everything "work" in an ecosystem.

The Transfer of Energy

As energy moves through an ecosystem, it takes different forms. Green plants use carbon dioxide and water to convert light energy from the sun into chemical energy during photosynthesis. Because green plants make their own food, they are called **producers.**

Green plants provide food for a variety of animals. Animals don't make their own food but eat other organisms. Animals are called **consumers.** There are three kinds of consumers. Animals such as dairy cows, sheep, zebras, and rabbits that eat only plants are called herbivores. Animals such as wolves, lions, and alligators that eat other animals are called carnivores. You might wonder if you are a carnivore or an herbivore. You are neither, actually. Humans are omnivores, organisms that can eat both plants and animals. Other omnivores include bears and raccoons.

Energy is transferred through a community as organisms produce and eat food. Energy flows from the sun to producers and then to consumers as each population eats and is eaten.

A food chain shows how the energy flows through an ecosystem. For example, energy from the sun flows to the grass that is eaten by mice. Then, it flows from the mice, which are eaten by owls. When the owls die, they are decomposed by organisms called decomposers. Decomposers are another group of consumers. They break down the dead tissue into simpler substances. Nitrogen, carbon, and other materials are returned to the soil by decomposers.

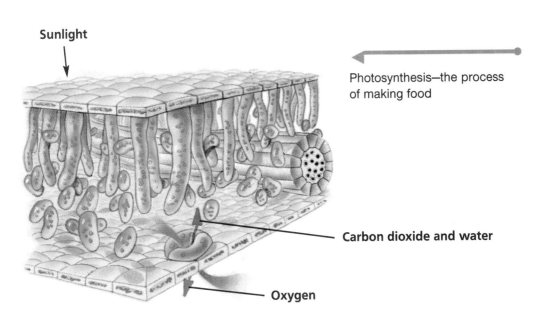

Sunlight

Photosynthesis—the process of making food

Carbon dioxide and water

Oxygen

Barn owl

Grasses

Field mouse

A **food web** is a series of interlinking food chains. A food chain shows one population that eats or is eaten by another population. A food web shows how one population can be part of more than one food chain. Food webs clearly show the interdependence of all biotic factors in an ecosystem.

A change in a food web has effects through the ecosystem. If a consumer organism no longer fills its niche in a food web, other organisms have more energy sources available in the ecosystem. If one or more of the producers in an ecosystem are taken away, it reduces the amount of energy available to the entire ecosystem.

Not all of the energy trapped by plants is converted to food for consumers. The plants themselves use some of the energy for their growth, reproduction, and survival. When herbivores eat plants, not all of the energy they eat is available to carnivores. The herbivores use some energy for their growth, reproduction,

A food web is made up of interlinking food chains. Which are producers? Which are consumers?

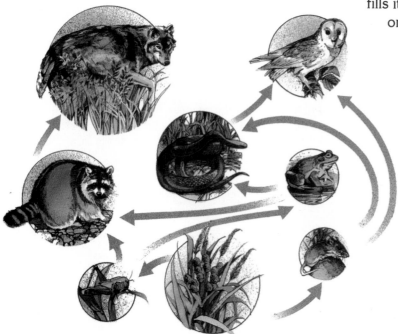

Energy Pyramid

The consumers in an ecosystem depend upon the producers for their food.

and survival. As carnivores eat herbivores, not all of the energy they eat is available for organisms higher on the food chain. The carnivores use some of this energy for their growth, reproduction, and survival.

A good way to show the flow of energy through an ecosystem is an energy pyramid. Remember that a pyramid gets narrower as it goes up. The bottom layer of the pyramid shows the amount of energy made available by producers. That energy is the base of all energy in the food chain. There are fewer consumers, such as grasshoppers and birds, at each new layer. As energy passes from one organism to another, only some of the energy converts to a usable form for the next layer in the food chain. Only about 10 percent of the energy eaten at one layer passes to the next layer.

In the energy pyramid example, for every 100 units of energy of corn eaten by grasshoppers, only 10 units of energy will be passed on to the birds that eat the grasshoppers. Only one unit of energy, of the energy provided by the original corn, is available to the animals that eat the birds. The energy available from food decreases at each higher level of the pyramid. An organism at higher levels depends on all the organisms below it for energy. The higher an organism is in the pyramid, the more organisms it needs to provide enough energy to grow and survive.

Interactions That Cycle Materials

All parts of an ecosystem work together to continuously cycle water and other substances important to life. Air, water, soil, and living organisms constantly exchange waste, carbon, and nitrogen. This cycling provides organisms with an ongoing supply of materials they need for survival, growth, and reproduction in an ecosystem.

The Water Cycle

Water is the most abundant resource on Earth, and one of the most important. All organisms depend on water for life. The **water cycle** begins when water falls to the surface of Earth in the form of precipitation. Once water falls to the ground, it follows several routes. Some of the water seeps into the soil, and some collects in rivers, lakes, and oceans. Water is constantly cycled between biotic and abiotic parts of an ecosystem. Heat energy from sunlight causes water held in soil or in bodies of water to evaporate and rise into the atmosphere. When the water vapor cools and falls to Earth as precipitation, the water cycle begins again.

The Water Cycle

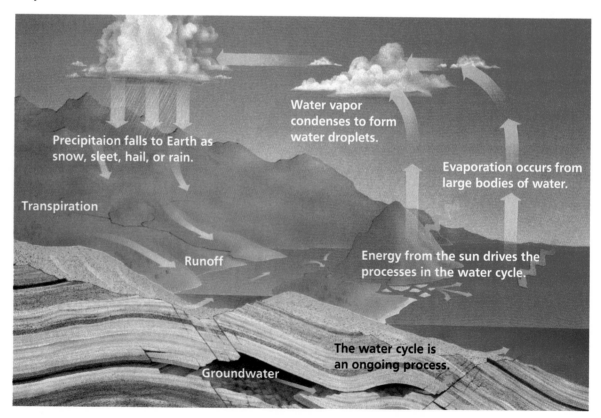

Precipitaion falls to Earth as snow, sleet, hail, or rain.

Water vapor condenses to form water droplets.

Evaporation occurs from large bodies of water.

Transpiration

Runoff

Energy from the sun drives the processes in the water cycle.

Groundwater

The water cycle is an ongoing process.

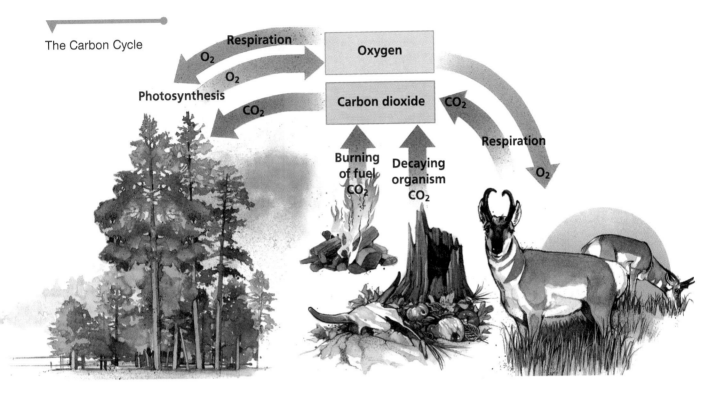

The Carbon Cycle

The Carbon Cycle

Just as water cycles through the ecosystem, so do the gases carbon dioxide and oxygen. These gases are needed by most living things. Look at the diagram above to follow the carbon cycle.

The carbon dioxide-oxygen cycle is the continuous exchange of carbon dioxide and oxygen among producers, consumers, and the atmosphere. The **carbon cycle** involves two basic life processes, photosynthesis and respiration. Green plants use carbon dioxide from the air during photosynthesis. Oxygen is then released into the air. The oxygen is used by plants and animals in respiration. During respiration, carbon dioxide is released into the air to begin the cycle again.

All organisms contain carbon. Waste products and the dead bodies of plants, animals, or simple organisms are broken down by decomposers. The carbon in waste and decomposing bodies is released as carbon dioxide and rejoins the carbon cycle.

The Nitrogen Cycle

Nitrogen is essential for living things. Earth's atmosphere is about 78 percent nitrogen. However, most living things cannot use nitrogen from air for their life processes. The nitrogen must be changed into another form for most living things to use it. Nitrogen is so important for plant growth that farmers and gardeners frequently use nitrogen-containing fertilizers.

The **nitrogen cycle** is the continuous movement of nitrogen in an ecosystem. Nitrogen cycles from the atmosphere to soil to organisms. Bacteria called nitrogen-fixing bacteria change nitrogen from air into a form usable by plants. Nitrogen-fixing bacteria live in lumps on the roots of plants called legumes. Nitrogen-fixing bacteria also change nitrogen in soil into a form that is usable by plants. Animals, in turn, eat the plants and obtain nitrogen. Some nitrogen in the ecosystem returns to the atmosphere. Other nitrogen returns to the soil when decomposers break down once-living things. The diagram illustrates the nitrogen cycle.

The Nitrogen Cycle

Some of this nitrogen is gaseous and is released into the atmosphere. Some is converted into other forms that are used by plants.

Some nitrogen gas is converted to nitrates by the action of lightning.

Lightning

African lion

Nitrogen also moves through the ecosystem when carnivores like the lion eat herbivores like the eland.

Eland

Bacteria that live in soil or in the roots of peas, beans, and clover change nitrogen gas from the air into compounds that can be used by the plant to make proteins and hereditary material.

Perennial peanut roots

Decomposers in the soil, including bacteria, break down nitrogen-containing compounds occurring in dead plant and animal bodies, waste products, or in the soil, into other forms of nitrogen.

The Role of Humans in Ecosystems

Humans live in the same ecosystems as other organisms. We are part of nature's communities and food webs. We also create a variety of complex habitats and communities for ourselves—cities, farms, and small villages all over Earth.

Humans have unique roles in their ecosystems. We keep pets such as cats, dogs, and parakeets. We plant gardens of vegetables and flowers. We use other animals such as horses, cows, and chickens. We raise plants and animals for a variety of purposes.

Because all parts of an ecosystem interact, a change in one part of an ecosystem affects the entire ecosystem. Humans have been responsible for a great number of changes to their ecosystems. Planting and harvesting crops, raising livestock, building cities, mining, and creating landfills are all human activities that can negatively affect the environment. Humans can positively affect the environment, too. We can reduce our use of natural resources, reuse materials and water, and recycle used materials for new uses. When we treat our ecosystems well, we protect them for ourselves and for the other organisms with which we share them.

CHECKPOINT

1. Where does energy in ecosystems come from?
2. Describe the water, carbon, and nitrogen cycles.
3. How do humans interact with their environment?
 How does energy flow through an ecosystem?

ACTIVITY

Testing Factors

Find Out

Do this activity to see how factors in the environment can affect organisms living there.

Process Skills

Predicting
Experimenting
Controlling Variables
Defining Operationally

WHAT YOU NEED

hand lens

one package
dry yeast

warm tap
water

brown paper
bag

one large
wide-mouthed
jar of brine
shrimp

ice cube

plastic
spoon

flashlight

masking tape

self-sealing
sandwich bag

rubber band

plastic shoe
box

Activity
Journal

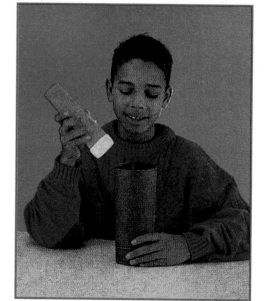

WHAT TO DO

1. Once you have a jar of live shrimp, feed them 5–6 grains of yeast in the water every day. If the water is milky, you are using too much yeast. Use the hand lens to check for live brine shrimp. They will be tiny, almost invisible, but you can see them as white dots swimming around.

2. Observe the shrimp with a hand lens after you have taken some out of the jar on a spoon. Draw a picture showing how the shrimp look.

3. Predict how the brine shrimp will react to light and to hot and cold temperatures. Write down your predictions.

4. **Experiment** to test your predictions. Wrap the sides of the jar with brown paper and secure it with a rubber band. Shine a flashlight onto the surface of the brine for three minutes. Hold the light in place and remove the paper. Record the location of the most shrimp.

5. Gently pour the brine and shrimp into a plastic shoe box. Seal an ice cube in a plastic bag and place it in the brine at one end of the box. After five minutes, record where most of the shrimp are located.

6. Remove the bag and dispose of the ice cube. Seal some warm tap water in the bag. Place the bag in the same place in the box. After five minutes, record where the shrimp are now.

CONCLUSIONS

1. How did the shrimp respond to light? To cold and warm water?
2. Based on your observations, were your predictions correct?
3. What did the shrimp eat?
4. What was the energy source for the environment in the jar?
5. Why was it important not to cover the jar?

ASKING NEW QUESTIONS

1. What physical conditions in the jar are similar to those in the ocean? What conditions are different?
2. Make a list of the environmental factors brine shrimp need.

SCIENTIFIC METHODS SELF CHECK

✔ Did I **predict** the brine shrimp's reactions?

✔ Did I **experiment** with different environmental conditions?

✔ Did I **control the variables** by changing only one factor at a time?

✔ Did I **operationally define** biotic and abiotic environmental factors?

Review

Reviewing Vocabulary and Concepts

Write the letter of the answer that best completes each sentence.

1. A ___ is all the organisms of the same species that live in an area.

   a. group   **b.** population

   c. gathering   **d.** community

2. ___ is the interactions of a variety of species of plants and animals that live in the same environment.

   a. Biology   **b.** An ecosystem

   c. Biodiversity   **d.** A biome

3. A nonliving factor that affects the environment of a region is ___ factor.

   a. an abiotic   **b.** a biological

   c. a chemical   **d.** a universal

4. The ___ biome covers three–fourths of Earth's surface.

   a. air   **b.** marine

   c. mobile   **d.** desert

5. A series of interlinking food chains is ___.

   a. a food web   **b.** an ecosystem

   c. an energy web   **d.** a gas net

Match the definition on the left with the correct term.

6. when organisms share the same habitat   **a.** biomes

7. process of plant and animal populations replacing each other over time   **b.** latitude

8. the distance north or south of the equator   **c.** nitrogen cycle

9. large, stable ecosystems   **d.** community

10. the continuous movement of nitrogen in an ecosystem   **e.** succession

Understanding What You Learned

1. What are some methods that scientists use to estimate a large population?

2. Write a short paragraph about succession. Be sure to include the cause of the start of succession, and use examples to explain why succession might happen.

3. What geographical features affect the climate of an area?

4. Name the land biomes.

5. How can humans positively affect their environment?

Applying What You Learned

1. Describe the stages of succession.

2. Describe the carrying capacity of an environment.

3. How is a grassland biome different from a tundra biome?

4. Explain why the first link in food chains and food webs is usually a green plant.

 5. Explain how communities make up Earth's ecosystems.

For Your **Portfolio**

Select an endangered species and prepare a detailed report about it. The report should contain information about where the animal is found, why it is endangered, and the steps being taken to protect it. Illustrations, maps, and charts or other data can also be included in your report.

3

Cells and Heredity

Whales and carrots, bacteria and beans—organisms come in all kinds and sizes. All organisms have at least one thing in common. Every organism from every kingdom is made of cells. Monera and protista are single-celled organisms. Most plants and animals are multi-celled organisms.

Every new organism begins life as a single cell—amoebas as well as the poppies shown here. Organisms reproduce more of their own kind. When organisms reproduce, traits are passed from parent to offspring. Living things inherit traits from their parents' genes.

The Big IDEA

Genes determine traits passed from one generation to the next.

CHAPTER SCIENCE INVESTIGATION

Make plants reproduce without seeds. Find out how in your *Activity Journal.*

A71

Cells

Find Out

- How cells can be arranged
- About different cell structures
- What some differences between plant and animal cells are
- About other types of cells

Vocabulary

cell membrane
nuclear membrane
cytoplasm
mitochondria
ribosomes
vacuoles
cell wall

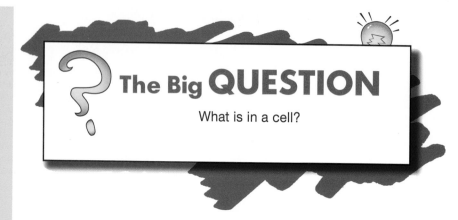

The Big QUESTION

What is in a cell?

In 1665, Robert Hooke, an English scientist, observed a slice of cork through a microscope. He saw that it was made up of small units that fit together and looked like a honeycomb. He named these "little rooms" cells. What he actually saw were the cell walls of the cork plant.

Cell Arrangements

Although there are millions of living things, every one of them is made of cells. Bacteria, beans, whales, and humans are all organisms made up of cells. Some organisms, like bacteria, have only one cell. Other organisms, like toadstools, are made of many cells of one type. Multicellular organisms, like beans, whales, and humans, are made of many different types of cells arranged in complex systems.

Cells exist in different shapes and sizes too. Most cells are too small to see without a microscope. The size of the organism usually depends on the number of cells it has, not the size of each of its cells. For instance, the smallest cells are bacterial cells, which are no more than 0.001 mm in diameter. The largest single-celled organisms are a type of marine algae that grow between 4 and 6 cm high.

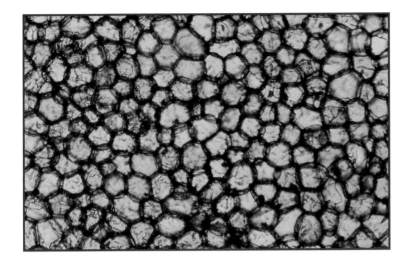

Cork cells showing cell walls

Single-celled organisms are able to carry out all the functions necessary for life. However, it is not necessary for every cell in a multicellular organism to perform all life functions. Instead, specialized cells work together to keep the organism alive. In complex, multicellular organisms, groups of similar cells form tissues. Muscle is a type of tissue. Similar tissues form organs. The heart is an organ made of muscle tissue. Complex organisms are made of systems, and the systems are composed of organs. These systems, organs, tissues, and cells all work together allowing multicellular organisms to grow, reproduce, and survive.

Tissues and organs are groups of similar cells. This plant leaf is an organ made up of similar tissues. The tissues, in turn, are made up of similar types of cells.

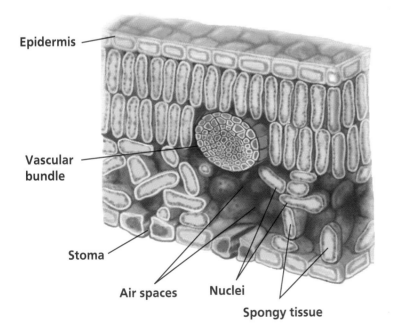

Epidermis

Vascular bundle

Stoma

Air spaces

Nuclei

Spongy tissue

Cell Structures

A cell is the smallest part of an organism that is capable of life. The main parts of most cells are the cell membrane, nucleus, nuclear membrane, cytoplasm, mitochondria, ribosomes, and vacuoles.

The outer covering of the cell is the **cell membrane.** The cell membrane allows water and nutrients into the cell. The cell membrane also lets water and waste products leave the cell.

The largest structure in the cell is the nucleus. It directs the cell's processes. The nucleus is surrounded by a **nuclear membrane.** The nuclear membrane controls what substances move in and out of the cell nucleus.

The nucleus contains chromatin. Chromatin contains material that controls the traits an organism has. The chromatin of a frog is different from that of a mushroom or a rose. Human chromatin is different from that of a dog or any other animal. Each type of organism has its own type of chromatin. Chromatin is located throughout the nucleus.

The inside of a cell is filled with a clear, jellylike substance called **cytoplasm** (sī′ to plazm). Cytoplasm is mostly water, but it also contains dissolved nutrients. Inside the cytoplasm, substances needed by the cell, including sugars, fats, and proteins, are made and stored.

Using modern microscopes, scientists have been able to identify many cell structures in the cytoplasm. These cell structures are organelles. Like organs, cellular organelles perform specific functions and contribute to the work of the cell.

The bean-shaped organelles in the cytoplasm are the **mitochondria** (mī′ tə con′ drē ə). Mitochondria are the power generators of the cell. They are responsible for cellular respiration. Inside the mitochondria, food energy is converted to energy the cell can use.

Ribosomes (rī′ bō sōmz) are complex protein organelles in the cytoplasm. Ribosomes are responsible for making the proteins used in chemical reactions in the cell. Some ribosomes float freely in the cytoplasm. Others look like small dots attached to ribbonlike membranes in the cytoplasm.

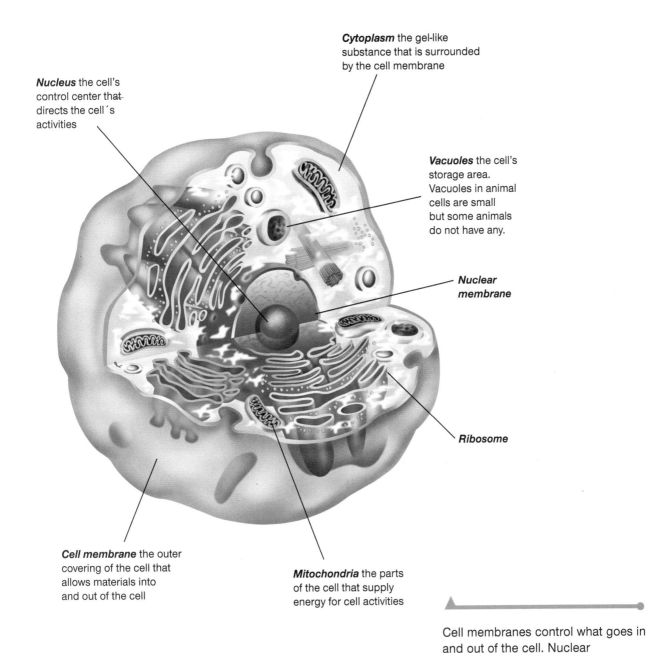

Cytoplasm the gel-like substance that is surrounded by the cell membrane

Nucleus the cell's control center that directs the cell's activities

Vacuoles the cell's storage area. Vacuoles in animal cells are small but some animals do not have any.

Nuclear membrane

Ribosome

Cell membrane the outer covering of the cell that allows materials into and out of the cell

Mitochondria the parts of the cell that supply energy for cell activities

Cell membranes control what goes in and out of the cell. Nuclear membranes control what goes in and out of the nucleus. The nucleus controls all cellular processes.

Most cells produce substances that are not immediately used. **Vacuoles** are the cell's reservoirs for water, minerals, other nutrients, and waste products. These fluid-filled organelles look like big, empty spaces when observed under a microscope. In plants, small vacuoles merge to form one large vacuole. In fact, plant cell vacuoles seem to occupy most of the cell.

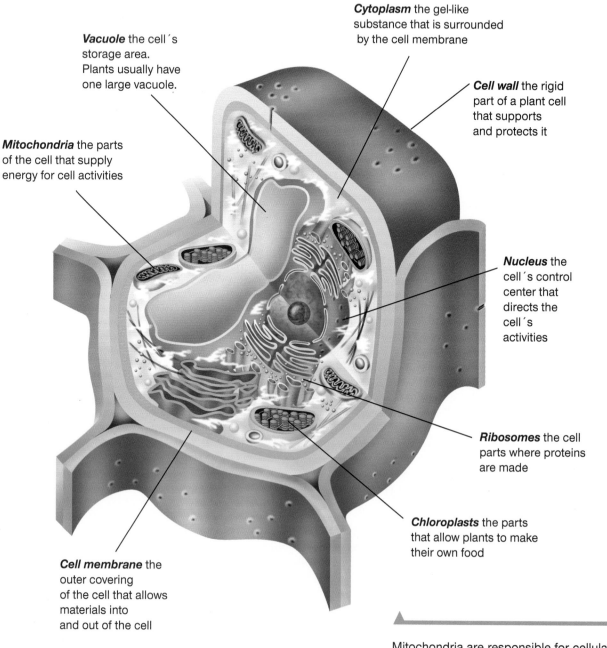

Cytoplasm the gel-like substance that is surrounded by the cell membrane

Vacuole the cell's storage area. Plants usually have one large vacuole.

Cell wall the rigid part of a plant cell that supports and protects it

Mitochondria the parts of the cell that supply energy for cell activities

Nucleus the cell's control center that directs the cell's activities

Ribosomes the cell parts where proteins are made

Cell membrane the outer covering of the cell that allows materials into and out of the cell

Chloroplasts the parts that allow plants to make their own food

Mitochondria are responsible for cellular respiration. Ribosomes make proteins essential for life. Vacuoles are cellular storage areas.

Plant and Animal Cells

The diagram on this page shows a typical plant cell and the one on the following page shows a typical animal cell. Each cell has a cell membrane, a nucleus, a nuclear membrane, cytoplasm, mitochondria, ribosomes, and one or more vacuoles. Similar structures within plant and animal cells have similar functions.

Plant cells differ from animal cells. The primary difference is that plant cells have a **cell wall.** The cell wall surrounds the cell membrane and helps give plant cells their shape.

Another difference between plant and animal cells is the size of their vacuoles. In both plant and animal cells, vacuoles are storage areas for water and other nutrients. In plants, large amounts of water are stored. Plant vacuoles fill with water, push against the cell, and help give the plant cell its specific shape.

There are other differences between plant and animal cells. Remember that most plants make their own food energy, while animals consume their food energy. There are organelles that aid in the processes of photosynthesis, food absorption, and digestion.

Typical Plant Cell

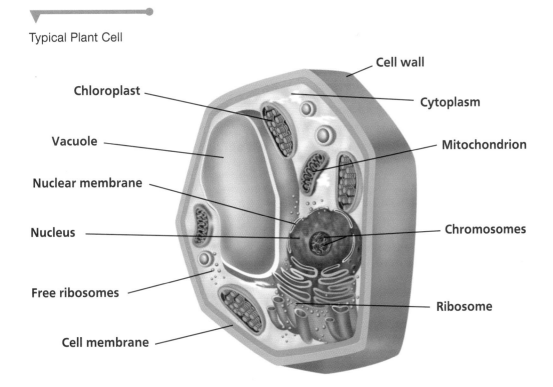

Cell wall

Chloroplast

Cytoplasm

Vacuole

Mitochondrion

Nuclear membrane

Nucleus

Chromosomes

Free ribosomes

Ribosome

Cell membrane

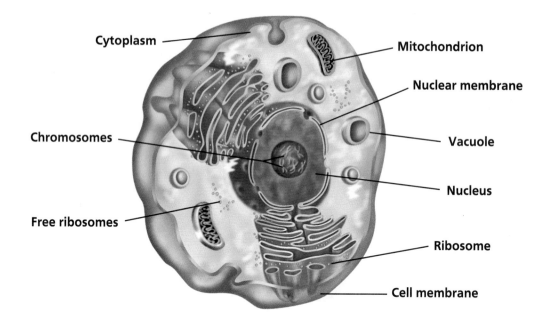

Cytoplasm

Mitochondrion

Nuclear membrane

Chromosomes

Vacuole

Nucleus

Free ribosomes

Ribosome

Cell membrane

In the diagram of the plant cell on A77, you can see that the cytoplasm contains dark green organelles called chloroplasts. Only cells that carry out photosynthesis have chloroplasts. The internal membranes of chloroplasts help trap light energy from the sun and convert it to chemical energy. Chloroplasts use the chemical energy to make sugars.

Lysosomes are cellular organelles usually found in animal or animal-like cells. Lysosomes contain digestive enzymes that break down food into smaller molecules. These smaller molecules can move into the cytoplasm across the lysosome membrane. Lysosome membranes protect the cell from harmful enzymes. Lysosomes also digest old, inactive organelles and return the chemicals to the cytoplasm.

Other Cells

Some living things are neither plant nor animal. Cells from the monera, protista, and fungi kingdoms are different from plant and animal cells and from one another. These organisms have structures found in both plant and animal cells. The presence or absence of one or more cellular organelles usually identifies these organisms.

Typical Moneran Cell

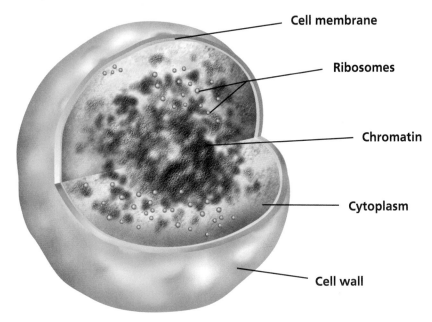

Cell membrane

Ribosomes

Chromatin

Cytoplasm

Cell wall

Plantlike protists have cells that closely resemble typical plant cells. Animal-like protists have cells that more closely resemble animal cells. Fungi have cells with characteristics of both plant and animal cells.

Monera are the most distinct. They have a cell wall, a cell membrane, cytoplasm, ribosomes, and chromatin. Monera are the only organisms that do not have a nucleus, nuclear membrane, or mitochondria.

CHECKPOINT

1. How do cells combine to form tissues and organs?
2. Name and explain at least six different cell structures.
3. What are some differences between plant and animal cells?
4. How are moneran cells different from animal and plant cells?

 What is in a cell?

ACTIVITY

Looking at Cells

Find Out

Do this activity to observe a plant cell and identify its structures.

Process Skills

Observing
Communicating
Classifying
Measuring
Interpreting Data

WHAT YOU NEED

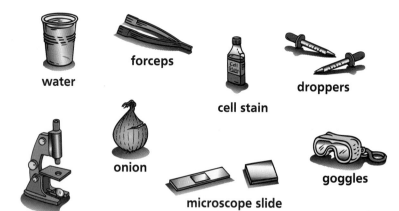

water

forceps

cell stain

droppers

microscope

onion

microscope slide and coverslip

goggles

rubber gloves

Activity Journal

WHAT TO DO

1. Wearing rubber gloves and goggles, place a drop of water in the center of a microscope slide. Using a different dropper, place a drop of cell stain in the water drop.

   Safety! *Be careful with cell stain, it can stain your clothes. If you get cell stain on your hands, be sure to wash them thoroughly. Do not put stained hands near your mouth.*

2. Use the forceps to peel the soft, slippery inner skin from a layer of onion.

3. Place the onion skin in the drop of water on the slide. Check to make sure the skin has no folds or wrinkles.

4. Use a pencil to lower a coverslip onto the slide.

5. Observe the onion skin under low power of the microscope and then under high power. Draw several cells. Label the cell parts you can see.

CONCLUSIONS

1. Compare your drawing with the diagram of the plant cell in your text. What structures did you see? Which structures were not visible?

2. Explain why you did not see chloroplasts in the onion skin.

ASKING NEW QUESTIONS

1. What would you expect to see if you placed part of the growing tip of the onion under the microscope?

2. Why do you think you needed to use cell stain to see the onion cells?

SCIENTIFIC METHODS SELF CHECK

✔ Did I **observe** the cells on the slides?

✔ Did I **record** my observations?

✔ Did I **identify** and **label** the parts of the plant cells?

✔ Did I **compare** my observations to the diagrams in the text?

✔ Did I **explain** why there were no chloroplasts?

Heredity

Find Out

- How traits pass from parents to offspring
- How cells multiply by dividing
- About reproduction through meiosis

Vocabulary

heredity
chromosomes
gene
mitosis
reproduction
meiosis

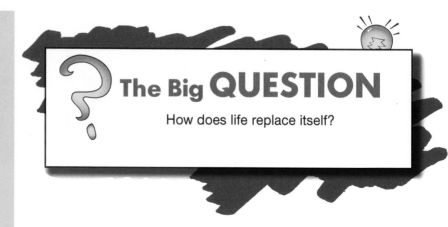

The Big QUESTION

How does life replace itself?

Codes are systems of sending information. For example, in baseball, catchers and pitchers make up a simple code of hand signals. When the catcher makes a hand sign, it is a coded message for the pitcher. The pitcher then knows what kind of pitch to throw to the batter. Codes are useful for sending large amounts of information in a short time.

Traits, and the genes responsible for them, pass from generation to generation by way of a chemical code. Chromosomes contain the chemical DNA, which carries the code for every trait of every living thing.

From Parents to Offspring

"He has his father's nose. She has her mother's eyes." Exactly what do people mean when they say people look like their parents? They mean the offspring and parents share common traits or features. **Heredity** is the transfer of traits from one generation to the next. All offspring inherit traits from their parents. Kittens grow to be about the same size as their parents and look a lot like them. The daisies in this year's garden look a lot like the daisies that grew there last year.

To understand heredity, recall from Lesson 1 that there is chromatin in every cell. Chromatin holds all of the information necessary to determine the traits of offspring. Chromatin is a mass of long, thin, intertwined strands. These strands are **chromosomes** (krō′ mə sōmz).

Scientists have known for many years that special chemicals exist on all chromosomes. The molecule DNA, or deoxyribonucleic (dē ok′ sē rī bō nōō klā′ ik) acid, stores the coded information that determines the traits of a living thing. All living things have DNA. However, its code, or the order in which the DNA chemicals appear is different for different organisms.

A **gene** is a group of DNA chemicals on a chromosome. Each gene controls one or more traits of the organism. The genes control the traits because they control which proteins and other molecules the cell makes. These different chemicals result in different traits.

Chromosomes can only create the same kind of organism from which they come. Cat chromosomes control cat traits, like hair length and color. Genes on daisy chromosomes control daisy traits, like plant height and petal colors. Human genes control human traits.

But genes don't determine everything about an organism's appearance. The environment also helps determine what an organism looks like. For example, genes determine the tallest we could be, but other factors help determine whether we actually reach that height. For instance, our diet and our health are factors that contribute to our exact height.

Heredity is the transfer of traits from one generation to the next.

Cells Divide to Multiply

Cells in your body, and in any living organism, are constantly changing. Your skin sheds old cells and creates new ones. New leaves emerge on plants. A caterpillar changes into a butterfly. All these changes require new cells.

Individual cells may not live for more than a short while. Most cells continuously grow, but there is a limit to how large any one cell can become. During an organism's maturation, its cells grow to a certain size and then divide.

When a cell divides, it makes two new cells. The new cells contain the same structure as the original cell. They perform the same functions too. The chromatin in the new cells is a replica of the chromatin in the old cell, because the DNA in the new cells is a replica of the DNA in the old cell.

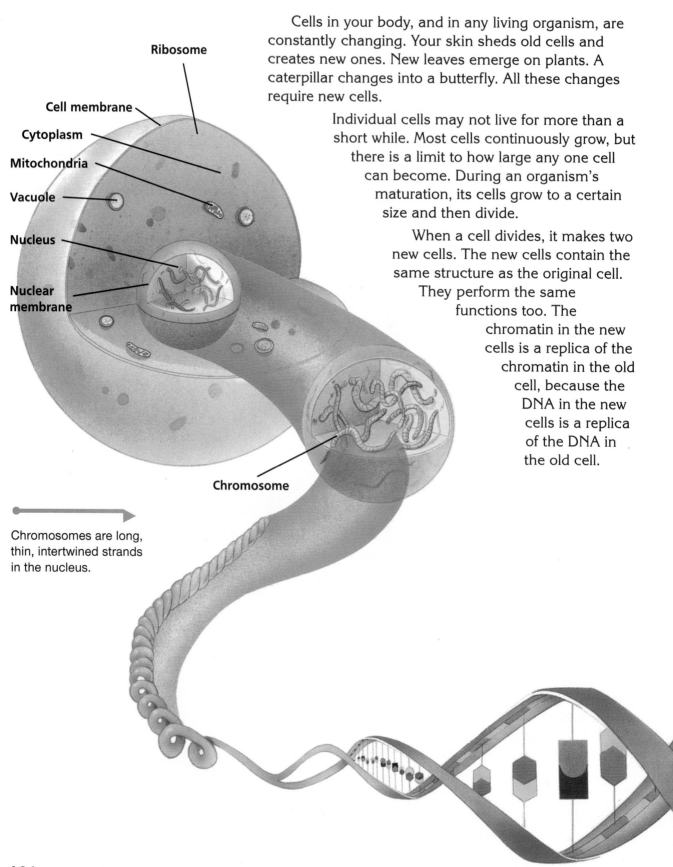

Ribosome

Cell membrane

Cytoplasm

Mitochondria

Vacuole

Nucleus

Nuclear membrane

Chromosome

Chromosomes are long, thin, intertwined strands in the nucleus.

All kinds of cells replicate. Skin cells make new skin cells. Leaf cells make new leaf cells. Amoebas make new amoebas. This type of cell division occurs by **mitosis.**

The photographs on this page show the different stages in the process of mitosis. During mitosis, the chromosomes in the nucleus of the original cell replicate, separate, and form two identical nuclei. The new cells have the same type and number of chromosomes as the original cell did. The new cells replicate any cell organelles and form new cell membranes. Usually, they are exactly like the original cell. Interphase is the stage between cell division. After cell division is complete, the cells are in interphase.

DNA stores the coded information that determines the traits of living things.

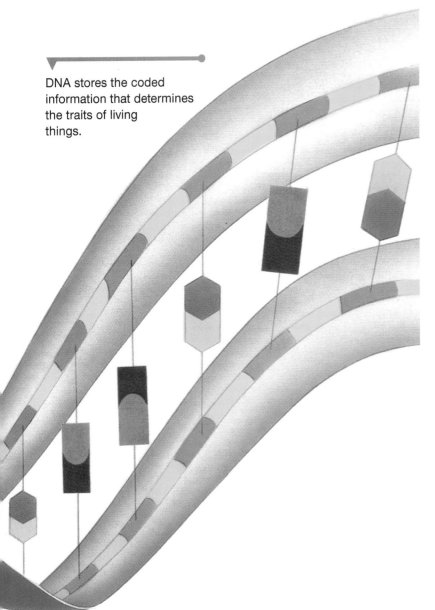

Prophase

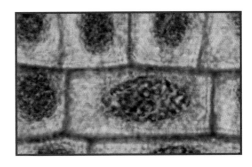

Metaphase

Anaphase

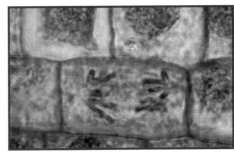

Telophase

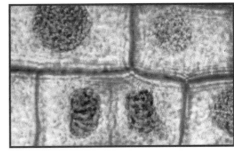

A85

Reproduction

Reproduction is the process through which a living thing produces new organisms like itself. Reproduction by one parent is called asexual reproduction. Asexual reproduction takes place through mitosis. A replica of the total DNA of the parent is passed along to each of its offspring. Therefore, the offspring cells are identical to the parent cell. Organisms such as amoebas, paramecia, yeast, and other one-celled organisms reproduce through mitosis. Two new organisms form from the division of one parent cell.

Meiosis Part I

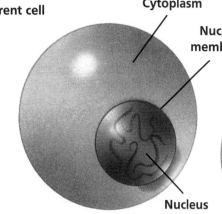

Parent cell | Cytoplasm | Nuclear membrane | Nucleus

Interphase

During interphase, the nucleus is the same as that in mitosis. Chromosomes come in pairs. There are two of each chromosome in the parent cell. The chromosomes are copied and remain attached to their copies. In this example you will see four chromosomes (two pairs) and their copies.

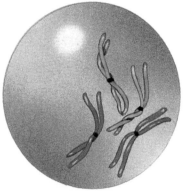

Prophase I

During prophase I chromosomes thicken and coil. Pairs of chromosomes with their replicated copies join together and move toward the equator of the cell. Instead of two attached chromosomes, as in mitosis, there are four attached chromosomes.

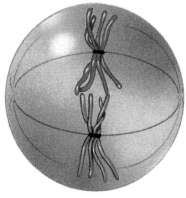

Metaphase I

During metaphase I the four attached chromosomes line up along the equator of the cell.

Anaphase I

During anaphase I each group of four attached chromosomes splits so that one pair goes to each side of the cell.

Telophase I

During telophase I the nuclear membrane re-forms. Afterwards two daughter cells form. Chromosomes begin to uncoil but remain attached. Each of the daughter cells has only one set of chromosomes, not two.

In organisms that have two parents, two cells join to make a new organism. The cells that join are sex cells, or gametes. Sex cells are formed by a different type of cell division. **Meiosis** (mī ō′ sis) produces cells that have only half the number of chromosomes of the parent body cells. Cells with half the number of chromosomes are sex cells.

The diagrams on pages A86 and A87 show all of the stages of meiosis.

Count the number of chromosomes in each daughter cell. How many are there? How many were present in the parent cell? What has meiosis done to the number of chromosomes in the daughter generation of cells?

Meiosis Part II

Prophase II

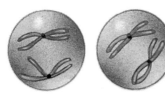

During prophase II the chromosomes coil again. There are only half the original number of chromosomes of the parent cell.

Metaphase II

During metaphase II the attached chromosomes move to the equator of the cell.

Anaphase II

During anaphase II chromosomes separate and one copy of each moves to opposite poles of the cell.

Telophase II   **Daughter cells**

During telophase II the chromosomes reach the poles, and the nuclear membrane re-forms. Each of the daughter cells has received one complete set of chromosomes.

Meiosis takes place in the cells of plant and animal reproductive organs. After meiosis, each sex cell has only half as many chromosomes as other cells. For example, a human body cell has 46 chromosomes. These form 23 matched pairs. Human sex cells, or sperm and egg cells, have only 23 chromosomes, one from each matched pair.

Sexual reproduction occurs when sex cells from two parents join to form a cell that has the same number of chromosomes as the parents. When the sex cells join, a

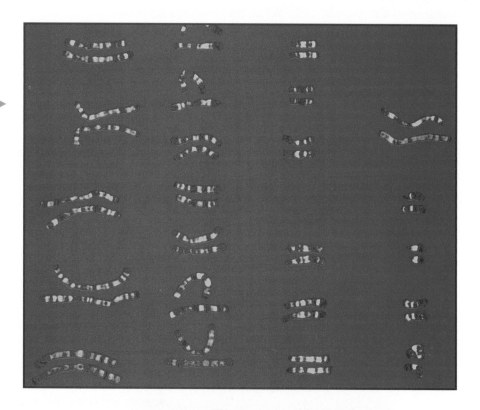

A karotype is a picture of a person's chromosomes.

Offspring do not look exactly like their parents.

zygote forms. The zygote is the new organism in its single-celled stage. It contains all of the hereditary information it needs to grow into a mature organism. The zygote undergoes mitosis to grow into a close replica of its parents. Because the new organism has DNA and chromosomes from two parents instead of just one, it is not identical to either parent.

Heredity is the transfer of traits from one generation to the next.

CHECKPOINT

1. How do traits pass from parents to offspring?

2. How do cells multiply by dividing?

3. How do cells reproduce through meiosis?

? How does life replace itself?

ACTIVITY

Modeling Mitosis

WHAT YOU NEED

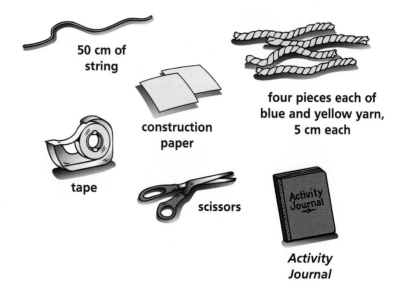

50 cm of string

construction paper

four pieces each of blue and yellow yarn, 5 cm each

tape

scissors

Activity Journal

Activity Journal

WHAT TO DO

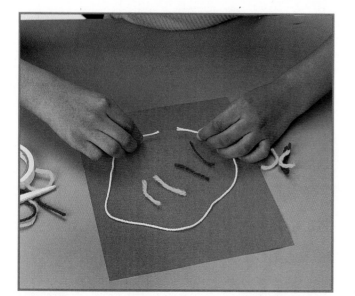

1. Use the construction paper as a base. Create a circle with your string. Place two strands of blue and two strands of yellow yarn in the circle.

2. Next to each yellow and blue strand of yarn, add a new piece of the same-color yarn. Tape the two sets of two yellow strands together at their center. Tape the two sets of two blue strands together at their center.

3. Remove the string from the paper. Place the pairs of blue and yellow yarn in the center of the paper so the tapes form a line. You should have a vertical line of *X*'s, one on top of the other.

4. Cut each tape lengthwise to separate the yarn pairs. The halves of each *X* should move in opposite directions to either end of the paper.

 Be careful with scissors.

5. Cut the string in half. Use each half of the string to make new circles on the paper around the yarn sets at either end of the paper. Each set contains two blue and two yellow pieces of yarn.

6. Cut the paper in half.

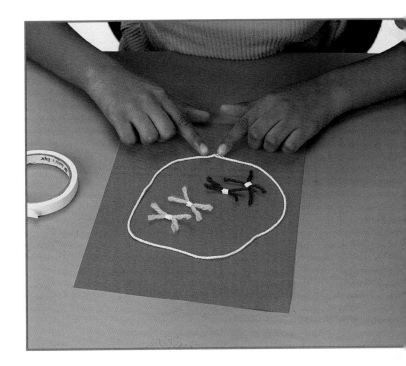

CONCLUSIONS

1. What did the construction paper represent?
2. What parts of the cell did the yarn represent?
3. What parts of the cell did the string represent?
4. Describe the process of mitosis.

ASKING NEW QUESTIONS

1. What kind of cell did the model most closely represent?
2. What would be true about two cells formed from mitosis joining to form a zygote?

SCIENTIFIC METHODS SELF CHECK

✔ Did I make a **model** that ended up as two identical "cells"?

✔ Did I **infer** what parts of a cell the construction paper, yarn, and string represented?

✔ Did I **operationally define** the process of mitosis?

CHAPTER 3

Review

Reviewing Vocabulary and Concepts

Match each definition on the left with the correct term on the right.

1. outer covering of a cell
2. surrounds nucleus
3. power generators
4. protein maker
5. fluid-filled organelles
6. gives a cell shape
7. process of transferring traits to offspring
8. intertwined strands of chromatin
9. group of DNA molecules
10. replica

   a. vacuole
   b. cell wall
   c. heredity
   d. reproduction
   e. cell membrane
   f. gene
   g. mitochondria
   h. nuclear membrane
   i. ribosome
   j. chromosome

Write the letter of the answer that completes each sentence.

11. The inside of a cell is filled with ___.

    a. jelly

    b. water

    c. cytoplasm

12. ___ are bean-shaped organelles in the cytoplasm.

    a. vacuoles

    b. ribosomes

    c. mitochrondria

13. A ___ controls an organism's traits.

    a. gene

    b. vacuole

    c. ribosome

14. Leaf cells make new leaf cells by the process of ___.

    a. mitosis

    b. meiosis

    c. mitochondria

15. The process by which sex cells form is ___.

    a. multiplication

    b. meiosis

    c. mitosis

Understanding What You Learned

1. What are tissues and organs?

2. What is a cell?

3. What are some similarities between plant cells and animal cells?

4. How is DNA like a code?

5. Why is meiosis important in organisms that have two parents?

Applying What You Learned

1. Describe what a vacuole is and what it does.

2. What kind of cells have cell walls?

3. List traits that you share with one of your parents.

4. Explain how cells multiply by dividing.

 5. Describe how living things can reproduce more of their own kind.

For Your **Portfolio**

Some diseases are hereditary, or passed from parents to offspring. Choose one inherited health problem to research. Use the information to write a brief report on your chosen disease. Keep your report for your portfolio.

Unit Review

Concept Review

1. How can there be more than one way to classify living things?
2. Describe Earth's ecosystems in terms of its communities.
3. Why does one generation often have the same traits as the one before it?

Problem Solving

1. Imagine you are a pet store owner and you sell a goldfish or a frog to a youngster. What would you tell him or her about the animal's needs and probable behavior? Write what you would say and explain the proper way to care for the pet. Include information from your Portfolio notes and *Activity Journal* that is helpful.
2. Create an imaginary organism that lives in your neighborhood. What features would you give it so that it could survive all year round? What would it eat? What would eat it?
3. Why is learning about an organism's DNA code considered a great scientific breakthrough?

Something to Do

Cutting down rain forests puts thousands of species of plants and animals in danger of becoming extinct. Rain forests are the home of half the plant and animal species living on Earth. Many people who live in or near rain forests need this land to grow food crops or to use for ranching. Many other people think this land shouldn't be used for any reason. They think it should be left alone. What do you think? Get together with several people in your class who have different opinions about this issue. Debate in your group whether rain forest land should be used for various purposes or left alone so that the diversity of plant and animal species will remain. Or perhaps your group can work out a compromise that would answer both needs.

UNIT B

Earth Science

CHAPTER 1

Exploring Weather and

Hot, dry desert; warm, humid tropics; areas with cold winters and warm summers—these are places on Earth with different climates. Scientists describe climate as the average weather of an area; that is, the average precipitation and average temperature over a long time. Weather is the condition of the air during a brief time. Even though a climate has typical characteristics, weather may still change from day to day and from season to season.

Weather is a constant presence in our lives, affecting how we live, what we do, what clothes we wear, and the food we eat. The sun's interactions with the atmosphere cause the great varieties of types of climate and weather around the world. Earth's shape, its movement, the contours of its surface, and the water vapor in the atmosphere all interact with the sun's energy to create wind, rain, drought, ice, hurricanes, and warm, sunny days.

The Big IDEA

Earth's climates and weather are affected by the sun's influence on the atmosphere.

Climate

CHAPTER
SCIENCE INVESTIGATION

Measure the wind pattern near your school. Find out how in your *Activity Journal.*

Properties of the Atmosphere

Find Out

- How the atmosphere helps Earth maintain an energy balance
- What the layers of the atmosphere are
- What is in air
- What air pollution is and how it can be monitored

Vocabulary

solar radiation
infrared rays
radiation balance
troposphere
stratosphere
mesosphere
thermosphere
exosphere

The Big QUESTION

What makes up Earth's atmosphere?

People in ancient cultures knew that air existed. Scientists looked up through the atmosphere that surrounds Earth and wondered: How high did it go? Was there air up there? Was the air high in the atmosphere different from air near the ground? After hot-air balloons were invented in 1783, scientists used them to travel far above Earth's surface. Scientists still use hot-air balloons, searching for answers to their questions.

Earth's Energy Balance

One of the factors that makes life possible on Earth is its distance from the sun. If Earth were just a little closer to or farther from the sun, there might not be life on Earth. The other planets in the solar system are much too cold or too hot to support life as we know it. Earth is heated by the energy in the sun's rays. We receive this energy from the sun in the form of **solar radiation,** or energy released by the sun.

An atmosphere of air surrounds Earth. This hot-air balloon rides higher in the atmosphere than breathable air does. The balloon flies so high that its passengers have to carry their own air to breathe.

Some of the solar radiation entering Earth's atmosphere never reaches the ground. Some is reflected back into space, and some is scattered by dust particles. Earth's surface also reflects some of the sun's energy back into space. The rest of the energy is absorbed by the atmosphere and clouds, and by the planet's surface. As Earth absorbs energy, it becomes warmer.

Earth eventually radiates the energy back to space in the form of **infrared rays,** or rays of energy that, when they are absorbed by an object, warm the object. Thus, Earth maintains a **radiation balance.** It receives solar radiation and releases an equal amount of energy.

As Earth absorbs energy, it becomes warmer. Animals can absorb warmth from rocks heated by the sun.

Earth loses and gains the same amount of energy over great spans of time. There were periods of time, though, when Earth was cooler, and sheets of ice covered much of its surface. At other times, it was warmer, and instead of ice, oceans covered much of North America and other continents. Life-forms have appeared and disappeared during such cycles. Scientists have concluded that Earth is in between ice ages at present. Overall, however, Earth has maintained an energy balance.

Gases in the atmosphere, including carbon dioxide and water vapor, allow the sun's energy to reach Earth but slow its escape into space. By slowing down this energy loss, these gases help keep Earth's average surface temperature about 30 °C warmer than it would be without these gases. The result of this natural warming process, called the greenhouse effect, is important for life on Earth.

Humans may be increasing this warming effect. When people burn fossil fuels such as gasoline and coal, they put more carbon dioxide gas into the air. Carbon dioxide pollution may increase the greenhouse effect and cause Earth to get even warmer. An overall increase in Earth's temperature is called global warming.

Warmer temperatures on Earth could cause much damage. Warming of Earth could cause glaciers and polar ice caps to melt. That would free enough water to flood much of Earth's coastal areas. If Earth warmed a few degrees, melting glaciers could raise the sea level. If the sea level rises as much as 6 m, ocean water would flood many coastal cities. Even a rise of just 1 m would affect the drinking water supplies of millions of people, since people cannot drink salt water.

Will people's pollution of the air with carbon dioxide contribute to such ecological changes? Scientists are working to discover the answer. This makes global warming and the prospect of rising sea levels challenging issues for everyone. How do you think your own activities might influence global warming?

Icebergs are found in polar regions. They contain freshwater.

Earth's Atmosphere

When you look up on a clear day, what do you see? You're looking up through hundreds of kilometers of atmosphere. Humans and most other living organisms live in a vast ocean of air. You may not think about the atmosphere very often, but you're aware of the changes that take place in it. The atmosphere is responsible for breathtaking sunsets, frost on windows, and dew on the grass.

Earth's atmosphere is made up of several layers. The energy absorbed by Earth warms the atmosphere above it. Temperatures in the atmosphere vary according to altitude. The atmosphere gradually thins with height above Earth's surface until the air molecules are so few and far between that you have reached space. The upper boundary between Earth's atmosphere and space is about 1000 km above Earth's surface.

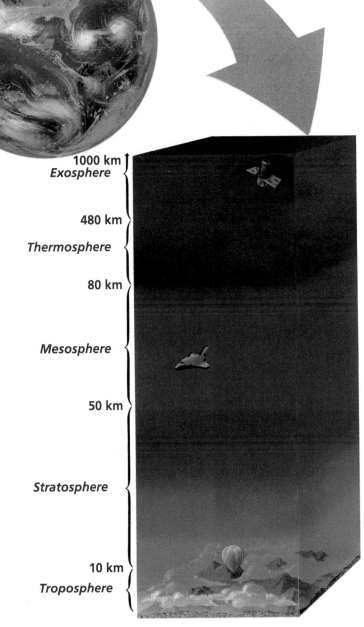

1000 km
Exosphere

480 km

Thermosphere

80 km

Mesosphere

50 km

Stratosphere

10 km
Troposphere

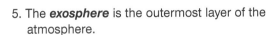

5. The **exosphere** is the outermost layer of the atmosphere.

4. The **thermosphere** is the layer of the atmosphere where the air is very thin and very hot.

3. The **mesosphere** is the middle layer of the atmosphere. The temperature of the air drops the higher you go.

2. The **stratosphere** is the layer of the atmosphere that contains an ozone layer. The temperature rises as you go higher because the ozone absorbs some of the sun's energy.

1. The **troposphere** is the lowest layer of Earth's atmosphere. This is where our weather takes place.

The atmosphere envelops Earth in several layers. These layers can be identified by the chemicals in them. The chemicals cause variations in temperature. As a result, Earth's atmosphere can be categorized by temperature.

The layer of the atmosphere closest to Earth is the **troposphere.** It contains the gases necessary for life. It extends about 12 km high in the middle latitudes, 18 km at the equator, and 8 km at the poles. Solar energy absorbed by Earth warms the troposphere, making it constantly churn and stir, giving us weather. All weather occurs in the troposphere. But temperatures drop steadily as you rise, about 6.5 °C for every 1000-m increase in altitude. The sun's energy heats this lowest layer of the atmosphere.

Usually, the air nearer Earth is the warmest. When it is not, pollution can get trapped near Earth.

The water vapor in the troposphere also helps regulate Earth's air temperature. The water vapor absorbs solar energy and thermal radiation from Earth's surface.

The troposphere is warmer near Earth's surface because the sun's energy heats the land and oceans. These in turn heat the air above them. However, sometimes just the opposite happens. At night and in the winter, air near Earth's surface can become cooler than air above it. The air temperature in a thin layer will then increase with altitude. This is a *thermal inversion*. It's the inverse of the normal pattern. *Inverse* means upside down. The worst air pollution occurs during thermal inversions because cold air near the ground traps the pollutants, preventing them from rising. Thermal inversions usually last until rain or wind breaks up the layer of warm air above.

At the upper end of the troposphere, the temperature stops falling. This point is the beginning of the tropopause. Although water vapor exists in the tropopause, the air is so cold at this altitude that clouds contain ice crystals. The coldest part of the tropopause is over the equator, where air rises so high that its temperature drops to –80 °C. The tropopause over the equator can be as much as 30 °C cooler than its temperature over the poles.

The **stratosphere** reaches from 11 to 50 km above Earth's surface. Because there is so little moisture, few clouds exist. Its lower layer has a nearly steady temperature of about –55 °C. Sometimes, turbulence from air currents in the troposphere can extend into the stratosphere. In the upper layer, the stratopause, temperatures increase with altitude to about –2 °C. Because the air temperatures increase with altitude, convection currents do not form.

Most of Earth's ozone lies in the stratopause. Ozone is a type of oxygen that forms by reactions between sunlight and gases in air. Ozone absorbs and retains some of the sun's energy, making the stratopause warmer. Temperatures increase as the amount of ozone increases. The ozone layer shields the planet from most of the sun's ultraviolet rays. Ultraviolet rays can disrupt plant life. They can also damage the eyes, weaken the immune system, and create health problems.

Chemicals injected into the atmosphere can react with ozone, destroying it. NASA satellites take photographs of the ozone layer above Earth. Over the Antarctic, a hole in the ozone layer appears to be growing. The ozone layer appears to be thinning over the northern hemisphere as well.

Chlorofluorocarbons, or CFCs, are manufactured chemicals that float up into the stratosphere. These chemicals are known to destroy the protective ozone layer. Aerosol sprays, Styrofoam, and freon, a coolant previously used in air conditioners and refrigerators, all contain CFCs. To limit the use and production of these chemicals, the world's nations agreed to stop making and using CFCs beginning in the year 2000. Some products that have CFCs in them could still be in use today if they were made before 2000.

The **mesosphere** layer extends from about 50 km to about 80 km above Earth. Temperatures again decrease with altitude in the mesosphere. Over the poles the air temperatures can drop as low as −100 °C. There is very little water vapor or ozone in the mesosphere. Hot gases and dust particles left by disintegrating meteors can be seen in the mesosphere. In this layer, strong winds blow from west to east during the winter and from east to west during the summer. The lowest temperatures in Earth's atmosphere occur at the top of the mesosphere, the mesopause.

Almost all of the atmosphere lies below the **thermosphere.** It begins 80 km above Earth's surface. It extends over the mesosphere to outer space, getting warmer the higher you go. The major components of the thermosphere are nitrogen and oxygen. However, the molecules of these gases are widely separated. The air in this layer is very thin. The thermosphere is completely exposed to the sun's radiation, which heats this thin air to very high temperatures. Temperatures in the thermosphere can reach as high as 2000 °C.

The part of the atmosphere farthest from Earth's surface is the **exosphere.** It begins about 480 km above Earth and extends as high as 1000 km. It has so little air in it that objects in it encounter almost no resistance. For this reason, most satellites are placed in orbit around the Earth in this layer.

There is almost no air in the exosphere. Satellites like this one encounter almost no resistance as they orbit Earth.

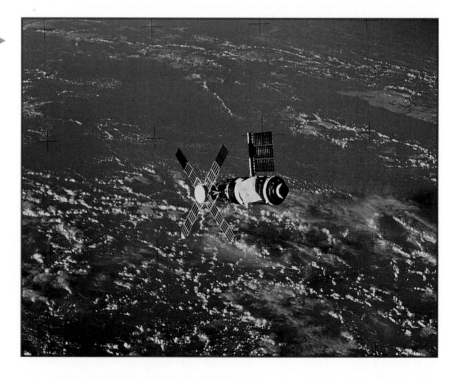

Winds carry particles that allow people to see how air moves.

Air

The atmosphere seems very thick, but compared to Earth's diameter the entire atmosphere is quite thin. If you made a scale model of Earth about the size of an apple, its entire atmosphere would be about as thick as the peel of an apple. In this model, the troposphere would be very thin indeed. Although the troposphere is thin compared to the outer layers of the atmosphere, it contains most of the gases in the atmosphere because of the force of gravity. Earth's atmosphere surrounds the planet. It has mass and is held by gravitational attraction close to Earth. The atmosphere revolves with Earth.

Most planets have atmospheres, including Earth. If there were no atmosphere at all, you would freeze at night and burn to a crisp in the daytime. But just having an atmosphere doesn't mean that a planet can support life. Mars has an atmosphere, but it wouldn't keep you alive. You need certain substances in the air you breathe. A slight change in Earth's atmosphere would make the planet unlivable for many forms of life.

The air in Earth's atmosphere contains a stable mixture of gases, liquids, and solids. Scientists theorize that the atmosphere began to form when Earth itself was first forming, about 5 billion years ago. Gases escaped from Earth's interior through volcanoes and other openings in Earth's newly formed crust.

By studying elements in rocks and gases that volcanoes release today, scientists speculate about what gases early volcanoes may have released. They theorize that Earth releases the same gases from its interior today as it did then. These gases include water vapor, carbon dioxide, nitrogen, ammonia, and methane. For about the first 500 million years of its existence, Earth's atmosphere was probably a mixture of hydrogen, water vapor, and oxides of carbon. The newly formed atmosphere contained about 10 percent carbon dioxide and no free oxygen. Life as we know it couldn't have survived in this early atmosphere.

However, the atmosphere changed over time. Condensation of water vapor helped form Earth's oceans about 4 billion years ago. Hydrogen molecules rose high into the upper atmosphere. Rain washed most of the carbon dioxide from the atmosphere into the oceans and onto land. There the carbon combined with other elements to form compounds such as methane. Methane reacts to form other gases or combines with other substances. With most of the water vapor and carbon dioxide gone from the atmosphere, nitrogen soon came to make up 78 percent of the air near Earth's surface. That is still true today.

Oxygen, the other major gas in Earth's air, wouldn't remain in the air on most planets. It combines easily and quickly with other elements to form compounds such as rust and carbon dioxide. On Earth, plants continually renew the supply of oxygen. In making food, the plants take in carbon dioxide. Early organisms, such as cyanobacteria, used the carbon dioxide in the atmosphere and gave off oxygen as a waste product. Over time, the oxygen content of the air increased. Earth's present atmosphere is 78 percent nitrogen and 21 percent oxygen. The remaining 1 percent of air is made up of tiny amounts of other gases, including carbon dioxide, water vapor, and argon.

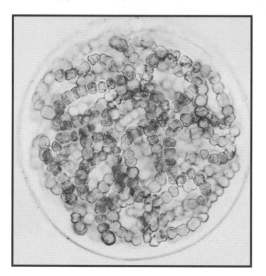

Plantlike organisms make food from the sun's energy and give off oxygen in the process.

Air Pollution

Plants use carbon dioxide and give off oxygen. People and other animals breathe in oxygen and give off carbon dioxide. It sounds quite stable, doesn't it? Until quite recently, Earth's atmosphere hadn't changed much for millions of years. But since the Industrial

The carbon dioxide emitted from these fires in Kuwait accounted for about 2 percent of worldwide emissions in 1992.

Revolution, which took place in the nineteenth century, large quantities of smoke, carbon dioxide, and other pollutants have been added to the air. From about 1850 to the present, Earth's atmosphere has changed relatively rapidly.

Everyone uses the same air that circulates around the planet. Human activity increases the amounts of carbon dioxide, nitrous oxide, and methane in the atmosphere. When people burn fossil fuels such as gas, coal, and oil, these chemicals pollute the air. Carbon dioxide allows sunlight to get through, but traps heat radiated back up from Earth. This is the *greenhouse effect*. It functions the same way as glass in a greenhouse does. The energy from the sun can penetrate through the atmosphere, but the heat radiated from Earth cannot. The heat remains trapped inside the atmosphere. The greenhouse effect may cause temperatures on Earth to get warmer.

Most of the carbon dioxide buildup is caused by burning fossil fuels, such as gas, coal, and oil. One extreme example of how increased pollution can affect weather was observed in 1992. During the Gulf War, several hundred oil fields in Kuwait were set on fire. At one time, more than 600 oil fires were raging out of control. The fires were put out in less than a year. About 1.5 million metric tons of carbon dioxide were emitted every day. Thick clouds of smoke blocked the sun.

Temperatures were 10–15 °C lower than in nearby
areas. Black rain fell throughout the Middle East. The top
of the smoke rose almost 5000 m high. Scientists
monitored the increased amounts of soot and ash
around the world. They hypothesized that the particles in
the air would cause water vapor in the atmosphere to
condense and increase precipitation. Two months after
the fires began, the soot content in places as far away as
Hawaii and Wyoming was five to ten times greater than
normal. However, only the weather in Kuwait, Saudi
Arabia, and Iran was affected by the Kuwait oil fires.

If Earth's atmosphere is warming, as some studies indicate, we need to know how and why. When we understand these changes, we may need to make lifestyle changes or identify ways to reverse the detrimental effects on the environment. Some countries and states have passed laws promoting cleaner air. Such laws have led to automobile emission systems that reduce solid particles and the gases that pollute and form smog. Catalytic converters were installed in cars beginning in 1975. Cars emit over 2.3 kg of carbon dioxide for each liter of gas they use.

One way to monitor emissions from cars is to use a pollution camera. Video cameras are hidden inside traffic cones attached to monitors. The monitor shoots infrared light beams through the exhaust fumes of passing cars. The exhaust changes the infrared beams. The beams are reflected into a detection unit that identifies what is in the fumes. This test could be faster and easier to use than current tests. The hidden cameras record license plates of cars that emit 100 or more grams of carbon monoxide per 1.6 km, well over the limits set by the Clean Air Act. Citations are mailed to people with cars that don't meet the standards.

To reduce carbon dioxide levels in the atmosphere, we can reduce our use of fossil fuels, or we can use fuels that give off little or no carbon dioxide. Of all known fuels, hydrogen is the most pollution-free when burned. Burning hydrogen gives off water vapor and traces of nitrogen. Some cars can burn hydrogen as fuel. However, hydrogen is dangerous to store. It can explode easily. Scientists are working on finding safer ways to store and transport hydrogen.

CHECKPOINT

1. How does Earth's distance from the sun make life possible?
2. What are the layers of the atmosphere?
3. What makes up air?
4. What is air pollution and how can it be monitored?

 What makes up Earth's atmosphere?

ACTIVITY

Finding Pollutants in the Air

Find Out

Do this activity to find out what solid pollutants are in the air.

Process Skills

Observing
Communicating
Predicting

WHAT TO DO

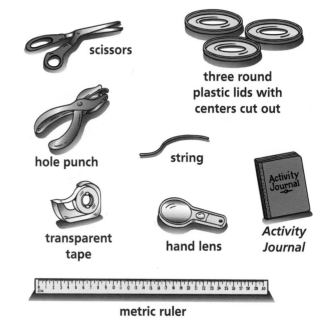

scissors

three round plastic lids with centers cut out

hole punch

string

transparent tape

hand lens

Activity Journal

metric ruler

WHAT TO DO

1. Punch a hole near one edge of each lid.

2. Cut three pieces of string, each long enough to hang the lids from various locations.

3. Put a piece of string through the hole in each lid. Tie a loop in the string so that you can hang the lid by the string. Place three strips of tape across the opening in each lid, with a space between the tape strips.

4. Label each lid. Examine the lids and tape with your hand lens. Record your observations.

5. Find different locations for each lid, indoors and outdoors. Hang the lids near areas with greater air circulation. What do you think will happen to the lids? Record your predictions.

6. The next day, collect the lids. Don't breathe or blow on them. Use your hand lens to observe any particles that collected on the tape. Record your observations. Compare your observations with your predictions.

CONCLUSIONS

1. What did you observe on the tape?
2. Where did you find the most solid air pollutants?
3. Which type of solid air pollutant occurred most often?

ASKING NEW QUESTIONS

1. Why were you to not breathe on the lids after you collected them?
2. What room in your home would have the most solid air pollutants?
3. How could you test that prediction?

SCIENTIFIC METHODS SELF CHECK

✔ Did I **observe** the lids before and after the experiment?

✔ Did I **record** my observations?

✔ Did I **predict** what would happen to the lids?

LESSON 2

The Sun's Role in Weather and Climate

Find Out

- How different amounts of sunlight create different climate zones on Earth
- What air pressure and wind are
- Where Earth's wind belts are

Vocabulary

tropical zone
temperate zones
polar zones
air pressure
wind

The Big QUESTION

How does the sun affect weather and climate?

*E*very place on Earth has a climate. Places far apart can have similar climates. Places close to each other, separated by a mountain perhaps, may have different climates. Climates are classified according to temperature, precipitation, humidity, sunshine, and wind. Air pressure, cloudiness, and seasonal variations also contribute to an area's climate.

Climate

Compare San Francisco and St. Louis. Although they have the same average yearly temperature of 15 °C, they have different climates. St. Louis has cold winters, hot summers, and precipitation throughout the year. San Francisco has mild, rainy winters and cool, almost rainless summers.

Differences occur within climates as well. The Midwest and New England can both have warm to cool summers and cold winters. But weather in Burlington, Iowa, is generally colder in winter and more humid in summer than in Burlington, Vermont. Differences in climates are caused by differences in the way Earth receives solar energy.

St. Louis, Missouri

San Francisco, California

The United States and Canada have seven major climate zones:

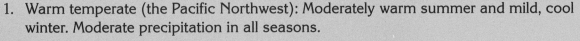

1. Warm temperate (the Pacific Northwest): Moderately warm summer and mild, cool winter. Moderate precipitation in all seasons.

2. Cool temperate (the Midwest and Northeast): Warm to cool summer and cold winter. Moderate precipitation in all seasons. Cool, moist air blows from the poles toward tropical zones. Most people live in temperate zones.

3. Subtropical (the Southeast): Warm to hot summer and cool winter. Moderate precipitation in all seasons.

4. Mediterranean (southern California): Hot, dry summer and mild rainy winter. Moderate precipitation in winter.

5. Mountain (Western mountain ranges): Affected by altitude and generally cooler and wetter than adjacent climates. Mountain zones in the U.S. and Canada include the Rockies, Cascades, and Sierras, and Appalachian Mountains in the United States. Sides of mountains facing wind may get more precipitation than sheltered sides. Air cools as elevation increases because the air is thinner. Snow and ice lie all year on some mountains. Fierce winds blow in the higher elevations.

6. Desert (Southwest): Arizona, Utah, Nevada, New Mexico. Hot to cold, with great changes in daily temperature except in coastal areas. Very little precipitation. Deserts get less than 100 mm of rain per year. Clouds are rare because of lack of moisture. Heat is lost at night because there are no clouds to trap heat.

7. Savanna (plains): Hot to cold, with great changes in daily temperature, except in coastal areas. There is little precipitation.

Sunlight and Temperature

Three main factors influence how Earth receives light and heat from the sun: latitude, topography, and surface temperatures. When the sun is high in the sky, the sun's rays strike Earth more directly than when the sun is low in the sky. In the tropics, the sun is relatively high in the sky all year long. These areas tend to be the warmest places. The sun's rays also explain why people need to avoid the sun at noon. In most locations, the sun is more directly overhead then, and its rays are stronger.

Even within one city, temperatures may vary dramatically during the year. During part of the year, a city warms in the sun, and its residents struggle to stay cool. A few months later, blizzards bury the city in snow. This happens in a given location because the angle of the sun's rays change in the course of a year.

Earth's axis is not perpendicular to the sun. It is tilted. Therefore, as it revolves around the sun, different parts of Earth receive the sun's rays at varying angles throughout the year. The sun's rays fall most directly within the **tropical zones** north and south of the equator. Tropical zones are located along the equator, where the temperatures are high. In the areas north of the Tropic of Cancer and south of the Tropic of Capricorn, the sun's rays are never directly overhead.

Even though it is in the tropics, Mount Kilimanjaro in Kenya has snow at its higher elevations.

In the **temperate zones,** the change in the angle at which the sun strikes Earth from winter to summer is very significant. Temperate zones are north and south of the tropics and have mild or moderate temperatures. As the angle of the sun's rays change, so do the seasons. Hours of daylight increase or decrease. Summers are warm or hot, and winters are cool or cold. Most of Earth's people live in the temperate zones.

During the summer, the polar zones receive 24 hours of daylight. **Polar zones** lie above 60°N or 60°S latitude at Earth's poles and have low temperatures all year. In the winter, these zones are dark for 24 hours. For example, the north pole has continuous daylight for 189 days starting about March 22, but beginning about September 22, the north pole is completely dark for 176 days and the south pole is in continuous daylight.

Areas within your community are also warmed unevenly. At this moment, if the sun is shining, different surfaces are absorbing different amounts of the sun's energy. Dark-colored surfaces, such as asphalt streets, absorb more energy than light-colored surfaces, which reflect energy. Soil and rocks heat up faster than water, but they also cool down faster. More energy is absorbed on a given surface at the time of day when the sun's angle is high. Less energy is absorbed when the sun's angle is low.

At any latitude, elevation also affects temperature. Air becomes less dense at higher altitudes. Even in the tropics, temperatures at high altitudes can be below freezing. For example, find Mount Kilimanjaro on a map. Notice that it is in the tropics. Can you explain why it has snow near its peak?

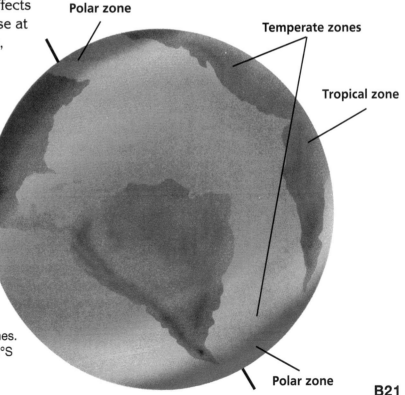

Polar zone

Temperate zones

Tropical zone

Polar zone

Earth has three major climate zones. Tropical zones are located along the equator. North and south of the tropics, between the latitudes of 30° and 60°, lie the temperate zones. Polar zones lie above the 60°N or 60°S latitudes.

This time-lapse photograph shows that the sun can still be seen at midnight during the summer in the arctic regions. The sun is lowest in the sky at midnight, yet it doesn't set below the horizon. Shortly thereafter, the sun begins to rise.

If you live in the northern hemisphere, the month of June may have little or no snow because this area receives the steepest sun rays and the most hours of sunshine in June. Yet, you may have noticed that lakes and oceans are usually warmer in July, August, and September than in June. Some people even wait until July or August before they go swimming in lakes. They know water warms very slowly. Water also cools slowly, in contrast to land, which cools quickly.

Air Pressure and Wind

Surface temperatures affect air temperatures. Think of the atmosphere as many air masses, each with its own temperature. Air masses are large bodies of air with similar temperatures and amounts of moisture. Temperature differences create differences in **air pressure.** Pressure is force acting over an area. Just as air in a balloon has pressure and pushes against the sides of the balloon, air in Earth's atmosphere has pressure and pushes against Earth and surrounding air masses.

Overall, our atmosphere has a mass of about 5.2×10^{15} metric tons. If you were to lie down at the beach and let your friends cover you with sand, you'd feel weight pressing on you. The more sand your friends piled on you, the more weight and pressure you'd feel. Air pressure is similar. The more air there is above you, the greater the weight of that air and the greater its pressure against you.

Most of the time you don't feel air pressure, but if the pressure changes suddenly, you may feel its effects. Have you ever ridden in a car in the mountains, flown in an airplane, or gone to the top of a tall building in a fast elevator? If you have, you may have felt your ears plug up, and you may have even felt them "pop." What causes this feeling?

Why do we care about air pressure? Differences in air pressure are a major factor in causing masses of air to move. The motion of air is vital in keeping the temperature of Earth just right for life. If the air moved only up and down, the tropics would become too hot for most life on Earth. In the polar zones, cold air would settle and the area would become exceedingly cold. In the temperate zones, weather and temperatures would change from season to season, but they would change very little from day to day. Air does move across Earth's surface, making temperatures all over the world more moderate and varied.

Differences in air pressure cause air to move. The movement of air is called **wind.** Differences in air pressure cause wind to blow from areas of high pressure to areas of low pressure. The greater the difference in air pressure, the faster the wind. If the difference is slight, you may feel a gentle breeze. If the difference is great, the wind may blow at speeds that can flatten buildings.

At a height of 5.5 km, air pressure decreases 50 percent from sea level value. Air pressure decreases 25 percent from sea level value at a height of 2.5 km.

Air pressure is greatest at sea level.

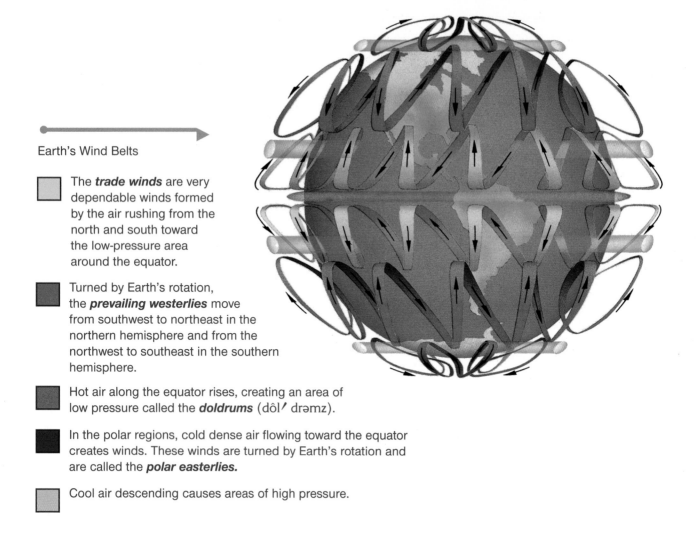

Earth's Wind Belts

The **trade winds** are very dependable winds formed by the air rushing from the north and south toward the low-pressure area around the equator.

Turned by Earth's rotation, the **prevailing westerlies** move from southwest to northeast in the northern hemisphere and from the northwest to southeast in the southern hemisphere.

Hot air along the equator rises, creating an area of low pressure called the **doldrums** (dôl′ drəmz).

In the polar regions, cold dense air flowing toward the equator creates winds. These winds are turned by Earth's rotation and are called the **polar easterlies.**

Cool air descending causes areas of high pressure.

Earth's Wind Belts

As air warms, its molecules move faster and it expands—that is, its molecules move farther apart. When air expands, its molecules take up more space without increasing in number. Cool air is more dense than warm air, meaning it has more molecules in a given amount of space. Thus, a cubic meter of warm air has less mass than a cubic meter of cool air. Therefore, a change in air temperature affects air pressure as well. When the air pressure changes due to a change in the temperature, a wind may spring up.

Winds flowing from an area of high pressure to an area of low pressure usually don't move in a straight line because of the rotation of Earth. Rather, the winds tend to spiral into low- and high-pressure centers.

You know that differences in pressure create winds. Did you know that unless the wind is very strong most objects in the path of wind can change the wind's direction or its velocity? Wind swirls around trees and buildings. When channeled into a narrow corridor between buildings or rocks, wind speeds can change dramatically.

Just as winds flow in patterns around buildings, certain predictable global wind patterns exist worldwide. Differences in temperature produce patterns of pressure systems called highs and lows all over Earth's surface. The diagram on the preceding page shows the major wind belts on the planet.

These pressure systems and prevailing winds influence weather all over the world. The winds influence the direction in which weather systems move. In which direction do you think weather systems move in the temperate zones?

The temperature and pressure of the atmosphere are always changing. Measuring and tracking them give us a better understanding of how the atmosphere affects us. The temperature and pressure of the atmosphere interact with one another and have a daily influence on you, whether you live at the top of a mountain, near the sea, or far inland.

CHECKPOINT

1. How do different amounts of sunlight create different climate zones on Earth?

2. What are air pressure and wind?

3. Where are Earth's wind belts?

 How does the sun affect weather and climate?

ACTIVITY

Testing Air

Find Out

Do this activity to learn how land and water absorb and release energy from the sun.

Process Skills

Predicting
Hypothesizing
Communicating
Using Numbers

WHAT YOU NEED

 two 475-mL glass jars

 soil

 water

 four thermometers

 masking tape

 safety goggles

 Activity Journal

WHAT TO DO

Safety! *Wear goggles when working with soil.*

1. Fill one container half full of soil. Fill the other container half full of water.

2. Tape one thermometer against the inside of each container so its bulb is 1 cm under the surface of the soil or water. Tape the other thermometers against the insides of the containers so that their bulbs are 1 cm above the surfaces of the water and soil.

3. Place the containers side by side in the room in the sunlight. Predict which thermometer will register the higher temperature. Form a hypothesis about the temperature of air over land and over water. Record your predictions and hypothesis.

4. Read and record the temperature of each thermometer every minute for 30 minutes.

5. Make a graph comparing the time in minutes with the temperatures for the soil, the water, and the air above each.

CONCLUSIONS

1. In which container did the temperature increase more?

2. How did the soil or water temperature affect the temperature of the air above it?

3. Do your data support your hypothesis about the temperature of air over land and over water? Explain why there is a difference in temperature.

ASKING NEW QUESTIONS

1. How do large bodies of water affect air temperatures around the world?

2. How do large areas of dark soil affect air temperatures?

SCIENTIFIC METHODS SELF CHECK

✔ Did I **predict** the temperatures of the different thermometers?

✔ Did I **hypothesize** why the temperatures would differ?

✔ Did I **record** my prediction and hypothesis?

✔ Did I **graph** my data?

Atmosphere and Weather Changes

Find Out

- What makes up weather
- How weather can be predicted
- What three types of severe storms are and how to protect yourself during those storms

Vocabulary

front
cold front
warm front
stationary front
occluded front
tornadoes
hurricanes

The Big QUESTION

What causes severe weather?

*D*o you remember learning about the water cycle? Through the process of evaporation, liquid water changes to water vapor, an invisible gas. Warm, moist air rises. It meets the cooler air of the upper atmosphere. Warmer air has more water vapor.

In clouds, the water vapor condenses on tiny particles that are always present in the atmosphere. These particles include dust, smoke, salt crystals, and soil. When water droplets combine to form larger drops and become massive enough to fall in the atmosphere, the process is called precipitation.

What Makes Up Weather

In large and small ways, the weather has always been important to humans. It influences our clothing, our activities, and where we take shelter. More importantly, weather can cause dangerous conditions and even deaths.

Meteorologists use weather maps to observe air masses carefully and track their movement. They know that air masses, their movement, and the way they interact with each other determine weather conditions.

The place where an air mass forms is called its source area. An air mass can be characterized by its temperature, humidity, and pressure. Meteorologists predicting weather changes can rely on their understanding of air mass characteristics.

As an air mass moves, it comes in contact with other air masses with different temperatures and amounts of moisture. The air masses interact with one another at their boundaries and produce changes that can often be predicted. The boundary between air masses, where the interaction takes place, is called a **front.** As the air masses move, the front moves with them.

Air masses seldom move at the same speed. The mass that is moving faster determines the way the two masses will interact, because the faster-moving mass overcomes the slower one. Most stormlike weather conditions take place along fronts.

A **cold front** forms when a cold air mass moves into a region occupied by a warm air mass. Warm air and cold air don't mix easily. When warm air is forced to rise, it cools and its relative humidity increases. Thus, the water vapor in the air condenses and forms a line of clouds.

As you can see from the diagram on the next page, when a warm air mass overtakes a cold air mass that's moving away, a **warm front** develops. The warm air is forced up, and the cooler air remains under the warm, rising air. As the warm air is forced upward, it cools, clouds form, and precipitation frequently develops.

As cold air moves into an area occupied by warm air, a cold front develops. Cold fronts usually mean stormy weather.

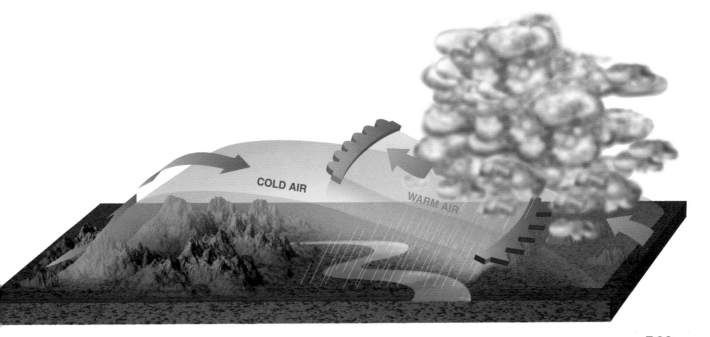

COLD AIR

WARM AIR

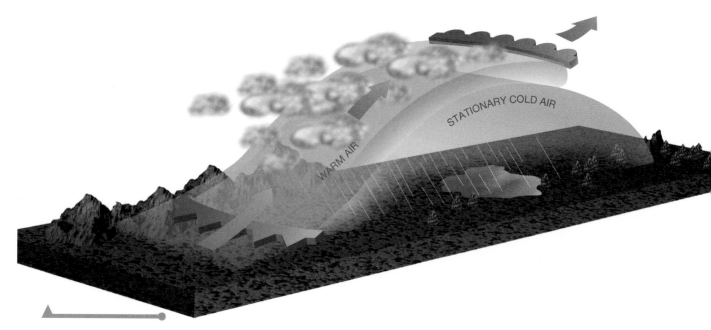

As warm air moves into an area occupied by cold air, a warm front develops. Warm fronts usually bring gentle, long-lasting showers.

In an occluded front, a cold front catches up with a warm front. The warm air is pushed up and away from Earth's surface.

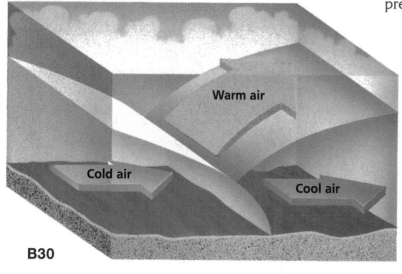

Warm air

Cold air

Cool air

A warm or cold front can stall, or stop moving, for a period of time. Such a front does not advance and is called a **stationary front.** Another type of front is formed when a cold front overtakes another cold front, lifting the warm air above the surface. This is an **occluded** (e klo͞od′ ed) **front.**

Fronts cause disturbances in the atmosphere, and therefore, they change the weather. Certain types of weather changes are associated with each type of front. Usually, cold fronts move faster than warm fronts. They also cause the air to rise more quickly and at a steeper angle than air along warm fronts. The rapidly rising air results in the formation of cumulus and cumulonimbus clouds that develop vertically, sometimes reaching great heights. Cold fronts and their clouds may bring heavy precipitation with large drops. However, because cold fronts move fast, the precipitation and other weather conditions they bring are often brief. The front often passes quickly and the skies clear. As the front passes and the cold air mass replaces the warmer one, the temperature drops.

The boundary of a warm front isn't as steep as that of a cold front. Thus, the air rises more slowly and is forced aloft, spreading out over a wide area. Usually this results in the formation of thick, layered stratus clouds. Because warm fronts are wide and move slowly, they generally bring steady, long-lasting rain or snow.

With any front, the amount of precipitation depends on how much water vapor is present in the warm air being forced aloft. If the air contains a lot of moisture, the front produces heavy clouds and precipitation as the air cools. If the air being forced aloft is dry, clouds may form but precipitation doesn't develop.

Predicting Weather

How do meteorologists predict the weather? Each morning, information is gathered by the National Weather Advisory Board. Weather balloons carrying instruments rise more than 32 km into the atmosphere and then burst. The instruments then fall by parachute back to Earth. Similar weather balloons are launched each day from 700 locations around the world.

Gathering weather information is a cooperative effort. Across the United States, more than 12,000 volunteer observers phone in their information. About 300 observers are located on merchant ships at sea, and almost 4000 commercial airplane crews report their observations. Hundreds of weather offices also report their information to the National Meteorological Service daily. There, giant computers organize the information and create models of the conditions in Earth's atmosphere. The computers also create national and regional weather maps. As you know, weather maps contain information about weather conditions such as wind speed, temperature, and cloud cover. They also show the location of air masses and fronts. These maps are updated every three hours. By comparing two maps made three hours apart, meteorologists can see the directions in which weather systems are moving and the speeds at which they're moving. This helps meteorologists predict where those weather systems will go next.

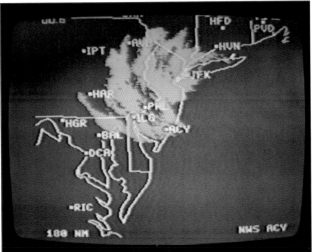

Doppler radar is one method of tracking storms and identifying severe weather. This radar image shows a storm over the east coast of the United States.

Severe Storms

When wind begins to blow hard and big raindrops start falling, do you ever wonder how a severe storm develops? How can we tell when these storms will occur?

In 1992, Hurricane Andrew raged through southern Florida. The strong winds of this hurricane smashed things in its path and ripped trees from the ground, roots and all. When Hurricane Andrew had moved on, southern Florida was a jumble of twisted and tangled wreckage of demolished buildings and trees. Andrew left 52 people dead and 250,000 people homeless. The price tag for rebuilding damaged areas was an estimated $20 billion, making Hurricane Andrew the costliest storm in United States history.

After battering Florida, Hurricane Andrew headed west and slammed into Louisiana. In areas that received warning, people were able to prevent loss of life and protect some property. Unfortunately, lives were lost in areas where people had no such warning. How do you think the path of the storm was predicted?

In August 1990, a tornado swept through the Illinois towns of Plainfield, Crest Hill, and Joliet with winds of 480 km/h. Nine people were pulled from their apartment buildings and thrown into a cornfield 12 m away. This tornado created a path of destruction 26 km long, injuring 90 people and killing 27 others.

Thunderstorm systems usually have high winds, but not all winds are dangerous. Winds move warm air to cold areas, and push cool air to hot regions. Even so, winds and precipitation can combine to bring disaster to living things. What makes winds and precipitation act this way?

Hurricane Andrew had winds that ranged from speeds of 225 km/h to 275 km/h.

Thunderstorms

Thunderstorms begin when warm, humid air rises upward rapidly. Warm air is less dense than the cooler air around it. The warmer and the more humid air is, the faster it rises and is cooled. As the warm air rises, the relative humidity increases until it reaches the dew point. Then, the water vapor condenses to form either water droplets or ice crystals.

In a thunderstorm rainfall can be so heavy that flooding results. Fortunately, high-speed winds usually push thunderclouds along, so the storm passes quickly before extensive floods develop. Meteorologists, by knowing the conditions that cause thunderstorms to form, can often predict the development and movement of these storms. Thus, they can warn people in the path of the storms to take shelter.

When water vapor condenses or freezes, it releases heat into the air that surrounds it. This heat warms the air further, causing more uplift. Moist air from the bottom of the system rushes in to replace the rising air. The rapidly rising air builds a towering cumulus cloud. Air and water vapor move up and down very rapidly within this cloud.

The friction of ice crystals whizzing through the cloud creates electrical disturbances. For reasons meteorologists do not entirely understand, the cloud may produce bolts of electricity called lightning. Extreme heat from a lightning bolt causes the air to become very hot—up to 25,000 °C. Thus, the air expands rapidly. When this sudden expansion occurs, it produces a loud noise—what we call thunder.

Because light travels faster than sound, you see the flash of lightning before you hear the crash of thunder. If you heard the thunder five seconds after you saw the flash, the lightning struck about a kilometer and a half away. If the amount of time between the flash and the thunder becomes shorter, the electrical storm is moving towards you. That means it's time to take precautions. Your chances of being struck by lightning are slim. However, lightning can cause serious injury or burn objects it strikes.

The rapid rising of warm, moist air results in heavy precipitation during thunderstorms. Lightning is probably caused by electrical disturbances within clouds.

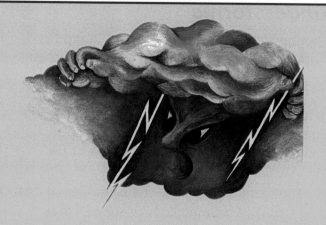

Thunderstorm Safety

1. Go inside if possible, but don't go into a small building that stands off by itself.

2. Avoid pipes, faucets, and electrical outlets.

3. If you can't go inside, stay away from places where you are taller than the objects around you. Don't stand on a hilltop or in an open field. If you are in the open, lie flat, even if you get wet or muddy.

4. Don't go into water. Lightning is attracted to water. Don't go out in a boat, because the boat will be taller than the surrounding water and attract the lightning.

5. Avoid anything made of metal. Lightning is attracted to metal.

6. Don't go under a tree. Head for a low spot if you're stuck in a forest.

7. A car is a safe place to be because the charge will travel through to the tires and into the ground. Be sure you aren't touching any metal parts of the car.

8. Don't use the telephone unless it's an emergency, because electricity can travel through the phone lines.

9. Lightning may be about to strike if you feel your hair stand on end. Immediately squat, lean forward, and place your hands on your knees, trying to make yourself as low to the ground as possible.

The chart tells how you can protect yourself during a thunderstorm. About 2 percent of thunderstorms produce tornadoes. Have you ever seen a tornado? How does the funnel shape spin and travel?

Tornadoes

A tornado is an extreme example of a wind system called a cyclone. In a cyclone, winds spiral around a low-pressure center. In the northern hemisphere, these winds move counterclockwise, and in the southern hemisphere, they move clockwise. Most severe storms develop in these cyclonic (sī klon′ ik) wind systems.

Tornadoes are powerful winds that form during other storms. They move over land in narrow paths. Their winds are so strong that they can pick up houses and smash factories. Tornadoes affect relatively small areas, but their fierce winds devastate almost everything in their path. The winds flatten buildings and hurl objects at speeds so great that a straw driven by the force of a tornado's wind can penetrate wood. These winds can also pick up huge objects such as trains. Some of these objects are crushed, and others are simply carried away.

Little can be done to avoid property damage in a tornado, but taking precautions can save lives. Tornado warnings don't come very far in advance, and sometimes they don't come at all. The path of a tornado is difficult to predict. A tornado can reduce one house to splinters and leave the one next door untouched. When meteorologists suspect that a tornado is forming, they warn everyone in the area to be prepared. Sometimes a tornado may approach without warning, but often you can see a tornado form.

Tornadoes appear as funnel-shaped extensions from clouds.

Tornado Safety Procedures

If you're at home:

1. Open the windows slightly, then get away from them.
2. Go to a storm cellar if you have one, or else go to a basement and stay underneath a staircase, mattress, or heavy piece of furniture, such as a table.
3. Don't go into a mobile home. Find shelter in a strong building.

If you're away from home:

1. Get away from the street.
2. Try to find a building to enter, but stay away from windows and doors.
3. If you can't find a building, lie in a ditch and cover your head with your hands.
4. If you're at school, go to an inside hallway on the lowest floor, bend over, and place your hands on your head.

As you may already know, tornadoes are most likely to form in thunderstorms with heavy rain or hail. How does this funnel of wind develop? As the warm, humid air rises upward within a cumulonimbus cloud, more warm air rushes in to replace the air that was forced upward. The air that rushes in also rises upward, and in some instances it begins to rotate. This rotating air extends beneath the cloud and may touch down toward the surface. Tornadoes can last a few minutes or as long as a few hours. They can move over the surface of land anywhere from 40 to 100 km/h, and they follow very unpredictable paths.

When a tornado has been spotted, you must take precautions immediately. The chart on the preceding page tells you what to do. Tornadoes can be tracked in order to warn people and provide them with time to use the information found in the chart.

Hurricanes

The cyclonic storms that cause the most widespread destruction are **hurricanes.** They are also known as typhoons in the South China Sea and the Indian Ocean, and as willy-willies in Australia. The wind speeds are usually 120–240 km/h; however, unlike tornadoes, hurricanes form over ocean waters and

Hurricane Precautions

1. Tape or board up all windows. Flying debris and wind pressure can break windows.

2. Secure outdoor objects that might be blown away—such as outdoor furniture and potted plants—or bring them inside.

3. Be sure to have plenty of canned foods, medical supplies, and freshwater on hand. Shipping and receiving such items may become difficult if a storm hits.

4. Leave all low-lying coastal areas, because they're likely to be swept by high tides and storm waves.

5. Stay at home if it's on sturdy, high ground. If not, then go to the appropriate shelter.

6. Beware of the eye of the hurricane. It may produce a lull for a few minutes to half an hour. At the other side of the eye, winds can again rise very quickly.

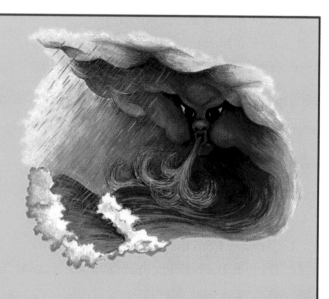

may be hundreds of kilometers in diameter. They can also last for several days and travel hundreds or thousands of kilometers. Hurricane Mitch, for example, formed in a low-pressure system off the coast of Africa and traveled to the United States. In 1998, Hurricane Mitch devastated areas in the Caribbean. It then traveled to the southeastern United States and caused some damage in Florida and South Carolina.

If you ever receive warning that a hurricane may strike your area, begin to take precautions. It's important to follow the advice of the authorities. You may be told to leave the area before the storm hits. Many people have died because they ignored such warnings. If you're not advised to leave the area, use the precautions listed in the chart on the preceding page.

The center of a hurricane is an area known as the eye. Within the eye, the air begins to sink because it is an area of low-pressure. The air within the eye is quite calm. The eye of a hurricane can be 20–200 km across. As the eye passes over an area, the wind speed drops and the sky may be clear and sunny. After the eye passes, fierce winds and heavy rainfall begin to pound the land and water again.

The formation of hurricanes usually takes place over tropical oceans, at latitudes between 5° and 20°. The ocean waters are warmed in the hot, direct rays of the sun, especially in late summer and early autumn.

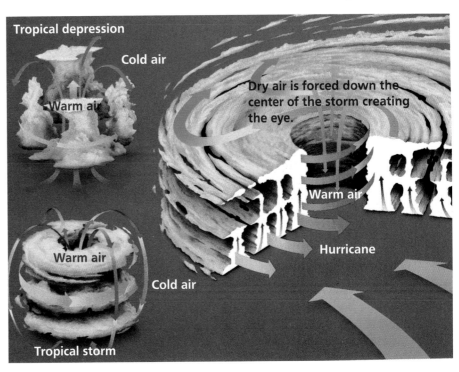

Warm, moist air rises rapidly, creating updrafts of air and an area of very low pressure called a tropical depression. Surrounding air rushes into the low-pressure center, sometimes at terrific speeds. In a hurricane, winds rage around this center at speeds of more than 200 km/h.

CHECKPOINT

1. What makes up weather?
2. How can weather be predicted?
3. What are three types of severe storms, and how can you protect yourself during those storms?

 What causes severe weather?

ACTIVITY

Classifying Storm Characteristics

Find Out

Do this activity to learn what the common characteristics of a thunderstorm, a hurricane, and a tornado are.

Process Skills

Predicting
Observing
Communicating
Inferring
Experimenting

WHAT YOU NEED

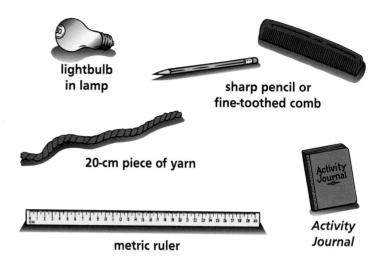

lightbulb in lamp

sharp pencil or fine-toothed comb

20-cm piece of yarn

metric ruler

Activity Journal

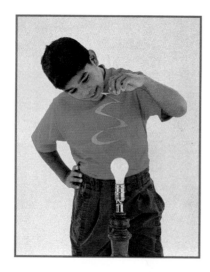

WHAT TO DO

1. Slowly and gently separate the threads at one end of the yarn with the pencil or comb. Predict what will happen when you hold the yarn over an unlit lightbulb. Record your prediction.

2. Hold the other end of the yarn over the unlit lightbulb so the bottom of the yarn is 10 cm above the top of the bulb.

3. Observe what happens to the yarn for about 1 minute.

4. Record your observations with words or drawings.

5. Predict what will happen when you hold the yarn over the lightbulb when it is lit. Now, turn on the lamp. Repeat Step 2, making sure the bottom of the yarn is about 10 cm above the lightbulb.

   Safety! *Do not look directly at the lit lightbulb or touch it. Don't let the yarn touch the lit bulb.*

6. After you observe what happens, turn off the lightbulb. Record your observations with words or drawings.

CONCLUSIONS

1. What effect did the unlit lightbulb have on the yarn? When you did the same thing with the lightbulb lit, what happened?

2. What do the yarn threads tell you about air movement? What happens to air above very warm land or water?

3. Why did you hold the yarn threads over the unlit bulb?

ASKING NEW QUESTIONS

1. What is the most common condition present during the formation of a thunderstorm, a tornado, or a hurricane?

2. How did you infer this from your experiment?

SCIENTIFIC METHODS SELF CHECK

✔ Did I **predict** what would happen to the yarn?

✔ Did I **observe** what happened?

✔ Did I **record** my prediction and observations?

✔ Did I **infer** the most common condition in the formation of a storm from the **experiment?**

Review

Reviewing Vocabulary and Concepts

Write the letter of the answer that best completes each sentence.

1. Energy from the sun comes to Earth in the form of ___.
   - **a.** global warming
   - **b.** light
   - **c.** thermal inversion
   - **d.** solar radiation

2. By receiving and releasing equal amounts of energy, Earth maintains ___.
   - **a.** the atmosphere
   - **b.** a radiation balance
   - **c.** a greenhouse effect
   - **d.** constant weather

3. The movement of air is called ___.
   - **a.** air pressure
   - **b.** climate
   - **c.** wind
   - **d.** humidity

4. When cold air moves into a region occupied by warm air, what forms is called ___.
   - **a.** a cold front
   - **b.** an air mass
   - **c.** a stationary front
   - **d.** a warm front

5. Powerful storms that move over land in narrow paths are called ___.
   - **a.** hurricanes
   - **b.** blizzards
   - **c.** weather systems
   - **d.** tornadoes

Match the definition on the left with the correct term.

6. layer of atmosphere closest to Earth
   - **a.** thermosphere

7. contains most of the ozone
   - **b.** mesosphere

8. has the coldest temperatures in the atmosphere
   - **c.** troposphere

9. found above most of the atmosphere
   - **d.** stratosphere

10. the boundary between air masses
    - **e.** front

Understanding What You Learned

1. Not all of the energy from the sun reaches Earth. Why is this so?
2. How does the atmosphere affect the temperature of Earth's surface?
3. Explain the difference between weather and climate.
4. How does the angle at which the sun's rays hit Earth affect the temperature?
5. How are tornadoes and hurricanes alike? How are they different?

Applying What You Learned

1. What are some things people could do to protect the atmosphere?
2. How could shifting wind patterns affect a region's climate?
3. A region has hot summers and cold winters. How would you describe the angle of the sun during both seasons?
4. A warm air mass is overtaking a cold air mass. As the warm air is forced up, the cooler air remains under the warm air. What probably will happen?

5. How are Earth's climates and weather affected by the sun's influence on the atmosphere?

For Your **Portfolio**

Imagine you live with a nine-year-old brother or sister and are visiting an area near a warm ocean. You have been warned that a hurricane is headed your way, but your area is not being evacuated. Write a dialogue in which you explain to the younger child what to expect if the hurricane hits, what you must do, and why.

2 Earth's Surfaces

Wave Rock, near Hyden, Australia, is a spectacular formation about 15 m high and several hundred meters long. Scientists estimate that the rock, which remarkably looks like an ocean wave, is more than 2700 million years old. The erosion that produced the wavelike appearance probably occurred during the last 1000 years.

Rocks look hard and unchanging, but in fact, they're constantly being changed by the forces of nature. Have you ever piled rocks in a stream to create a dam? Over time, the force of the stream's running water will change the appearance of the piles.

The forces that sculpt, or change, Earth's rocky surface occur all the time. Around the clock, rivers pick up rocks, carry them along, change them, and put them down someplace else. Day and night, winds blow sand grains against rocks, grind them down, and carry them off. Inside Earth, other processes also work without stopping to create rocks or to change them.

The Big IDEA

Earth's surface has land, water, and natural resources.

CHAPTER SCIENCE INVESTIGATION

Make and erode rocks. Find out how in your *Activity Journal.*

The Rock Cycle

The Big QUESTION

How do rocks change over time?

Planet Earth is undergoing constant and continuing changes. Some of these changes occur daily; others take thousands, or even millions, of years. Some Earth changes result in awe-inspiring events such as volcanic eruptions or powerful storms of wind and water. Other changes happen unseen, deep within Earth or in quiet streambeds. Earth's crust is made of rock. Through our investigation of rocks, we can identify their composition and infer their origins and histories.

Minerals

Minerals are one of Earth's important natural resources. Minerals are the basic materials that make up Earth. Minerals all have a definite chemical composition. They can be elements or compounds. Minerals occur in nature, are inorganic, and have their own crystalline shapes. An inorganic compound is one that does not come from living things.

Many of the products you use have some sort of mineral as an ingredient—soft-drink cans, electrical wiring, coins, computer chips, pencils, jewelry, automobiles, and pots and pans. Minerals can also be found in living things, but minerals do not come from living things.

Diamond is a mineral. A manufactured diamond, even though it looks the same, is not a mineral. It does not occur in nature. A pearl is not a mineral because it comes from an oyster. Oil is not a mineral for two reasons. It is not a solid, and it is made from ancient once-living organisms.

The properties of some minerals make them so pretty that people in cultures all over the world wear them. They wear them on their fingers, in their ears, and around their necks. The minerals in jewelry look different from the raw minerals within Earth's crust. Raw minerals are mined, or taken from Earth, and polished before they become gemstones.

But minerals add more to our lives than beauty. Minerals have many practical, day-to-day uses. For example, from minerals we obtain iron, copper, and aluminum that are used in making pots and pans, cars and machinery, and many synthetic fabrics and medicines.

Suppose your teacher told you that two new students, Maya and Michael, would be joining your class. Would it be possible to figure out beforehand which student was shy, which had musical talent, and which had a good sense of humor? Of course not! You'd need to meet and talk to Maya and Michael before drawing any conclusions about their unique characteristics. This same "seeing is believing" principle is also important when it comes to identifying minerals. To identify minerals, you must look for their unique characteristics.

These materials and products each contain at least one mineral.

Properties of Minerals

Clear quartz has a glassy luster.

Talc is a nonmetallic mineral with a pearly luster.

Asbestos has a silky luster.

Exactly what are these things called minerals? A substance must meet five requirements to be classified as a mineral. A mineral is solid, nonliving, and formed in nature. It has atoms that form a crystalline pattern, and its chemical composition is definite.

Minerals are compositions of one or more Earth elements, such as silicon, oxygen, carbon, and iron. Elements combine to form more than 500 different minerals, but there are fewer than 100 common minerals. Some minerals are found in Earth's crust, in caves, streams, rivers, and oceans. Other minerals are buried deeper inside Earth's crust and in the mantle.

As an analogy, consider the millions of different kinds of people in the world. How are they alike? What distinguishes them from one another? Think of your family. Each of you has something in common, making you members of the same family, yet each of you is unique. The same is true of minerals. Minerals can be distinguished by their physical as well as their chemical properties.

Luster: The luster of a mineral is simply the way it reflects light. Have you ever noticed how a gemstone diamond glitters? The cut and polish of the diamond makes it appear to sparkle. A mineral's luster can be described as being either *metallic* or *nonmetallic*. Minerals with a metallic luster shine like metal. Pyrite, commonly called "fool's gold," has a metallic luster.

Minerals that don't shine like metals have nonmetallic luster. The luster of nonmetallic minerals may be described in many ways. Some look pearly. Other nonmetallic lusters are said to be glassy or silky.

Cleavage: Another way to identify a mineral is to observe the way it breaks. If a mineral breaks, or cleaves, along smooth, flat planes, it has cleavage. Calcite has cleavage in three directions. As a result, when force is applied to calcite in a certain direction, it splits into blocks. Micas have cleavage in only one direction. They break into sheetlike pieces. Some minerals do not break along even planes. Instead, these minerals fracture, or break, along irregular surfaces. Quartz and garnet are two minerals that fracture.

Color: Minerals can be every color of the rainbow. The color of some minerals is determined by the composition and the kinds and amounts of impurities in the minerals. However, certain minerals, such as quartz, exhibit a range of colors naturally. Some single crystals of quartz are even multicolored.

Streak: A mineral's streak is another way to identify it. The streak is the color of the powder left by the mineral when it is rubbed across a piece of unglazed porcelain tile called a streak plate. The streak left by a mineral may be a different color from the mineral itself. For example, pyrite, which looks like gold, leaves a greenish-black streak. Gold, on the other hand, leaves a yellow streak. Minerals harder than the streak plate won't leave a streak.

Hardness: Another property commonly used to identify minerals is hardness, or the mineral's resistance to being scratched. *Diamond* comes from the Greek word *adamas,* meaning "unconquerable." That is a good description of a diamond's qualities. Most minerals are made of two or more elements, but a diamond is composed of only one element—carbon. The diamond is the hardest natural substance on Earth because of the way the carbon atoms combine. The beautiful diamonds you are used to seeing in jewelry have been carefully cleaved and polished to reflect light.

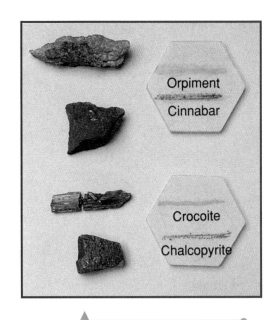

Streak plate

The Mohs Scale of Mineral Hardness is a ranking of ten minerals according to hardness. This scale is very useful because any other mineral can be compared to the minerals on the Mohs scale as a standard for "scratch ability." You have probably heard that diamonds can cut glass. This is supported by the Mohs scale, as shown at the right. It shows diamond as having a hardness rating of 10, while a piece of glass has a hardness rating of 5.5.

Any unknown mineral can be tested for hardness. Scratch its smooth surface with another known mineral or test material, such as a fingernail, copper penny, or knife. If you can scratch the unknown mineral, you know that it is lower on the Mohs scale than the material that scratched it.

Mohs Scale of Mineral Hardness		
Hardness	Mineral	General Features
1	Talc	soft, flaky, slightly greasy
2	Gypsum	can be scratched by your fingernail
3	Calcite	can be scratched by a penny
4	Fluorite	can be scratched by a knife
5	Apatite	barely scratched by a knife
6	Orthoclase	can scratch glass easily
7	Quartz	can scratch a steel file
8	Topaz	can scratch a quartz
9	Corundum	can scratch a topaz
10	Diamond	cannot be scratched

Rocks

When you stand on the edge of the Grand Canyon and look down, you can see about 2.5 km deep into Earth. The Colorado River at the bottom looks like a thin green ribbon. Any river rafters passing by appear to be the size of ants and cannot see you waving. Walking down the canyon is like walking back into time. You can see different layers of rocks as you descend into the canyon because they are different colors—red, green, and purple. What do they tell us? The walls of the Grand Canyon have been called the world's oldest history book because their rock record goes back two billion years. In order to understand this history, we have to learn how rocks are formed and what they say.

Rocks provide important clues to our environment. The rocky walls of a canyon tell what happened a million years ago, and how the canyon formed. Rocks act as Earth's record of past events, even before there was such a thing as a written record.

What are rocks made of? Rocks are combinations of different minerals that have gone through a natural process to make them into rocks. Minerals are the ingredients that make rocks, just as flour, sugar, and chocolate chips are cookie ingredients. Rocks may be made of a single mineral or a combination of minerals. Rocks are classified into different types by the ways that they were formed.

Many things that happened over millions of years formed the Grand Canyon in Arizona. Rivers, seas, and deserts formed layers of sedimentary rock over very old igneous and metamorphic rocks.

Igneous rocks are rocks formed from molten Earth materials. Igneous rocks all began as a material called magma, which is the hot, liquid rock in Earth's interior. When magma erupts at the surface of Earth in a volcano, it is called lava. When the magma cools into solid rock, it becomes an igneous rock. Some types of igneous rock are obsidian, pumice, and pitchstone. Granite is another type of igneous rock which is cooled underground.

Sedimentary rocks are rocks formed as a result of weathering and deposition of loose Earth materials, or by taking material out of solution. Sedimentary rocks are composed primarily of clay and the minerals calcite and quartz. They are created when loose debris of other rocks, called sediment, is washed away and settles in a place with other loose gravel, sand, and pebbles. Commonly, sediment gathers at the bottom of the ocean, having been washed there by rivers. Over time, various forces act on the sediment in order to form it into new rock. As the loose materials pile onto one another, they are packed closer together. In addition, spaces in the sediment may be filled with other mineral matter, which acts as a cement and holds the packed sediment together. Over many years, sedimentary rock forms.

In many parts of Earth, the most common type of rock that we see at the surface is sedimentary rock. The walls of the Grand Canyon are sedimentary rock. Many areas on Earth that are now land were once under water, and sedimentary rock formed at that time. Later, these old submarine beds were raised above sea level. Some types of sedimentary rocks are sandstone, mudstone, and limestone.

Metamorphic rocks are rocks formed from pre-existing rocks as a result of temperature or pressure changes. Metamorphic rocks are formed when igneous, sedimentary, or other metamorphic rocks undergo major changes due to heat, pressure, or chemical fluids. The changes that occur create an entirely new rock.

Meta is a word that means "change." *Morph* is a word that means "form." Metamorphic rocks come from other rocks that change form. For example, the igneous rock granite, and the metamorphic rock schist, will both turn into the metamorphic rock gneiss at high temperatures and pressures. At medium temperatures and pressures, the sedimentary rock limestone can turn into marble.

Three kinds of rock: igneous, sedimentary, and metamorphic. Can you identify which rock is which?

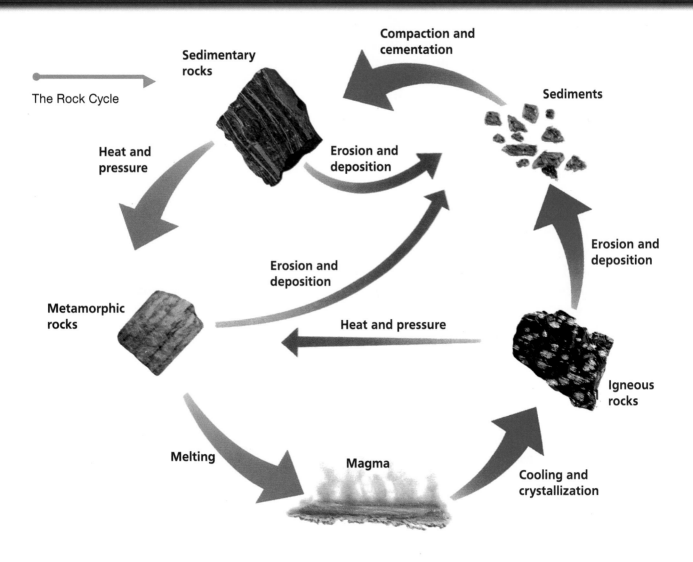

The Rock Cycle

Sedimentary rocks

Compaction and cementation

Sediments

Heat and pressure

Erosion and deposition

Erosion and deposition

Metamorphic rocks

Erosion and deposition

Heat and pressure

Igneous rocks

Melting

Magma

Cooling and crystallization

Rocks and other Earth materials are constantly changing. These changes are caused by chemical and physical processes occurring both on and below Earth's surface. On Earth's surface, air, wind, water, and other forces cause change. Heat and pressure act on rocks below Earth's surface. Together, these processes make up what is called the **rock cycle.** This continuous cycle affects all three kinds of rock.

The rock cycle begins with igneous rocks, which are created when magma has cooled and become solid. Rain, wind, freezing, and other natural processes wear down igneous rocks that are exposed at Earth's surface. This debris is deposited and turns into sedimentary rocks after undergoing years of pressure and cementing. The resulting sedimentary rock may, through burial, heat, or pressure, be changed into metamorphic rocks. Metamorphic rocks, which are deeply buried, may melt and become magma again. Rock formation and change are a continuous cycle.

Earth's rocks, landscapes, and human-made structures are being continually changed by the forces of nature. Many rocks change colors, composition, firmness, or form because of weathering. **Weathering** is the breaking down of rocks into smaller pieces by natural processes. Wind and water are important agents in the weathering process.

The breakdown of rocks involves two types of weathering that work together—physical weathering and chemical weathering. Physical weathering reduces rocks to smaller fragments without changing their composition. Rocks that have been physically weathered provide much of the material, or sediments, for the formation of sedimentary rocks.

The other kind of weathering, chemical weathering, causes the minerals that make up rocks to undergo chemical changes. These changes weaken a rock's structure so it is more easily broken down by physical weathering processes.

Rock fragments and particles are formed by weathering processes. They are commonly carried away by the agents acting on the original, larger rock, such as mass wasting, water, wind, and glaciers. **Erosion** is the process by which weathered particles are carried away and redeposited by nature's agents of change. The forces of erosion are constantly removing and redepositing loose, weathered materials on Earth's surface.

Like other cycles in nature, the rock cycle is a sequence of changes happening over and over again. Trace the steps of the rock cycle on the diagram. Notice that chemical and physical weathering and erosion are parts of the rock cycle.

The appearance of this gravestone is the result of weathering.

CHECKPOINT

1. What is a mineral?
2. Name at least three mineral properties.
3. What are rocks?

 How do rocks change over time?

ACTIVITY

Classifying Rocks and Minerals

Find Out

Do this activity to find out how to classify rocks and minerals.

Process Skills

Observing
Classifying
Hypothesizing

WHAT YOU NEED

rock and mineral samples

hand lens

glass plate

Activity Journal

steel file

penny

WHAT TO DO

1. Observe and examine the whole group of rocks and minerals.

2. Describe the minerals and rocks in your sample by visual appearance.

3. Describe the general texture of each item. Is it smooth or rough? Is it layered? Are there any holes? Are the edges of each piece smooth or angular?

4. Put your items into groups according to their similar properties. Write down this classification list.

5. Hypothesize about the hardness of each sample and whether it is a pure mineral or a sedimentary, igneous, or metamorphic rock. Record your observations.

6. **Observe** each item with your hand lens. Add to your descriptions.

7. After using the hand lens, would you change your original groupings?

8. Rank each mineral from softest to hardest. Scratch each mineral with your fingernail. Set aside those you are able to scratch.

9. Scratch the minerals you did not set aside with a copper penny. Set aside those you are able to scratch.

10. Scratch the minerals you set aside with a steel file. Set aside those you are able to scratch.

11. Finally, see if the minerals you have left will scratch a glass plate.

12. **Classify** your sample items according to the Mohs scale. **Record** this classification list.

CONCLUSIONS

1. How did each additional test (touch, hand-lens inspection, mineral properties tests) help you **classify** your sample?

2. Is there only one way to **classify** your rocks? Explain.

3. Explain why you grouped your items the way you did.

ASKING NEW QUESTIONS

1. What properties were the most useful in **classifying** your samples?

2. What other properties might be examined to help tell rocks and minerals apart?

SCIENTIFIC METHODS SELF CHECK
✔ Did I **observe** each item carefully?
✔ Did I **classify** each item according to its observable properties?
✔ Did I **hypothesize** about each item's hardness?

Water and Land

Find Out

- What causes erosion
- How water erodes Earth
- How glaciers change Earth's surface
- What changes landforms

Vocabulary

sediment
glaciers
topography
canyon
discharge
landslides
tsunami

The Big QUESTION

What shapes Earth's surface?

*E*arth has a wonderful diversity of rain forests, deserts, mountains, and valleys. Its surface is covered by many different kinds of rocks. New Earth features are continually created and torn down through a variety of ongoing systems and interactions. Rocks within Earth's crust shift and collide, forming mountains or deep basins. A glacier scours the surface over which it moves. When it melts or moves on, sharp peaks and deep valleys are left behind. Windblown material, water, and other agents of change act on the peaks and valleys in the mountain ranges, eroding them and changing their appearance.

Agents of Erosion

Wind erosion is one type of erosion. Wind erosion was responsible for the Dust Bowl in the 1930s, and it continues to be responsible for many interesting formations on Earth. During the 1930s, massive amounts of soil were moved by strong winds in southwestern Kansas, Colorado, northeastern New Mexico, and parts of Texas and Oklahoma. In this region, which was described as the Dust Bowl, the winds stirred up dust storms so thick that people choked to death from the dust.

The Dust Bowl, which existed between 1935 and 1938, was also an environmental disaster. The winds lifted dry, loose soil from 20 million hectares of land. The land was ripe for wind erosion because of overgrazing by cattle. Because of overgrazing, the topsoil was not anchored by crops or groundcover plants.

Dust storms like those that occurred in the Dust Bowl can carry 875 metric tons of dust, clay, and silt at speeds of 40 km/h. That's as much dirt as could be carried by eight railroad cars. Some people call these dust storms "black blizzards."

Scientists make a distinction between sandstorms and dust storms. Both are produced by wind, but the material raised by sandstorms consists of grains of sand about 0.25 mm in diameter. These fairly large sand particles are normally raised less than 64 cm off the ground. In contrast, dust storms blow material finer than 0.06 mm in diameter and raise that material throughout the lower level of the atmosphere. The dust storms of the Dust Bowl "blotted out the sun," according to the people there. The blown material was so fine that the dust blew right into the houses through cracks in the doors and window frames. The cause of this catastrophe was poor agricultural techniques coupled with severe drought. Contour farming and extensive irrigation systems have helped bring the land back into agricultural production.

Winds moved massive amounts of soil in thick clouds over many of the Great Plains states in the 1930s.

Gravity also contributes to the process of erosion by exerting a force on everything on Earth's surface. The force of gravity causes loose materials to move toward lower elevations. This movement is caused by the difference in mass between the two objects (Earth and the loose material). As these materials move, they erode Earth's surface. Sometimes, the erosion is gradual. Cliff rocks, weathered for centuries, may break loose and tumble downhill. Erosion due to gravity can also occur quickly, such as in landslides, rock slides, and avalanches. When masses of mud, soil, rocks, or snow move, destruction of property and loss of life may result.

Plants can also break rock apart. Seeds growing in cracks in rocks are amazingly powerful. As they swell with moisture, they can separate rocks into pieces. The heat of sunlight can also crack rocks over time. Many natural forces—sun, wind, gravity, and plant roots—have a part in the weathering and erosion of rocks. Another natural cause of erosion is water.

Erosion by Water

Moving water is by far the most powerful agent of erosion. It does more to reshape Earth's surface than all the other agents combined. Valleys, gullies, canyons, waterfalls, and certain types of lakes are among the landforms created by running water.

The water that forms surface streams is the runoff from rain and snow that isn't absorbed by openings and spaces in Earth's surface. Streams wear away Earth's surface, picking up rocks and other materials as they flow. The force of water carries rocks ranging in size from huge boulders to tiny grains of silt. Each year, streams of water carry about a billion tons of sediment and deposit it in Earth's oceans. **Sediment** is the solid matter of rocks or earth that are left by agents of erosion. In the oceans, these sediments eventually form beds of sedimentary rocks.

Bryce Canyon, in southern Utah, is a dramatic example of how the energy of running water has changed a part of Earth's crust. Flash flooding, combined with the effects of rain, wind, and other agents of erosion, causes the rim of the canyon to erode at the rate of about 1 m every 150 years.

Precipitation that seeps into the pores and cracks of soil is groundwater. Groundwater is also an agent of erosion. Most groundwater contains an acid formed from decaying plants combined with air and water. This acid erodes rocks such as limestone and dolomite, by chemically dissolving them and carrying away the minerals in the water solution.

Water also causes erosion when it falls as acid rain. Acid rain, a popular topic in today's news, isn't a modern problem. It was a problem in England a century ago. Polluted rain was reported in the factory town of Manchester, England. Several decades later, Scandinavian scientists made the term popular when they investigated the cause of fish dying in their lakes and streams. The problem, they hypothesized, was caused by acid rain.

Scientists discovered that acid rain is formed when toxic substances such as oxides of sulfur and nitrogen are released into the air from the burning of coal. The gases are absorbed into clouds, where they mix with water droplets to form sulfuric acid. It falls back to Earth as acid rain.

Acid rain damages the leaves and needles of plants. It gets into rivers, lakes, and groundwater. It speeds up the weathering of rocks, buildings, and monuments on Earth's surface. The few remaining marble statues around the Parthenon in Greece have been etched and pitted by acid rain. The faces of the presidents carved into Mount Rushmore, in South Dakota, have also been affected by acid rain.

Over millions of years, water has eroded the limestone, sandstone, and shale in Bryce Canyon to form a fantastic collection of spires and craggy columns. Shown here is the Rock Spire Trail below Bryce Canyon at sunset.

Before glaciation

Valley glaciers form at high elevations.

During glaciation

Moving glaciers erode the rocks beneath them.

After glaciation

Erosion widens valleys.

Erosion by Glaciers

Glaciers are large masses of ice in motion. Glaciers form when vast amounts of snow become compressed and compacted into dense ice. Glaciers form in areas where snow gathers faster than it melts. Where on Earth would you expect glaciers to form?

Earth processes create glaciers. Like water in its liquid form, glaciers cause erosion. Glaciers flow slowly, picking up rocks and other Earth materials and depositing them elsewhere. Glacial erosion occurs along all boundaries of large ice masses. As the ice melts and the water refreezes in these places, rocks and sediments are frozen into the ice. These "passengers" cut and scrape the land over which the glacier moves. Then, glaciers deposit these rocks and sediments.

There have been several ice ages in Earth's past, when massive glaciers covered up to 30 percent of Earth's surface. During the most recent ice age, which ended about 10,000 years ago, glaciers covered northern Europe, most of Canada, and parts of the United States. At that time, glacial erosion and sediment deposits created the Great Lakes and the rocky farmland in the New England area of the United States.

Today, only about 10 percent of Earth's surface is covered by glaciers. They are most common in Greenland and Antarctica. It is estimated that glaciers contain about 75 percent of Earth's freshwater.

This is the Svartisen Glacier in Norway.

Changing Landforms

The **topography,** or features of Earth's surface, are constantly changing. Some landforms change quickly. Waves crash on beaches, moving sand out to sea. The ocean currents then deposit the sand somewhere else. Heavy storms and floods move rocks and soil, changing the shape of the land. Earthquakes and volcanoes can change Earth's surface in just a few minutes.

Running water forms much of Earth's landscape and is very important to people. Rivers provide transportation, irrigation, and energy. People have built dams on rivers, changing the nature of the rivers and of the topography and providing electricity.

As you have already learned, water is a major force of erosion. It transports soil and rocks from the weathering of Earth's surface and deposits them in another place, usually the ocean. This constant force of erosion cuts into Earth and forms a channel for the stream to move along. Over time, moving water will form a **canyon** or a valley. A canyon is a narrow gorge or ravine with steep cliff walls, formed by a river or stream.

Discharge is the amount of water running through a channel in a given period of time. When the discharge increases so much that its channel is unable to hold it, a flood is created. A flood happens when the water rises over the banks of the channel and moves into the low-lying land next to the river or stream. Commonly, when a river or stream floods, the sediments that it is transporting are deposited on the land next to the river's channel. This makes the soil very rich, and flooded areas are often excellent agricultural fields.

Floods are usually predictable. The area that will be covered with water if a flood should occur is called the floodplain. Scientists can identify where the floodplains are located. They can sometimes predict when floods will occur as well. Floods often occur in the spring, when significant amounts of ice and snow are melting, or after several days of rain. In both examples, the ground has become saturated and can no longer absorb any more water. The runoff into the rivers and streams increases, and the channel can no longer contain the discharge. The water overflows onto the soaked ground.

The area near Jefferson City, Missouri, is part of the floodplain of both the Mississippi and Missouri rivers. In 1993, both rivers flooded and covered the ground.

Water often plays a role in mass movements when it gets into pores and cracks among rocks and soil on hills with steep slopes. **Landslides** are movements of large amounts of materials on Earth's surface due to gravity. Landslides on hillsides sometimes follow flash floods that have loosened soil and rock. The constant movement of river water can cause landslides by wearing away the supporting structures under cliffs and hillsides. Sudden melting of snow can also cause landslides. The destruction of plant life by fire can make slopes unstable, resulting in landslides when the rain comes.

Landslides and mud slides occur when debris on a slope becomes loosened, perhaps by rainfall or perhaps by an earthquake. Often, landslides occur on steep slopes where there are no plants to anchor the soil. Maybe a road was cut through a mountain, leaving steep slopes. Or maybe the wave action of the ocean has worn away the underside of a cliff. A landslide may also be referred to by geologists as a slump, slide, flow, avalanche, or creep, depending on what caused it and how it moves. Whichever type it is, a landslide will move a great deal of topsoil downhill very quickly. For this reason, landslides can be very dangerous.

Rock slides send rocks down a mountainside in seconds.

Mud slides move masses of very wet mud down a slope.

In the past 30 years, people have increasingly picked lakes and seashores as locations for homes. Development of coastal areas has accelerated as beachfront condominiums, houses, hotels, and resorts have been built on shifting sands.

Not too long ago, a family purchased their dream home with a view of San Francisco, California, and the sea. Less than ten years later, their guest-room deck was hanging over the surf, and the foundation was at the cliff's edge. Luckily, this family was able to move the home—at a considerable cost, further away from the cliff. The problem was coastal erosion, a natural process that alters the shorelines of Earth. Other property owners have not been so lucky. They have had to abandon their homes.

Barrier islands, small strips of sand dunes and marshes that protect much of the East Coast of the United States from the direct force of waves, have become prime spots for commercial development. Sand dunes tend to keep barrier islands intact by their very nature, which is to shift and change shape as a result of the buffeting of the sand and ocean currents. They deflect and reduce the effects of the stronger wind and ocean currents, reducing those effects upon the coastlines they protect. Problems occur when there are buildings on the beach or when sand has been removed to enhance the view. There is no place for the dunes to move, and coastal erosion becomes evident.

Coastal erosion is a worldwide problem in countries where coastal property has been heavily developed, such as the U.S., Great Britain, Germany, and the Netherlands.

Sudden undersea movements like earthquakes or volcanic eruptions can produce a very long wave called a **tsunami** (tsoō na′ mē), or seismic sea wave. A tsunami results from a very rapid displacement of an area of ocean bottom. Water rushing in or out of this area sets off the wave. A tsunami can also be produced by underwater landslides. Huge deposits of soft mud and sediment cover the steep slopes of the underwater continental shelf. If these slip down suddenly, they give the water a great push.

Tsunamis have extremely long wavelengths, as much as 240 km long. They also can travel nearly 960 km/h. When a tsunami comes close to shore, its speed slows down and its height increases. A tsunami may suddenly rise into a wave that is 3–30 m high. These large waves can be very destructive to coastal areas and communities.

In the United States, shorelines that border the oceans, as well as those on the five Great Lakes, have many waterfront homes.

CHECKPOINT

1. What causes erosion?
2. How does water erode Earth?
3. How do glaciers change Earth's surface?
4. What changes landforms?

 What shapes Earth's surface?

ACTIVITY

Ice Carving

Find Out

Do this activity to learn how glaciers cause erosion.

Process Skills

Measuring
Hypothesizing
Experimenting
Observing
Communicating

WHAT YOU NEED

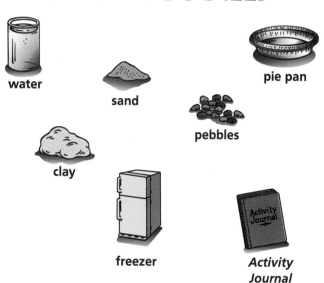

water

sand

pie pan

pebbles

clay

freezer

Activity Journal

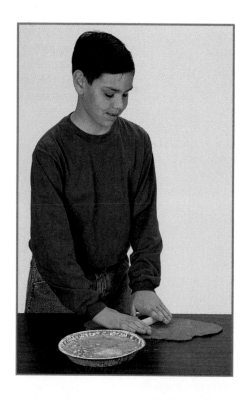

WHAT TO DO

1. Mix the sand and pebbles together in the pie pan. Add enough water to almost cover the mixture.

2. Put the mixture in the freezer and let it freeze solid. This will be your model glacier.

3. Roll out the clay to make a smooth, rectangular surface that measures about 20 cm wide, 40 cm long, and at least 3 cm thick.

4. Make a hypothesis based on what you know about erosion. Record your hypothesis about the effects of the glacier on the clay.

5. Remove the glacier from the pie pan. Place it at one end of the slab of clay with the roughest side down.

6. Push the glacier across the clay. Record your observations about what happened to the clay and glacier.

CONCLUSIONS

1. Evaluate the results of your test.

2. What happened to the surface of the clay?

ASKING NEW QUESTIONS

1. What properties of a glacier might affect the markings and debris it leaves behind?

2. What do you think would happen if a glacier passing across land suddenly melted?

SCIENTIFIC METHODS SELF CHECK

✔ Did I **construct a model** of a glacier?

✔ Did I **predict** what would happen after the glacier crossed the clay?

✔ Did I make a **hypothesis** about the effect of the glacier based on my knowledge of erosion?

✔ Did I **test** my hypothesis?

✔ Did I **observe** what happened?

✔ Did I **record** my hypothesis, observations and results?

LESSON 3

Natural Resources

Find Out

- Why some minerals are so valuable
- What fossil fuels are

Vocabulary

metallic minerals
nonmetalic minerals
ores
hydrocarbons
strip mining

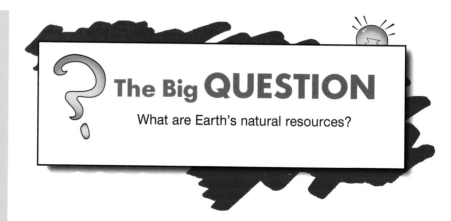

The Big QUESTION

What are Earth's natural resources?

What resources are found in Earth's crust? How do people use them? Minerals and fossil fuels are used every day by nearly everyone. How long will they last?

Minerals—Part of Earth's Crust

Have you ever realized that almost everything around you comes from Earth? Think about your cotton blue jeans, the bricks that make up buildings, a hammer, a pair of eyeglasses, a wooden rocking chair—nearly everything you can think of (except maybe a meteorite from outer space) comes from Earth.

The processes of formation differ among the different kinds of minerals. However, all minerals were formed as a result of natural processes. Fossil fuels, such as coal and oil, are deposited or trapped in Earth in predictable ways.

Many of the products in your home are made from natural resources. Glass is made from the mineral quartz. Steel is a mixture of iron and carbon. Quartz, iron, and carbon are only a few of the hundreds of substances found in Earth's crust. How do we obtain such resources from Earth's crust?

What products and materials in the photo above can you identify as natural resources?

It has been known for thousands of years how useful minerals are. Stone Age people used minerals for tools and jewelry. If you use talcum powder after a bath, pencils at school, or salt on your food, you are using minerals. The quartz crystals in most watches are also minerals. Most modern paints include mineral pigments for coloring, and rocks such as chalk and clay provide minerals that thicken paint.

Minerals are often extracted from Earth by mining. Here, copper is being mined in Butte, Montana.

The pigments used to make paint colors come from minerals.

Geologists have identified over 500 minerals. These scientists conduct research to find deposits of minerals. Minerals such as copper, gold, and silver are called **metallic minerals**. Other minerals, such as quartz, diamond, and sulfur, are **nonmetallic minerals**.

Today, many rocks and minerals are used in construction. The outsides of some buildings are made of granite or sandstone. Elements such as iron, aluminum, copper, and tin are extracted from certain minerals and used to make beams and wiring. How do we know so much about minerals? Scientists known as mineralogists study minerals to obtain information about each one.

Rocks and minerals that are found in quantities large enough to make them worth mining are called **ores.** Ores have been mined for thousands of years. For example, ancient Egyptians mined emeralds to use for jewelry. They also used the process of electroplating to coat jewelry with a thin layer of gold. How are gold deposits mined from Earth's crust?

Gold deposits form close to igneous rocks, such as granite. These rocks become weathered. Gold-bearing rocks wash down from mountains and may be found in sand and gravel deposits near riverbeds. Sand and gravel are deposited by streams or rivers in areas where the velocity of the water decreases. When the river current slows, it can't carry as much sediment as when it was moving quickly. As the current slows, the heavy gold particles and sand and gravel settle to the bottom.

One method of gold mining is known as placer mining. It works by separating the dense gold from sand grains that aren't as dense. Placer mining is the oldest method of gold mining. How does it work? Miners fill a pan with water and place handfuls of dirt and sand into the pan. The pan is then swirled, and the dense materials settle in the center of the pan.

Miners panning for gold near a riverbed

Energy Resources

Fossil fuels are organic materials. Fossil fuels, mined for their energy value, are substances formed from organisms that lived on Earth millions of years ago. Coal, oil, and natural gas are fossil fuels.

The sun supplies energy for Earth's processes, which enables plants and animals to live and grow. Often, when these organisms die, they become buried by loose sediments. As the remains of organisms decay and become compressed by the mass of overlying sediments, all the water is squeezed from them. Over millions of years, pressure and heat turn the organic material into fossil fuels. Most organisms contain the elements hydrogen and carbon. When they die and their bodies are subjected to heat and pressure by overlying sediments, the elements hydrogen and carbon remain. Therefore, fossil fuels contain hydrogen and carbon and are known as **hydrocarbons.**

Coal was used for fuel as early as 3000–4000 years ago in the country of Wales. As early as the twelfth century A.D., the Hopi people mined coal by scraping and digging. They used coal for cooking and in ceremonial chambers.

How do you think people use coal today? Approximately 23 percent of the electrical energy in the United States is generated by coal burning plants. We obtain coal by mining it from Earth's surface or from underground mines. Mining near Earth's surface is called **strip mining** because layers of soil and rock overlying the deposits are stripped away. In strip mining, cuts are made side-by-side and trenches are dug to reach the coal seam. Then, mechanical shovels are used to dig out the coal. As each new trench is excavated, the material that is dug out is dumped into an old trench.

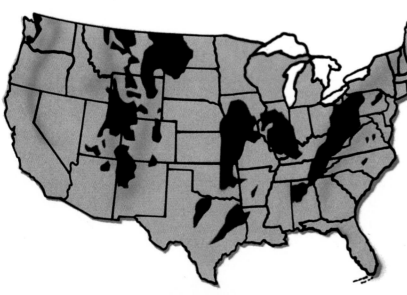

This map shows where the major coal deposits are located in the United States.

Coal has been used for fuel for thousands of years.

In some places, the coal can't be reached directly from the surface. A gently sloping entry shaft, known as an adit, is dug and used to reach coal seams that are within a few hundred meters of the surface. When coal seams are far beneath the surface, a vertical shaft is dug. This type of mine is difficult to build and operate. Why do you think this is so?

Another fossil fuel, petroleum, was used by many ancient civilizations. The ancient Egyptians used it to help preserve mummies. Our word *mummy* comes from the Persian word *mum,* meaning "a type of tar." The ancient Chinese used petroleum to heat and light their homes and to cook. Tar pits supplied crude oil that was used for fuel, cooking, and lighting in ancient Central America. At the same time, petroleum was used in Europe for lubricating wagon wheels and in ointments that stopped swelling and helped cuts heal. We still use petroleum products today for some of these purposes.

Another type of fossil fuel is natural gas, also a hydrocarbon. Natural gas is usually found in oil reservoirs above the surface of the oil. It's not as dense as liquid petroleum, and it rises above the petroleum within the reservoir.

This train has a coal-powered steam engine. Eventually, coal-powered engines were replaced with petroleum-powered engines.

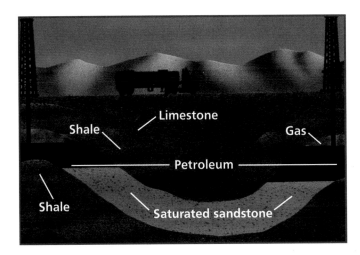

Shale

Limestone

Gas

Petroleum

Shale

Saturated sandstone

Petroleum is a liquid formed from organisms that lived millions of years ago. This oil then became trapped in porous rock, such as sandstones and limestones. In places where vast amounts of oil became trapped, oil reservoirs were formed. These reservoirs are drilled today for oil and natural gas.

Although fossil fuels provide most of our energy resources today, another energy source is also being more widely used. One kind of nuclear power, fission, is based on the energy released by atoms as they split. Because all matter is made of atoms, atoms could be considered renewable resources.

However, scientists have only been able to produce atom-splitting energy by using the mineral uranium. Uranium is a nonrenewable resource, and it is found in the United States in New Mexico, Wyoming, and Texas. Uranium is also mined in South Africa, Australia, and Tadzhikistan.

The atoms in the mineral uranium can be split to release nuclear energy.

By 1988, there were about 575 commercial nuclear reactors in operation. But uranium resources are quite limited. If all existing nuclear plants continue to use uranium at today's rates, our estimated supply will last for only 100 years.

This type of nuclear energy is quite costly and dependent upon limited mineral resources. In addition, its by-products are very dangerous radioactive wastes. These deadly wastes must be stored away from humans forever. There is no known way at this time to control or change the radioactivity.

Another type of nuclear energy that is under development is called fusion. It is based on the energy created when atoms combine. If we can create a nuclear fusion power plant, the fuel supply would be inexhaustible because we would never run out of atoms.

Our use of fossil fuels has changed throughout history. Coal was the main source of fuel in 1900, but as inventions changed from steam-driven to petroleum-driven motors and power sources, petroleum products overtook coal as the main fuel. Today, petroleum is still the most widely used fossil fuel.

Since 1900, energy consumption has doubled approximately every 20 years. Because of the use of such large amounts of fossil fuels, the sources are running out. They are nonrenewable, which means they can't be replenished. If people better understand the limited amounts of minerals and fossil fuels, they can work to conserve them. Think about how much energy you may use with just one appliance—a refrigerator.

The longer you keep the refrigerator door open, the more energy you use.

Did You Know?

We open our refrigerators almost 22 times a day. That's over 8000 times a year for each one of us! When you open the refrigerator, the inside of the refrigerator becomes warmer. Lots of extra electricity is needed to cool the inside of the refrigerator back down.

What You Can Do

Don't open your refrigerator unless you have to. Once you've opened it, quickly get what you want and close the door. Think about what you want before you open it.

See for Yourself

Keep a record of how many times you open the refrigerator during the day. Are you opening it more than you really need to? And how long do you keep it open?

By conserving energy, people will use less fossil fuel. Your ideas can make a difference in decreasing consumption of fossil fuels. What advice can you give people to help them use energy more wisely?

CHECKPOINT

1. Why are some minerals so valuable?
2. What are fossil fuels?

 What are Earth's natural resources?

ACTIVITY

Finding Earth's Resources

Find Out

Do this activity to learn how to find and mine Earth's natural resources.

Process Skills

Constructing Models
Observing
Communicating
Predicting

WHAT YOU NEED

two sheets of typing paper

toothpick

timer

transparent tape

hardcover book

chocolate-chip cookie

paper towel

index card

art brush

Activity Journal

WHAT TO DO

1. Roll and tape the sheets of paper to form two large tubes.

2. Place the index card at the corner of the table, and then push it about 20 cm toward the center of the table. Tape the index card down.

3. Position and tape the tubes along the edge of the index card that are farthest away from the edge of the table. Make sure that one of the tubes extends over the edge of the table by 2.5 cm.

4. Set the timer for about three minutes. Construct a model of sonar reflection by placing the timer at one of the open ends of the tube.

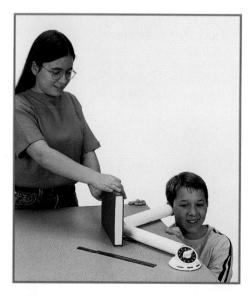

5. Place your ear next to the end of the open tube and note the sound of the ticking timer. Record your observation.

6. Predict what will happen to the ticking when your partner places a book next to the open ends of the tubes. Record your prediction.

7. Stand a book next to the open ends of the tubes.

8. Record what happened to the ticking.

9. Spread out a paper towel and place a chocolate-chip cookie in the center of it. Assume the cookie is Earth and the chips are mineral deposits you want to mine.

10. Using a toothpick, scratch the "earth" away from one "mineral deposit." Do not scratch any chips or break the cookie.

11. Use the brush to sweep pieces of "earth" away from the chip.

12. Continue gently scratching and brushing until you have removed the chip from the cookie. Record your observations.

CONCLUSIONS

1. Compare your predictions with your results.

2. Why did the ticking become louder when the book was placed at the open ends of the tubes?

3. How was the book a model of a layer of petroleum?

4. How was the cookie a model of Earth?

ASKING NEW QUESTIONS

1. How do you think sound can be used to find petroleum?

2. What types of natural resources can be mined like the chips?

3. What other ways could people use to find natural resources?

SCIENTIFIC METHODS SELF CHECK

✔ Did I **construct models** of sonar reflection and mining?

✔ Did I **predict** what would happen?

✔ Did I **observe** the results of the experiment?

✔ Did I **record** the results?

Conservation of Resources

Find Out

- What some environmental effects of using natural resources are
- How salt water can be turned into freshwater
- How to maintain clean water supplies
- How nature recovers from pollution
- What you can do to conserve resources

Vocabulary

conservation
environmental impact
desalination
siltation

The Big QUESTION

How can resources be conserved?

*P*eople use minerals and fossil fuels every day. But the use of many minerals and fossil fuels harms the environment.

Environmental Effects of Using Natural Resources

Humans use resources from every part of Earth. They use resources from the atmosphere and from inside Earth's surface. They also use resources on Earth, such as water and forests. This book is made of paper, which comes from wood. The wood comes from Earth's forests. The dyes that make the ink come from minerals inside Earth. In fact, everything you can point to probably comes from a natural resource.

Soil, land, water, and air are important natural resources. These are materials in the environment that are useful and, therefore, valuable to people. Not only are these natural resources useful, but they are also necessary to our lives.

Climate, mineral resources, soil, and water determine where people live. In turn, as people live and work, they change their surroundings. The way humans live affects their environment. In fact, human activities usually change the environment more rapidly and in ways different from natural activities. Usually humans contribute more negative changes to the environment than positive ones.

Coal mining in Pennsylvania

With proper care, we can use Earth's natural resources for a long time. **Conservation** is the planned use of natural resources to prevent their depletion, destruction, or neglect. Conservation of natural resources provides us with an opportunity to make a positive impact on our environment. The effect of human activity on the total environment is called **environmental impact.** Not all environmental impacts are negative. Careful planning and using resources wisely can lead to positive environmental impacts.

For example, mining coal can pollute groundwater supplies. The water coming into contact with sulphur changes to form sulfuric acid. Sulfuric acid can wash into rivers and groundwater sources. The problem can be controlled by changing and directing the course of water flow near a coal mine. This can reduce pollution, erosion, and water treatment costs.

Reclaimed strip mine in Oklahoma

People who are concerned about the environment oppose strip mining because of the damage it does to the landscape. Waste rock removed from the mines used to be left in unsightly piles and heaps. Now, most states require strip-mining operations to reclaim or restore the land. Environmental regulations require the waste rock to be replaced and then covered with topsoil. The land that was once stripped of its mineral resources can be made ready to grow crops, forests, or grassy fields. However, reclaimed areas do not look like the area did before the area was mined.

Salt Water

Salt left behind after desalination

Desalination is a process in which seawater is boiled and the steam is piped into a cool bottle. As evaporation occurs, the salt is left behind. The steam that cools in the bottle condenses into freshwater.

We use water every day, and our demand for it is increasing. Now, it's more important than ever that we make better use of our supplies. In one sense, the supplies are limited—all the water we'll ever have is present on Earth now. Yet in another sense, supplies are unlimited—water goes through a cycle, and people keep reusing the water present on Earth. The more we learn about water, the more we'll be able to conserve it, protect it, and use it wisely.

The water cycle is very stable and continues to circulate everywhere on Earth. If water is always going through a cycle, why should we be worried about running out? After all, 70 percent of Earth's surface is covered by water. The problem is that most of this is not freshwater, but salt water. Can we use salt water?

Much of the salt in seawater is compounds of various dissolved minerals. The primary mineral is sodium carbonate. When this mineral combines with chlorine, it forms sodium chloride, or salt. A person can safely drink water that contains less than 0.5 kg of salt for every 100 kg of water. But seawater has about seven times that amount of salt. Therefore, a person who drinks only seawater can't survive.

It's possible to change salt water into freshwater through a process called desalination. **Desalination** is the removal of salt from seawater to make freshwater. The costs of both removing the salt and then getting the freshwater to the places where it is needed are high.

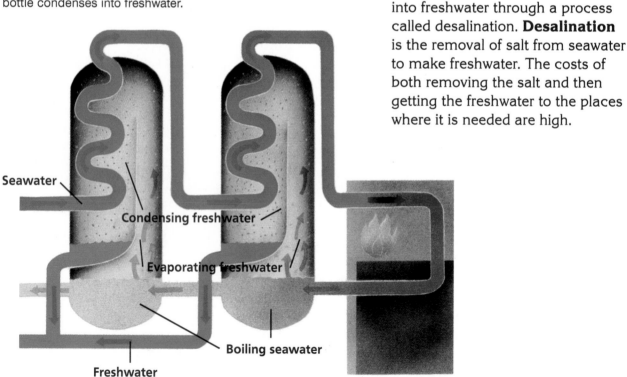

Seawater

Condensing freshwater

Evaporating freshwater

Boiling seawater

Freshwater

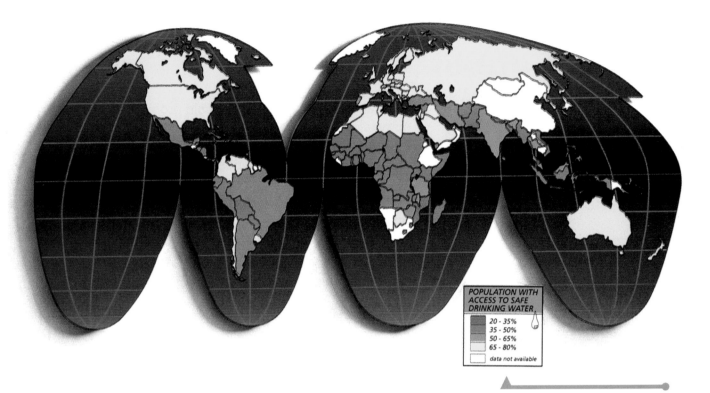

POPULATION WITH
ACCESS TO SAFE
DRINKING WATER

20 - 35%
35 - 50%
50 - 65%
65 - 80%
data not available

World populations with access
to safe drinking water

Because Earth has vast amounts of salt water, desalination may soon be more widely used for obtaining freshwater. Natural sources of freshwater are limited. In addition, freshwater supplies are not evenly distributed across the globe. Some areas have plentiful supplies, while other areas have very little freshwater available.

Most of northern Africa and most of Asia, as well as central Australia and the Middle East—about half of the landmasses on Earth—are dry areas that do not receive sufficient rain. The most heavily populated areas of the world, however, are usually regions where enough rain falls for the needs of the population. Northwestern Asia, Southeast Asia, China, Europe, India, and the eastern part of the United States are heavily populated areas that receive enough rain for the people living there.

Water isn't distributed evenly, either. For example, in the 1980s, severe droughts baked the midwestern and the southeastern United States as well as parts of Argentina, Australia, Brazil, Ethiopia, Paraguay, and Uruguay. But during the same decade, floodwaters soaked the land in the south-central United States and parts of Bangladesh, China, and India.

The distribution of water has always been uneven, and people have had to adjust to varying water supplies. For example, in the western United States, people have made adjustments that have changed the Colorado River.

Before it reaches its destination at the Sea of Cortes, the Colorado River evaporates and leaves branch-like patterns in the land.

B77

Maintaining Clean Water Supplies

Water pollution is a large-scale problem. What are some sources of water pollution? Raw sewage pumped into rivers, lakes, and oceans pollutes many city water supplies. Fertilizers, pesticides, and insecticides that seep into groundwater supplies are common in farming regions. Liquid wastes from large manufacturing plants pumped into bodies of water, materials leached from landfills, and careless disposal of hazardous wastes are other common sources of water pollution.

Antipollution efforts since the 1960s and 1970s resulted in declines in the levels of many toxic, or poisonous, substances in Lake Erie and other parts of the Great Lakes. The Cuyahoga River in Cleveland, Ohio, was so polluted in the summer of 1969 that the river caught fire and burned as a result of the chemicals in the water. The Great Lakes are now cleaner than they were many years ago. Some of the beaches have reopened, and untreated sewage no longer flows into the lakes to cause high levels of bacteria.

Water supplies can also be maintained through conservation. Think of all the ways your family uses water. The average American uses more than 240 L of water a day in his or her home.

The Great Lakes

Suppose there was a water shortage in your community. Think about two water conservation plans. The first plan should be one that your family can practice on a daily basis to conserve water. The second should be in case of a severe water shortage. In what ways would you conserve water?

The Cuyahoga River was so polluted in 1969 that it caught fire and burned for days.

Today the Cuyahoga River is much cleaner.

Natural Pollution-Recovery Systems

Name some ways a forest fire can impact a local environment.

A forest is a large area of land covered with trees. However, a forest is much more than just trees. There are many kinds of plants in a forest. How many different kinds can you name? The trees make it possible for these other plants to grow. Forests provide food and shelter for many different animals too.

Forests are important to people for many reasons. Prehistoric people lived in forests and obtained food there. Today, forests are one of Earth's resources due to their economic value, their environmental value, and the recreational area they provide.

The products people obtain from forests are lumber, paper, plastic, latex for making rubber, oils, waxes, and clothing fibers such as rayon. Many of these products are produced directly from specific forests. Others are manufactured by-products from trees.

How do you think forests are valuable to the environment? The soil within a forest is usually permeable and is able to absorb water to help prevent erosion and water runoff. The plants living in forests help to keep the oxygen and carbon dioxide in balance in Earth's atmosphere. This balance is essential for all life on Earth. In many parts of the world, there are vast areas of dense forests with very few people nearby.

In some cases, natural systems pollute the environment. For example, after a forest fire, rain will carry more soil, ash, and soot to rivers and streams. The streams will fill up with fine matter in a process called **siltation.** Volcanoes also cause pollution when they pump greenhouse gases into the air. For instance, when Mount Pinatubo in the Philippines erupted in 1991, a huge amount of sulfur dioxide was spewed into the air. Sulfur dioxide emissions from volcanoes can cause worldwide cooling by a few degrees Celsius.

Nature can recover from a small amount of almost anything. When large amounts of toxic substances are introduced into an environment, there is no natural mechanism for recovery. Some substances, like phosphates, throw nature off track and cause an ecosystem to crumble. People are often responsible for this type of pollution.

Conserving Resources

One advantage to conservation is that there is no need to wait for governments, businesses, and homeowners to take action. Everyone can take immediate action and individual responsibility. You use energy every day, and you have some control over how you use it.

If you are the last to leave a room, turn off the lights. If you are the only one in the room, use only the lights you need. Many appliances use more energy than lights. Turn off all appliances when you are not using them.

Heating water also uses a lot of energy. Do not leave the hot water running except when you are using it. When you take a shower, turn off the water while you soap and scrub. Then turn it on to rinse.

Conserving energy used for transportation is important too. You can plan your travel routes to conserve as much fuel as possible. You could consider walking or riding your bike. Carpooling and public transportation conserve energy as well.

Recycling some things, such as cans, bottles, and newspapers, uses less energy than making them from raw materials. Reusing things is even better than recycling them because it creates no pollution at all. Use both sides of a sheet of paper. Buy drinks in returnable bottles. Repair clothing and other possessions instead of buying new ones. Do not throw away anything that someone else can use. Have a garage sale or give away things to a charity or a thrift shop. There is an old saying that one person's junk is another person's treasure. So look for ways to let others reuse your possessions. And be on the lookout for treasures!

CHECKPOINT

1. How can use of natural resources be harmful?
2. How can salt water be turned into freshwater?
3. What are some sources of water pollution?
4. How do forests help the environment?
5. What can you do to conserve resources?

 How can resources be conserved?

ACTIVITY

Conserving Resources

Find Out

Do this activity to see how different techniques can conserve a valuable resource—soil.

Process Skills

Constructing Models
Predicting
Measuring
Experimenting

WHAT YOU NEED

several sheets of newspaper

metric ruler

water

pebbles

sprinkling can

400-mL beaker

five aluminum pans

leaves or grass clippings

potting soil

dishpan

Activity Journal

WHAT TO DO

1. Fill all of the pans with soil to within 1 cm of their rims. Level and pat the soil down until the surface is firm. Pour 100 mL water into each pan. Allow the water to soak in before doing Step 2.

2. Set one of the pans aside. This is the control. Set up one of the following techniques in each of the remaining pans:
   • Mulching—Cover the surface of the pan with a thin 1-cm layer of grass clippings or leaves.
   • Artificial soil—Lay strips of newspaper across the surface of the pan. Leave a 5-mm space.
   • Terracing—Use pebbles to build two small stone walls across the surface of the soil.
   • Contour plowing—Use your fingers to make 1-cm deep parallel grooves over the surface of the soil.

3. Which model will have the least soil erosion? Record your prediction.

4. Hold the control pan so that one side touches the edge of the dishpan and the opposite side of the pan is elevated 10 cm. Measure 200 mL of water into the sprinkling can. Hold the sprinkling can above the soil. Pour the water onto the soil at the upper side of the pan. The water should run across the soil and into the dishpan.

5. Hold the pan above the dishpan until the water stops draining. Transfer the water and soil from the dishpan into the beaker. Measure how many milliliters of soil and water went into the dishpan. When the soil settles to the bottom of the beaker, measure the volume of the soil lost by erosion. Record your results.

6. Repeat Steps 4 and 5, for each of the other pans. For the terracing and contour-plowing pans, be sure to hold them over the dishpan so the water runs across the pebbles and across the grooves. Record your results for each pan.

CONCLUSIONS

1. Which technique was best at preventing soil from being carried into the dishpan by the running water?

2. Rank the conservation techniques from 1 to 5. Number 1 is the technique that allows the least amount of soil to erode, and number 5 allows the most soil to erode.

ASKING NEW QUESTIONS

1. How might plants affect erosion?

2. Would different soil conservation techniques be better for different kinds of terrain?

SCIENTIFIC METHODS SELF CHECK
✔ Did I **predict** which technique would prevent soil erosion?
✔ Did I **experiment** with **models** to test my prediction?

CHAPTER 2

Review

Reviewing Vocabulary and Concepts

Write the letter of the answer that best completes each sentence.

1. Deposited debris after years of pressure and cementing becomes ___ rocks.
   - **a.** metamorphic
   - **b.** hard
   - **c.** sedimentary
   - **d.** mineral

2. Sediments are deposited on land when flooding causes ___.
   - **a.** discharge
   - **b.** weathering
   - **c.** siltation
   - **d.** strip mining

3. A wave caused by sudden, undersea seismic movements is ___.
   - **a.** a landslide
   - **b.** an earthquake
   - **c.** a rock slide
   - **d.** a tsunami

4. When valuable metallic or nonmetallic minerals are found in large quantities, they are called ___.
   - **a.** ores
   - **b.** hydrocarbons
   - **c.** diamonds
   - **d.** sediments

5. The process of changing seawater to freshwater is ___.
   - **a.** strip mining
   - **b.** conservation
   - **c.** desalination
   - **d.** tsunami

Match the definition on the left with the correct term.

6. solids that are nonliving, formed in nature, inorganic, and have a definite crystalline shape
   - **a.** topography

7. weathering that causes erosion is part of this process
   - **b.** glaciers

8. large masses of ice in motion
   - **c.** conservation

9. the features of Earth's surface, like a mountain, canyon, or gorge
   - **d.** rock cycle

10. the planned use of natural resources to prevent their depletion, destruction, or neglect
    - **e.** minerals

Understanding What You Learned

1. What is the difference between a metamorphic and igneous rock?
2. What is the difference between chemical and physical weathering?
3. What were the causes of the dust storms in the Dust Bowl in the 1930s?
4. Since 1900, why has energy consumption doubled every 20 years?
5. How are forests important to people and the environment?

Applying What You Learned

1. Why is a scale for ranking the softness or hardness of minerals useful?
2. How do people interfere with or speed up the natural process of erosion?
3. Why is the depletion of fossil fuels such a concern?
4. Why might conservationists be opposed to mining for diamonds?

 5. What are the processes that give Earth's surface its land, water, and natural resources?

For Your **Portfolio**

Write a letter to the editor of an imaginary newspaper describing your concerns about human-caused landslides or waste of natural resources. Include your ideas for correcting or avoiding the situation. Share your letter with the class.

3 The Changing Earth

In order to understand Earth's processes, you can create a model of it by making observations of its changes and patterns. In scientific terms, a model is a picture, either in your mind or in some solid form. It helps you see a process or an object that might otherwise be difficult to see or understand. An example of a model you have used is a map or a globe that represents Earth.

Scientists take the first steps toward understanding Earth's ever-changing features when they start to gather evidence that will eventually become part of a model. A model of Earth's processes would tell how natural processes of change shape many of the features on the planet's surface. When natural processes act on Earth's surface, certain predictable chemical and physical changes occur in the rocks and landforms of Earth's crust. When scientists know the effects of change, they can begin to understand why Earth's surface looks like it does.

The Big IDEA

Earth's surface moves and changes over time.

SCIENCE INVESTIGATION

Investigate plate movements
and volcanic eruptions.
Find out how in your
Activity Journal.

Earth's Layers

Find Out

- How nature's forces stay the same over time
- What Earth's structure is
- How pieces of Earth can move

Vocabulary

crust
metallic core
mantle
lithosphere
crustal movement

The Big QUESTION

What is inside Earth?

Have you ever stood outdoors and imagined what was under your feet? We know that directly beneath us are soil, rocks, water, and maybe even some oil or coal. But is that all? No. There are powerful processes that are occurring constantly deep inside Earth, far beneath our feet.

Nature's Forces

Scientists believe that the present is a key to the past. To understand the order of events that have occurred on Earth, scientists study how Earth processes operate today. They use current observations to make a model of how Earth processes have acted through time to change Earth. They believe that the processes at work in and on Earth today must have worked in much the same way in the past.

For instance, if you drop a rock from your hand, gravity causes the rock to fall to the ground. You could assume that if you had been around 20 million years ago, gravity would also have caused a rock to fall to the ground then. If water flows downhill today, it is safe to assume it has flowed downhill ever since water started flowing. In other words, you use what you observe happening in the world today to try and understand what happened in the past.

Nature's forces are always changing Earth's surface.

However, the rates at which change happens today may be different from the rates at which changes happened long ago. If you found an ancient river, you could assume that its banks eroded in some places and sand was deposited in other places. If you measured the amount of erosion that was happening today and found that it was 1 cm/y, you could not assume that the ancient river always eroded at that rate. It may have eroded by 20 cm/y or by 0.25 cm/y. The process of erosion would be the same, but the rate at which it occurred might be different.

Earth is undergoing constant and continuing change. Some of these changes occur daily; others take thousands, or even millions, of years. Some Earth changes result in awe-inspiring events such as volcanic eruptions or earthquakes. Other changes happen unseen deep within Earth. To understand these processes of change, let's start by examining the structure of Earth.

Earth's Structure

Earth consists of three major zones: a surface crust and a dense nickel-iron core with a flexible mantle between them. The surface of Earth is the **crust.** Like your skin, which is thin on your face and thick on the soles of your feet, the thickness of Earth's crust also varies. Where do you think Earth's crust is thickest and thinnest? Earth's crust is thickest where there are continents. Continents are the major land areas of Earth. Earth's crust averages about 40 km in thickness under continents. Under the oceans, Earth's crust is thinnest. Earth doesn't have huge landmasses under its oceans. The crust averages only about 8 km in thickness under the oceans.

The center of Earth is the **metallic core.** It is the most interior zone of Earth. This layer is under immense pressure from the rest of Earth. The pressure makes the core extremely hot. Scientists believe that the core has a temperature of 6100 °C. This heat causes many of the events and changes that occur throughout Earth. Believe it or not, the core is actually cooling down from much higher temperatures from when Earth formed 4.5 billion years ago.

The core has two layers: the inner core and the outer core. The outer core is composed of iron and nickel. The core's extreme heat keeps these metals in the form of melted liquids. The inner core is solid iron and nickel. It is the hottest layer because it has the most pressure being exerted on it from the layers above it. Why is the inner core solid although it is the hottest layer? The inner core is under extreme pressure. It is not able to become liquid.

The **mantle** is the middle zone of Earth. This mantle is made of rocks composed chiefly of iron, magnesium, silicon, and oxygen. It makes up about 82 percent of Earth's volume. The mantle has two main parts—the lower mantle layer and the upper mantle layer.

The lower mantle sits on top of the outer core, but is made of solid rock. Temperatures in the lower mantle can reach as high as 3000 °C. To get an idea of how hot this is, consider that most recipes call for oven temperatures of less than 220 °C!

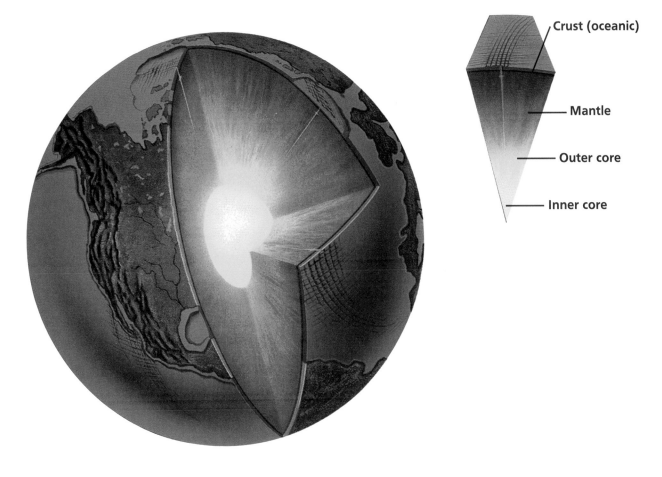

Crust (oceanic)

Mantle

Outer core

Inner core

The upper mantle extends nearly to Earth's surface. The temperatures in the upper mantle may reach as high as 1500 °C. Two layers at the top of the upper mantle are important in shaping Earth's surface. The lower of these two layers is called the asthenosphere (es thē′ nō sfēr). The rocks of the asthenosphere are hot and semi-molten. They can flow, but not easily. They move the way taffy candy does when you pull on it.

Above the asthenosphere lies the top layer of the upper mantle. Unlike the asthenosphere, this last layer is stiff and somewhat brittle. Together with the crust, the top layer of the upper mantle forms a layer called the **lithosphere.**

Moving Pieces of Earth

Scientists have discovered that the layers of Earth are not quite as simple as three neatly organized zones. They now know that the solid top layer of the upper mantle and the crust are attached and work together as a special layer called the lithosphere. The lithosphere is divided into seven large pieces and several smaller pieces. Each piece is a huge slab of rock called a plate. Each plate has continents and mountains on it, or it makes up part of the ocean floor.

Take a look at the map on this page. Do you notice anything about the shape of the continents? Does South America's east shore look like it could fit like a puzzle piece with the west shore of Africa? Can you find any other continents that look like they could fit together?

In 1620, Francis Bacon, an English scientist, noticed how the plates or continents could fit together. By that time, mapmakers had started producing more accurate maps of the world's continents. For the next several centuries, scientists examined the possibility that the continents were pieces in a puzzle.

Continental Puzzle

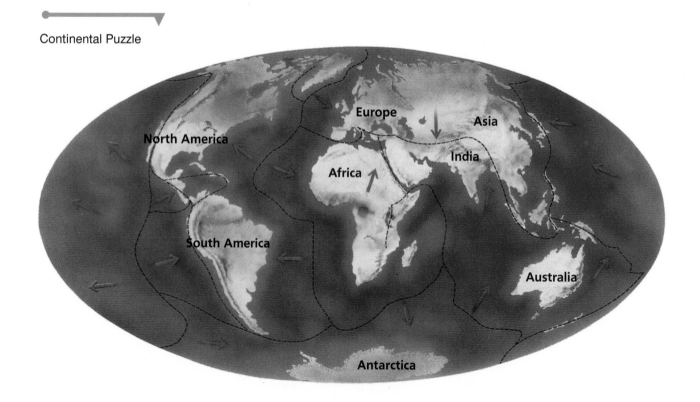

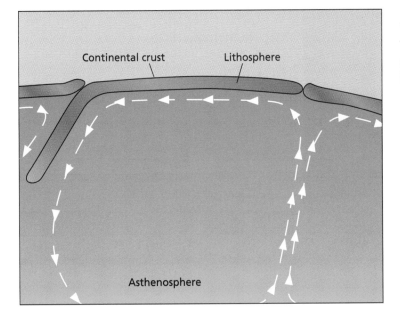

The convection currents of the asthenosphere can move the lithosphere.

By the 1960s, scientists concluded that the convection currents in the asthenosphere pushed the lithospheric pieces around. The asthenosphere is a semimolten layer in the mantle that acts rather like soft plastic. Convection currents in the asthenosphere are caused by differences in temperature in the asthenosphere. They move materials up and down throughout the mantle.

The pattern of motion caused by the convection currents in the asthenosphere can be compared to a conveyor belt. At one edge of the system, hot, less-dense rock is rising and forming new crust. As the hot rock cools, it becomes more dense. More hot rock forms new crust, pushing the cooler crust farther away from the place where plates are moving away from one another.

Eventually this ocean crust may reach the edge of a continent. If it collides with enough force, it may be forced downward into the mantle beneath the continent. When it slips under, it can form a deep ocean trench. The material of the plates is moving in a cycle. The **crustal movement,** or moving of the lithospheric pieces, is what causes the continents to move or shift. Scientists believe crustal movements shifted the continents around to where they are now.

Also in the 1960s, other evidence led scientists to deduce that the continents had been joined millions of years ago. One profound piece of evidence is the fossil

Tangiers, Morocco, on the Atlantic shore of Africa

Rio de Janeiro, Brazil, on the Atlantic shore of South America

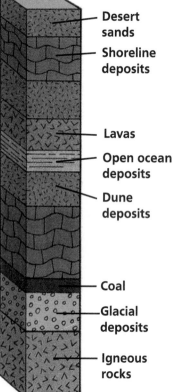

Rock Columns From Brazil and Africa

Brazil

Rain forest deposits

Shoreline deposits

Lavas

Open ocean deposits

Dune deposits

Coal

Glacial deposits

Igneous rocks

Southwest Africa

Desert sands

Shoreline deposits

Lavas

Open ocean deposits

Dune deposits

Coal

Glacial deposits

Igneous rocks

record. Geologists have discovered identical fossils from the same period on coasts of different continents. For example, millions of years ago, the same small garden snail lived on the shore of Europe and in the eastern part of North America. This snail could not have crossed the ocean. These two continents must have been joined at one time.

Geologists also discovered that the Atlantic shores of South America and Africa have the same layers of rocks. They match up perfectly. Again, the two continents had to be attached at one time for this to happen.

In 1912, a German meteorologist named Alfred Wegener proposed a model of Earth's land before its continents separated. He called the single landmass Pangaea (pan jē′ uh). *Pangaea* in Greek means "all lands" or "all Earth." The illustration on this page shows how Earth's seven continents might have been joined together in Wegener's model. Wegener's ideas were originally rejected because he could not offer a good explanation of how the continents moved. After the discovery that the asthenosphere could move the continents, Wegener's ideas were reconsidered.

Pangaea

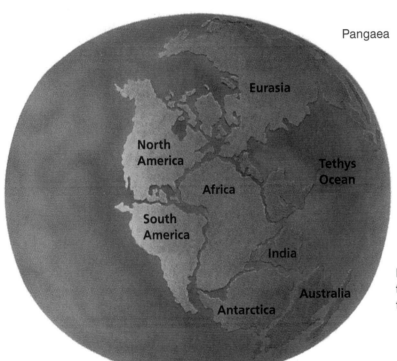

Pangaea is the ancient continent that included landmasses of all the present-day continents.

CHECKPOINT

1. How do nature's forces stay the same over time?
2. What is Earth's structure?
3. How can pieces of Earth move?

 What is inside Earth?

ACTIVITY

Putting the Pieces Together

Find Out

Do this activity to find out if the continents could once have been joined.

Process Skills

Classifying
Communicating
Interpreting Data

WHAT YOU NEED

world map with geologic and surface features

colored pencils

scissors

pencils and paper

sheet of white tracing paper

Activity Journal

WHAT TO DO

1. Trace the continents from a world map onto paper.

2. Mark the world map as shown with surface features and geologic features. Color each a different color. Cut out the continents.

3. Match the continents in as many ways as you can by shape alone. Record that number.

4. Match the continent pieces by surface features. Record the number of matches.

5. Next, match them by both features at the same time. When you have what you think is the best fit, make a good drawing of it. Make up a key. Use the key to classify where the geologic and surface features are on your map.

6. For comparison, make a map of the present-day positions of the continents. Using your key from Step 5, draw in the surface features and geologic features.

7. Write a paragraph about your new map.

CONCLUSIONS

1. How many different ways did the continents fit together with shapes and features? With shapes alone? With features alone?

2. Compare your map in Step 5 with the map in Step 6. How do they differ? Are any of the continents in the same place? Where would the north pole be on the map in Step 5? How do you know?

3. What do the fit of shapes and resources tell you about how likely your arrangement is?

4. Did your paragraph include all of the information about your map, including your results?

ASKING NEW QUESTIONS

1. What does the evidence of fit for shapes and features tell you about the continents and their relative positions?

2. If you lived 10 or 20 million years from now, how would you be able to figure out the relative positions of the continents of the twentieth century?

3. How could your paragraph be useful to others who want to find out if the continents have been joined?

SCIENTIFIC METHODS SELF CHECK

✔ Did I **classify** the features of my map pieces?

✔ Did I **write** a paragraph about my new maps?

✔ Did I **interpret** my **data** to understand how the continents could have been joined?

Major Geologic Events

Find Out

- What earthquakes are
- What volcanoes are
- How mountains form

Vocabulary

fault
epicenter
Richter scale
magma
lava
compression

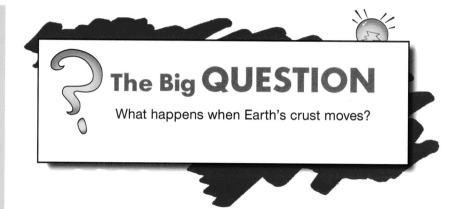

The Big QUESTION

What happens when Earth's crust moves?

What's inside Earth can change landforms that you can see on Earth. Earthquakes, volcanoes, and mountains are caused by what's inside Earth. Earthquakes and volcanoes are mighty expressions of Earth's energy. Both are awesome Earth processes. Both are distributed across the globe in a predictable pattern that contributes evidence to our model of Earth processes.

Earthquakes

Your house is shaking, the ground is rolling, pictures are falling off the walls, and you are having a difficult time standing up. Why? You are experiencing an earthquake. You can't believe it's happening. Did you know that small earthquakes occur somewhere on Earth every 30 seconds? Most earthquakes are so weak that they are only detected with sensitive scientific equipment.

Why do these earthquakes occur? Earthquakes usually happen where two plates of the lithosphere move against each other and create a fault. A **fault** is a place in Earth's crust where the rocks have broken and moved in relation to one another.

As you learned in the last lesson, the lithospheric plates move across the asthenosphere. Some plates push past one another at different rates. The rocks along the fault zone bend for a while. But when the pressure becomes too great, they suddenly snap, and an earthquake occurs.

The center of this movement below ground is called the focus of the earthquake. Directly above the focus, where the movement on the surface of Earth is most intense, is the **epicenter** of the earthquake. Most of the movements are small, but a few are so great that they produce horribly destructive earthquakes. Cities with large buildings and dense populations that are located near the epicenter of an earthquake are the most prone to disaster.

The epicenter is located directly above the source of the earthquake. The place deep within the crust where the energy is generated and released is called the focus of the earthquake.

Epicenter

Focus

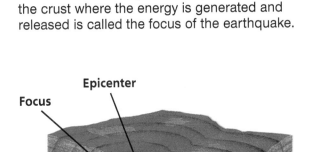

1. Sometimes rocks move smoothly along a fault, but often a rock gets stuck against neighboring rocks and can't move. When this happens the two rocks begin to act as one.

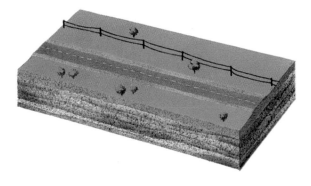

2. The rock must be bent and broken apart again. The pressure acting on the rock builds. Eventually the pressure becomes so great that the rock breaks and slips.

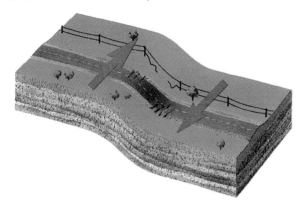

3. The energy generated from the movement depends on the pressure that has built up on the rock. If there is only a little pressure, the energy generated and released will be small. If the pressure is great, the energy is also great and the release of that energy can cause an earthquake. The pressures that act on rocks will be discussed in a later lesson.

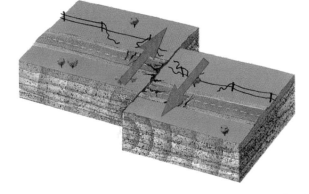

This highway near Oakland, California, collapsed during an earthquake.

Detecting Earthquakes

If the focus of an earthquake is far underground, how can scientists detect where it is? When an earthquake occurs, it sends waves of energy through Earth. This energy is much like the ripples that radiate across a pond when you drop a stone into the water. Scientists have machines called seismographs to detect and measure these waves of energy.

Scientists measure three types of waves: *P* waves, *S* waves, and *L* waves. *P* (or pressure) waves are like sound waves, with an accordion-like expansion and compression through the particles of solid rock. *P* waves make a great booming noise when they hit the surface. *S* (or shake) waves travel about half as fast as *P* waves. *S* waves move through the rock in a side to side motion. *L* (or long) waves are called surface waves because they happen only on top of the ground. *L* waves are the slowest of the three types. They produce an up-and-down rolling motion. The diagram on this page shows the characteristics of seismic waves.

Much of what geologists know about Earth's interior has come from studying seismic data from energy waves. The waves act like X rays of Earth. Geologists know that *P* waves travel through solid rock and liquid

Characteristics of Seismic Waves

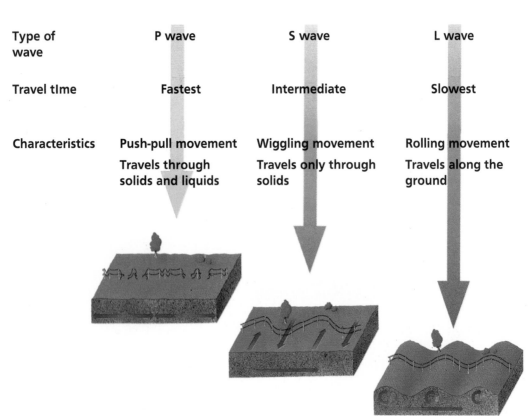

Type of wave	P wave	S wave	L wave
Travel time	Fastest	Intermediate	Slowest
Characteristics	Push-pull movement Travels through solids and liquids	Wiggling movement Travels only through solids	Rolling movement Travels along the ground

Richter Scale Magnitude	Estimated Number Per Year	Effects at Epicenters
Less than 2.5	900,000	Not usually felt
2.5–5.4	30,000	Very minor damage
5.5–6.0	500	Slight damage
6.1–6.9	100	Can be destructive in areas with large populations
7.0–7.9	20	Major earthquakes
Greater than 8.0	1 every 5 to 10 years	Major destruction

and that *S* waves travel only through solid rock. Therefore, a liquid somewhere in Earth would stop the *S* waves, and the *S* waves wouldn't be recorded on the other side of Earth. This is how scientists concluded that the outer core is a liquid.

Measuring Earthquakes

The magnitude or strength of an earthquake is measured by a seismograph. The seismograph records the earthquake's waves on a strip of paper. This record is called a seismograph. Scientists can tell the strength of an earthquake by the height, or amplitude, of the lines on the seismograph.

A scale called the **Richter scale** gives meaning to the measurement of the strength of earthquakes. It is the most commonly-used scale to measure the force of an earthquake. The Richter scale goes from 1 to 10.

An earthquake which occurred in 1976 in northern China measured 7.8 on the Richter scale. Thirty-two square kilometers of one city were damaged. It was estimated that 250,000 people died and another 700,000 people were injured.

The damage to this highway near Santa Cruz, California, was caused by an earthquake.

Volcanoes

Volcanoes form where melted materials well up from inside Earth. When the molten rock, called **magma,** rises to Earth's surface, a volcanic eruption occurs. Magma that rises to Earth's surface is called **lava.** Many famous volcanoes form large mountains. Years and years of eruptions put new and higher layers of lava on the mountain with each eruption.

Volcanoes are classified into three main types: cinder cones, shield volcanoes, and composite volcanoes. The cinder cone is the simplest type of volcano. Cinder cones are generally small and have steep sides. They are composed of cinders and ash ejected from volcanic vents. The western United States has many cinder cone volcanoes.

A shield volcano is very large and has gently sloping sides. Hawaii is made up of a chain of shield volcanoes. Mauna Loa is the world's largest shield volcano. It is 4 km above sea level and rises more than 8.5 km from the ocean floor. Shield volcanoes are formed from quick-flowing lava.

The composite volcano, as its name suggests, is a combination of a shield and cinder volcano. It is larger than a cinder cone and has steep sides. It is smaller than a shield volcano. Composite volcanoes often produce thick, slow-moving lava and explosive eruptions. The Cascade Mountains in California, Oregon, and Washington have many composite volcanoes.

This diagram shows the locations of frequent volcanic and earthquake activity. Why do you suppose some areas of Earth are more active than others?

▲ Active volcano

■ Earthquake zone

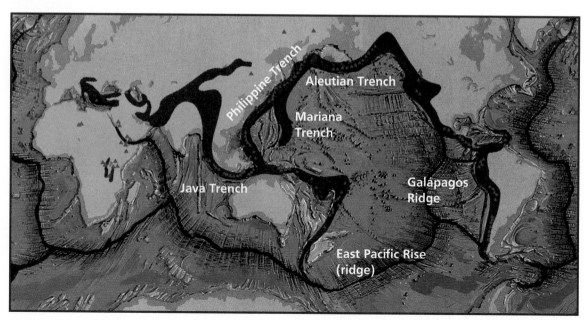

Philippine Trench

Aleutian Trench

Mariana Trench

Java Trench

Galápagos Ridge

East Pacific Rise (ridge)

The Cascade Mountains in California, Oregon, and Washington are composite volcanoes.

Obviously, molten lava and gases from an erupting volcano are dangerous, but not as dangerous as the enormous mudflows and giant avalanches that follow some eruptions. The mudflows, called lahars, have killed thousands of people without warning while destroying huge areas of cities and land.

Major volcanic eruptions also spew large amounts of ash into the atmosphere. This can cause damage hundreds or thousands of kilometers from the actual volcano. Some historic eruptions have even caused widespread famine because ash blocking the sun changed weather patterns, causing crops to grow poorly or not at all.

In the summer of 1816, for example, one year after a huge eruption of the Tambora volcano in Indonesia, ash still in the atmosphere caused weather changes that resulted in summer frost and snow. The unseasonably cold weather severely damaged crops in Europe and the northeastern United States.

This volcano is on the island of Montserrat in the Caribbean.

An extinct volcano is one that scientists believe will not erupt again. An active volcano is one that is still erupting. A dormant volcano is inactive but has the potential to erupt again. With all the dangers volcanoes present, why do people live in the shadow of an active or dormant volcano? Many people settle near volcanoes because crops thrive in the mineral-rich soil of ancient eruptions. Some countries, such as Iceland, use volcanoes to provide energy for heat and power.

Mountain Building

As you have just learned, a volcano can create a mountain after years of repeated lava flows. However, most mountains are created when two lithospheric plates collide. When two continents collide, the rocks get pressed together. This results in a **compression** of the rocks that produces mountains that are folded together and shoved upward. Compression is the process of squeezing together. These types of mountains are called *folded mountains*. The Alps in Europe and the Appalachians in the U.S. are good examples of folded mountains.

The Alps in Chamonix, France, are examples of folded mountains.

All mountains are formed by the complex processes that continue to shape Earth's crust.

Fault

Block

Dome

Sometimes so much pressure is applied to rocks at Earth's surface that they break rather than fold. These breaks in the rocks, along which movement occurs, are called faults. Rocks slide past each other along faults when force is applied. *Fault-block mountains* are formed when enormous blocks of rock move up and down relative to the surrounding bedrock. California's Sierra Nevada Mountains and the Andes Mountains in South America are good examples of fault-block mountains. All of these mountain-building processes—volcanic activity, folding, and breaking—are still occurring.

The Andes Mountains in Patagonia, Chile, are examples of fault-block mountains.

CHECKPOINT

1. What are earthquakes?
2. What are three different types of volcanoes?
3. How do mountains form?
 What happens when Earth's crust moves?

ACTIVITY
Making It Quake

Find Out

Do this activity to find out what happens during an earthquake.

Process Skills

Constructing Models
Predicting
Communicating
Observing
Controlling Variables
Experimenting

WHAT YOU NEED

two pieces of cloth or plastic wrap

safety goggles

toy cars, houses, bridges

32-cm x 22-cm cake pan

sand or dirt

Activity Journal

WHAT TO DO

1. Place the two pieces of cloth or plastic wrap in the bottom of a cake pan. Make sure a lip of cloth or wrap hangs over the opposite ends of the pan.

2. Cover the strips of cloth or plastic wrap with slightly moist sand or dirt.

    Safety! *Wear your goggles when working with sand.*

3. Create a model of a village with the toy cars, houses, bridges, and other objects down the center of the pan on top of the moist sand or dirt.

4. **Predict** what will happen if you grasp one lip of the cloth or plastic wrap and your friend grabs the other strip as you both pull each strip in the opposite direction. **Record** your prediction.

5. Now do the above. **Observe** what happens. **Record** the results.

6. If you have time, repeat Steps 1 through 5 by re-creating the village exactly as you built it before. Change only the amount of force you use when pulling the strips.

CONCLUSIONS

1. Why did you need cloth or plastic wrap at the bottom of the pan?

2. What does the space between the two cloths represent?

3. What happened when you pulled each strip in the opposite direction?

4. If you had time, what happened when more force was used to pull the strips?

ASKING NEW QUESTIONS

1. Can you imagine how real cities could be damaged during an earthquake?

2. What steps could you take to minimize damage and injury if you lived in an area prone to earthquakes?

SCIENTIFIC METHODS SELF CHECK

✔ Did I **construct a model** of an earthquake?

✔ Did I **predict** what would happen?

✔ Did I **observe** the effects of pulling on the strips?

✔ Did I **record** my predictions and observations?

✔ Did I **control the variables** by only changing the amount of force used in pulling the strips when I repeated the **experiment?**

Plate Tectonics

Find Out

- What plate tectonics theory is
- What new landforms result from plate movements
- How the plates move

Vocabulary

theory
plate tectonics theory
plates
convergent boundary
subduction
divergent boundary
transform boundary

The Big QUESTION

How does Earth's surface move?

Earthquakes, volcanoes, and surface features of Earth—what do all of these add up to? Earlier, you learned that Earth's crust is made up of several large pieces. These plates of the lithosphere slide around on the convecting asthenosphere. Earth is a network of forces and systems that are always changing.

Plate Tectonics Theory

The pattern of the continents suggests that they were once joined. Earthquakes and volcanic eruptions occur in a pattern around the world. You have a great deal of evidence already about how Earth works.

How do the patterns you have seen so far relate to one another? Do they, in fact, add up to one model of Earth? Put together, they may help you see your planet as a network of systems that interact and bring about changes.

A **theory** is an organized set of observations, ideas, experimental evidence, and thought that is designed to predict or explain an event or phenomenon. **Plate tectonics theory** is the idea that Earth's lithosphere is broken into several large pieces of land that move around on Earth's convecting asthenosphere. These large, moving pieces of Earth's crust and mantle are called **plates.** These plates are constantly moving at a rate of 2–20 cm per year. That's about as fast as fingernails grow. As the plates move and interact with one another, new crust forms and old crust moves, changes, or is destroyed.

Remember the "continental puzzle" map? It shows the boundaries of the world's plates and the direction in which they are moving. There are three major types of boundaries: convergent, divergent, and transform. At each type of boundary, one or more interactions can occur.

Fault-block mountains in Grand Teton National Park, Wyoming

Continental Puzzle

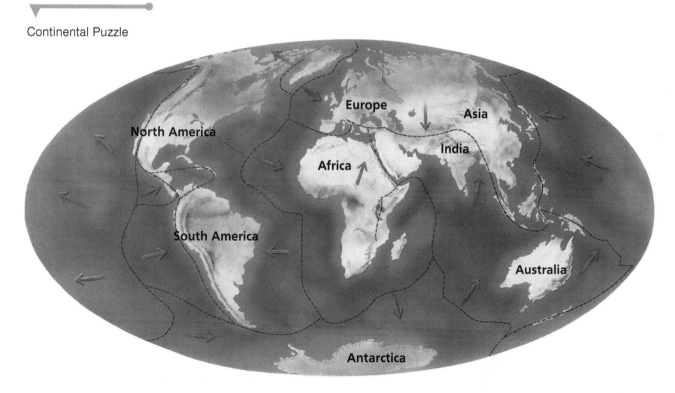

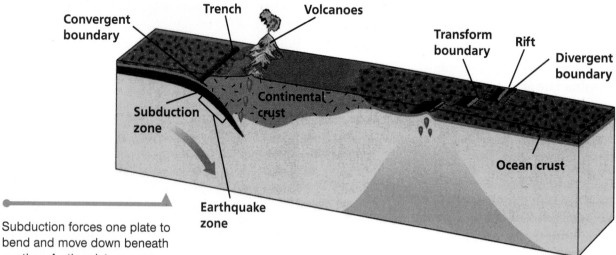

Convergent boundary

Trench   Volcanoes

Transform boundary   Rift

Divergent boundary

Subduction zone

Continental crust

Ocean crust

Earthquake zone

Subduction forces one plate to bend and move down beneath another. As the plate moves downward, it enters the heated rock of the mantle and melts. The molten rock is less dense than the material around it. Some of the molten rock rises and melts through the crust in places. As a result, volcanic eruptions occur.

This system of interactions explains the pattern of intense earthquake and volcanic activity in certain zones of the world. Look at a map of the west coast of South America. Would you expect some of the Andes Mountains to be active volcanoes?

The Lesser Antilles Islands were formed by subduction.

Convergent Boundaries

A **convergent boundary** is where two plates meet and converge or collide. Many of the world's earthquakes and volcanoes occur at convergent boundaries.

At a convergent boundary, a process called **subduction** occurs. In the process of subduction, one of the plates slides under the plate with which it is colliding.

There are three kinds of subduction. The first type takes place when an ocean plate meets another ocean plate. One of the ocean plates subducts by going under the other. The plate that is subducting creates a deep ocean trench. The plate that stays on top develops volcanoes. One example of what can result from an ocean-to-ocean subduction is what happened in the Lesser Antilles Islands in the East Caribbean. After millions of years of ocean plates colliding, volcanoes grew from the ocean floor and created an island chain.

In the second type of subduction, an ocean plate collides with a continental plate. The heavier oceanic crust subducts by sliding under the lighter continental crust. This type of subduction causes the continental plate to push up mountains and develop volcanoes. Again, the subducting oceanic plate creates a deep ocean trench.

The final type of subduction is continental plate to continental plate. The continental crusts push against each other to form mountains. The Himalayan Mountains in central Asia are a good example of this. Some of the highest mountains in the world are located here, including Mount Everest.

It is important to note that the volcanoes formed at convergent boundaries are known for their violent eruptions. The lava of these volcanoes contains a lot of silica. The silica makes the lava thick and sticky, which holds back mounting volcanic pressures until huge explosions blast skyward.

Divergent Boundaries

A **divergent boundary** is where two plates move away from one another. Divergent boundaries are marked by mid-ocean ridges.

Mid-ocean ridges were an exciting discovery. Many people had thought of the ocean floor as flat. Then, geologists discovered that under the sea, a ridge of mountains snakes its way around the globe. In the center of the ridges are valleys or rifts between the edges of the two plates pulling apart.

When the plates pull back from each other, magma comes to the surface and creates new crust. When this happens in the ocean, it causes the seafloor to get larger. This is called seafloor spreading. Seafloor spreading has been shown to occur at ocean ridges. The Atlantic Ocean is spreading by 2 cm per year. The East Pacific Rise is spreading by 20 cm per year. That rate is the fastest seafloor spreading in the world. If the spreading continues at that rate, the seafloor in the Pacific Ocean will be 2000 km wider in ten million years.

Mount Everest in Nepal is more than 8000 m above sea level.

A black smoker

Seafloor spreading at a divergent boundary can cause a rift or a valley in the middle of the ocean floor. If the boundary is a very active one, there will be a continuous flow of molten lava and jets of water containing lots of dark minerals. These jets are called black smokers. Certain bacteria feed on the minerals. They begin a food chain that scientists have only recently discovered. Near the top of this food chain are clams and brilliantly colored tube worms. Scientists have only recently developed the equipment to handle the pressure of going down more than 2000 m to study the bottom of the ocean.

Transform Boundaries

A **transform boundary** occurs when two plates slide past one another or when two plates slide in the same direction but at different speeds. They are also called faults. As you learned in Lesson 2, earthquakes can occur at these boundaries. The rocks along the plates bend for a while, then snap and create an earthquake. The most well-known transform boundary is the San Andreas Fault, located in California.

New Landforms

As you now know, enormous forces are exerted where two continental plates come together. The pressure causes layers of the crust to deform. They crumple up, some of them rising in mountain crests and others sinking into the mantle. Regardless of whether this change is fast or slow, we can interpret how Earth has changed by reading the record left in the rocks. For instance, limestone is often formed from the skeletons of sea animals. If you find limestone in the mountains, you might hypothesize that the area you now see as mountains was once covered by water. The process of creating landforms does not happen overnight.

Occasionally, at or near a divergent boundary, a volcano will grow to great heights. After millions of years these volcanic mountains get so tall that they reach sea-level and form an island. The Hawaiian Islands and Iceland are two examples of islands formed from volcanic mountains.

If you had lived on Iceland in 1963, you could have seen an island being born. Off the southwest coast of Iceland were numerous eruptions throughout several months. The volcano that rose out of the water was named the island of Surtsey. It is 2.6 km^2 and is the newest landmass on Earth.

Island of Surtsey, Iceland

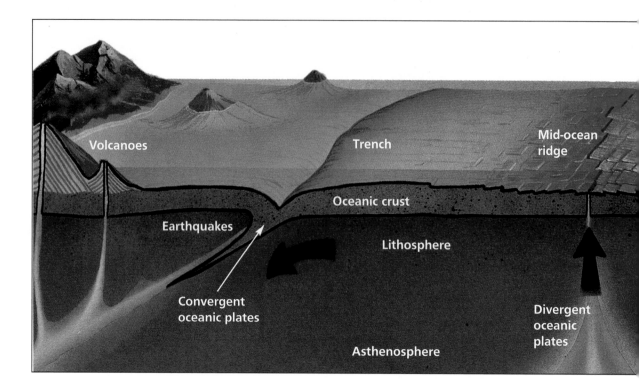

Volcanoes

Trench

Mid-ocean ridge

Oceanic crust

Earthquakes

Lithosphere

Convergent oceanic plates

Divergent oceanic plates

Asthenosphere

Moving Plates

Now that you are familiar with the different ways Earth's surface can move, you may wonder, "Why does it move?" You may remember that there is a layer of the mantle called the asthenosphere. In it, rock melts as it gets close to the core. As it rises toward the crust, it cools and sinks back down. These patterns of circulation are convection currents. They are currents that move in a series of circular motions.

New rock continually forms at the mid-ocean ridges, and old rock continually melts down below the trenches. In this sense, Earth is recycling. It is returning the material taken out of the mantle back to the mantle to be reused. Our planet is good at conserving its own resources.

The theory of plate tectonics could provide people with a solution to many of the social issues and questions we face today. For instance, because we know that Earth's crust is continually recycled, it seems possible that we could dispose of hazardous wastes by emptying them into areas that are likely to be subducted and soon remelted.

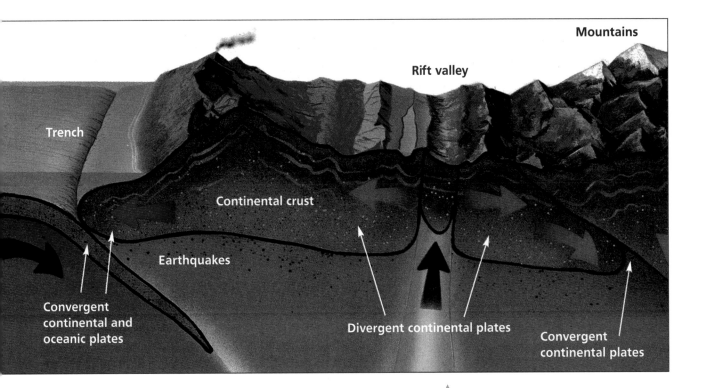

Mountains

Rift valley

Trench

Continental crust

Earthquakes

Convergent
continental and
oceanic plates

Divergent continental plates

Convergent
continental plates

A cross-sectional diagram of Earth's crust and asthenosphere, showing the processes that result in the recycling of Earth's materials

Some scientists have suggested that radioactive waste might be dumped at subduction zones. The idea is that the waste would be carried deep into the asthenosphere with the descending ocean plate. It is supposed that it would melt in with the other rock and become part of the mantle. Other scientists are concerned that this may not work and could cause widespread pollution.

A good theory helps us make predictions based on evidence. The theory of plate tectonics might help us uncover valuable resources. Oil deposits often form in the sediments along continental-shelf margins. Metallic ores form in deposits near large magma bodies or along sea-floor spreading ridges. Scientists and engineers are looking for these resources based on the predictions from the theory of plate tectonics.

CHECKPOINT

1. What is plate tectonics theory?
2. What new landforms result from plate movements?
3. How do the plates move?

 How does Earth's surface move?

ACTIVITY

Investigating Plate Tectonics

Find Out

Do this activity to see how plates on Earth's surface interact in many different ways.

Process Skills

Observing
Communicating
Constructing Models
Inferring

WHAT YOU NEED

hard-boiled egg

water

paper towel

Activity Journal

WHAT TO DO

1. Gently crack the shell of the hard-boiled egg.

   Safety! *Do not eat your egg. Discard it where your teacher tells you.*

2. Peel off the pieces of eggshell and place them gently on your paper towel. Put your peeled egg in a small amount of water to get it wet.

3. Take your egg out of the water. Choose a few of the medium-to-large pieces of eggshell that were adjacent to each other.

4. Slide the pieces of shell around the egg toward each other, away from each other, and past each other.

5. Draw pictures of the "puzzles" you have made.

CONCLUSIONS

1. Did the pieces fit together perfectly? Why or why not?

2. Explain what happened to your eggshell when you pushed two pieces toward one another. What type of boundary did it model?

3. Explain what happens when you push the shells away from each other.

4. What part of Earth did the water represent?

ASKING NEW QUESTIONS

1. What other Earth processes did the egg and shell represent?

2. Imagine that your egg has been cut in half. Can you infer a comparison of the structure of Earth to the egg?

SCIENTIFIC METHODS SELF CHECK

✔ Did I **observe** how the pieces of eggshell could slide past each other?

✔ Did I **draw** pictures of the eggshell puzzle?

✔ Did I **construct a model** of Earth's plates using the pieces of eggshell?

✔ Did I **infer** how the different layers of Earth could be represented by the hard-boiled egg?

Continental Drift

Find Out

- What continental drift is
- What geologic time is
- How we can infer Earth's processes

Vocabulary

continental drift
geologic eras
Ring of Fire
hot spots

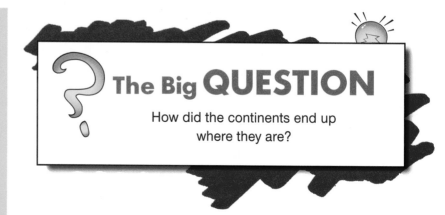

The Big QUESTION

How did the continents end up where they are?

*D*o *you like putting together puzzles with lots of pieces? It's challenging and sometimes a bit frustrating. That's the kind of puzzle that scientists confronted as they tried to answer the question: "Could the continents have been joined at one time?"*

Moving Continents

You know that Earth's plates are moving and causing events such as earthquakes and volcanoes. Earth's processes are also responsible for forming mountains. What did Earth look like millions of years ago, before the continents moved to where we see them now? What will Earth look like millions of years from now? What other evidence have scientists discovered that supports these theories?

Around the beginning of the 1900s, one model of Earth's processes was beginning to take shape. First, scientists observed, analyzed, and interpreted the rock record on the boundaries of the different continents. They dated the rocks to find out when they formed. (In terms of Earth's history, a 100-million-year-old rock is recent.) They compared the rocks and surface features on two continents that looked as though they fit like puzzle pieces.

In many places, older rock layers along continental boundaries fit well. Recently formed layers showed differences. The differences could represent what happened after the continents split apart.

Fossils provided further evidence. They showed that long ago, the same plants and animals existed on different continents at the same time. This is quite unusual because, as you know, specific plants and animals are limited by their habitats and their environments.

These fossils were found in layers that had formed hundreds of millions of years ago. Therefore, scientists concluded that the organisms lived hundreds of millions of years ago. However, fossils that represented a more recent time—say, only 50 million years ago—often didn't match when these same continental areas were compared. Scientists interpreted this evidence to mean that the point at which the fossil record began to differ showed the approximate time when the continents separated. This separation of the continents is **continental drift.**

The Pacific Coast shoreline of the United States near Santa Cruz, California

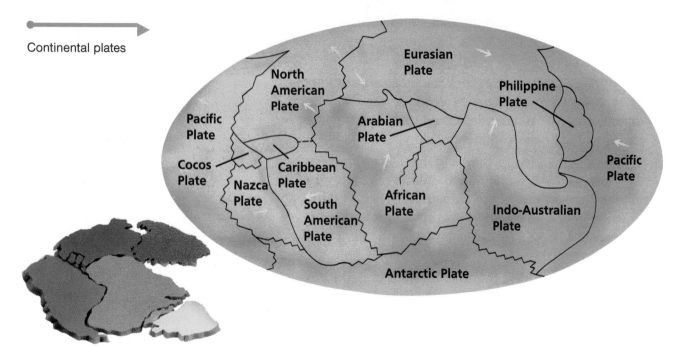

Continental plates

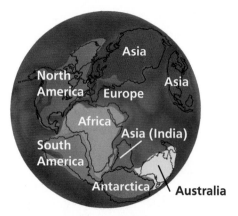

Pangaea

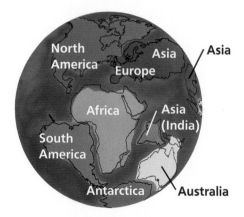

About 250 million years ago

About 70 million years ago

Francis Bacon was the first scientist to notice that the shapes of the world's continents seemed to fit together. In 1620, he published his ideas in the book *Novum Organum*. Of course, most people then thought that his ideas were foolish, and not much was heard about moving continents again until the early 1900s. In 1912, the German meteorologist Alfred Wegener noticed the same similarities. He believed that all of the continents were once joined together in a supercontinent that he named *Pangaea*.

Wegener theorized that about 200 million years ago, Pangaea split into a northern continent he called Laurasia and a southern continent he called Gondwana. Laurasia later split apart to form North America, Europe, and Asia. Gondwana split to form Australia, India, Africa, South America, and Antarctica. These landmasses, Wegener thought, drifted like stone rafts on the more dense material below them.

Wegener was on the right track but he could not describe what made the continents move. In the early 1900s no one could imagine a force strong enough to move continents. It wasn't until the 1960s that scientists had enough evidence to propose that the convection currents in the asthenosphere were strong enough to move the continents. The fossil record, the rock layers, and the convection currents in the asthenosphere all support the theory of continental drift.

Geologic Time

Scientists have put together a time scale that allows them to place all of the important events that took place on Earth's surface into one long sequence. They use the fossils present in rocks to help divide geologic time. By this process, they put together a time line of the planet's history based on changes observed in the geologic record.

At different times, different kinds of events occurred. Different kinds of life forms existed at these different times. The rocks provide a record of these events and life forms.

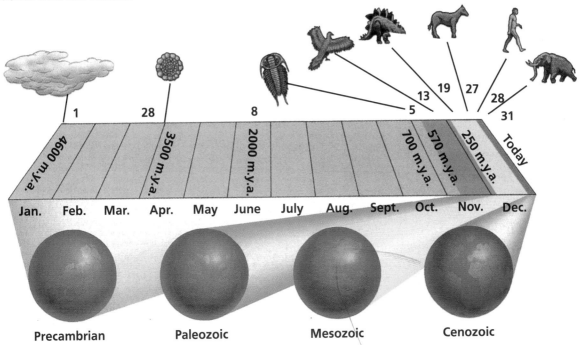

Precambrian   Paleozoic   Mesozoic   Cenozoic

m.y.a. = million years ago

Geologic eras, or the major geologic time divisions, are based on changes in Earth's crust and the changes in the types of life forms present. The four main geologic eras divide up the time from the formation of Earth to the present. That is about 4.6 billion years.

It is difficult to put such vast amounts of time into something meaningful. How long ago was 4.6 billion years? 600 million? 60 million? In order to understand geologic time, use the diagram on this page to compare Earth's geologic eras to one calendar year.

Throughout these different periods, Earth's crust was in motion. There is evidence that changes in the location of the continents also match changes in the geologic eras.

Earth is 4.6 billion years old. That period of time is represented in this diagram by one calendar year. The dates of the year indicate when important things happened—the formation of Earth, the appearance of cells, and other events in life history. The globes represent the position of the continents during the different geologic eras.

Understand Earth's Processes

Earth changes continually. Its slow process of change can be observed in Earth's features. If you examine Earth's mountains, volcanoes, and other landforms, you can figure out when some of the changes happened. You can also figure out what caused the changes. For example, the Rocky Mountains are high, jagged, and pointed because they are made of three types of rock and have been deeply eroded by mountain glaciers. By contrast, the Appalachian Mountains are low, smooth, and rounded and are made only of folded sedimentary rocks.

Mountains form because of upward thrust as two plates collide. They slowly wear down as gravity and the forces in Earth's atmosphere work on them. Think about the forces that wear away at Earth's surface. Exposed rock erodes over time. Erosion is the process by which wind, water, or ice wears away the rock. Since these processes have been wearing away at both sets of mountains, the mountains must have formed at different times.

What happens to the bits of rock that wear off in erosion? Earth conserves its resources. The rock formed at divergent plate boundaries, for example, is recycled into magma at a convergent boundary. What do you think Earth does to recycle the material eroded from rocks?

The Rocky Mountains are made of igneous, sedimentary, and metamorphic rocks.

The Appalachian Mountains are made of folded sedimentary rocks.

Earth's Ring of Fire

Ring of Fire

Most of Earth's volcanoes are located near areas where strong earthquake activity occurs. In fact, 80 percent of the world's volcanoes are located on that zone of strong earthquake activity that circles the Pacific Ocean. So many volcanic eruptions occur in this zone that it has been named the **Ring of Fire.**

Look at the photo and compare it to the map on B102. Do you see a connection? Can you connect these locations with any recent earthquakes or volcanoes? You may have heard about an earthquake in San Francisco that interrupted the 1989 baseball World Series. You may also know of the spectacular eruption of Mount St. Helens in the Cascade Mountains of Washington State in 1980. These are only two examples of earthquake and volcanic activity in this area of the United States.

Japan and the Philippines are two other countries where many volcanoes and earthquakes occur. Did you know there was a devastating earthquake in Kobe, Japan, in 1995? Take a moment to explore your map. You can probably find many more examples of volcanic and earthquake activity around the Ring of Fire.

The Hawaiian Islands developed as a result of a hot spot under the Pacific Ocean plate.

Hot Spots

Hot spots provide one more piece of evidence to help support the theory of continental drift. **Hot spots** are areas with extremely powerful pressures that push magma up through the crust to form volcanoes. As the crust moves the volcano away from the hot spot, the volcano becomes dormant. But the pressure at the hot spot pushes magma up through the new area of crust above it to form a new, active volcano.

The Hawaiian Islands are a chain of dormant and active volcanoes caused by a hot spot that has existed for thousands of years. Mauna Loa and Kilauea are active volcanoes now. As the Pacific Plate continues to move over time, these volcanoes will become dormant. Already, there is a new volcanic island active and growing underwater. When it reaches the ocean's surface, it will be added to the Hawaiian Island chain.

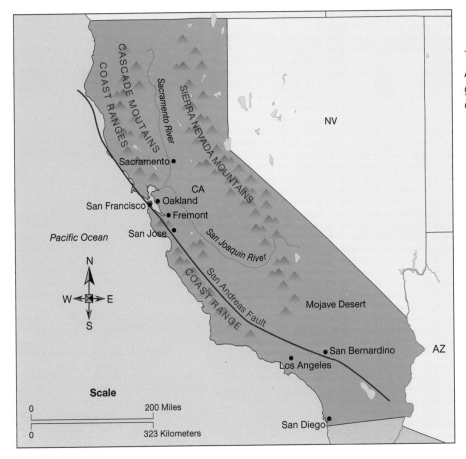

A map showing the geographic features of California

A Final Example

California is where excellent examples of continental drift occur. One of the most well-known geologic areas is the San Andreas Fault. It is responsible for many small and a few large earthquakes. It enters California in the north at Point Arena and extends into the southern part of the state. The San Andreas Fault is where the Pacific Plate is very slowly edging northwest and the North American Plate is moving west. The rocks of the Sierra Nevada were once on California's Pacific shore. They are being uplifted into a gigantic fault-block mountain along their east edge. Can you find other examples of continental drift?

CHECKPOINT

1. Describe continental drift.
2. What is geologic time?
3. How can we infer Earth's processes?

 How did the continents end up where they are?

B125

ACTIVITY

Moving On

Find Out

Do this activity to find out what Earth might look like in the future if continental drift continues.

Process Skills

Interpreting Data
Predicting
Constructing Models
Communicating

WHAT YOU NEED

map of the continents that you can cut out

large sheet (28 cm x 43 cm) of colored paper

pencil

scissors

Activity Journal

WHAT TO DO

1. Cut out each continent. Place them in their current relative positions on the sheet of colored paper. Interpret the data for the current continental positions and what you know about continental drift to predict where the continents will be ten million years in the future.

2. Use your model and make the continents "drift." When a continent drifts to the edge of the paper, it must reappear on the opposite edge. Move each continent once.

3. Draw a rough sketch of their relative positions.

4. You may continue to move the continents, drawing a sketch of relative positions after each move.

5. Record what the continents look like in their new position.

CONCLUSIONS

1. What did you predict about the position of Earth's continents ten million years from now?

2. Will they be in the same places or different ones? How do you know?

ASKING NEW QUESTIONS

1. How is predicting different from guesswork?

2. What further evidence do you need to better predict the future positions of the continents?

3. How could you test your predictions?

SCIENTIFIC METHODS SELF CHECK

✔ Did I **interpret data** about current positions of continents and the theory of continental drift?

✔ Did I **predict** the location of the continental plates?

✔ Did I use the **model** to make the continents drift?

✔ Did I **draw** a sketch of the continents in their new positions to **record** my observations?

CHAPTER 3

Review

Reviewing Vocabulary and Concepts

Write the letter of the answer that best completes each sentence.

1. The center of Earth is called the ___.
   - **a.** mantle
   - **b.** metallic core
   - **c.** crust
   - **d.** lithosphere

2. The outermost layer of Earth is the ___.
   - **a.** crust
   - **b.** epicenter
   - **c.** lithosphere
   - **d.** convergent boundary

3. A ___ is a place in Earth's crust where the rocks have broken.
   - **a.** convergent boundary
   - **b.** fault
   - **c.** mantle
   - **d.** metallic core

4. ___ is when one of the plates slides under the plate with which it is colliding.
   - **a.** Compression
   - **b.** Crustal movement
   - **c.** Continental drift
   - **d.** Subduction

5. ___ is the theory that Earth's continents have moved over time.
   - **a.** Plate tectonics
   - **b.** Subduction
   - **c.** Crustal movement
   - **d.** Continental drift

Match the definition on the left with the correct term.

6. the middle layer of Earth

7. area directly above the focus in an earthquake

8. the scale used most often to measure the scale of earthquakes

9. molten rock

10. an organized set of observations, ideas, experimental evidence, and thought

11. large, moving pieces of Earth's crust and mantle

12. where two plates meet and collide

13. where two plates meet and one slides under the other

14. major geologic time divisions

15. pressures that push up magma to form volcanoes

   a. mantle

   b. theory

   c. Richter scale

   d. convergent boundary

   e. geologic eras

   f. hot spots

   g. plates

   h. magma

   i. epicenter

   j. subduction

Understanding What You Learned

1. What are the names of seven large pieces of Earth's lithosphere?
2. How is the pattern of motion caused by convection currents in the asthenosphere like a conveyor belt?
3. How can volcanoes be destructive?
4. Why do volcanoes form at convergent boundaries?
5. What makes continents drift?

Applying What You Learned

1. Why can't you dig a tunnel through Earth?
2. Why are cities susceptible to devastation from earthquakes?
3. Why was the discovery of ocean ridges so exciting?
4. Why is the zone of strong earthquake activity encircling the Pacific Ocean called the Ring of Fire?
5. Based on what you have learned, how would you describe how Earth's surface moves and changes over time?

For Your **Portfolio**

Trace the map of California on page B125. Use your map to answer these questions. What kind of plate boundary runs through it? How do you know? Describe the processes that probably occur along the boundary. What features would you expect to find there? Write your answers on a sheet of paper and save them in your portfolio.

Earth in Space

The night skies have captured the imagination of civilizations for thousands of years. Fascination with the heavens has given rise to a variety of legends and myths that people have created to try to explain our place in the universe.

In ancient times, people thought that Earth was the center of the universe. However, as time went on and people began to understand more about the universe, we have come to realize that our planet is only a small planet within a much greater system.

We have learned a great deal about space over the years. Advances in technology and increased interest in space exploration continue to fuel the drive for a greater understanding of the universe. Science plays the key role in trying to answer the many questions we still have about space.

The Big IDEA

Our solar system is part of the universe.

CHAPTER SCIENCE INVESTIGATION

Research space technology. Find out how in your *Activity Journal.*

The Sun, Moon, and Earth

Find Out

- How the sun and Earth affect time and the seasons
- How the moon affects tides
- What an eclipse is

Vocabulary

rotation
orbit
ellipse
semidiurnal tides
diurnal tides
eclipse

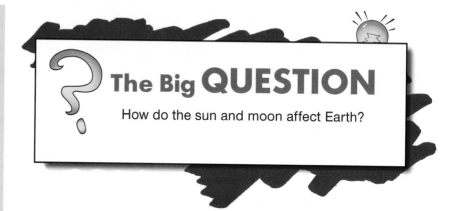

The Big QUESTION

How do the sun and moon affect Earth?

How will investigating the relationships among the sun, Earth, and the moon help you to understand the various cycles that are experienced on our planet? You can understand day and night, the calendar year, the seasons, and the tides better. Interactions among the sun, moon, and Earth result in the phases of the moon and can produce eclipses.

How the Sun and Earth Affect Time and the Seasons

How could you tell time if clocks or watches didn't exist? How could you tell when a month had passed without using a calendar? What if you lived near an ocean—how could you keep track of time? Which seasonal changes can be measured where you live? Did you know that there are more seasonal changes in some places on Earth than there are in others?

Animals and plants seem to react to time changes by instinct. For example, you've probably seen birds migrating at different seasons. Gray whales also migrate with the seasons. But some animals even react to the passage of hours during a single day! Fiddler crabs change color as the day progresses. Silvery gray in the morning, they grow steadily darker until noon. The darker color protects them from enemies and the sun. Your life, too, is affected by the length of the day and the year, the change in seasons, and maybe even the tides.

In ancient times, people thought that the sun moved around Earth because it appeared that the sun rose in the morning, and moved across the sky to set at night. Now we know that the sun does not move around Earth. It is Earth's rotation on its axis that results in sunrises, sunsets, and day and night.

The amount of solar energy, heat, and light given off by the sun is about the same year round. In addition, Earth is always about the same distance from the sun. However, the amount of solar energy received on Earth depends on the angle of Earth's tilt.

The angle of sunlight received at any place on Earth changes during the year because Earth is tilted 23.5 degrees on its axis. This tilt is also responsible for changes in the length of daylight and seasons throughout a year. Examine the diagram on pages D134 and D135 to see why.

It takes the moon about 29.5 days to go through a complete cycle of its phases.

What Causes Night and Day?

Earth is not only tilted on its axis, it also rotates. **Rotation** (rō tā′ shen) is a spinning motion, like a toy top. Every 24 hours, Earth makes a complete rotation on its axis. As you know, the amount of solar energy each hemisphere of Earth receives during a day depends on the time of year.

Because different parts of Earth are exposed to sunlight at different times, Earth is divided into 24 time zones, roughly by lines of longitude (those lines that run north-south on maps). The starting point for the time zones is the prime meridian, or the line of longitude that passes through the Greenwich Observatory in Greenwich, England.

There are 12 time zones to the west of the prime meridian, and 12 to the east. The clocks in the time zone east of you are set one hour later than yours, while clocks to the west are set one hour earlier.

If you travel around the world, you'll cross all 24 time zones and either gain or lose a day, depending on which direction you're going. The International Date Line, a longitudinal line running through the Pacific Ocean, is a part of the human-made timekeeping system. If you cross this line going west, you add a day. If you cross it going east, you subtract a day.

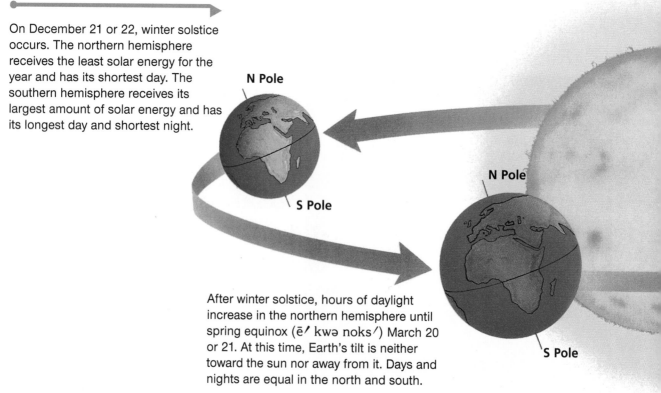

On December 21 or 22, winter solstice occurs. The northern hemisphere receives the least solar energy for the year and has its shortest day. The southern hemisphere receives its largest amount of solar energy and has its longest day and shortest night.

N Pole

S Pole

N Pole

S Pole

After winter solstice, hours of daylight increase in the northern hemisphere until spring equinox (ē′ kwə noks′) March 20 or 21. At this time, Earth's tilt is neither toward the sun nor away from it. Days and nights are equal in the north and south.

Here's how time zones work. As Earth rotates and sunlight reaches the East Coast of the United States, the time might be 6:00 A.M. As the rotation continues, sunlight stretches westward across the continent. When it reaches Chicago about an hour later, clocks there will read 6:00 A.M. because this city is in the next time zone. One hour later the sun will rise in Denver and the clocks there will show 6:00 A.M. This becomes slightly more complicated when some states use daylight savings time from April through October and other states do not. For daylight savings time, people set their clocks one hour ahead of the usual time in that zone. That means they actually get up an hour earlier than usual every day, but they enjoy an extra hour of daylight in the evening.

The path Earth travels through space around the sun is called an **orbit.** The shape of Earth's orbit is not a perfect circle, but an **ellipse.** An ellipse is an oval. That's why Earth is slightly closer to the sun at certain times.

One complete revolution around the sun requires 365.25 days, or one year. Every fourth year, we total up the fractions of days, add a day to February, and call this a "leap year."

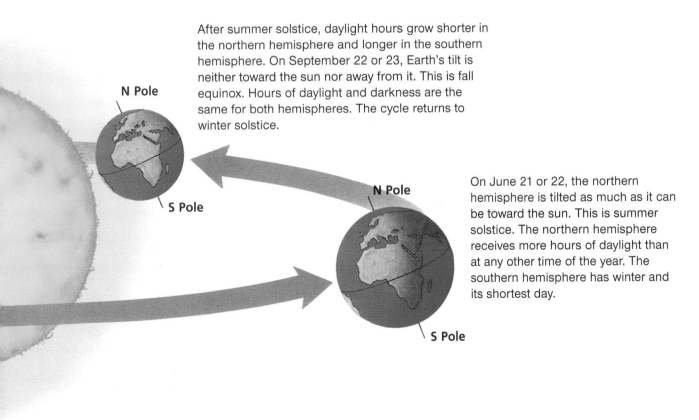

After summer solstice, daylight hours grow shorter in the northern hemisphere and longer in the southern hemisphere. On September 22 or 23, Earth's tilt is neither toward the sun nor away from it. This is fall equinox. Hours of daylight and darkness are the same for both hemispheres. The cycle returns to winter solstice.

N Pole

S Pole

N Pole

On June 21 or 22, the northern hemisphere is tilted as much as it can be toward the sun. This is summer solstice. The northern hemisphere receives more hours of daylight than at any other time of the year. The southern hemisphere has winter and its shortest day.

S Pole

The Moon and the Tides

To understand how the moon affects tides, you need to know how the moon moves around Earth. While Earth rotates on its axis as it revolves around the sun, the moon also rotates on its axis and revolves around Earth. The same side of the moon always faces Earth. We never see its other side. If the moon did not rotate, we would see different faces of the moon.

You know that Earth takes a year to orbit the sun. The moon takes about 29.5 days to orbit the Earth. It travels in a slightly elliptical orbit, just like Earth. If the moon takes about 29.5 days to orbit Earth, why does the moon look different at different times of the month?

Moonlight is actually sunlight reflected off the moon toward Earth. The moon doesn't generate any light or heat of its own, so we can see only the part of the moon receiving light from the sun.

▼
Moon Phases

2. As the moon moves a quarter of its orbit around Earth, we see more of its lighted half. When we see half of its lighted half, it is called the first quarter phase.

1. When the moon's orbit takes it between the sun and Earth, the side facing Earth is dark. The moon is not visible at night during this time, called the new moon phase.

3. When the moon reaches the opposite side of Earth from the sun, the entire side toward Earth reflects the sun's light—the full moon phase.

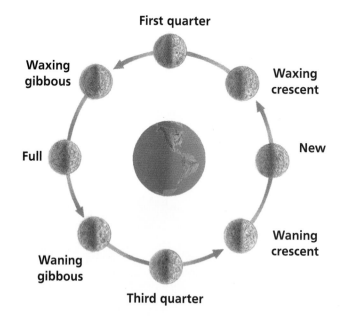

First quarter

Waxing gibbous

Waxing crescent

Full

New

Waning gibbous

Waning crescent

Third quarter

Light from sun

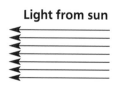

5. The moon completes its cycle of phases in 29.5 days by becoming a new moon again, with its dark side toward Earth.

4. As the moon completes its orbit, its other side gradually slips into shadows, the third quarter phase.

Both the sun and the moon affect tides on Earth. They both exert a gravitational attraction that affects the water on Earth's surface.

The gravitational attraction between Earth and the moon results in a bulge in the ocean water facing the moon and another bulge in the water on the opposite side of Earth. When these bulges are present, it is high tide in these areas. The shallower water between the bulges is low tide.

As the moon revolves around Earth, the moon's gravitational attraction with Earth creates tides in Earth's oceans. Some areas, such as the Atlantic Coast, have two high tides and two low tides every day. These are called **semidiurnal** (sem′ ē dī ur′ nel) **tides.** In other places, including the Gulf of Mexico, the shape of the coast and depth of the water result in only one high and one low tide each day, called **diurnal** (dī ur′ nel) **tides.**

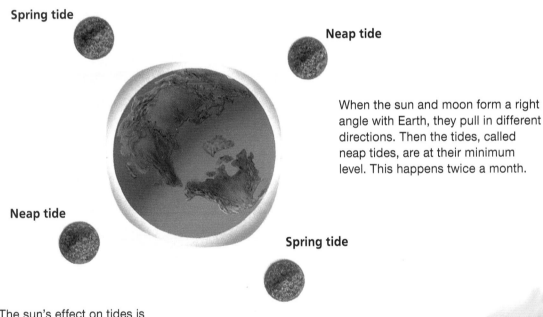

Spring tide

Neap tide

Neap tide

Spring tide

When the sun and moon form a right angle with Earth, they pull in different directions. Then the tides, called neap tides, are at their minimum level. This happens twice a month.

The sun's effect on tides is particularly noticeable when the sun, the moon, and Earth are in line, resulting in extra-high tides called spring tides. The name is misleading because spring tides also occur twice a month, not just in the springtime.

Eclipses

Sometimes, we can see Earth's relationship with the sun and moon with something as simple as a shadow. An **eclipse** occurs when one object passes into the shadow of another object. There are two kinds of eclipses, lunar and solar. Both cast a dark inner shadow called an umbra (um′ brə) and a lighter outer shadow, the penumbra (pi num′ brə).

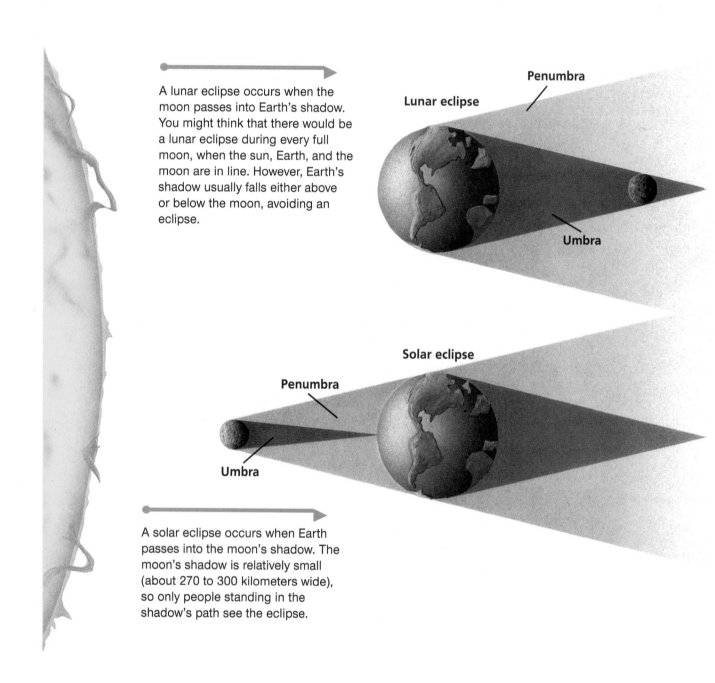

A lunar eclipse occurs when the moon passes into Earth's shadow. You might think that there would be a lunar eclipse during every full moon, when the sun, Earth, and the moon are in line. However, Earth's shadow usually falls either above or below the moon, avoiding an eclipse.

Lunar eclipse

Penumbra

Umbra

Solar eclipse

Penumbra

Umbra

A solar eclipse occurs when Earth passes into the moon's shadow. The moon's shadow is relatively small (about 270 to 300 kilometers wide), so only people standing in the shadow's path see the eclipse.

This time-lapse photograph shows a solar eclipse.

You may not be aware of it, but all living things are affected by the interaction of the sun, the moon, and Earth. Earth's orbit around the sun determines the length of a year. This orbit and the tilt of Earth determine when farmers must plant and when they must harvest. Birds and whales migrate with the seasons. The tides, caused by the gravitational attraction of the sun and the moon with Earth, determine when ships will sail and when fish will spawn. The sun and the moon are responsible for a great many natural occurrences on Earth's surface.

CHECKPOINT

1. How do the sun and Earth affect time and the seasons?
2. How does the moon affect tides?
3. What is an eclipse?

 How do the sun and moon affect Earth?

ACTIVITY

Creating an Eclipse Model

Find Out

Do this activity to learn how to create a model to understand solar eclipses.

Process Skills

Constructing Models
Controlling Variables
Observing
Communicating

WHAT YOU NEED

2-cm marble as the moon

new tennis ball as the sun

Activity Journal

metric ruler

WHAT TO DO

1. Take the tennis ball and the marble and set them up in a position modeling a solar eclipse.

2. Take the marble between your thumb and forefinger and hold it 7 cm away from your eye. Take the tennis ball in the other hand and put it at arm's length away from your body about 37 cm. The marble and the tennis ball should be in line with your open eye, which represents your view from Earth. Move the marble toward and away from you until it blocks out any view of the tennis ball.

3. Use the tennis ball and marble to create a lunar eclipse. The tennis ball (sun) should block out any view of the marble (moon).

4. Sketch your models.

CONCLUSIONS

1. What is a solar eclipse?
2. What is a lunar eclipse?

ASKING NEW QUESTIONS

1. How would you show a partial eclipse? What would be different from a full eclipse?
2. If you lived on the moon and observed Earth from there, would you see any eclipses? If so, describe them.

SCIENTIFIC METHODS SELF CHECK

✔ Did I use a **model** to create an eclipse?

✔ Did I use the same model in a different **experiment?**

✔ Did I **observe** what happened and **record** the results?

Our Solar System

Find Out

- Where the asteroid belt is
- What the solar system is
- What the characteristics of the inner planets are
- What the characteristics of the outer planets are
- How Pluto was discovered

Vocabulary

asteroids
terrestrial planets
Jovian planets
solar system
space probes
comet
meteors

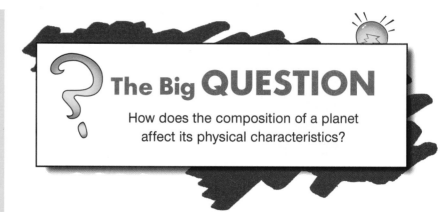

The Big QUESTION

How does the composition of a planet affect its physical characteristics?

The solar system is an important part of our universe. It is made up of our sun and the nine large objects that orbit the sun. These nine planets are Mercury, Venus, Earth, Mars, Jupiter, Saturn, Uranus, Neptune, and Pluto. The solar system contains the moons that orbit the planets and the thousands of other celestial bodies that orbit the sun. The sun is actually a star, and it is the only star in the solar system. The sun controls the orbits of all the planets. The closer a planet is to the sun, the shorter its year. Each planet rotates on its own axis.

The Asteroid Belt

For thousands of years, people have gazed up into the night sky. They noticed that some bright lights wandered around the sky and dreamed about what they looked like. You know the answer to a question that puzzled astronomers for thousands of years. Does the sun revolve around Earth, or does Earth revolve around the sun?

Of course, we now know for sure that Earth is one major planet that orbits our sun. But we still have much to learn about the other planets.

We know that one planet is more than 11 times bigger than Earth, and one is about half the size of our moon. One planet is circled with rings of ice, and one has surface temperatures that reach 482 °C. Some planets have many moons, while other planets have none. Some planets are hard and rocky, and some are made largely of gas.

Asteroid

Why are all the planets so different? Is there life on another planet? Does that life look anything like life on Earth? Could we live on Mars or our moon, or someplace else in our solar system? And what keeps the planets in orbit? Why don't they all just go flying off into space?

In the late 1700s, the German astronomer Johann Bode (bo′ de) calculated a scale of planetary distances. He measured the distances of all the planets from the sun, and then compared them. He put Mercury's distance at a value of 0. For the next planet from the sun, Venus, he made the distance equal to 3. From there on, each planet was given a value double the prior value (3, 6, 12, 24, 48). Bode then added 4 to each number. From this he developed a formula called *Bode's law*. Look at the diagram on this page to see what Bode's law shows. It shows a fairly regular pattern of the relative distance between each of the then-known planets and the sun—4 (Mercury), 7 (Venus), 10 (Earth), 16 (Mars), 28 (no planet), 52 (Jupiter), and 100 (Saturn).

The absence of a planet at point 28 drew attention to the wide gap between Mars and Jupiter. Since Bode's time, astronomers have discovered a belt of more than 10,000 **asteroids** where the "missing planet" would be. No one is sure whether asteroids are debris from a planet that met with disaster or bits of material that never condensed into a planet. While most of the asteroids in this belt are held by the sun's gravity to their solar orbit, there can be asteroids that stray. One such asteroid's orbit brought it to within less than 804,672 km of Earth.

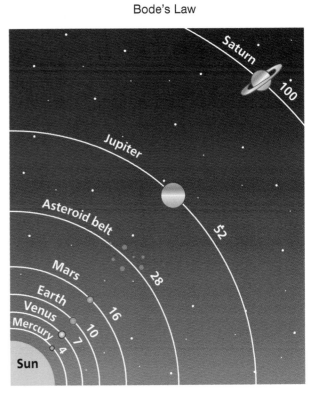

Bode's Law

The Solar System

The study of the planets began long ago. Early astronomers noticed that five "stars" were brighter than the others. Today we know those "stars" are the planets we can see without using a telescope. Because these five "stars" seemed to move in relation to other stars, the Greeks called them *planets,* which comes from the word *wander.*

Present-day scientists label the planets as "inner" and "outer." The inner planets, Mercury, Venus, Earth, and Mars, are called **terrestrial planets.** Terrestrial planets are similar to Earth in their composition. They are solid, rocklike, and dense.

Four of the outer planets, Jupiter, Saturn, Uranus, and Neptune, are called **Jovian,** or Jupiter-like, **planets.** Jovian planets are made of gas and are bigger but less dense than the terrestrial planets. The fifth outer planet, Pluto, is unique among all the planets because it is made of a mixture of rock and ice. These nine major planets and our sun make up our **solar system.**

The *Atlantis* space shuttle launching the *Magellan* spacecraft on its Venus mission

The sun is the biggest object in the system by far. It has 99.86 percent of the total mass of the solar system. Its gravitational attraction with each of the other planets holds the planets in their orbits.

We can't see much of the other planets from Earth. No one has traveled to any of the planets yet. Now that you have an idea of the distances that lie between Earth and the planets, you may understand why. Scientists on Earth have launched deep-space probes. These have expanded our knowledge tremendously. **Space probes** are rocket-launched vehicles. They contain instruments and cameras that gather data as they fly by, orbit, or land on planets and other objects in space. Because of data collected by space probes, you can learn more about the planets than even scientists knew when your parents were in school.

The Inner Planets

Mercury Mercury is the second-smallest planet, less than half the size of Earth. Until the *Mariner 10* space probe flew by Mercury in the early 1970s, little was known about this planet. It's so close to the sun that the sun's glare makes it nearly impossible to see.

Mercury is surrounded by a very thin layer of gases, mostly hydrogen, helium, and neon. Without an atmosphere, temperatures soar to more than 425 °C in the sun and drop to – 173 °C on the dark side of the planet. Mercury's temperature changes make it one of the hottest planets and the coldest of the inner planets.

Venus Because Venus is Earth's closest neighbor, it was the first planet to be studied with space probes, starting back in 1962. As you can see from the photograph, Venus has a thick, cloudy atmosphere that hides the surface of the planet. *Pioneer Venus 2* helped determine that Venus's atmosphere is 97 percent carbon dioxide. Its clouds are mostly sulfuric acid, which gives Venus its yellow-white color.

Because Venus is so close to the sun, the sunlight it receives is very intense. Venus's thick layer of carbon dioxide traps the heat, sending surface temperatures as high as 482 °C, hot enough to melt lead. Venus still has active volcanoes, which suggests that there are forces under the planet's surface much like Earth's. One of the volcanoes stands 12 km high and is more than 240 km wide at the base. The planet's core is nickel and iron, like Earth's.

Mercury

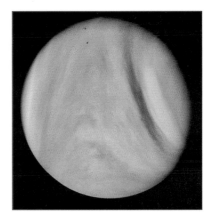

Venus

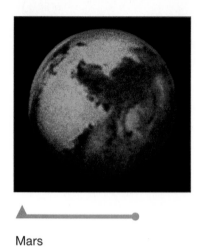

Mars

Mars While space probes haven't detected any evidence of life, they've discovered that Mars is similar to Earth in several ways. For example, the atmosphere on Mars is mostly carbon dioxide, as on Venus, but it also has small amounts of nitrogen and oxygen, as on Earth. Mars also has some water in its atmosphere, about 0.001 as much as Earth's atmosphere has. That's enough to condense and form clouds and fog.

The days on Mars are almost the same length as on Earth, 24 hours and 37 minutes. But because Mars is farther from the sun, it takes about twice as long as Earth to complete its orbit, 687 Earth days. Mars's axis is tilted about the same amount as Earth's, causing seasons. But summer temperatures may reach only –21 °C. Winter temperatures may dip below –124 °C, freezing carbon dioxide into ice caps on Mars's polar regions.

The Outer Planets

Jupiter

Jupiter Jupiter, the largest planet in our solar system, is more than 11 times the size of Earth. It contains 318 times more mass than Earth. This amount of mass means Jupiter has a great gravitational attraction with other objects. This allows Jupiter to function as the center of a miniature solar system orbited by 16 moons. It also has a very small, faint set of rings.

Space probes began studying Jupiter in 1972. After passing through the Asteroid Belt, the probes sent back pictures of a whirling ball of hydrogen colored by small amounts of methane and ammonia. This planet has more in common with the sun than it does with any of the planets. At its core, Jupiter is 30,500 °C. It sends twice as much energy into space as it receives from the sun. Yet at cloud level, the temperature is only –160 °C.

There is a permanent storm on Jupiter, seen as a red spot on the photograph on this page. Swirling clouds surround the Great Red Spot, a feature as long and wide as three Earths.

Saturn Similar to Jupiter, Saturn is a gaseous planet composed mostly of hydrogen. It has drizzling ammonia rain and more methane in its atmosphere than Jupiter does.

Saturn is huge, second in size only to Jupiter and 9.5 times the size of Earth. It radiates even more energy into space than Jupiter, three times as much as it receives from the sun. Scientists are not sure why, but they speculate that the ammonia rain contributes to the mystery. Still, the temperature at cloud level is a chilly –180 °C.

Unlike Jupiter, Saturn is surrounded by thousands of butterscotch-colored rings held in place by its gravitational attraction with them. The rings consist of particles of ice and rock, varying in size from dust to boulders. Scientists aren't sure whether the rings are bits of material that never quite joined into a planet, or a moon that was torn apart by Saturn's gravitational force.

Uranus Uranus is the third-largest planet, about four times the size of Earth. It has an atmosphere of mostly hydrogen with some helium, ammonia, methane, and water vapor. The methane makes Uranus look blue-green from Earth.

Beneath Uranus's relatively calm atmosphere is a scalding ocean of water and ammonia. Beneath that is a molten core the size of Earth. Uranus radiates the same amount of solar energy as it receives. Its temperature at cloud level is –200 °C.

Uranus's axis isn't in the center of the planet, and it's tilted more than any other planet, more than 82 degrees. As a result, its north pole faces the sun for about a quarter of its 84-year revolution. Then, half a Uranian year later, its south pole faces the sun.

Neptune Neptune is the eighth planet from the sun. It is a little smaller than Uranus and four times larger than Earth. Like the other Jovian planets, its atmosphere is composed of methane, hydrogen, and helium. Neptune seems to have continuous, violent weather storms.

After passing by Uranus in 1989, *Voyager 2* reached Neptune, the last stop in its 12-year mission through space. Data sent back show that Neptune has at least eight moons, and has four rings made of rock, dust, and ice.

Saturn

Uranus

Neptune

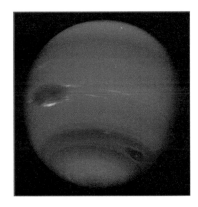

The Discovery of Pluto

Pluto and its moon, Charon, from a NASA artist's view from 1983

Pluto Pluto has been described as a snowball, a mix of rock and frozen methane and ammonia with a surface temperature of -237 °C. It has a thin nitrogen atmosphere. The smallest planet, about the size of Earth's moon, Pluto has an irregular orbit that sometimes takes it inside Neptune's orbit. Between 1979 and 1999, Neptune was the outermost planet in the solar system, not Pluto.

How do scientists know whether they have found all the objects in the solar system? The other planets had been seen by the eye and telescope for hundreds of years. But it was only 60 years ago that Pluto was discovered at the edge of our solar system.

Scientists had observed Neptune's and Uranus's slightly unusual orbits. In order for the orbits of these two planets to move the way they did, scientists hypothesized that there must be an object, like a planet with mass and gravitational force, that interfered with the orbits.

Using a specially engineered telescope, scientists took hundreds of pictures of the sky and analyzed them. Upon careful examination, they found a small object that moved in relation to the background stars. This object was Pluto.

Comets and Meteors

Beyond the planets is a region of space that seems to be the birthplace of most comets in our solar system. A **comet** is a mass of frozen gases, dust, and rocky particles, often called a "dirty snowball."

Like planets and asteroids, comets orbit the sun. When a comet nears the sun, the heat causes its carbon dioxide ice to vaporize, making the comet brighter the closer it gets to the sun.

The force of the vaporizing gases can alter the comet's orbit. That's why some comets are seen only once. Others, like Halley's comet, have a predictable orbit.

Solar wind sweeps comets' glowing tails back, away from the sun. The tails sometimes extend 165 million km into space. The interrelationship of a comet, the sun, and the solar wind is illustrated by the diagram on the next page.

Comet Hale-Bopp

Meteoroids are small chunks of matter, possibly bits of comets, that also orbit the sun. Often, their orbits cross Earth's. When they reach our atmosphere, meteoroids are called **meteors.** As meteors move rapidly through the atmosphere, friction acts on the meteor, and intense heat results. Many burn up in the atmosphere, producing "shooting stars." But meteors are not stars. The meteors that fall to a planet's surface are much more solid and are called meteorites.

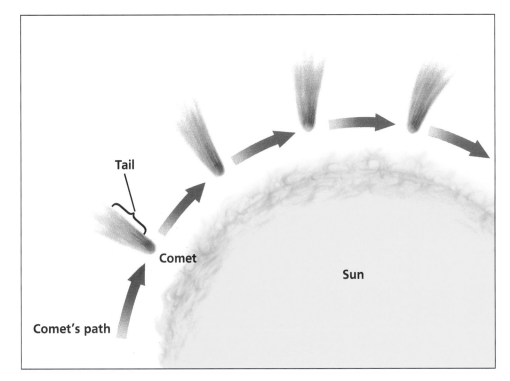

Tail

Comet

Comet's path

Sun

The tails of comets are in part a result of the solar wind sweeping back gases vaporizing at the comet's surface.

CHECKPOINT

1. Where is the asteroid belt?
2. What is the solar system?
3. What are the characteristics of the inner planets?
4. What are the characteristics of the outer planets?
5. Describe the discovery of Pluto.
 How does the composition of a planet affect its physical characteristics?

ACTIVITY
Comparing Planets

Find Out
Do this activity to find out how to make a chart that compares information about the planets.

Process Skills
Interpreting Data
Classifying

WHAT YOU NEED

reference books

the Internet

pencil

Activity Journal

WHAT TO DO

1. Use the information in the lesson, reference books, or the Internet to create a chart about the planets.

2. Brainstorm with a partner about all the things you know that make one planet different from another; for example, how long their days are, how many moons they have, and what they are made of. Organize the data.

3. List as many ways as you can of classifying planets, for example, by color, size, and the presence or absence of an atmosphere.

4. Make each item on your list the heading for a column. Prepare a chart that lists the planets, including Earth, in a column on the left. The other column headings should come from your data lists.

CONCLUSIONS

1. Is classification by size a good way to separate the planets?

2. What is the best way to distinguish each planet?

ASKING NEW QUESTIONS

1. What are some other facts about planets that would be interesting to find out?

2. What would you tell an imaginary visitor from another galaxy about the planets in our solar system?

SCIENTIFIC METHODS SELF CHECK

✔ Did I collect and **organize data** on all of the planets?

✔ Did I **classify** the planets based on the data I collected?

The Stars

Find Out

- What tools are used to observe stars
- What starlight is
- What the phases of a star's life are
- What galaxies are

Vocabulary

parallax
supernova
nebula
black hole
spiral galaxy

The Big QUESTION

What happens to a star in a star life cycle?

For thousands of years, people have looked up at the skies to see the stars. Sailors have used the stars to navigate across oceans. But what are stars, and what happens to them over the course of time? Do they stay the same, or do they change?

Tools of Observation

For years, people observed the sky with only the naked eye. The invention of the telescope had a tremendous impact on how scientists were able to see the stars, planets, and other objects in space. The telescope helped astronomers see farther than our eyes are capable of seeing. Telescopes can magnify images, collect light, and even collect information about the light and radio waves being transmitted by stars. Nowadays, we not only have telescopes and observatories on Earth, but we also send telescopes up in balloons, airplanes, rockets, and spacecraft to receive information that might be blocked by Earth's atmosphere.

All stars, like the sun in our solar system, send energy out into space. Some of this energy is in the form of visible light. *Optical* telescopes are instruments that use large lenses or mirrors to collect light. The first scientist to use this kind of telescope to study the skies was Galileo, in the early 1600s. *Refracting* telescopes are optical telescopes that use a lens to collect light to produce an image. The first telescopes were refracting telescopes. A *reflecting* telescope is an optical telescope that uses mirrors to produce images that can be analyzed later. Sir Isaac Newton built the first reflecting telescope in 1668. The largest optical telescope in the world is located in Mauna Kea, Hawaii.

The Hubble telescope

Another way we can collect astronomical data is to use *radio* telescopes, which pick up the radio waves being transmitted by objects that are too dim or too distant to view through other telescopes. Many radio telescopes use large, curved surfaces to collect radio waves from space and focus them toward a large receiver.

Our ability to collect information from the sky improved considerably with the creation of the Hubble space telescope in 1990. The Hubble space telescope allows us to take astronomical readings from space as it orbits Earth's atmosphere. This way, we can see the whole sky, which is not possible from the ground. Once information is received, it is recorded and transmitted to space stations on the ground for further analysis. Sending a telescope into space is very expensive and difficult because all repairs need to be made in space. After the launch of the Hubble telescope, scientists realized that there were problems and discovered that the mirror in the telescope was polished to the wrong curve. In 1993, a space shuttle was sent into space with astronauts specially trained to make all necessary repairs.

Photo of the gas pillars in the Eagle Nebula taken from the Hubble telescope

Starlight

Stars are so far away from Earth that it wasn't until the invention of the telescope that we were really able to study them. We are able to learn the most information about stars from the light that they emit, or send out. Starlight is really energy given off from the star's surface. Besides the light that we are able to see with our naked eye, a star also emits other forms of electromagnetic energy.

Although it may look white to us, starlight is a mixture of colors that travels through space at the speed of light, 299,792 km/s. A light-year is the distance that light travels in one year in a vacuum.

Astronomers can measure a star's distance from Earth. If you hold up one finger, then look at it first with one eye and then with the other, what seems to happen? Did you notice how the finger seems to change position in relation to more distant objects when you look at it first with one eye and then with the other? This apparent difference in direction is called **parallax.** Astronomers chart the position of a star, then do it again six months later when the star has moved. They can then figure out the change in position and find out how much movement has taken place.

In the early 1900s two astronomers, Ejnar Hertzsprung and Henry Norris Russell, discovered a relationship between a star's real brightness and its color. Although stars have different brightnesses as seen from Earth, this doesn't always reflect their real brightness. A nearby dim star may outshine a brighter star that is farther away.

Solar Flare

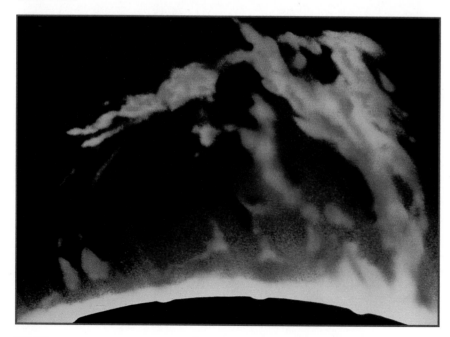

Hertzsprung and Russell investigated this relationship by taking a sample of stars for which they knew the distance from Earth. By comparing the stars' known distances to their apparent brightnesses, they were able to determine how bright the stars really were.

Next, a star's real brightness was compared to what was known about the star's temperature. That is, hot stars tend to be blue in color, while cooler stars look reddish. This information gave Hertzsprung and Russell a handy way to arrange and categorize stars according to temperature and real brightness.

Some stars, however, vary in brightness. These stars are called variable stars and can change their brightness in as short as a few hours or over a period of years! Polaris, the North Star, changes its brightness slightly every four days. Some variable stars are binary stars—two stars that revolve around each other. These pairs are so far away from Earth that they appear to be one star. However, when one eclipses the other, we see only one star, which makes the pair seem less bright.

We know that our sun is yellow, but stars come in a variety of colors. There are blue, blue-white, white, yellow-white, yellow, orange, and red stars. A star's color shows how hot its surface is. The hottest stars are blue, and the coolest are red.

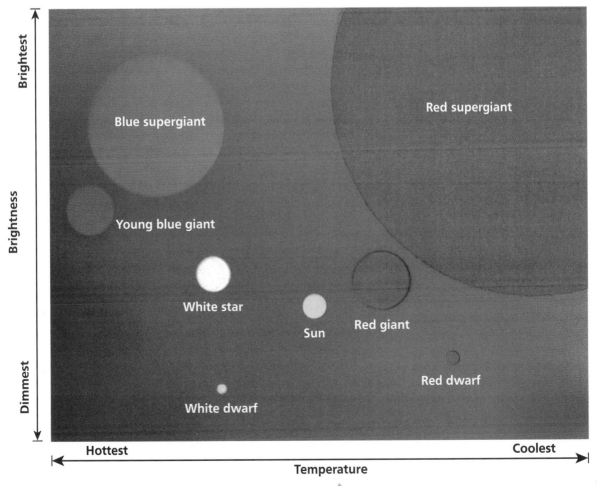

B155

Phases of a Star's Life

At night, when we look up at the sky, we are able to see only a few thousand stars, although there are actually billions of them in the universe. Stars are made primarily of hydrogen and helium.

The life of a star begins when clouds of hydrogen dust and gas begin to collapse because of their own gravitational forces. As its mass increases and its particles start to collide, the temperature rises. When it reaches one million degrees, a nuclear reaction takes place. Hydrogen atoms fuse together to form helium, which releases energy, and the new star begins to shine. This process can take millions of years.

Spiral galaxies like this one can contain hundreds of billions of stars.

The death of a star begins when all of its hydrogen is used up. At this point, the star starts to expand as its outer layers turn a reddish color and begin to cool down. When a star looks like this, it is called a red giant. If the star is extremely large, we call it a supergiant. When a red giant loses its cool outer layer, it becomes a white dwarf.

The death of a star may also come as a **supernova.** This is an explosion in which most of the star's matter is hurled into space. A **nebula** is a cloud of dust and gas in space. At this point, what was once a giant star becomes a neutron star. This "dead" star is extremely dense and is thought to be the stage during which a black hole could develop.

When a star explodes, it produces a supernova.

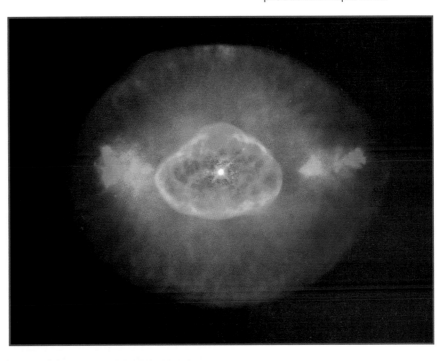

The Crab Nebula is the remains of a supernova recorded in A.D. 1054 by Chinese astronomers.

The name *black hole* gives the impression that there is an actual hole in space, doesn't it? Scientists believe that a **black hole** is formed from the death of an extremely large star with a mass of at least 30 times that of our sun. Scientists hypothesize that very large stars, those that began with a mass 30 to 50 times greater than our sun, can become black holes.

A black hole is such an unusual feature in the galaxies that it can't be defined like other stars. It must be described by its gravity. A black hole's gravity is so strong that even light can't escape. As material is accelerated into the black hole, it emits radiation.

Scientists may have located sources of X rays and measured changes in time and space that are caused by black holes. Currently, the best candidate for true black-hole status is Cygnus (sig′ nəs) X-1, which is in a constellation of stars that resembles a swan.

Galaxies

The scale of a galaxy (ga′ lək sē) challenges the imagination. A galaxy is defined as a group of billions or trillions of stars. No one knows how many galaxies are in the universe, but scientists have found clusters of 10,000 of them. Although the structure of each galaxy is different, we classify them by their general shape.

Irregular galaxies are smaller. They have many stars and great clouds of dust and gas, but no definite shape. Most of these galaxies may be in the early stages of their lives. Elliptical galaxies are oval-shaped, with trillions of older stars, but little dust or gas.

Many of the brightest galaxies are spiral galaxies, including the Milky Way. Our solar system is part of the Milky Way galaxy. A **spiral galaxy** is disk-shaped with arms that rotate around a dense center.

The Milky Way contains 100 to 200 billion stars and is about 100,000 light-years in diameter. A light-year is the distance light travels in one year. Just one light-year is 9.46 trillion kilometers!

Astronomers have hypothesized that the center of the Milky Way contains a massive black hole. The stars in and surrounding the center are old and red. They, in turn, are surrounded by a disk of dim, red stars and younger, more yellow stars. Hot blue and white stars and clouds of dust and gas form the spiral arms. Our solar system with its yellow sun is about two-thirds of the way out from the center of the galaxy, near one spiral arm.

Just as Earth orbits the sun, the sun and the rest of our solar system orbit the center of our galaxy. One of these orbits takes about 250 million years!

Our galaxy is also in orbit. Sometimes, the orbits of galaxies cross and the galaxies collide. Scientists have found a number of distorted galaxies, apparently formed by collisions.

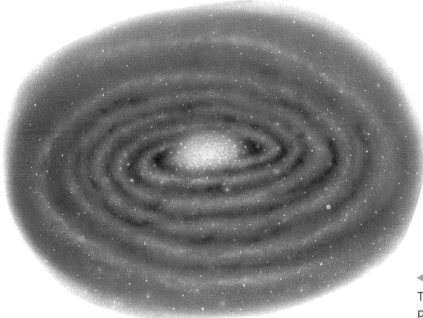

The yellow dot shows the position of the solar system in the Milky Way galaxy.

CHECKPOINT

1. What tools are used to observe stars?
2. What is starlight?
3. What are the phases of a star's life?
4. What are galaxies?
 What happens to a star in a star life cycle?

ACTIVITY

Seeing Stars

Find Out

Do this activity to learn why all the constellations are not visible all over Earth.

Process Skills

Observing
Communicating
Constructing Models

WHAT YOU NEED

a large globe

colored pencils

Activity Journal

ruler

WHAT TO DO

1. Your partner should hold a globe so that northeastern America is visible, and then slowly rotate the globe. Observe the areas of the globe and record what you see.

2. Next, have your partner turn the globe so that the continent of Antarctica is visible.

3. As the globe is rotated, what parts of Earth do you see? Can you see Sweden? Record your observations.

4. Switch places with your partner, and repeat steps 1, 2, and 3.

5. Draw a circle that represents Earth. Draw one dot on the perimeter of the circle to approximate a latitude of 40°N and one at the south pole of 90°S.

6. With your ruler, draw a line touching only the edge of the circle at one point.

7. Repeat for the second point.

8. Use a different colored pencil for each line. Shade in the area from the lines to the edge of your paper with your colored pencil. This represents the area of stars visible from that point on Earth.

CONCLUSIONS

1. Do the two shaded areas overlap anywhere?

2. Is it possible that some stars would be visible from both places?

3. Are there some stars that could be visible only from one of the two places?

ASKING NEW QUESTIONS

1. How does Earth's curvature affect what stars you can see?

2. Who would be a good person to talk to if you wanted to learn more about stars?

SCIENTIFIC METHODS SELF CHECK

✔ Did I **observe** the shaded areas of the globe?

✔ Did I **record** my observations?

✔ Did I **construct a model** of starlight seen on Earth?

Exploring Space

Find Out

- What one theory about how the universe began is
- What some tools of space observation are
- How we fly and live in space

Vocabulary

Big Bang theory
red shift
rockets
artificial satellite
shuttle
International Space Station

The Big QUESTION

How does exploring space help us understand the universe?

You know that Earth is part of the solar system, with the sun at its center and planets revolving around the sun. Our solar system is part of a galaxy called the Milky Way. The universe contains billions of other galaxies. Consider what the future may hold in space exploration. Can you imagine living in space? It may be possible one day.

The Universe

Where did the universe come from? The most widely-accepted theory of the origin of the universe is called the **Big Bang theory.** This theory was first offered in 1929. This theory states that a fireball exploded 13 to 21 billion years ago (the "big bang") and caused space, matter, and energy to spread apart in all directions. It was the energy of this first explosion that began the expansion of the universe.

As the material cooled, hydrogen and helium condensed into clouds. Over the next half-billion years, the clouds became galaxies, and within them, stars formed. As the first generation of stars lived and died, they created other heavier elements. From these elements came planets and moons. Our own solar system formed from a cloud of gas and debris about five billion years ago. Every atom in and on Earth and the other planets is part of this original matter.

The universe is still cooling and expanding. Do we have any proof or observations to support the theory of an expanding universe? We do. In fact, we can measure how fast other galaxies are moving away from ours.

This representation of the Big Bang gives you an idea of the time span involved in the development of the universe.

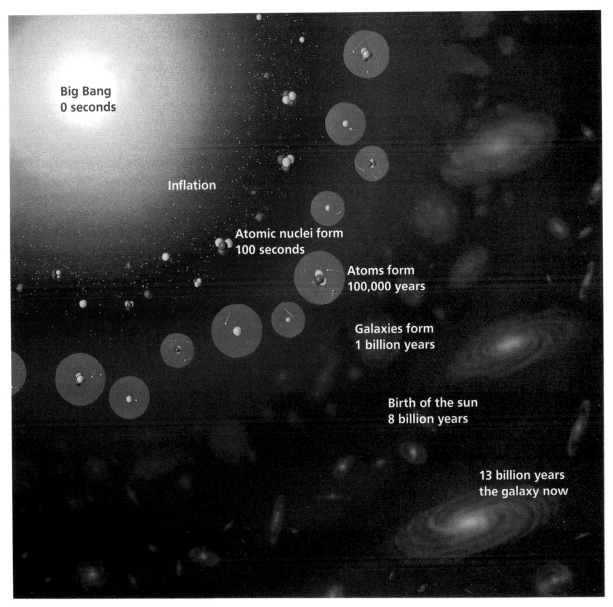

Big Bang
0 seconds

Inflation

Atomic nuclei form
100 seconds

Atoms form
100,000 years

Galaxies form
1 billion years

Birth of the sun
8 billion years

13 billion years
the galaxy now

Observer

Blue shift

Moving light source

Red shift

Observer

When U.S astronomer Edwin Hubble used a spectroscope to analyze the light from other galaxies, he discovered that this light had shifted toward the red end of the spectrum. Called a **red shift,** it indicates when a light source is moving away from an observer. This red shift is important for the theory of the expanding universe. The galaxies farthest away have more red shift than the closer galaxies. They are moving away faster.

This means the electromagnetic waves are spreading out and lengthening, indicating that these galaxies are moving away from us. If they were moving toward us, the wavelengths would be bunching up and shortening, causing a shift to the blue end of the spectrum.

Tools of Space Observation

How have we learned all of this information about our universe? One way we learn about space is to record and study the observations we make about space from here on Earth. Another way is to send instruments into space to make observations. A third way is to send people into space.

People have been observing space for thousands of years. Over 4000 years ago, early astronomers began building Stonehenge, a ring of stones in Great Britain, to record their observations of the solar system. Stonehenge is the oldest known structure to be used as an observatory. Other ancient peoples have built observatories. Africans in Kenya, the Anasazi from areas in the western United States, and the Maya in Mexico also built observatories.

Diagram showing the expected shift in spectrum of a moving object. There is a blue shift as the object moves toward an observer and a red shift as an object moves away.

What makes these achievements all the more notable is that the astronomers who were doing this work did not have the advantage of complex equipment to aid them. All of their observations were made by looking at the sky with an unaided eye. However, the invention of the telescope opened a new era of astronomical observation.

Today, astronomers use different observatories to view space. One type of observatory has optical telescopes. These telescopes use lenses and mirrors to collect light and magnify images of distant objects. These observatories must be built in places where there are no strong disturbances in the atmosphere, no air pollution, and no bright lights. They are usually found on the tops of high mountains, where the sky is clear most of the time.

Another kind of observatory is used to "listen" to space. Radio telescopes are used to study radio waves. These radio telescopes use very large antennae to catch radio waves from space. These antennae are usually built in valleys. The mountains protect these observatories from radio interference that comes from cities and other areas with dense population.

Stonehenge in England

Mayan observatory in Chichen Itza, Mexico

Big Horn Medicine Wheel Observatory in Wyoming

These are two of the five dish antennae at the Greenbank National Radio Observatory, which is located at Deer Creek Valley, West Virginia.

Although most large telescopes are positioned in observatories on mountaintops, their view is still blurred by Earth's atmosphere. This blanket of air distorts and sometimes blocks ultraviolet rays, X rays, and other radiation from space. This is good for things living on Earth, but it is not good for gathering data from space. Sometimes, the lights from the ground can also interfere with a land-based observatory.

As you learned, NASA launched the Hubble space telescope on a space shuttle. It orbits about 610 km above Earth's surface, transmitting data by radio waves to astronomers on the ground at the Goddard Space Flight Center in Greenbelt, Maryland. Operating outside of Earth's atmosphere allows the space-based observatory to return clearer images of objects in space. For instance, a picture of a star taken by the Las Campanas Observatory in Chile showed only a blob of light. When viewed by the Hubble space telescope, it was clear the star was really a binary star. Astronomers have used the Hubble telescope to find other information about black holes and other heavenly bodies.

The Nordic Optical Telescope at the Roque de los Muchachos Observatory is in La Palma in the Canary Islands. The observatory is at an altitude of 2.4 km. The high altitude and clear air minimize any distortions.

Light from space

Motion from atmosphere

Reflected by atmosphere

Absorption by atmospheric particles

Diffusion by particles

Observatory

As light enters Earth's atmosphere, it can be distorted through diffraction by particles in the atmosphere.

Space Flight

Every space flight starts with a rocket. **Rockets** are basically tubes filled with fuel. As the fuel burns, the gases expand and exert force on the inside of the tube. The gases escape through the open end of the rocket. The escaping gases create a force that provides the power to launch the rocket into space.

More advanced rockets are now built with stages. A rocket's first stage sends a spacecraft into the upper atmosphere. The first stage then drops away, and the second stage of the rocket takes over. The second stage has enough force to put the spacecraft into orbit. Rockets can be used only one time.

In 1957, the Soviet Union launched *Sputnik*. *Sputnik* was the first **artificial satellite** put into orbit. This satellite had no humans aboard to control its path. Then, in 1961, the Soviets sent Yury Gagarin into space. Gagarin was the first person in space. In 1962, John Glenn became the first U.S. astronaut to orbit Earth. He was strapped into a capsule on the top of a simple rocket. The capsule orbited Earth three times, then used a parachute to land in the ocean.

In 1968, the United States spacecraft *Apollo 8* orbited the moon ten times and returned safely to Earth. The *Apollo 11* astronauts, Neil A. Armstrong and Edwin E. Aldrin, Jr., actually landed on the moon on July 20, 1969. Armstrong was the first person to step onto the surface of the moon.

The *Mercury* orbiter

John Glenn preparing for his 1962 *Mercury* mission

The U.S. space shuttle *Columbia* was launched on April 12, 1981. This **shuttle** was the first reusable spacecraft. It could land at a regular airfield. On January 28, 1986, some of the dangers of space travel were realized. The U.S. space shuttle *Challenger* exploded soon after launch. All seven astronauts aboard were killed. The U.S. redesigned the shuttle and began new flights in 1988.

Thirty-six years after John Glenn first orbited Earth, he returned to space with six other astronauts on the space shuttle *Discovery*. At age 77, Glenn became the world's oldest space traveler. On the nine-day space mission, he performed a wide range of experiments to study the relationship between aging and space flight.

Discovery on its 1998 mission

The crew of the 1998 *Discovery* mission

In December 1998, astronauts completed the first phase of the **International Space Station.** This is a cooperative program, drawing on the talents of scientists from 16 nations. By 2000, an international crew of three astronauts should be living on the space station. They will perform many medical experiments and educational activities. Some of these astronauts have already learned to meet the challenge of living in space.

Space travelers must make a lot of effort to stay in shape. Exercises that imitate the effects of gravity on Earth are important in an environment with no gravity. In the weightless environment of space, muscles and bones can weaken.

What about a space flight to Mars? The 1999 Mars Millennium mission was a national project designed to get students thinking about living on Mars. Recent Mars *Explorer* missions have been very successful. How likely is it that humans will live on Mars? It is probably not likely within the next few years. But what about 100 years from now?

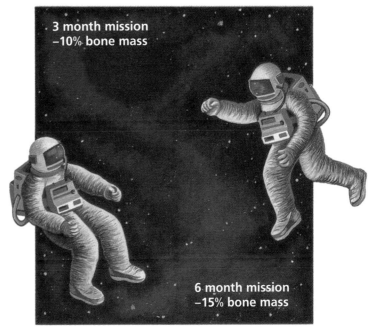

3 month mission
−10% bone mass

6 month mission
−15% bone mass

Working against gravity helps bones and muscles stay in shape. Without gravity, bones lose calcium and muscles weaken. The calcium loss seems to begin as soon as the flight begins.

CHECKPOINT

1. What is one theory about how the universe began?
2. What are some tools of space observation?
3. How are rockets and shuttles used for space flight and living in space?

 How does exploring space help us understand the universe?

ACTIVITY

Expanding the Universe

Find Out

Do this activity to learn how to construct a model of the expanding universe.

Process Skills

Communicating
Measuring
Constructing Models
Using Numbers
Interpreting Data
Inferring

WHAT YOU NEED

one white, round balloon

black, felt-tipped pen

safety goggles

10 cm of string

rubber bands

Activity Journal

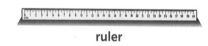

ruler

WHAT TO DO

1. Use the pen to mark the balloon before you inflate it. Mark ten dots randomly on one side of the balloon. Number each dot. Keep the dots in the center of the flattened balloon. Record the position of each dot. Measure and record the distances between the dots.

2. On the other side of the balloon, put a dot *A* and a dot *B* about 0.5 cm apart. Put a dot *C* about 2 cm away from dot *A*.

 Safety! *Blow up only your own balloon.*

B170

3. Blow up the balloon less than halfway and close it with a rubber band. Use the string to measure the distance between dots. Measure and record the new distances between the ten dots. Measure and record the distance between dot A and dot B and between dot A and dot C with your string ruler.

4. Remove your rubber band and blow more air into the balloon. Measure and record the new distances between the dots again.

5. Blow the balloon up to about 20 cm. Do not allow the balloon to pop. Once more, measure and record the distances between dots. Record the new distances between dot A and dot B and between dot A and dot C.

6. Figure the change in the distances between dot A and dot B and between dot A and dot C.

CONCLUSIONS

1. What happened to the distances between the ten dots as the balloon got bigger?

2. What do you think would happen to the distances if the balloon could stretch forever without popping?

3. Did the distance between dot A and dot B change the same amount as the distance between dot A and dot C each time you put more air in the balloon?

4. What would happen to the distances if the inflated balloon was left for a long time? (Think of what happens to balloons left over from parties.)

ASKING NEW QUESTIONS

1. What do these models tell you about the way scientists think the universe is changing?

2. What other model might test the same ideas?

SCIENTIFIC METHODS SELF CHECK

✔ Did I construct **models?**

✔ Did I **measure** distances **using numbers?**

✔ Did I **interpret** information to make **inferences?**

✔ Did I **record** my data correctly?

Review

Reviewing Vocabulary and Concepts

Write the letter of the answer that best completes each sentence.

1. The path of Earth in space, or its orbit, is not round but is ___.
   - **a.** around its moons
   - **b.** an ellipse
   - **c.** a straight line
   - **d.** diagonal

2. Beaches with semidiurnal tides have two high and low tides daily, but beaches with one high and one low tide daily have ___.
   - **a.** rip tides
   - **b.** diurnal tides
   - **c.** strong tides
   - **d.** ebb tides

3. Unlike meteors that plunge into our atmosphere, we call these tiny planets that revolve in their own orbits ___.
   - **a.** comets
   - **b.** space probes
   - **c.** asteroids
   - **d.** dirty snowballs

4. We have seen photos of the planets that revolve around the sun, and that make up our solar system, thanks to ___.
   - **a.** comets
   - **b.** radio waves
   - **c.** space probes
   - **d.** telescopes

5. A red giant star may be turned into a black hole by immense gravity, while a smaller red giant may explode and become a ___.
   - **a.** planet
   - **b.** meteor
   - **c.** supernova
   - **d.** comet

Match the definition on the left with the correct term.

6. the time when one celestial body casts a shadow that we can see

7. sometimes we can see the spectacular tail of one in the night sky

8. a cloud of dust and gas in space

9. because they understand this, astronomers can use sightings many months apart to chart the movement of a star

10. disk-shaped cluster of stars with arms that rotate around a dense center

- **a.** comet
- **b.** nebula
- **c.** spiral galaxy
- **d.** eclipse
- **e.** parallax

Understanding What You Learned

1. What is the difference between a solar eclipse and a lunar eclipse?
2. How did Bode's law help in the discovery of the asteroid belt?
3. What is a black hole?
4. What are the advantages of the three different kinds of observatories?
5. What are the ways we can learn about space?

Applying What You Learned

1. What are some advantages and disadvantages of sending either space probes or people into space?
2. Why do scientists study space?
3. Pretend you are talking with someone who lived 2000 years ago. How would you explain that Earth is not the center of the universe?
4. What keeps the planets in our solar system?

5. How is studying space helpful in understanding our solar system's place in the universe?

For Your **Portfolio**

Begin a two-week log of space information. Each day, read a newspaper or a newspaper Web site for information about space exploration. Enter what you find in your log and explain how what you have learned in this chapter helps you understand what the story is all about.

Unit Review

Concept Review

1. Explain how the sun affects weather and climate.

2. Describe a life cycle of a natural resource that was produced by Earth, extracted and used by people, and then finally if it can be reused, or recycled, or becomes refuse or pollution.

3. What are some significant geologic occurrences that have happened in your lifetime?

4. Explain how our solar system is part of the universe.

Problem Solving

1. How do computers help people predict the weather?

2. Compare two sides of a debate concerning the use of a limited natural resource.

3. Make a diagram that illustrates the cycle of changes that affect mountain systems on Earth.

4. Consider the opportunities that await scientists for doing research on the International Space Station. Imagine that you might be able to join the crew—if you qualify. Explain the training and experience a person would need to qualify.

Something to Do

Design and then build a model of a craft that will enable you to investigate Earth from the land, water, or sky. Choose one feature or process of Earth or the solar system that you want to know more about. Design an instrument that will enable you to research this, then make a model of it and put it on your craft. Write what you think your craft might discover.

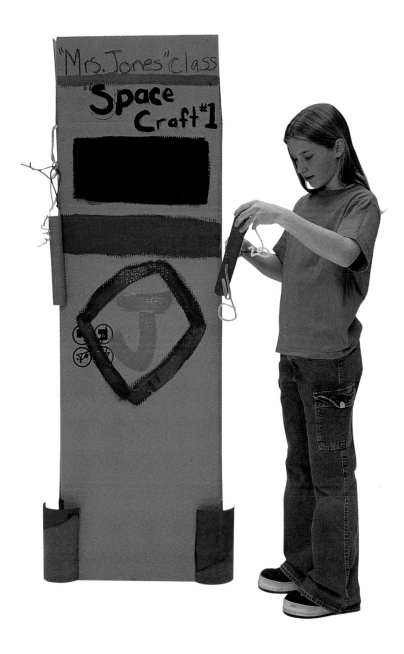

UNIT C

Physical Science

Solar

All living things on Earth depend on energy from the sun. Plants capture the sun's energy and use it to change carbon dioxide and water into simple sugars and oxygen. Animals and other organisms eat the plants.

The sun's energy evaporates water. In the atmosphere, water vapor traps heat around Earth. In fact, almost all of Earth's energy comes from the sun. There appears to be no end to the sun's supply of energy. Unlike other forms of energy that we use, the sun's energy creates virtually no pollution on Earth.

The energy of the sun is everywhere. We can see it as light. We can feel it as it warms our skin.

The Big IDEA

The sun is Earth's energy source.

Radiation

Properties of Solar Radiation

Find Out

- What wave energy is
- What different uses of electromagnetic waves are
- How the sun's energy gets to Earth

Vocabulary

waves
wavelength
amplitude
electromagnetic waves
frequency
radiant energy

The Big QUESTION

What kinds of energy come from the sun?

Think about being on a surfboard. When the right wave comes along, your board is lifted, and you travel toward the shore. After a while, the wave slows down and you bob up and down in place as shallow waves pass by. The surfboard is a good example of how waves can transfer energy from one place to another.

Wave Energy

Waves are rhythmic disturbances that carry energy through matter and space. Some waves, such as sound waves, need a medium through which to travel. The medium can be a solid, liquid, gas, or a combination of these. Other waves do not need a medium. Waves, such as light or radio waves, can travel through the emptiness of space as well as through matter.

Radio waves and the waves on the surface of water are examples of transverse waves. Transverse waves move up and down at right angles (90°) to the direction in which they travel.

We can measure the energy that a wave carries. To do that we first have to measure the wavelength. A **wavelength** is the distance between a point on one wave and the identical point on the next wave. In the diagram below, the wavelength is measured from the crest, or top, of the first wave to the crest of the second wave. In fact, as long as we pick identical points on the waves, we can measure the wavelengths of waves from any location on the waves.

The energy in a water wave can move things in its path. The surfer is taking advantage of energy in this water wave.

What is the difference between a ripple in a pool and a huge ocean wave crashing on shore? The ocean wave carries a lot of energy. As a result, it is very tall. A ripple has little energy and is very low. The height of a wave is its **amplitude.** The amplitude of the wave tells us how much energy it carries. High amplitudes carry lots of energy. Low amplitudes carry less energy.

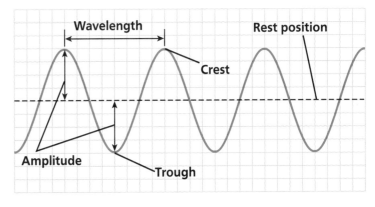

A Transverse Wave

Electromagnetic Waves

What do a radio station, a microwave oven, dental X rays, and a lamp have in common? All are examples of the use of electromagnetic (ə lek′ trō mag ne′ tik) waves. **Electromagnetic waves** transfer energy by means of alternating electric and magnetic fields at right angles to each other. That means they are transverse waves. Electromagnetic waves travel in a straight line. In empty space, or a vacuum, electromagnetic waves travel at 300,000 km/s. They move more slowly when they pass through matter.

Like other waves, electromagnetic waves can have almost any wavelength. This range of wavelengths is called the *electromagnetic spectrum*. The chart shows electromagnetic waves classified by their wavelengths on the electromagnetic spectrum. The spectrum is divided into segments that relate to the ways we use or experience these wavelengths.

Refer to the diagram of the electromagnetic spectrum. Each electromagnetic wave has its own frequency and wavelength. Electromagnetic waves with short wavelengths have high frequencies. The waves with long wavelengths have low frequencies.

The Electromagnetic Spectrum

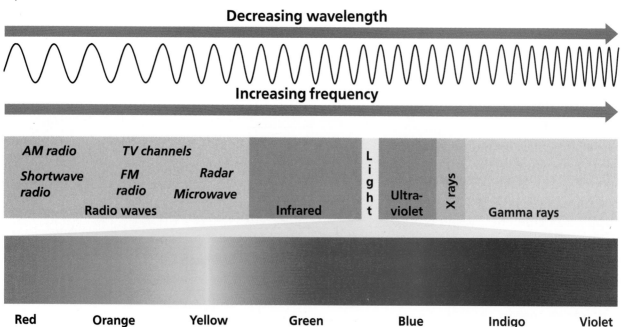

All electromagnetic waves are classified by their wavelengths on the electomagnetic spectrum.

You have probably heard the word frequency. Different stations broadcast on different frequencies. When you tune a radio from one station to another, you are adjusting the receiver to pick up a different frequency. When you change channels on a television, you are adjusting the television set receiver to pick up radio waves of different frequencies.

What is a frequency? The **frequency** of a wave is the number of wave crests that pass a place in one second. The measure of frequency is hertz (Hz). One hertz is the same as one wave per second at the measuring point. Wave frequency depends on the rate of vibration of the object producing the wave. Most radio stations give their frequency when they announce their call letters.

Uses of Electromagnetic Waves

In addition to broadcasting TV and radio programs, radio waves have other uses. Have you ever used a cellular or cordless telephone? They operate by means of radio waves being transmitted to and from the handset and the base. Besides sound and pictures, radio waves can carry computer information, or cook food in microwave ovens. The microwaves pass through food to the water molecules in it. The energy causes the molecules of water to vibrate faster. It heats the food from the inside out. We use glass, paper, and some plastics in microwave ovens because microwaves pass easily through these materials.

Warm objects give off infrared radiation, which has higher frequencies and shorter wavelengths than radio waves. Infrared cameras can detect infrared waves. Night-vision goggles and some medical equipment can detect infrared radiation given off by warm objects.

Heat loss from your body can be detected by infrared cameras and shown in pictures called thermograms. This thermogram shows a human hand.

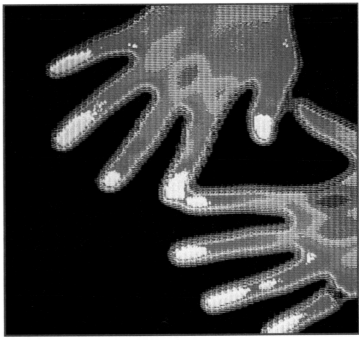

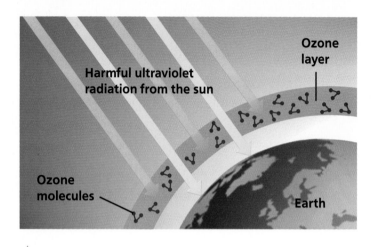

Harmful ultraviolet
radiation from the sun

Ozone
layer

Ozone
molecules

Earth

Ozone blocks most of the sun's
ultraviolet rays.

In this X ray, the area where
the skull is shows up white
on the X-ray film.

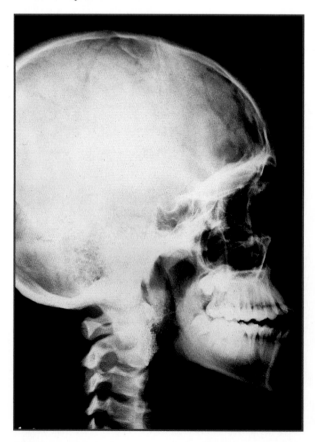

The part of the electromagnetic spectrum that you can see is visible light. The range of wavelengths of visible light appears as the colors of the rainbow. These wavelengths are shorter than infrared radiation and have higher frequencies. Visible light is only a small part of the total electromagnetic spectrum. We will investigate the properties of visible light in the next lesson.

Sunlight includes a large portion of ultraviolet (UV) light. These waves have much shorter wavelengths and higher frequencies than visible light. This type of electromagnetic radiation can change the pigments of our skin, such as giving us a suntan or sunburn. It can also alter skin cells and cause cancer. Many people use sunscreen to protect their skin cells from these waves. Fortunately, Earth's atmosphere contains a layer of ozone molecules. They absorb about 90 percent of the sun's ultraviolet waves, preventing these rays from reaching Earth's surface.

X-ray waves have a higher frequency and shorter wavelength than UV light waves do. These high-energy waves can travel through many types of matter. They travel easily through soft tissues, such as skin and blood cells. X rays are absorbed by harder materials, such as bones. X-ray machines pass X rays through your body and onto photographic film. X rays cause reactions in film similar to the way visible light does. When the film is developed, your bones show up white on the black film because they absorb the X rays.

Gamma rays and cosmic rays have the highest frequencies and the shortest wavelengths of all electromagnetic waves. Because of their high frequencies, gamma rays transfer a lot of energy. These waves can penetrate all human tissues causing damage along the way. The damage can result in illness or even death. Some radioactive materials emit gamma rays. Cosmic rays have more energy than gamma rays, and some are able to pass through Earth without being absorbed.

How Energy Comes From the Sun

You may know that thermal energy is the total kinetic energy of the particles in matter.

The temperature of matter is a measure of the average kinetic energy of the particles in a sample of matter. Kinetic energy comes from the vibrations and movement within and between particles of matter. Warm objects have faster-moving particles. If you had a cup of hot tea and an identical cup of cold tea, which would have more kinetic energy?

Heat flows from warmer objects to cooler objects. Heat can move from a warmer object to a cooler object when the two are not in direct contact. This process of energy transfer is called radiation. Energy transferred in this way is **radiant energy**, which consists of electromagnetic waves.

Radiant energy is how the sun warms Earth from 150 million km away—through mostly empty space. If you've ever gotten into a car that was in direct sunlight for a long time, you know that the energy from the sun can be changed to thermal energy.

Nearly half of the sun's radiation that reaches Earth does so as visible light. However, sunlight also includes gamma rays, X rays, UV rays, and radio waves. Scientists estimate that about 34 percent of the sun's rays that reach Earth reflect back into space and another 19 percent are absorbed by Earth's atmosphere. That means almost half (about 47 percent) of the energy from the sun's rays that reach Earth is absorbed by Earth's surface. The absorbed radiant energy converts to thermal energy, warming Earth's surface.

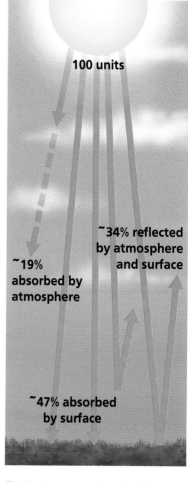

100 units

~34% reflected by atmosphere and surface

~19% absorbed by atmosphere

~47% absorbed by surface

Radiant energy absorbed by Earth's surface can be converted to thermal energy.

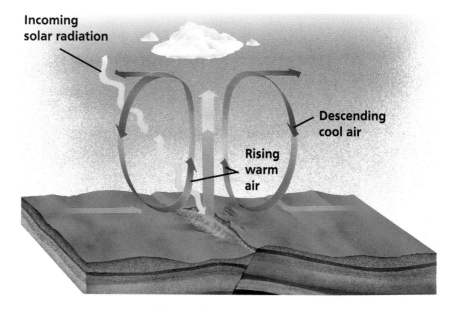

Incoming solar radiation

Descending cool air

Rising warm air

Energy from the sun creates Earth's wind currents. They are a result of convection.

Earth's Energy

Almost all of Earth's energy comes from the sun. In the Life Science unit, you learned that plants transform some of the light energy into chemical energy through the process of photosynthesis. The green pigment in the chloroplasts of plants cells absorbs light and uses the energy in photosynthesis. Energy from the sun is also stored in Earth in the form of fossil fuels. These fuels form over millions of years from the remains of organisms that once lived on Earth. Burning these fuels releases the energy they absorbed from the sun millions of years ago. The fossil fuels that are mined for their energy value are coal, oil, and natural gas.

In the Life Science and Earth Science units, you learned how Earth reuses its water in the water cycle. It is the energy from the sun that causes water to evaporate from Earth's surface and rise into the air above it. The water doesn't just go away. As air cools, the water vapor condenses and falls back to Earth as precipitation.

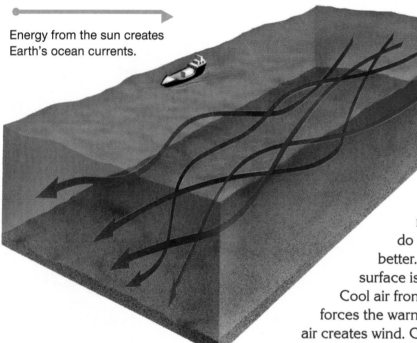

Energy from the sun creates Earth's ocean currents.

The energy from the sun also creates Earth's weather. Incoming solar radiation heats Earth's surface. Not all parts of Earth have the same type of surface. Some surfaces receive more thermal energy than others do and some surfaces absorb it better. When air above a warm land surface is warmed, its density decreases. Cool air from other regions rushes in and forces the warm air upward. This movement of air creates wind. Convection currents are currents driven by air density differences. Land and sea breezes, thunderstorms, and wind belts such as the trade winds are the result of these convection currents caused by the sun's energy reaching Earth.

Convection also creates ocean currents. An ocean current changes the location of water caught up in its flow. An ocean current can travel horizontally through an ocean like a river or circulate from the surface to the ocean floor and back.

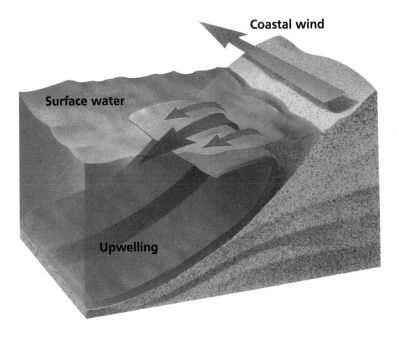

Coastal wind

Surface water

Upwelling

Energy from the sun creates wind, which in turn creates upwelling in Earth's oceans.

Deep-water and circulation currents are driven by differences in water density. Cold ocean water with high salinity is very dense. Warm ocean water diluted by tropical rainfall is lower in density. The currents are produced by the denser, colder water pushing the less dense, warm water ahead of it.

Earth's winds also affect water far below the surface of the ocean. When wind blows surface waters away, the colder, deeper waters of the ocean rise and replace it. This causes upwelling. Upwelling is the rising up of colder, denser waters to the ocean surface. Upwelling occurs when winds cause surface waters to move offshore. This upwelling of deeper waters brings nutrients to organisms living near shorelines.

CHECKPOINT

1. What is wave energy?
2. What are some of the different uses of electromagnetic waves?
3. How does the sun's energy get to Earth?
 What kinds of energy come from the sun?

ACTIVITY

Making Waves

Find Out

Do this activity to learn how to make transverse waves.

Process Skills

Constructing Models
Observing
Predicting
Communicating
Controlling Variables
Inferring

WHAT YOU NEED

rope (3 m)

stationary
object

*Activity
Journal*

WHAT TO DO

1. Work with a partner. Decide who will make waves and who will record observations.

2. Tie one end of a 3-m rope or coiled cord to a stationary object such as an object on a wall or a doorknob.

3. Model a wave by moving the other end of the rope up and down with your hand. Observe the wave you make.

4. Predict what will happen if you increase the speed of movement. Record your prediction.

5. Increase the speed of the movement. Record your observations.

6. **Predict** what will happen if you increase the height of the movement of your arm. **Record** your prediction.

7. Increase the height of the movement of your arm. Raise the rope to a higher point. **Record** your observations.

CONCLUSIONS

1. What happened to the frequency and wavelength when you increased the speed of movement?

2. What happened to the wave when the rope hit the stationary object?

3. What type of wave was modeled?

4. Describe the relationship between the source and the wave.

ASKING NEW QUESTIONS

1. How many ropes would you need to demonstrate electromagnetic waves?

2. What would you need to demonstrate sound waves?

SCIENTIFIC METHODS SELF CHECK

✔ Did I **model** transverse waves?

✔ Did I **observe** changes in the waves?

✔ Did I **predict** changes in the waves?

✔ Did I **record** my observations?

✔ Did I **control the variables,** height and movement, one at a time?

✔ Did I **infer** how waves move energy?

Visible Light

Find Out

- What transparent, opaque, and translucent materials are
- How reflections work
- How refraction and reflection differ
- What lenses are
- How the eye works
- What colors are in white light

Vocabulary

transparent
opaque
translucent
reflection
angle of incidence
refraction

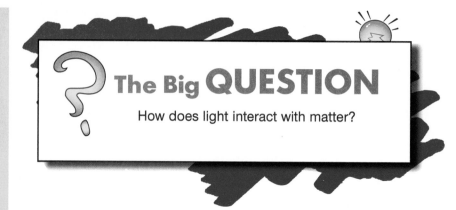

The Big QUESTION

How does light interact with matter?

Did you look in a mirror this morning? When you comb your hair or brush your teeth, a mirror helps you see what you are doing. We use mirrors for grooming because they reflect our image back to us. Mirrors can also help us understand the properties of light.

Light Rays

You know that visible light is a part of the electromagnetic spectrum. The sun's energy that reaches Earth includes both visible and invisible light waves. Humans have tried to explain the properties of light throughout history. The first person to explain that light is reflected from an object to the eye was an Arab mathematician named Alhazen, who lived about A.D. 1000. He also attempted to explain why things farther away appeared smaller than nearby things. These theories helped form our current theories about light.

Scientists know that visible light travels in straight lines. If you shine a flashlight in some dusty air, you can see that light waves travel in a straight line from their source. When a ray of light reaches an object, several things can happen. Light rays can bounce off, pass through, or be absorbed by objects.

The type of matter in an object determines what happens to light rays. Materials that light rays easily pass through are **transparent.** Most types of clear glass, such as eyeglasses and windows, are good examples of transparent materials. Materials that light rays do not pass through are **opaque.** Opaque materials absorb or reflect all light. You cannot see through opaque materials.

Other materials have properties somewhere between these two types. These materials let the light rays pass through them but scatter the light so that you cannot see clear images through them. This type of material is **translucent.** Frosted glass and waxed paper are examples of translucent materials.

The flower is opaque. Opaque materials do not allow light to pass through them. Objects that allow light to pass through them without forming a clear image are called translucent. The vase is translucent. Objects such as the eyeglasses that allow light to pass through them and enable you to see images clearly are transparent.

Reflection

Light, like other electromagnetic waves, has the ability to bounce off some surfaces. This is called **reflection** (rē flek′ shun). The angle at which the waves strike the surface determines the angle at which the waves reflect. To understand the reflection of light rays, imagine you're a basketball player. Passing the ball to a teammate by bouncing it on the floor is similar to the principle of reflection. The ball hits the floor and bounces upward at the same angle.

Because light rays travel in a straight line, the angle the rays make coming out of a reflection is equal to the angle they make coming from the source of the light. This is called the *law of reflection,* which states that the **angle of incidence** (in′ si dens) is equal to the angle of reflection. *Incidence* means the act or manner of falling. So the angle of incidence is the angle at which the light ray from a source *falls* on a surface.

When light rays from an object reflect from a smooth, glossy surface, almost all the rays reflect in the same direction. This is why you can sometimes see your reflection on a pond. But if a breeze disturbs the surface of the pond, your reflection disappears. Rough surfaces also reflect light. But they have many surfaces on which the light rays fall. When light rays fall on rough surfaces, the light rays reflect in many directions. When light rays are scattered, no image is produced.

What you see when you stand in front of the mirror is actually an image of yourself. Light falling on you reflects off you onto the mirror. Some of that light is reflected from the mirror back to your eyes. However, the image is reversed!

Whenever you look into a mirror, the image you see appears to be turned around.

A flat mirror is a plane mirror. What happens if the mirror is not flat like a plane mirror? If a smooth mirror curves inward, like the inside of a spoon, it is a concave mirror. A concave mirror doesn't reflect light in the same way as a plane mirror does. A concave mirror makes the light rays converge, or come together. Concave mirrors are found in flashlights, car headlights, and spotlights. If a light source is placed at the right spot in front of a concave mirror, the light rays reflect outward as parallel lines.

If a smooth mirror curves outward, it is convex. Convex means that something curves outward like the outside of a spoon. A convex mirror makes the light rays diverge, or spread apart. Convex mirrors are good to use where a wide area has to be seen. Convex mirrors are also called wide-angled mirrors. You've probably seen convex mirrors near the ceiling in stores or near driveways. People and stores use them for safety and security.

Telescopes use mirrors to capture images of objects in space. The Hubble telescope, named for the astronomer Edwin Hubble, is a large, orbiting telescope with a mirror that is 240 cm in diameter. In 1990, it was launched into space so scientists could get clearer images of objects in space. After the Hubble telescope was placed in orbit, it began sending images to Earth. These images were a little blurry. The problem was a wrong curvature in the telescope's mirror. The wrong curves in the mirror caused distorted images to form.

In 1993, astronauts from the space shuttle *Endeavour* repaired the telescope by equipping it with a device that used mirrors to correct the problem. As a result, the Hubble telescope now sends near-perfect pictures of space back to Earth.

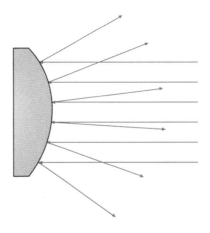

Parallel light rays striking a convex mirror reflect outward as shown.

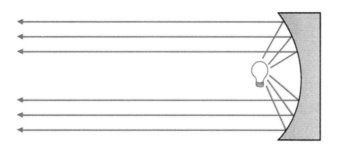

A lightbulb placed at the right spot in front of a concave mirror can reflect parallel light rays.

A close-up look at a fiber optic cable.

A particular color of laser light has the same wavelength and frequency. The crests and troughs of these waves stack up similarly to the way lasagna noodles stack up in a box.

Light and Fiber Optics

An interesting phenomenon occurs when a light ray in a dense medium meets the surface of the medium at a shallow angle. Instead of passing out of the dense medium, the ray reflects off the surface and stays entirely within the dense medium. The result is the phenomenon known as *total internal reflection.*

Fiber optics is the science of transmitting images through transparent fibers by repeated total internal reflection. The most common fibers used are thin strands of extremely pure glass. Regardless of how the fiber is bent, light flows along the inside of the fiber. The light is totally internally reflected within the fiber. Fiber optics have many uses, such as laser surgery and communications. Phone lines transmit calls using light as a signal via fiber optics.

Laser light is usually the light conducted along the inside of a fiber. *Laser* stands for "light amplification by stimulated emission of radiation." Some kinds of lasers produce such a powerful beam of light that their energy can cut a hole through steel. Lasers produce light of only one color of the spectrum. The light has only one wavelength and frequency.

The Universal Product Code (UPC) found in many stores is read by lasers that scan product labels. Geologists use lasers to predict earthquakes and volcanic eruptions. They beam lasers across faults in Earth's crust. The reflections of the laser light can measure the smallest of movements in Earth's crust.

Lenses

We use the principles of refraction to make lenses. One of the most common uses for lenses is to correct vision. If you wear eyeglasses or contact lenses, you know that lenses can help you see better. They clear up blurry images. Other common uses for lenses are in microscopes, telescopes, binoculars, and cameras.

What is a lens? A lens is a transparent object that has at least one curved side. Most lenses are transparent glass or plastic. Some lenses are even made of quartz. The material is carefully ground and shaped. We use lenses to magnify or reduce images, or to concentrate or separate light rays. Lenses, like mirrors, can be concave or convex (or both).

Light refracts when it passes through either kind of lens. Light rays that pass directly through the center of a lens keep going in their original direction. Light rays that strike the lens anywhere else are bent, or refracted. The amount of bending is determined by where the light enters the lens. The farther away from the center of the lens, the more bending there will be.

Convex lenses are curved outward on at least one side. The middle of a convex lens is thicker than its edge. Convex lenses cause incoming rays of light from distant objects to meet on the other side of the lens. When parallel rays of light pass through a convex lens, they refract toward each other. The point at which parallel light rays converge is the focal point of the lens. Convex lenses magnify images. Microscopes, magnifying glasses, and eyeglasses that correct farsightedness are examples of convex lenses.

Concave lenses are curved inward on at least one side. The middle of a concave lens is thinner than its edge. Concave lenses make incoming rays of light diverge on the other side of the lens. When parallel rays of light pass through a concave lens, they refract away from each other. Concave lenses, which reduce images, are used in cameras and eyeglasses that correct nearsightedness.

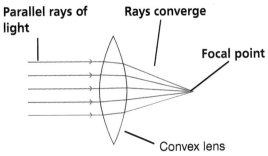

Light passing through a convex lens

Parallel rays of light — Rays converge — Focal point — Convex lens

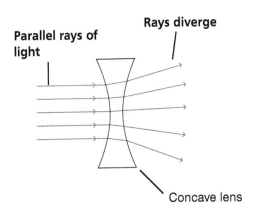

Parallel rays of light — Rays diverge — Concave lens

Light passing through a concave lens

Refraction

Light travels through air and space in straight lines, in all directions, and at constant speed. It can also travel through other media, such as water and glass. When light waves traveling in air pass into another medium, they usually change speed. The change in the speed of light rays depends on the nature of the medium. Different media have different densities. Light passing into a denser medium slows down. Light passing into a less dense medium speeds up. A ray of light that enters a different medium at a right angle (90°) to the surface changes speed but does not change direction. If a light ray enters a different medium at an angle less than 90°, the light ray changes direction. The change in direction is due to the change in speed.

The change in direction means that sometimes, when light rays pass through objects, they seem to bend slightly from their original path. You can observe this by looking through a clear glass of water. If you lean a straw into the glass and look at it from the side of the glass, you'll see a "break" in the straw. The straw appears bent. It may even appear to be in two separate pieces. This happens because light travels at different speeds in different media. Light rays travel at 300,000 km/s in air. They slow down to 197,000 km/s in glass.

As the light ray moves from the air to the glass, the light ray's path moves closer to the normal. As the light ray moves from the glass into the air, the light ray's path moves farther away from the normal.

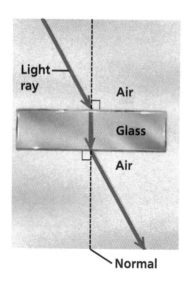

Light ray

Air

Glass

Air

Normal

The bending you see is an angle of refraction (rē frak′ shun). **Refraction** is the bending of a light wave as it enters a different medium. There is an angle of incidence in refraction, just like in reflection. The angle of incidence in refraction is the angle at which the light hits the surface of the refracting medium. Scientists measure refraction with the help of an imaginary line. The imaginary line stands at a right angle to the surface of the medium. The name for this imaginary line is the normal. When light rays pass into a denser medium, the light rays' path moves closer to the normal. When the light rays pass into a less dense medium, they move away from the normal.

Imagine if you went roller skating down a straight sidewalk toward grass at the bottom of a hill. Both of your skates would hit the grass at the same time. They would slow down together by the same amount, so neither skate could pull you to one side. You would keep going in a straight line. You have slowed down, but not changed direction.

Now, imagine you are skating down a sidewalk again. Only this time, the wheels of one skate veer off the sidewalk onto the grass. The skate in the grass slows down. The skate on the sidewalk is still going fast. What happens to you? You turn away from your original path down the sidewalk and shift toward the slower skate. Suddenly you're moving over the grass at a considerably slower speed. This is similar to the way light changes speed and direction in refraction.

How the Eye Works

Light waves bring the world to your brain through your eyes. How do the eyes work? The cornea and the lens of your eye are convex lenses. They focus light rays on the retina, the back surface of the eye. Light-sensitive cells in the retina change the energy of the light to electric signals that then go to the brain. The brain interprets the signals as upright images.

The retina is thin and extremely fragile tissue. The cells in the tissue are called rods and cones, which are named for their shapes. The center of the retina houses 6,000,000 cones. The cones are sensitive to bright lights and colors. The cones create the image on which the eyes focus. It is the cones that produce sharp images of objects and scenes. The cones also help you see colors. Human cones can distinguish more than 200 different colors.

Around the outer edges of the retina are 120,000,000 rods. The rods help you see in dim light. Rods don't respond to colors the way cones do. They absorb reflected light and create different shades of gray. So the images you see in very dim light look like gray shadows.

Your eyes contain lenses.

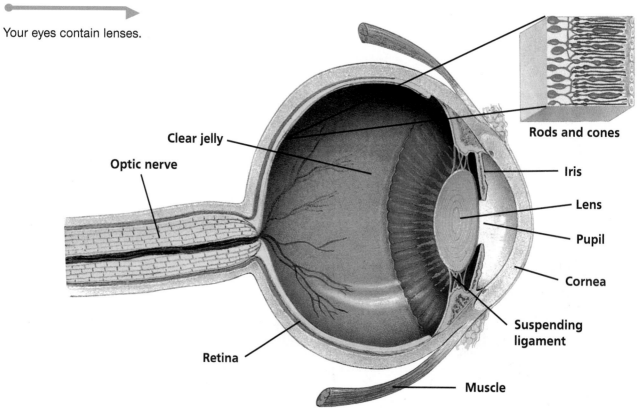

Clear jelly

Optic nerve

Rods and cones

Iris

Lens

Pupil

Cornea

Suspending ligament

Retina

Muscle

Light Waves and Eye Vision

You know that light can be refracted or reflected. The cornea is the first refracting structure that light passes through as it enters the eye. Next is the pupil, which controls the amount of light that enters the eye. The lens of an eye lies behind the pupil. The lens can change shape. It becomes thicker or thinner, depending on the distance of an object viewed.

The lens focuses light rays onto the retina. The lens of the eye is a natural, transparent object that has at least one convex curved side. Both convex and concave lenses are used in eyeglasses to help correct vision problems. Concave lenses assist people who are nearsighted. Because their eyes' focal length is too short, they see nearby objects clearly but not those in the distance. In people with nearsightedness, the eyes' lenses focus images of distant objects *in front* of the retinas rather than on them. Concave lenses correct this by spreading light waves that enter the eye. This extends the focal length and makes light focus on the retina properly.

Convex lenses help people who are farsighted. Farsighted people see objects clearly at farther distances but not those that are close. Their eyes' lenses focus behind the retina instead of on it. Convex lenses cause light rays to begin to converge before they enter the lens in the eye. The resulting images carried by the light then focus correctly on the retina. Close-up vision is no longer blurry.

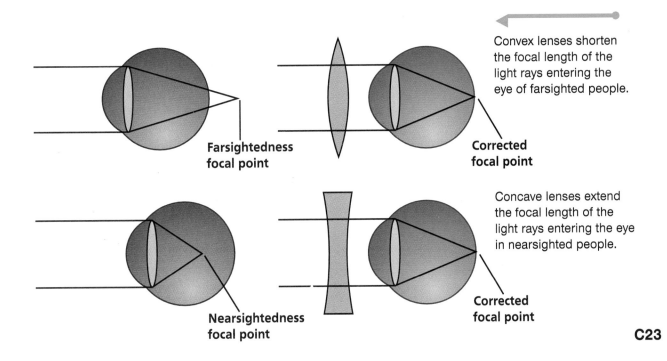

Convex lenses shorten the focal length of the light rays entering the eye of farsighted people.

Farsightedness focal point

Corrected focal point

Concave lenses extend the focal length of the light rays entering the eye in nearsighted people.

Nearsightedness focal point

Corrected focal point

Wavelength and Color

Remember that light travels through the transmission of waves. The main differences among various electromagnetic waves are their lengths and frequencies. This makes the wave either visible to us or invisible. We can't see microwaves or radio waves. Their wavelengths are too long. We can't see X rays because their wavelengths are too short.

We can see waves that make visible light. Our eyes recognize these particular frequencies and wavelengths. When all the colors of the spectrum are blended together, we see *white light.*

The color you see when you look at an object depends on the color of light it reflects. An object that looks green in white light appears that way because it absorbs all the colors of the spectrum *except* green. The green light is reflected off its surface.

A green plant will appear black in red light because it absorbs all the light within the wavelength of the red. In white light the plant also absorbs the red light. In fact, it reflects only the green light. Therefore, it appears to be green.

Each raindrop forms many colors. But the color that reaches our eyes from a particular raindrop depends on the angle between it and the line formed from the sun's rays. Many raindrops, each sending colored light at certain angles, can form a complete rainbow.

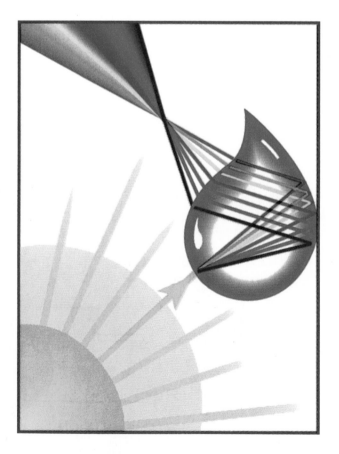

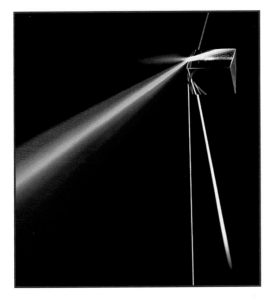

A prism is a piece of cut and polished glass or plastic. White light shining through a prism is separated into all the colors of the visible spectrum.

When white light passes through a prism, the colors of the spectrum separate according to their wavelengths. Each wavelength of light refracts by a different amount as it travels through a prism. This results in a familiar pattern of colors: red, orange, yellow, green, blue, indigo (deep blue), and violet. An easy way to remember this pattern is *ROY G BIV.*

Colors with shorter wavelengths refract more than those with longer wavelengths. For this reason, violet light, which has the shortest wavelength, refracts the most. Red light, which has the longest wavelength, refracts the least. This effect is also responsible for rainbows. When rain is falling in front of you and the sun shines behind you, you can see a rainbow. The drops of water in the sky act like tiny prisms.

CHECKPOINT

1. Describe transparent, opaque, and translucent materials.
2. How does reflection work?
3. How do refraction and reflection differ?
4. What is the difference between a concave lens and a convex lens?
5. How does the eye work?
6. What colors are in white light?

 How does light interact with matter?

ACTIVITY

Making Colors from Light

Find Out

Do this activity to learn how all the colors of visible light in the electromagnetic spectrum make white light.

Process Skills

Observing
Predicting
Measuring
Communicating
Hypothesizing
Designing an Investigation

WHAT YOU NEED

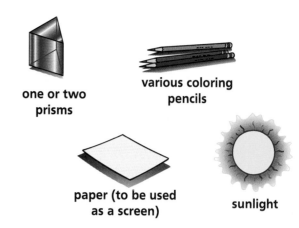

one or two prisms

various coloring pencils

paper (to be used as a screen)

sunlight

WHAT TO DO

1. Place the prism between a sunlit window and the paper.

2. Turn the prism until a ray of sunlight passes through it onto the paper.

3. Notice what happens to the white light. Observe the colors you see. Record them.

4. If two prisms are available, predict what color(s) of light will result if you place the second one between the first prism and the paper screen. Record your prediction.

5. Take the second prism and place it between the first prism and the paper screen, holding them all up by a sunlit window.

6. Notice what happens to the light. Observe the colors. Record the color(s). Compare them to your predictions.

7. Illustrate the effects of using one or two prisms using colored pencils.

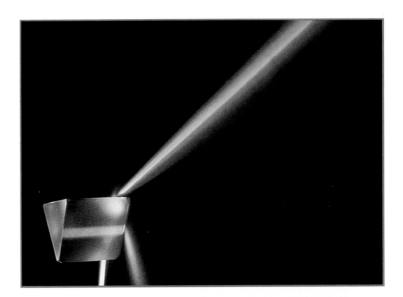

CONCLUSIONS

1. How does the prism change the white light?

2. What colors do you see?

3. What happens when two prisms are used?

ASKING NEW QUESTIONS

1. When you look at the visible light spectrum, what is the order in which the bands of color appear?

2. Make a hypothesis about what would happen if only one color of light shined through the prism.

3. Design an investigation to test your hypothesis.

4. Write a report to include the steps and results of your investigation. Present your findings to your class.

SCIENTIFIC METHODS SELF CHECK

✔ Did I **observe** the spectrum?

✔ Did I **predict** the colors in the spectrum?

✔ Did I **record** my observations and predictions?

✔ Did I **compare** my results to my predictions?

✔ Did I **illustrate** my observations?

✔ Did I **hypothesize** about what would happen if only one color of light was directed through the prism?

✔ Did I **design an investigation** to test my hypothesis?

Radiation and Earth's Energy

Find Out

- What renewable and nonrenewable resources are
- What the advantages and disadvantages of solar energy are
- How hydroelectric power can produce electricity
- What geothermal energy is
- How wind energy is used
- What biomass is

Vocabulary

nonrenewable resources
renewable resources
inexhaustible resources
turbines
hydroelectric power
geothermal
wind farms

The Big QUESTION

How do we get alternative sources of energy?

Human energy demands are very high in our society. Many people no longer grow their own food. Many don't know how to preserve it without electric freezers or refrigerators. Most people don't make their own clothing, build their own houses, or make their own furniture. Most people have jobs that are too far from their homes for them to walk to work. As a result, we depend on the mass production of many things that we need and use on a daily basis. Our society has become dependent upon the use of energy.

Sources of Energy

Water waves, wind, sound waves, and electromagnetic waves carry energy. Water waves can bob a toy boat in a pond or wreck land and property. Wind forces can topple trees or help us fly a kite on a warm spring day. Sound waves allow us to hear music. But if they have enough compression, or are too loud, sound waves can shatter glass. Light waves allow us to see the world as well as live in it.

Humans are not very efficient at converting energy from one form to another. For example, we use electricity to make a lightbulb work. The lightbulb converts electrical energy to light energy. But the lightbulb does not completely convert the electrical energy into light energy. The lightbulb also gives off heat. It is inefficient in changing energy from one form to another.

Generally, when humans transform mechanical energy to another form, some of the useful mechanical energy is lost. But when humans use energy that comes directly from the sun, they are sometimes being energy-efficient. Let's look at some ways humans use energy from the sun.

Solar Radiation

The sun's energy comes to Earth, is absorbed by Earth's crust, reflects into the atmosphere, converts to thermal energy, or is used by things living on Earth. Mechanical energy is the total amount of kinetic and potential energy in a system. Kinetic energy is energy in the form of motion. Kinetic energy does work. Potential energy is stored energy.

We know something about the physical properties of using and storing energy. One of the physical properties of energy is that the amount of energy in a system is always the same, or constant. Regardless of how energy changes form, it can be neither created nor destroyed. This concept is known as the *law of conservation of energy*. We can classify Earth's energy resources by whether we must convert the energy to another form before we use it or whether we can use the energy directly.

All energy conversions have thermal energy as a by-product. The lightbulb converts some of the electrical energy to light. The remainder becomes thermal energy, which warms the surrounding air.

Humans use many sources of energy. Some are nonrenewable, others are renewable, and still others are inexhaustible. Can you classify the kind of energy resource in each of the pictures on these pages?

Energy sources can also be classified as either conventional or alternative sources. Conventional means usual. Conventional sources of energy are those we usually use, such as nuclear power, fossil fuels, and wood. Oil, natural gas, and coal are fossil fuels that must be removed from within the ground. Wood comes from trees that are cut down from forests. Alternative sources of energy are all other sources of energy. These include solar energy, geothermal energy, wind power, and water power.

Another way to look at energy is to see how quickly it is replenished. Most conventional energy resources exist in supplies that cannot be replenished within 30 years. These are **nonrenewable resources.** Oil, natural gas, and coal are nonrenewable resources. So are the elements used in nuclear fission reactors. **Renewable resources** are those that are replenished within 30 years, such as wood, geothermal energy, the elements used in nuclear breeder reactors, and energy from biomass. Resources that are always available are **inexhaustible** (in/ ex aus/ ti bul) **resources.** Inexhaustible resources include all of the alternative resources listed above—solar energy, wind power, and water power.

Solar Energy

Large amounts of energy from the sun strike Earth every day. Energy produced on the sun travels to Earth in about eight minutes. Energy from the sun is called solar energy. Each day, the amount of solar energy that strikes the United States is greater than the energy in 22,000,000 barrels of crude oil. That's 10,000 times more than all the energy used in the world in 1990. If we can find ways to use solar energy directly, we can reduce our dependency on nonrenewable energy sources. In order for us to use solar energy, we must first collect it. Then, we must use it right away or store it. Sometimes we have to concentrate the solar energy before we use it.

One use of solar energy is to help heat our homes and buildings. We know that light energy travels through glass. If we make houses and buildings with large windows that face the sun, solar energy can pass through them. Many homes in the northern hemisphere have few windows on their north side and many windows on their south side to take advantage of this fact. In winter, the sun helps warm the inside of the house. Shades on the windows in summer keep the sunlight out of the house so the house stays cooler. This is one type of passive solar heating. Passive solar heating means that no special equipment collects or converts the energy of the sun to provide heat.

Some types of equipment that collect solar energy are solar reflectors, solar collectors, and solar cells. A solar collector is a device that absorbs solar energy. In a solar collector, glass or plastic covers dark-colored energy-absorbing material. The absorbed energy changes to heat and the covering holds the heat in the collector. Any air or liquids that pass through the collector become heated. The hot air or liquids can circulate through a building, warming it. Solar collectors can also provide hot water for washing, bathing, cleaning, and swimming. Many buildings have solar collectors on their roofs.

Solar reflectors do what their name says. They reflect and focus sunlight on one spot. Solar reflectors are good for heating water, cooking food, and starting fires. Mirrors are good reflectors. Scientists and engineers are experimenting with creating mirror farms to collect solar energy.

Solar electric generating system in the Mojave Desert in California

These mirrors are solar reflectors, which focus sunlight on one spot to generate steam. The steam is used to produce electrical energy.

Solar cells are thin strips of material that produce an electric current when struck by sunlight. Solar cells convert sunlight directly into electrical energy when sunlight strikes the materials. You may have used a solar cell in a calculator or a clock.

Some electricity-generating plants use solar energy to produce steam for driving their turbines. **Turbines** are wheels with blades powered by a fluid. Turbines are used to help convert steam energy to electrical energy. Solar cell panels also power irrigation pumps, telephone booths, lighthouses, and aircraft navigation beacons. Satellites and many scientific research stations also use solar cells. The cost of electricity produced from solar cells is higher than that from conventional energy sources. In 1991, the cost of electricity generated by panels of solar cells cost at least 20 percent more per kilowatt-hour than energy generated by fossil fuels.

This race car is powered by the energy produced by the solar cells on its frame.

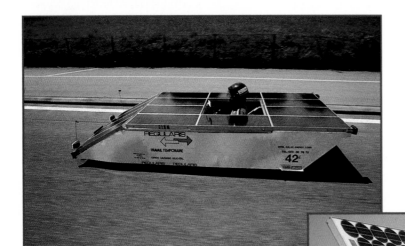

The electric current to operate this telephone booth in Mystic, Connecticut, comes from the solar cells in the panel above the booth.

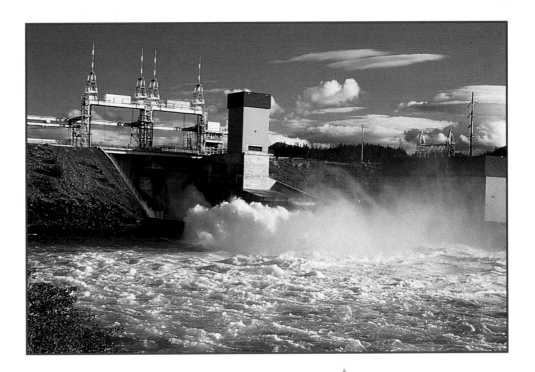

Hydroelectric Power

Potential energy is the energy an object or particle has because of its position or condition. When you lift a ball, it gains potential energy because of its position. The higher an object, the more potential energy it has. Energy from falling water works on this principle. For centuries people have used waterwheels to convert the power of falling water into mechanical energy to drive small mills, grindstones, saws, or other machines. The first large factories used machines powered by moving water.

Hydroelectric power is the production of energy by water power. Hydroelectric plants use large amounts of water to generate electrical energy. At a dam, as water levels rise, the water gains more potential energy. The higher the dam, the more potential energy the water behind the dam has. When the water is released, it crashes down. The energy of the falling water is kinetic energy. The kinetic energy can be channeled by power plants to turn turbines, which in turn generate electricity.

Electricity generated at a hydroelectric plant that is not needed right away can be stored in batteries. This stored energy can replace fossil fuels for a variety of uses, even to power vehicles. Some utility companies shut down their fossil-fuel plants during times of low demand (such as at night) and let nearby hydroelectric plants supply electricity.

Whitehorse hydroelectric dam along the Yukon River in Canada

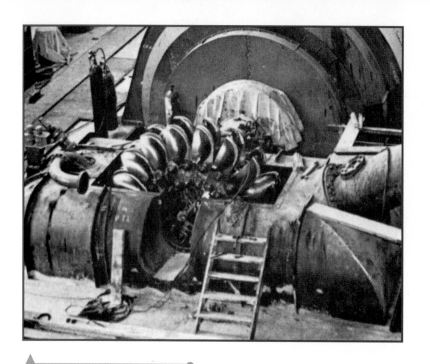

A Pelton wheel can generate electricity for household use.

It is possible to increase hydroelectric power production without building more big dams. There are almost 50,000 small dams already in the United States. Small power plants could be built at many of these dams. However, the cost per kilowatt of energy generated at small electric plants is much higher than the costs at larger plants.

Another way to increase hydroelectric power is for homeowners who live near streams to build small dams with waterwheels. As long as the community approves, the waterwheels can power generators to supply electricity for the household. The Pelton waterwheel is a small waterwheel that can generate electricity, even from a small, fast-flowing stream. It is a wheel with bowl-shaped cups mounted on its rim. It turns at high speed. The wheel generates electricity efficiently. Waterwheels can be an inexpensive source of power for households, farms, or remote locations. They are nonpolluting, although they may interfere with fish migration. A company in Scotland uses several Pelton wheels. Each wheel can generate enough electricity for the needs of a small town.

Similar to hydroelectric power, ocean tides can also be used to generate electrical energy. Tide generators in the Bay of Fundy, Canada, make use of the large differences between low tide and high tide. There are not many places on Earth with such big differences between high tide and low tide. In the 1970s, Stephen Salter, a British engineer, created a floating tidal energy collector. This device can be used with any regular tides. Because the collectors come to a point on one side, like a duck's beak, they are called "ducks." Salter ducks float on the surface of water and gather kinetic energy from the tides. The up-and-down motion of the waves rocks the "duck." This motion drives pumps, which push liquid through a generator. The generator then converts the energy to electricity.

Geothermal Energy

Geothermal energy is another alternative energy source. **Geothermal** means heat from Earth. Geysers and hot springs are sites where naturally hot water is near or at the surface of Earth. The hot water can be pumped directly to homes or used by a power station to generate electricity. Remember that to generate electricity, water must reach temperatures high enough to turn to steam and power turbines. Most geothermal sites already have water hot enough to make steam. For some uses, geothermal energy can cost about the same as conventional energy sources. However, hot springs and geysers are not usually located near areas where large amounts of electrical energy are needed. They are usually located in remote and undeveloped areas. Transferring the electricity away from natural geothermal sites is usually hard to do.

Hot rocks near the surface of Earth are also potential sources of geothermal energy. As with geothermal water sources, most hot rocks are in remote areas. Areas with hot rocks usually don't have enough water nearby to generate steam. Scientists are looking for ways to drill deep into Earth to reach hot, dry rocks inside Earth. They hope to use these hot rocks for energy.

This geothermal energy site in Wairakei, North Island, New Zealand, is being used for thermal energy transfer.

Wind Energy

Wind is the result of the convection of thermal energy. When Earth absorbs energy from the sun, it converts it to thermal energy. Wind power was one of the first forms of energy humans learned to control. Sails on ships let people travel across lakes, seas, and oceans. The same principles drive windmills. Windmills, like waterwheels, were once used to power machines. Today's windmills can generate a lot of electric power. The turning blades can turn generators, which make electricity. When windmills are grouped together to produce electrical energy, they are called **wind farms.** Some wind farms can generate as much electricity as a hydroelectric power plant.

However, finding the right environment for windmills or wind farms is not easy. Wind farms need large areas of land to supply a large amount of electricity. A wind farm that can make as much electricity as a solar energy station may need five times more land. The blades of all windmills must be high enough so that the wind will cause them to turn almost constantly. In the Midwest, that can be as high as 25 m. Most wind farms in the United States are in California, which has the right conditions for windmills to be efficient.

Windmills in the Netherlands

Rotational blade wind farm in Alberta, Canada

Propeller blade wind farm in Gorgonio Pass in southern California

Biomass

Biomass is material from living things that can be used to provide energy. When biomass is burned, it produces thermal energy. Compost is a good example of biomass. Burning biomass produces fewer pollutants than burning fossil fuels does. Scientists estimate that more than 50 percent of most landfill waste is usable biomass energy. However, it takes much more biomass to create the same amount of energy as from a small amount of fossil fuels. This makes biomass more costly to use than some other energy sources.

Burning biomass is one way to produce thermal energy. This Puente Hills, CA, landfill gas energy recovery facility can produce enough electricity to provide daily energy to almost 70,000 homes.

CHECKPOINT

1. What are nonrenewable and renewable resources?
2. What are the advantages of solar energy?
3. What is hydroelectric power?
4. What are some of the advantages of geothermal energy?
5. How is wind power converted to energy?
6. How can landfills be used to produce thermal energy?

 How do we get alternative sources of energy?

ACTIVITY
Making Wind Work

Find Out
Do this activity to learn how to make a wind-powered device.

Process Skills
Predicting
Constructing Models
Experimenting
Communicating
Using Numbers

WHAT YOU NEED

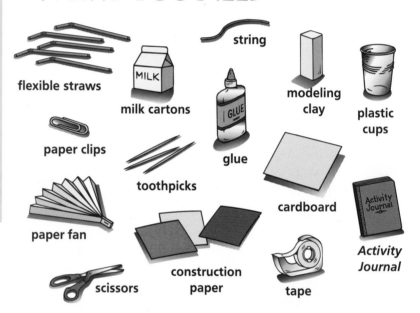

flexible straws

string

milk cartons

modeling clay

plastic cups

paper clips

glue

toothpicks

cardboard

paper fan

Activity Journal

scissors

construction paper

tape

WHAT TO DO

1. Draw a plan for a device that can use wind energy to pick up paper clips.
2. Predict how many paper clips your device will pick up.
3. Make a model. Use the materials provided to build your machine.
4. Test your device at different wind speeds. Record your trials.
5. Make a chart of your paper clip data.
6. Revise at least one part of your device so that it will work better.
7. Predict how many more paper clips your improved device will pick up.
8. Repeat Steps 4 to 7 as often as time permits.

Conclusions

1. How many paper clips did your device pick up when you first built it?
2. How well did it work at different wind speeds?
3. Did your changes result in more paper clips being picked up?
4. Why was it important to design the windmill before it was built?

Asking New Questions

1. Wind speed can vary a lot. How could you control the work your windmill does at different speeds?
2. How could your machine be useful?

SCIENTIFIC METHODS SELF CHECK

✔ Did I **predict** the number of paper clips my device would pick up?

✔ Did I **create** a model?

✔ Did I **experiment** with different wind speeds and designs?

✔ Did I **record** my observations?

✔ Did I **chart** my data?

Review

Reviewing Vocabulary and Concepts

Write the letter of the answer that best completes each sentence.

1. The distance from the crest of a wave to the rest position of the medium is the ___.
   - **a.** reflection
   - **b.** hydroelectric power
   - **c.** amplitude
   - **d.** frequency

2. The number of wave crests that pass a place in one second is the ___ of the wave.
   - **a.** angle of incidence
   - **b.** frequency
   - **c.** wavelength
   - **d.** amplitude

3. ___ are materials that light rays pass through most easily.
   - **a.** Transparent materials
   - **b.** Opaque materials
   - **c.** Translucent materials
   - **d.** Renewable resources

4. Materials that allow light to pass through them but scatter the light so that no clear image forms are___.
   - **a.** transparent
   - **b.** turbines
   - **c.** translucent
   - **d.** opaque

5. Resources that are always available are ___.
   - **a.** inexhaustible resources
   - **b.** renewable resources
   - **c.** opaque
   - **d.** electromagnetic waves

Match the definition on the left with the correct term.

6. electric and magnetic fields that vibrate at right angles to each other
   - **a.** reflection

7. light rays do not pass through these materials
   - **b.** nonrenewable resources

8. light that bounces off surfaces
   - **c.** turbines

9. energy supplies that cannot be replenished within 30 years
   - **d.** electromagnetic waves

10. large machines that convert steam energy into electrical energy
   - **e.** opaque

Understanding What You Learned

1. Describe a transverse wave. Give some examples of transverse waves.

2. Where does radiant energy come from?

3. What happens to water in the water cycle?

4. How does visible light travel?

5. What happens when light rays fall on rough surfaces?

6. What is the difference between convex and concave lenses?

7. Who or what is *ROY G BIV?*

8. What is the law of conservation of energy?

9. Briefly describe how a solar collector works.

10. What would you need to produce electrical energy from water?

Applying What You Learned

1. What kind of devices use radio waves for energy?

2. How would you describe to a friend that the sun's energy can cause sunburn?

3. Explain how you can see your reflection.

4. Think of different ways to use solar energy. Explain which one would be the most practical one for your home.

5. Explain how the sun is Earth's energy source.

For Your **Portfolio**

Survey ten people between the ages of 10 and 18, ten people between the ages of 20 and 35, and ten people over the age of 40. List each person's age, whether they wear glasses or contact lenses, and if so whether they are nearsighted or farsighted. Make a graph of the results for each age group. Write a report. What conclusions can you make based on your data?

CHAPTER 2

HEAT

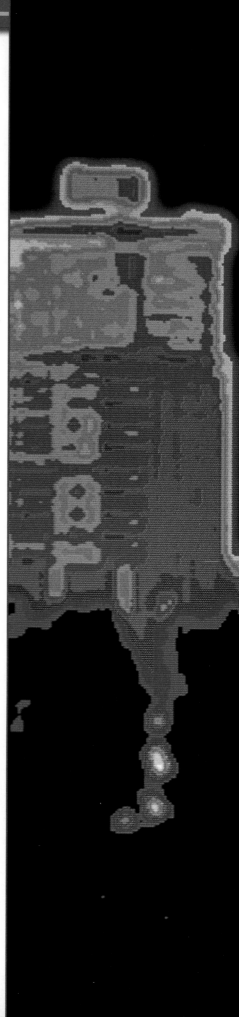

Were you ever so cold that your teeth chattered? Or maybe you shivered and goose bumps broke out on your arms. Your body was responding to sensations of cold by automatically conserving heat energy.

Were you ever so hot that you started to sweat? Or panted after long, hard exercise? Sweating and panting are your body's reaction to being overheated.

The ability to transfer energy, especially heat energy, is one of the first skills humans learned. As a result, people can live everywhere on Earth. People live in hot tropical forests. They live in cold Arctic tundra. They have learned how to stay cool in hot places. They have learned how to stay warm in cold places. People can produce and transfer energy for heating and cooling.

The Big IDEA

Energy can be produced and transferred.

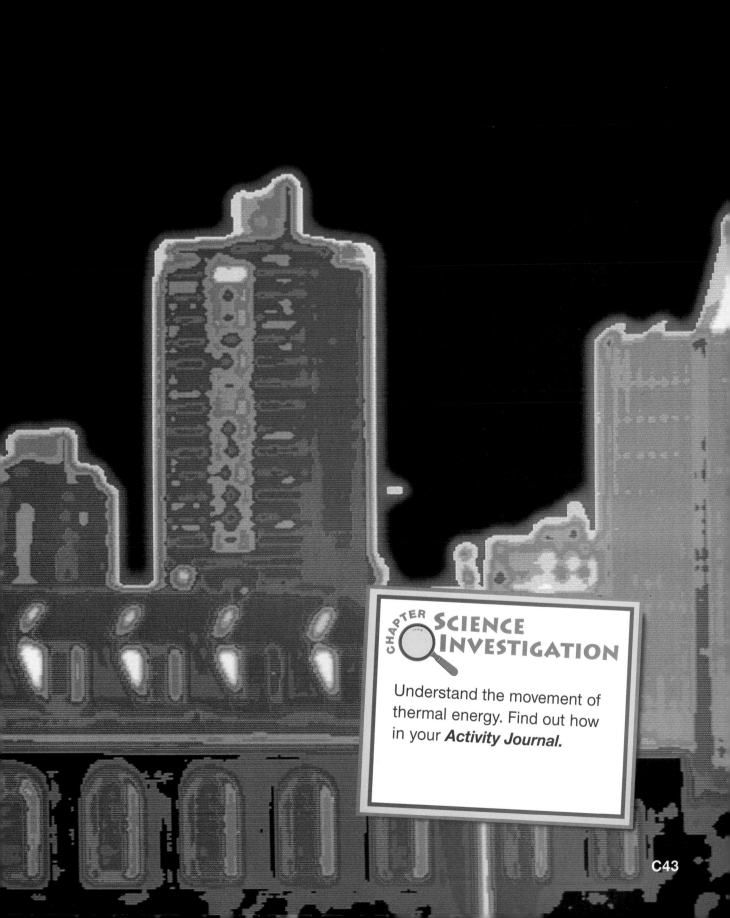

CHAPTER SCIENCE INVESTIGATION

Understand the movement of thermal energy. Find out how in your *Activity Journal.*

Thermal Energy

Find Out

- Where energy in matter comes from
- What thermal energy is
- What the three ways to transfer heat are

Vocabulary

thermal energy
heat
temperature
conduction
conductors
convection
radiation

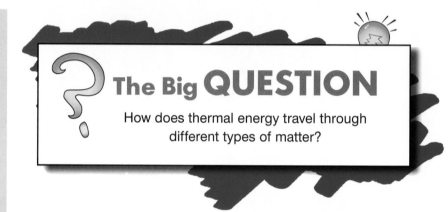

The Big QUESTION

How does thermal energy travel through different types of matter?

Fire has been important to humanity for a long time. Fires were used for warmth and cooking. The first matches were invented in China in A.D. 577. At that time people used sparks and tinder, or small, dry twigs, to start new fires. Some women in a Chinese kingdom under siege ran short of tinder. So, the women coated tiny sticks with sulfur. When they brushed the sulfur tip against a gritty surface, the stick burst into flame. Today, we know these tiny sticks with sulfur tips as matches. We also know of ways to make things hot without fire.

Energy and Matter

Let's recall what energy is. Energy is the ability to cause change. You have learned that energy is the total amount of potential and kinetic energy in a system. Potential energy is the energy an object or molecule has because of its position or condition. When water is held behind a dam, the potential energy of the water is high. Kinetic energy is the energy of motion. When water flows from behind the dam, the falling water has kinetic energy.

You know that the water behind a dam has potential energy. Did you know that the water behind a dam also has kinetic energy? That's because the molecules that make up the water are constantly moving. When things are in motion, they have kinetic energy. All matter is made up of molecules, and the molecules are always moving. The moving molecules give matter its kinetic energy.

Thermal Energy

Scientists know that in any given situation, energy may change from one form to another, but the total amount of energy in a system remains constant. You know this principle as the *law of conservation of energy*. In the water and dam system, falling water changes position from a high level to a low level. For the energy in the system to be the same, some of the water's potential energy changes to kinetic energy.

When water falls over a dam, it has energy of motion, or kinetic energy. The water held behind the dam also has kinetic energy. It is in each molecule of water.

The total kinetic energy of the molecules in a sample of matter is its **thermal energy.** The thermal energy of matter depends on the total kinetic energy of each molecule in it. For example, a 20 °C baseball has thermal energy whether it's sitting on the ground or speeding through the air. The molecules that make up a baseball have kinetic energy. The thermal energy of the baseball comes from its molecules.

The ability to transfer thermal energy is important for our survival. We need it to cook food, keep warm, or cool off. You put a pot on a stove and turn on the burner. The burner gets warm and heats the pot. The soup inside gets hot. As your older sister gets ready for school, she may use an electric curling iron. The curling iron uses electricity to transfer thermal energy from it to her hair.

A baseball has thermal energy whether it's flying through the air or lying on the ground. The thermal energy of a baseball comes from its molecules.

Meteoroids are destroyed by thermal energy. Friction between a meteoroid and Earth's atmosphere generates enough heat to vaporize the meteoroid. Friction generates heat energy.

Have you guessed that thermal energy is somehow related to heat? Thermal energy is the energy coming from an object's vibrating molecules. **Heat** is the transfer of thermal energy between objects because of their difference in temperature. The flow of thermal energy always goes from higher temperatures to lower temperatures. When we ask someone to "heat dinner" we are asking the person to add thermal energy to the food and make the food warmer. Cooking food adds heat to it.

The electricity heats the curling iron. The heat can be transferred to her hair.

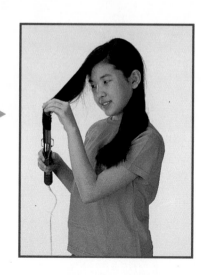

Friction between this meteorite and Earth's atmosphere generates heat.

Hot and Cold

If you have a cup of soup in your hands, how does the cup feel? If you hold a bowl of ice cream in your hands, how does the bowl feel? When the air temperature outside is high, you probably say it feels hot. When you take something from the freezer, you probably say it feels cold.

The words *hot* and *cold* aren't very scientific. When you talk about how hot or cold something feels, you are talking about its temperature. *Hot* usually means high temperature. *Cold* usually means low temperature. In fact, **temperature** is a measure of the average kinetic energy of the molecules within matter. Temperature helps us estimate the amount of thermal energy in matter. Our sense of touch also lets us estimate the amount of thermal energy in something. But our senses are sometimes fooled.

When we hold a cup of hot cocoa, we can feel its warmth in our hands. If we put the cup of cocoa on the counter in the kitchen, after a while we feel that the cocoa is cold. The cocoa is the same temperature as everything around it. Where did the thermal energy of the cocoa go?

At first, the cocoa in the cup is hot. Its molecules have a lot of kinetic energy. The fast-moving molecules in the cocoa move around. Some of them bump into the slower-moving molecules of the cup. This slows down some of the molecules in the cocoa. But the molecules in the cup start to move faster. Some of the faster-moving molecules in the cup bump into the slower-moving molecules in the air and the countertop. This slows down some of the molecules in the cup. But the molecules in the air and countertop started moving faster. After a while, all of the molecules in the cocoa, the cup, the air, and the countertop are moving at the same speed.

This is an example of kinetic energy being transferred from an object with higher energy to one with lower energy. The object with higher temperature has faster-moving molecules, or higher kinetic energy. The object with lower temperature has slower-moving molecules, or lower kinetic energy. When the molecules come in contact (bump into each other), the faster molecules slow down and the slower molecules speed up.

Thermal energy that flows from an object at a higher temperature to an object at a lower temperature is heat. Notice that heat always flows from objects with higher temperature to objects with lower temperatures. That's how we can feel that the cup of cocoa is hot. How do we feel that things are cold? The energy from your hand flows *to* something that is cold. What you feel as cold is the heat leaving your hand.

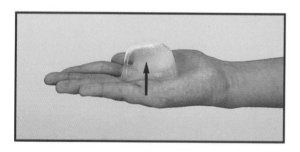

Heat flows from the hot cocoa to the cup to your hand. It makes your hand feel warm. Heat flows from your hand to the ice cube. It makes your hand feel cold.

Conduction, Convection, and Radiation

Heat flows in three ways, by conduction, convection, and radiation. In **conduction,** thermal energy flows from one body of matter to another because they touch. The examples of the warm cocoa on the counter and the ice cube in your hand were both methods of transferring heat by conduction. The thermal energy flows from one body to another without carrying any of the first body's matter with it. If you heat soup in a pot on the stove, the whole pot becomes warm. By applying heat from the stove's burner, the bottom of the pot gets warm. The thermal energy is conducted from the warm part of the pot to the rest of the pot. The pot then conducts thermal energy to the soup inside it.

Some substances conduct heat better than others. Wood, plastic, air and glass do not conduct heat as well as metal does. Solids conduct heat better than liquids or gases do. That's because the molecules in solids are closer together. It's easy for tightly packed molecules to conduct the transfer of thermal energy. Substances that conduct heat easily are **conductors.** They easily conduct thermal energy to things that touch them. Metals, such as iron and copper, are good conductors.

The soup inside the pot gets warm by conduction.

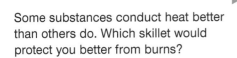

Some substances conduct heat better than others do. Which skillet would protect you better from burns?

The continuous exchange of hot and cold in a fluid is a convection current.

Convection is the transfer of thermal energy in a fluid. Gases and liquids are both considered fluids because they flow. When a fluid is heated, the warmer parts of the fluid expand and become less dense. The less dense parts rise because of their buoyancy (boy′ en sē′), or ability to float. Rising, warm fluid transfers heat to the surrounding cooler fluid. As thermal energy is transferred, the temperature of the warmer fluid drops. The fluid contracts, becomes denser, and sinks back down. This helps drive more warm fluid upward. This continuous exchange of warm and cold fluids is a convection current.

You can observe a convection current in hot water. If you put a pot of water on the stove to boil, the stove burner transfers thermal energy to the pot through conduction. The pot transfers thermal energy to the water through conduction. As the water begins to heat, air bubbles and warm water rise to the surface. Heat transfers to the cooler water at the surface through convection. The cooler water is more dense. The cooler water sinks and more hot water is forced upward. If the thermal energy continues to be transferred into the water, the water will change to gas. The gas will evaporate into the air. If left long enough, the pot will boil dry.

Convection currents in air can also cause air turbulence. Columns of warm air move upward. When the warm air reaches cooler air, thermal energy is transferred between the air layers. The cooler, denser air sinks downward. The faster this transference of thermal energy occurs, the more turbulence there is.

When a plane passes through an area of air turbulence, passengers get a bumpy ride!

Radiation is the transfer of thermal energy through air and space. Radiation does not require the presence of any matter to transfer thermal energy. Radiant heat is thermal energy transferred by radiation. It can travel through a vacuum. Conduction and convection, on the other hand, require the presence of matter to transfer thermal energy. The sun's energy reaches Earth by radiation.

During the past decade, various manufacturers have been researching new ways to harness radiant heat. The halogen hot plate, which transfers thermal energy from light, is one such invention. With a conventional hot plate, an electric coil transfers heat to a piece of lab equipment through conduction. With the halogen hot plate, a halogen lamp generates the heat. The heat is transferred by radiation. A halogen hot plate can boil 800 mL of water in 12 minutes. A conduction hot plate heats 800 mL of water in 20 minutes.

The lamp heats food through radiation.

CHECKPOINT

1. How do molecules give matter its potential and kinetic energy?

2. How can we use thermal energy?

3. Describe three ways that heat can be transferred.

? How does thermal energy travel through different types of matter?

ACTIVITY

Flowing Heat

Find Out

Do this activity to see which way heat flows.

Process Skills

Predicting
Measuring
Communicating
Inferring

WHAT YOU NEED

570-mL insulated foam cup

two 250-mL beakers

graph paper

two lab thermometers

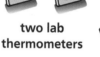

two heavy-duty, self-sealing plastic bags

clock or watch with a second hand

hot water

cold water

Activity Journal

WHAT TO DO

1. Place both self-sealing bags into the insulated foam cup. Make sure their openings are open. Push the bottoms of both bags firmly into the cup's bottom. Predict what will happen to the water temperature in each bag.

2. Measure 250 mL of hot water and pour it into one bag. Immediately pour 250 mL of cold water into the other bag.

3. Seal all but 1 cm of each bag closed. Leave just a small opening to insert a thermometer.

4. Put a thermometer in each bag. Hold them to make sure the tip is in the middle of the water and just above the bottom of the cup. Do not let the thermometers touch the bottom of the cup.

5. Use the thermometers to stir the water around inside the bag. Record the water temperature in each bag every 30 seconds for 15 minutes. Record your data.

6. Graph your data.

CONCLUSIONS

1. What happened to the temperature in the bag of hot water? In the bag of cold water?

2. Which bag of water gained thermal energy? What evidence do you have that this bag of water gained thermal energy?

3. Which bag of water lost thermal energy? What evidence do you have that this bag of water lost thermal energy?

4. How would you explain the temperature changes?

5. Infer which way the thermal energy flowed. Explain how you know this.

6. How do your results compare with your prediction from Step 1?

ASKING NEW QUESTIONS

1. What would happen if you had two bags of hot water and a bag of cold water in the cup?

2. What would happen if you used twice as much cold water?

SCIENTIFIC METHODS SELF CHECK

✔ Did I **make a prediction?**

✔ Did I **measure** and **record** my data?

✔ Did I **infer** the direction of the heat flow?

Energy Conversion

Find Out

- How to measure heat
- What happens when matter warms or cools
- How thermal energy can be used
- What insulation does

Vocabulary

**thermal expansion
contraction
expansion joints
mechanical energy
insulators**

The Big QUESTION

What happens when energy is transformed?

*K*nowing about thermal energy transfer is important for many reasons. When you know about conduction, you know that a metal spoon will get hot if you leave it in a pot on a hot stove burner. When you know about convection, you know that the heat from your home will escape if you leave the front door open in cold weather. When you know about radiation, you know that plastic cassettes or compact discs can be melted by the sun if left outside. Knowing about the transfer of thermal energy allows us to control it.

Measuring Heat

Thermal energy is the total kinetic energy of all the molecules in an object. Temperature is an estimate of thermal energy. But, it is not the same as thermal energy. Temperature does not take into account the number of molecules present in matter. Temperature does measure the average amount of kinetic energy that a sample of matter has. Low temperatures mean the average kinetic energy in the sample is low and the molecules are not moving very fast. High temperatures mean the average kinetic energy in the sample is high and the molecules are moving much faster.

Heat is the transfer of thermal energy between objects because of a difference in their temperatures. Heat is measured by its effect on a body of matter. The way we measure heat is by the calorie. A calorie is the amount of heat needed to change the temperature of 1 g of water 1 °C. The absorption of 1 calorie will change the temperature of a gram of water by 1 °C.

Four factors are involved in heat flow: the amount of energy added or removed, the amount of temperature change, the type of matter, and the amount of matter. The factors are used to measure specific heat. Specific heat is the amount of heat energy required to raise the temperature of 1 g of a substance 1 °C.

Every substance stores heat differently. Each substance has its own specific heat. Iron absorbs and loses heat quickly. It has a low specific heat. Water absorbs and loses heat slowly. The high specific heat of water is important. Because living things are mostly water, they can absorb heat from direct sunlight and still maintain their body temperature.

The molecules within matter are constantly moving. The faster the molecules within matter are moving, the higher its kinetic energy is.

Low kinetic energy

Medium kinetic energy

High kinetic energy

Thermal Properties of Matter

The amount of thermal energy an object has depends on its mass. Things with greater mass have more thermal energy. An iceberg has more thermal energy than a pan of boiling water because the iceberg has more mass.

Matter of the same size can have different thermal energies, too. The thermal energy in 5 kg of ice is different from the thermal energy in 5 kg of ice cream. There is more thermal energy in matter with greater densities.

Even when mass and temperature are the same, different kinds of matter can have different kinds of thermal energy because of their densities.

The state of matter depends on its temperature. At very cold temperatures, materials are usually solids. Their molecules are close together and stay in a tight order. When solids gain thermal energy, their molecules move faster. They move a little farther apart from each other, but they stay in their patterns. If you add more thermal energy to the matter, the molecules begin to lose some of their order and move even farther apart. When matter gets warm, its molecules take up more space. The transfer of thermal energy makes the molecules spread out. This is **thermal expansion.**

All matter undergoes thermal expansion when warmed. Whether matter is a gas, a liquid, or a solid, its molecules take up more space when heated. When cooled, some matter undergoes **contraction** and takes up less space. You've probably seen the results of this in a sidewalk. A sidewalk has different sections. Between each section is a space. Sometimes, the space is filled with some spongy material. Other times, the space is just empty. When it is cool outside, the spaces between the sidewalk sections get bigger. When it is hot outside, the spaces between the sections get smaller. The spaces are **expansion joints.** The builder puts them in intentionally. If there weren't any expansion joints, what would happen to the sidewalk when it got very hot or very cold?

If enough thermal energy is added or removed, the state of matter will change. When enough thermal energy is added, solids become liquids and liquids become gases. When enough thermal energy is removed, gases become liquids and liquids become solids. One of the physical properties of matter is the temperature at which it changes from one state to another.

Builders put expansion joints between sections of these bridges to avoid problems caused by thermal expansion or contraction.

Types of Energy

You have learned that energy is the ability to do work. Energy can change from one form to another. Different forms of energy are not very different from each other. Different types of energy include electromagnetic, thermal, chemical, nuclear, and mechanical.

Chemical energy is the energy in the bonds between atoms in molecules. In a chemical reaction, the bonds between molecules change. Nuclear energy is the energy in atoms. In a nuclear reaction, atoms are changed. During these reactions, energy is either released or it is absorbed. (You will learn more about the atom and molecules in Chapter 3.)

Mechanical energy is the energy of moving parts. For example, consider an electrical motor. When a motor is running, each part of the motor has mechanical energy. You know that motors can do all kinds of work. They can move fan blades, run air conditioners and furnaces, and more. Motors may have different sizes and shapes, but they all must have coils that produce magnetic fields. Electricity is the presence or movement of electrically charged particles called electrons. The principles that allow us to make motors are the same ones we use to make generators. Motors transform electrical energy into mechanical energy. Generators change mechanical energy into electrical energy.

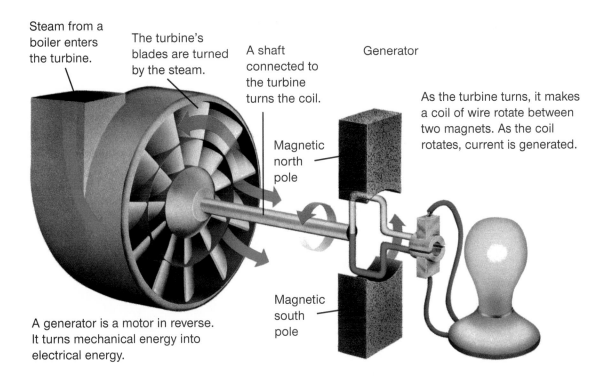

Steam from a boiler enters the turbine.

The turbine's blades are turned by the steam.

A shaft connected to the turbine turns the coil.

Generator

As the turbine turns, it makes a coil of wire rotate between two magnets. As the coil rotates, current is generated.

Magnetic north pole

Magnetic south pole

A generator is a motor in reverse. It turns mechanical energy into electrical energy.

Efficiency of Heat Conversion

You know that energy cannot be created or destroyed. It can be transferred, though. When energy is transferred from one body of matter to another, the amount of energy in the system stays the same. People can convert energy from one form to another. But, the conversion is never perfectly efficient. Energy is not lost. It is simply converted to a less useful form.

For instance, suppose you wanted to burn a stick of wood. You would add thermal energy to the wood. As the wood burns, not all of its energy becomes heat. When wood burns, chemical reactions change the wood into ash. You can see the wood change form. Some of the energy changes to light. You can see that too. Most of the potential energy stored in the wood, however, is released as heat. The thermal energy radiates out into the room. You can feel its warmth. Even though not all of the energy in the wood is transferred as thermal energy, the total amount of energy stays the same.

The forms of energy are similar. When energy is converted from one form to another, the total amount of energy in the system stays the same.

Using Thermal Energy

Knowing how to transfer thermal energy helps make our lives more comfortable. We can cook with it. We can generate electricity with it. We can run our vehicles with it. One of the most common ways we use thermal energy is to control the temperature inside of our homes.

We use our knowledge of the ways thermal energy can be transferred to heat our homes. Houses with furnaces have ducts, or tubes, that transfer thermal energy by convection. The ducts coming out of the furnace carry heated air up and away from it. Other ducts allow cooler air to return to the furnace. Some houses have hot-water heating systems. The water is heated by a boiler. Pipes carry hot water from the boiler to the rooms in the house. The water circulates in the pipes by convection. As the heated water passes through the pipes in a cold room, thermal energy heats the air in the room by radiation.

Air conditioners seem to violate the principles of thermal energy transfer. They seem to move thermal energy from a cooler place (inside) to a warmer place (outside). However, it is really thermal energy transfer that makes these cooling devices work.

Part of a window air conditioner is located outside. Tubes full of condensable gas or coolant run from inside to outside.

INSIDE — Expansion valve — **OUTSIDE**

Evaporator — Compressor — Fan — Condenser

Motor — Heated air

Blower

Cool dry air

Wall — Cooler outside air

Outside, the coolant vapor is compressed until it becomes a liquid. Compressing it forces it to release thermal energy.

Liquified coolant moves, still under pressure, into the building. It enters an evaporation coil where it has room to expand. It can become a vapor, but energy is required. Thermal energy is transferred from the room to the coolant.

The coolant returns outside. The thermal energy is released as the coolant is compressed. If you stand near an air conditioner outside, you notice that the exhaust thermal energy is warmer than the air around you.

In an air conditioner, an electrically powered compressor sprays a gas through the coils that are inside the house. The gas picks up thermal energy from the room air, becoming warmer as it travels through the coils. The gas is then compressed until it is a liquid. This liquid is hot, both from the compression and from the room heat it absorbed. When pumped through the coils on the outside of the house, the hot liquid gives up thermal energy to the outside air, which is cooler than the coils are. After losing some thermal energy, the liquid comes back indoors, expands into a gas, and flows into the coils inside the room. The gas temperature is now much lower than that of the room air. As the gas picks up thermal energy from the room, it cools the room air. This cycle continues as long as the air conditioner is turned on.

Insulators

Some materials work better than others in preventing the movement of thermal energy. Dry clothing feels warmer than wet clothing. Carpeted floors feel warmer than the bare floor next to them. The rate at which thermal energy moves through a substance is its heat conductivity. Substances that allow thermal energy to flow through them rapidly have high heat conductivity. They are conductors. Substances that slow down or prevent the flow of thermal energy have low heat conductivity. They are **insulators.**

Good insulators are materials like wool, wood, air, plastic, rubber, glass, and sulfur. These materials don't have high heat conductivity. Think about an insulated bottle. You can put hot cocoa in it and take it with you on a cold day. When you open the bottle, the cocoa inside is still warm. However, if you leave the bottle outside long enough, the cocoa eventually becomes cold. An insulated bottle is made of materials like glass or plastic that are separated by a space. These materials and the space keep hot things hot and cold things cold. An insulated bottle is not a perfect insulator. It just slows down the transfer of thermal energy.

We can use insulating materials to keep our homes from exchanging thermal energy with the outside air. Building insulation helps stop the flow of thermal energy into and out of our homes. When it is cold

What do these objects have
in common?

outside, the insulation in the walls keeps the thermal
energy inside the building from transferring outside.
When it is warm outside, the insulation keeps the
building from gaining thermal energy.

Different substances have different heat
conductivity. You probably know something about
conductors from studying electricity. The reason metals
are good conductors of thermal energy is the same
reason why they are good conductors of electricity. The
kinetic energy inside the molecules controls the flow of
thermal energy. Temperature affects the conductivity of
a material. Metals gradually lose conductivity as their
temperatures rise. On the other hand, nonmetals
gradually gain conductivity as their temperatures rise.

CHECKPOINT

1. What does temperature measure?
2. What happens to matter when it warms or cools?
3. How can knowledge of thermal energy transfer help
   us heat and cool our homes?
4. What makes a material a good insulator?

 What happens when energy is transformed?

ACTIVITY

Insulating for Energy Conservation

Find Out

Do this activity to learn ways to use energy more efficiently.

Process Skills

Measuring
Communicating
Experimenting
Using Numbers
Inferring

WHAT YOU NEED

large cooler full of ice

small cardboard box with lid

stack of newspapers

thermometer

clear plastic wrap

tape

hot water

scissors

plastic margarine tub

Activity Journal

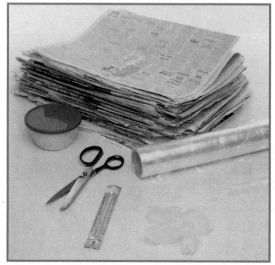

WHAT TO DO

1. Use your box to make a model house. Cut windows and doors into the sides. Cover the outside of the windows and doors with one layer of plastic wrap. Leave spaces around the window and door openings.

2. Place a thermometer inside the model house near one of the windows. Put very hot tap water into the margarine tub and place the tub inside the model house. This will act as the furnace for your house.

3. Put the model house into the cooler.

4. **Measure** and **record** the temperature inside the model house after 5 minutes, 10 minutes, and 15 minutes. Do your measuring quickly. Try not to leave your house exposed for more than 10 seconds.

5. **Experiment** with insulation. Remove your house from the cooler. Crumple some newspaper (about 2 cm thick) and place it near the walls and ceiling of your model. Double-pane the windows by putting another layer of clear plastic on the inside of the window and door openings. Make sure the door and windows are sealed tight, leaving no spaces.

6. Repeat Steps 3 and 4 as often as time permits.

7. **Chart** your data.

CONCLUSIONS

1. How much longer than the house *without* insulation did the house *with* insulation stay above 20 °C?

2. How did your results compare to those of others in your class?

3. Explain what the crumpled newspaper does.

ASKING NEW QUESTIONS

1. Make an **inference** about which house would need the least energy to keep it comfortable on a cold day.

2. How could you test materials for use in insulating buildings?

SCIENTIFIC METHODS SELF CHECK

✔ Did I **measure** and **record** changes in temperature?

✔ Did I **experiment** with different amounts of insulation?

✔ Did I **chart** my data?

✔ Did I **infer** one way in which energy can be conserved?

Energy Transfer and Consumption

Find Out

- How to figure energy efficiency
- How fossil fuels were formed
- How turbines convert kinetic energy to electrical energy
- What some of the problems with using fossil fuels are

Vocabulary

efficiency
electric power
fossil fuels
reservoirs

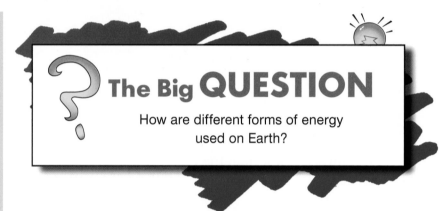

The Big QUESTION

How are different forms of energy used on Earth?

Before 1900, humans used plants and animals as their main energy resources. Animals were used for land transportation and to clear fields. Hand tools like saws and axes were used to cut trees. Wood was used to make furniture, to build houses, for heat, and to cook food. Laundry was washed by hand. In fact, throughout most of history, people have lived without frozen food, motor vehicles, and electrical appliances.

Using Energy

Today, more energy is used to do work than ever before. Machines do most of the work that was once done by animals. Trains, planes, cars, and trucks are used for transportation. Power tools are used to cut trees and wood. Other machines are used to make our furniture, cook our food, and warm our homes. Water is piped directly into our homes. We use machines to clean our clothes and our dishes. All of these machines need a different kind of energy resource than animals do. Energy resources used for machines are fuels.

This electric power substation in Detroit, Michigan, takes in high-voltage power and sends low-voltage power out to homes and businesses.

Energy Efficiency

People and other living things almost always need to change energy from one form to another in order to use it. You can't get warm by sitting next to a lump of coal or stick of wood. The energy in the coal or wood has to be converted into a usable form. You have to burn the coal or wood to make heat. When you change energy from one form to another, only part of the energy is changed into the form of energy desired. The remainder becomes energy that isn't used. **Efficiency** (e fish′ in sē′) is the percentage of the energy that is converted into the desired form.

Electricity that comes from electrical energy is one of the forms of energy you use most often. Electricity influences the daily lives of people throughout the world. Many of us depend on electrical devices to make our lives safer, healthier, easier, and more enjoyable. People who use electrical devices often depend on them. They don't even notice them most of the time— until something goes wrong.

Electrical energy is usually described in terms of how fast it is used. **Electric power** is measured by the rate at which energy is used. Electric power is measured in watts, or joules of energy used in a second. One kilowatt is 1000 watts. A 100-watt lightbulb uses 100 watts of electric power. When you watch TV, your television uses about 200 watts of electric power. A kilowatt-hour is the amount of energy used when you consume one kilowatt of electric power in one hour. If a 100-watt lightbulb is turned on for 1000 hours in a year, it consumes 100 kilowatt-hours in a year. If you watch TV for 365 hours per year, you consume 73 kilowatt-hours per year. An electric power plant can produce as much as 300 billion kilowatt-hours per year.

All energy conversions have thermal energy as a by-product. For example, 90 percent of the electrical energy in a lightbulb is converted into thermal energy. When you were younger, you may have noticed that a lightbulb can get hot enough to burn you. Only about 10 percent of the electrical energy that comes to a lightbulb is converted into light. This means the lightbulb is about 10 percent efficient. No one has been able to create a machine that is 100 percent efficient.

Fossil Fuels

Coal is a fossil fuel that is mined from the ground.

Fuels are substances that are burned for energy. The most common sources of power are fossil fuels. Fuels that are formed in Earth from once-living things are **fossil fuels**. Fossil fuels are coal, oil, and natural gas. These fuels supply about 90 percent of the energy we use in the United States. As you know, fossil fuels are not renewable energy resources. Therefore, engineers and other scientists are working to develop renewable forms of energy. They are also working to design machines that require less use of these energy resources. How would you classify fossil fuels?

Fossil fuels formed on Earth millions of years ago in two main ways. Coal formed from the matter of once-living plants that decayed in places with no oxygen. The matter was compacted and heated. Chemical reactions occurred that eventually produced coal. Coal formed in layers, or seams. The seams can be near the surface of Earth or deep within it. Coal seams range in thickness from about 2 cm to more than 30 m.

Coal is dug or mined from the ground. Coal that is almost pure carbon is hard coal or anthracite. Coal that is mixed with other elements, like sulfur, is soft coal or bituminous coal. In the United States, soft coal is the preferred choice for use in coal-fired power plants because it burns easily and has a high heating value. However, coal with too much sulfur in it will cause pollution. Coal is not very explosive. It is safe to transport and store.

People have been burning coal as an energy resource since at least the 1200s. In the 1900s, most of the energy used in the United States came from coal. By 1988, coal supplied 57 percent of the electricity used in the United States. It was the source of more than 25 percent of the total energy used in the United States. In 1989, the average coal-burning electric plant could generate 230 megawatts of electricity. That's enough power to supply a city of 100,000 people with electricity every day.

Oil and natural gas formed from the matter of once-living things deposited on the ocean floor. The dead matter was covered with sand, silt, and clay. These coverings increased the pressure on and temperature of the dead matter. At high temperature and pressure, chemical reactions occurred in the matter. The results of these reactions are oil and natural gas.

Oil is a liquid and natural gas is a gas. Liquids and gases can flow or move. When newly formed, the oil and natural gas moved through the sediments below the ocean floor into spaces in the sandstone. Usually, bends or blockages in the sandstone would stop the flow of oil or gas. These places formed pockets called **reservoirs.** Reservoirs of natural gas and oil are usually found together. The sandstone at the bottom of a reservoir is usually saturated with oil. Natural gas sits above the oil in the spaces in the sandstone. This happens because natural gas is less dense than liquid oil.

Like coal, natural gas and oil are taken from the ground. People use drills to reach the reservoirs of natural gas or oil. Pipes are put in the drill hole and oil and gas are pumped up through the pipes. The pipes and pumps are oil and gas wells. Have you ever seen a gas or oil well?

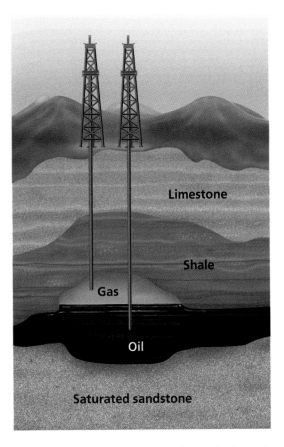

Natural gas and oil usually form at the same time.

These wells in California remove oil from the ground.

C67

Natural gas and oil burn easily because they are compounds of hydrogen and carbon. In fact, natural gas is very explosive. In 1989, natural gas supplied more than 10 percent of the energy used to generate electricity in the United States and more than 22 percent of its total energy. At that time, more than half of the homes in the United States used natural gas as their major heat source.

Oil is also explosive, but it is not as explosive as natural gas. Because oil is a liquid, it is the easiest fossil fuel to transport. A small amount of oil provides a lot of energy. So, it takes up the least space for the energy it provides. Oil is usually converted to transportation fuels. Oil is used to make plastics and other synthetic materials. Oil can also be burned for fuel.

Using Fossil Fuels

Fossil fuels contain stored energy. The stored chemical energy in fossil fuels is concentrated. It is easy to use and, when burned, produces intense heat. Unlike some of the energy sources you learned about in Chapter 1, fossil fuels can be stored and transported to where they are needed. Finding new places where fossil fuels are in the ground is an area of active scientific research.

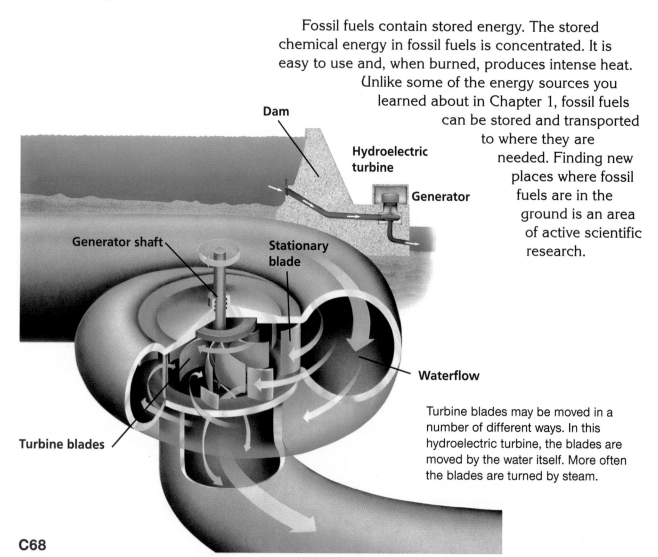

Dam

Hydroelectric turbine

Generator

Generator shaft

Stationary blade

Waterflow

Turbine blades

Turbine blades may be moved in a number of different ways. In this hydroelectric turbine, the blades are moved by the water itself. More often the blades are turned by steam.

When fossil fuels are burned, their stored chemical energy is converted to thermal energy. The thermal energy may be used to heat something. Usually, it is converted to another form, such as mechanical or electrical energy.

Electricity is created by converting another kind of energy (usually mechanical) to electrical energy. You reviewed mechanical energy in the previous lesson. You learned that it is converted to electrical energy with a generator. One way to power a generator is with a turbine. A turbine is a wheel with blades that is powered by a fluid. Some large turbines are powered by steam created from heating water with burning coal or oil. In making steam, some of the energy becomes heat. The efficiency of most oil-burning electrical turbines is 30–40 percent. This means that 30–40 percent of the energy in the oil is converted to electricity. The rest of the energy escapes from the turbine as heat.

Steam Turbine and Generator

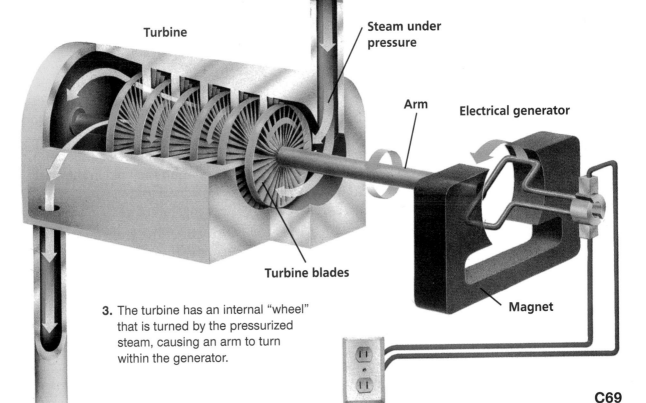

1. Water is heated until it turns to steam, which is put under tremendous pressure.

2. The pressurized steam is passed through a pipe into the turbine.

4. The generator is a giant magnet. As the arm turns within the magnet, electrons are freed and move through wires to become electricity.

Turbine

Steam under pressure

Arm

Electrical generator

Turbine blades

3. The turbine has an internal "wheel" that is turned by the pressurized steam, causing an arm to turn within the generator.

Magnet

Problems with Fossil Fuels

Most people would prefer to use energy resources that do not cause pollution. At this time, unfortunately, we do not have the necessary technology to make those alternative resources as useful as fossil fuels. Many renewable and inexhaustible energy resources are more costly to use than fossil fuels. Currently, fossil fuels account for about 90 percent of the world's energy use. Fossil fuels are used directly by motor vehicles and other gasoline-powered machinery. They are also used indirectly as sources of electricity. They can be taken from Earth, stored, and transported to where they are needed.

There is a limited supply of the three main fossil fuels in the world. At the current rate of world use, known supplies of oil and natural gas will be gone before the end of the twenty-first century. Plus, getting more oil and gas out of the ground will likely become more difficult. Known supplies that are easy to get to have already been used. If new supplies are found, they are likely to be in areas that make it more difficult to take them from the ground. For instance, new oil and natural gas supplies may be discovered in Antarctica. The extreme climate and transportation problems would make the use of these supplies very difficult.

Besides the limited supply, there are other problems with using fossil fuels for energy. Gasoline, which is made from oil and burned to power our cars, is a huge part of our fossil-fuel use. One of the main by-products of burning oil resources is pollution. Smog and air pollution are two of the most obvious problems resulting from the use of oil. Scientists and engineers are working on reducing the amount of gasoline needed to power many engines. Cars have been designed that get more kilometers per liter of fuel than they did in the past. Other cars have been designed that use natural gas or electric-powered motors instead of gasoline engines.

Because of concern about the limited supplies of oil and natural gas, coal is the fuel used in most electrical plants in the United States. One advantage of coal is that it is more plentiful than oil or natural gas. In fact, the United States has more coal deposits than any other country in the world. However, much of the coal buried in the United States is difficult to obtain and use. New methods for mining coal are needed for us to reach and remove some of these coal deposits.

Burning gasoline creates pollution.

Also, U.S. coal resources include coal that creates a lot of pollution when it is burned. This type of coal has not been used in the past because of this pollution. If coal has a lot of sulfur in it, the sulfur becomes sulfur dioxide when the coal is burned. Acid rain occurs when sulfur dioxide combines with nitrogen oxide, water, and other substances in the atmosphere. These substances eventually produce acids that fall out of the atmosphere with rain. Acid rain damages almost all matter it comes in contact with. There are ways to burn coal and reduce acid rain as shown in the illustration below.

Crushed coal is burned on a bed of limestone, producing energy more efficiently than by conventional methods. In one such method, coal is converted to gas. The gas is used to generate electricity. As a result of this process, sulfur becomes sulfur crystals, rather than sulfur dioxide.

A Method of Burning High-Sulfur Coal to Reduce Sulfur Emissions

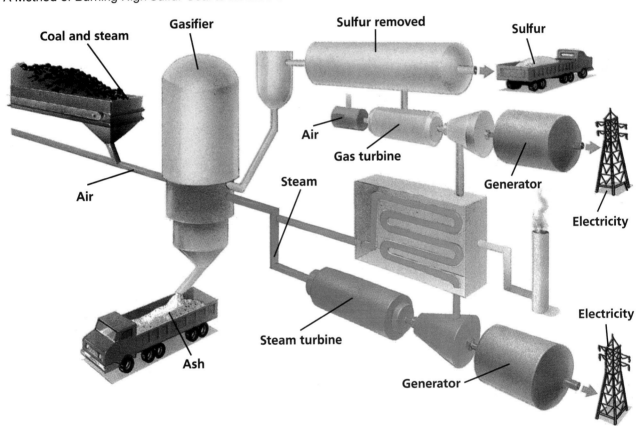

CHECKPOINT

1. What is energy efficiency?
2. How were fossil fuels formed?
3. How do turbines work?
4. What problems occur with fossil fuel use?
   How are different forms of energy used on Earth?

C71

ACTIVITY
Transferring Energy

Find Out

Do this activity to learn how long it takes to heat water using two different heat sources.

Process Skills

Experimenting
Measuring
Communicating

WHAT YOU NEED

cardboard box

clear plastic wrap

black plastic

thermal mitts

newspaper

funnel

thermometer

20-cm rubber hose

water

two 250-mL glass beakers

pushpin

Activity Journal

two straws

hot plate

clay

masking tape

WHAT TO DO

1. Construct a solar energy collector (see the illustration of a completed collector). Line a box with crumpled newspaper. Tape black plastic in place over the newspaper. Plug one end of a straw with clay. With your pushpin, punch 12 holes in one side of the straw. Put a piece of rubber hose on the open end of the straw. Tape the straw in place at the top of the box. Attach the other end of the hose to the end of the funnel. Cover the box with the clear plastic wrap and tape it in place. Cut the other straw to make a drainage pipe. Make a hole at the base of the box and place the straw in it. Seal the area around the straw with clay and masking tape so that the straw is not sticking up too much inside the box.

2. Place the box in the sun. Tilt it so that the bottom is perpendicular to the sun's rays. Place one beaker under the drainpipe of the box. Start with 250 mL of cold tap water. Measure and record the starting water temperature. While holding the funnel, slowly pour the water into it. Record how long it takes for all of the water to run into the beaker. Measure and record the water temperature.

3. Repeat Step 2 twice more, using the same water. Add all of the times together and record the total.

 Use thermal mitts in Step 4.

4. Measure 250 mL of cold water (the same starting temperature as in Step 2) into the beaker. Heat water with the hot plate. Record the temperature every 30 seconds. Note the time when the water temperature equals the final water temperature from Step 3.

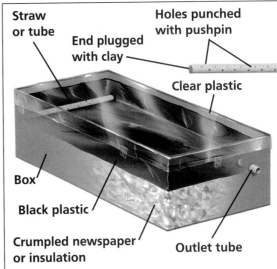

Straw or tube — End plugged with clay — Holes punched with pushpin — Clear plastic — Box — Black plastic — Crumpled newspaper or insulation — Outlet tube

CONCLUSIONS

1. What was the final water temperature using the solar collector?
2. How long did it take the hot plate to heat the water to that temperature?

ASKING NEW QUESTIONS

1. What are some of the benefits of using solar heating?
2. What are some of the drawbacks of using solar heating?

SCIENTIFIC METHODS SELF CHECK

✔ Did I **experiment** with two ways to heat water?

✔ Did I **measure** and **record** the time and temperatures accurately?

Review

Reviewing Vocabulary and Concepts

Write the letter of the answer that best completes each sentence.

1. ___ is the transfer of thermal energy between objects because of a difference in their temperatures.
   a. Movement
   b. Convection
   c. Heat
   d. Fueling

2. In conduction, thermal energy flows from one body of matter to another through ___.
   a. metal
   b. direct contact
   c. glass
   d. air currents

3. Thermal expansion is the transfer of thermal energy, which makes molecules ___.
   a. contract
   b. spread out
   c. bigger
   d. smaller

4. Substances that slow down or prevent the flow of thermal energy are ___.
   a. conductors
   b. insulators
   c. walls
   d. thick

5. ___ is the rate at which energy is used.
   a. Electric power
   b. Electricity
   c. Heat
   d. Mechanical energy

Match the definition on the left with the correct term.

6. the total energy in matter
7. measure of the average kinetic energy of molecules in matter
8. the energy of moving parts
9. areas within Earth where oil is trapped
10. a rotary engine in which steam or water powers the blades

a. turbine
b. mechanical energy
c. temperature
d. thermal energy
e. reservoirs

Understanding What You Learned

1. Explain three ways to transfer heat.
2. What is used to measure heat in different kinds of matter?
3. How is energy transferred when no matter is present?
4. How do insulating materials help save energy?
5. How does a turbine convert mechanical energy to electricity?

Applying What You Learned

1. How are temperature and thermal energy related?
2. How can thermal energy be removed from matter?
3. How does a hang glider or a soaring bird use convection currents?
4. Why should heating vents be placed near the floor and air conditioning vents be placed near the ceiling?
5. Explain why wooden spoons are safer to use than metal spoons when cooking.
6. Where would you need to include expansion joints in a building or construction project?
7. Why are some windows made of two panes of glass separated by a space filled with air?
8. Why is energy efficiency important?
9. What are some problems that result from using fossil fuels for energy resources?
 10. How can energy be produced and transferred?

For Your Portfolio

Write a list of as many songs as you can think of that mention fire, ice, heat, or coldness. Then, write a paragraph about whether any of the songs convey the importance of heat or fire to people.

3

Chemical Properties

Matter is anything that has mass and takes up space. Each kind of matter has characteristics that can be observed without changing the makeup of the substance. These characteristics are the physical properties of matter. Mass, volume, and density are physical properties of matter. The color, shape, taste, odor, hardness, and state of matter are physical properties, too.

Everything we feel, hear, see, smell, and taste exists because of matter. Most of our knowledge of the world around us depends on our knowledge of matter. We can identify its structure. We can take matter apart and put it back together again. We can figure out how different types of matter interact with each other. We can observe the way matter reacts or doesn't react with other matter. We can also understand how and why the properties of matter exist the way they do.

The Big IDEA

Matter has identifiable properties and can change when interacting with other matter.

CHAPTER SCIENCE INVESTIGATION

Identify and classify materials according to their physical and chemical properties. Find out how in your *Activity Journal.*

Properties of Matter

Find Out

- What some physical properties of matter are
- What some chemical properties of matter are
- What the parts of an atom are

Vocabulary

chemical property
atom
electrons
nucleus
proton
neutron

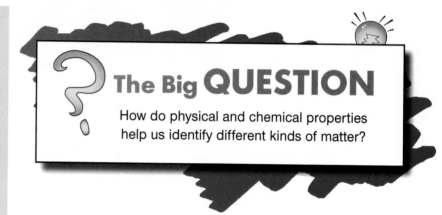

The Big QUESTION

How do physical and chemical properties help us identify different kinds of matter?

We experience changes in matter so often that sometimes we are not even aware when they happen. We see ice melting in a glass. We bake a cake using flour, water, baking soda, and other ingredients. We digest food. How are these changes alike and how are they different?

Physical Properties of Matter

Matter has both physical and chemical properties. You know that by adding thermal energy to matter you can change the state of matter. The state of matter is one of its physical properties. A physical property is a property, or characteristic, of a substance that can be observed without changing its chemical nature. Matter does not change chemically when it changes from one state to another. Matter can exist in the form of a solid, a liquid, or a gas, depending on the temperature and the pressure. Its chemical properties stay the same.

The temperature at which matter changes from one state to another is one of its physical properties. Solids change to liquids at the melting point. Liquids change to solids at their freezing points. The melting point and freezing point of a substance are the same temperature.

The temperature at which a liquid changes to gas is the boiling point. When a gas changes to liquid, the process of condensation happens. Condensation and boiling happen at the same temperature for a substance. Most types of matter have their own specific temperatures at which they freeze and boil. For example, water freezes at 0 °C. It boils at 100 °C.

Two other physical properties of matter that you might know something about are mass and volume. The mass of something is the amount of matter it contains. The volume is the amount of space it occupies. You can use mass and volume to find out another physical property of matter—its density. Density is the amount of mass per unit volume of matter. Density explains why some things float. A balloon filled with air will float on water. A balloon filled with hot air will rise above the more dense surface air. Air is much less dense than water, so the air-filled balloon floats on water. Hot air is less dense than cool air, so a hot-air balloon will float into the air.

Knowing the physical properties of matter allows us to use them in different ways. Heating the air in this hot-air balloon will make the balloon float.

Other physical properties of matter are texture, odor, and hardness. Texture is the physical property of how matter feels to the touch. Rough, grainy, slippery, and smooth are all different ways to describe how matter feels. Odor is also a physical property of matter. Sometimes you can easily tell what you're going to have for dinner by its odor. Baked turkey smells different from baked fish. You can also tell a gas leak by its odor. Natural gas companies add a distinctive-smelling chemical to natural gas. It has an unpleasant smell, like rotten eggs.

Hardness is a physical property that tells us how hard something is compared to something else. Pencils have the soft mineral graphite in them. Graphite is a form of carbon. Graphite is one of the softest minerals. Diamonds are also a form of carbon. Diamond is the hardest mineral. Scientists use hardness to classify some minerals and gems.

Color and shape are also physical properties of matter. How can you use color and shape to help you identify objects such as the ones shown here?

Chemical Properties of Matter

The ingredients used to make a cake change when they are baked. They are no longer the same substances. When you eat the cake, you digest it. The food changes into nutrients for your body's cells. The cake changes into different substances. Chemical changes create new and different substances.

A **chemical property** describes how a substance can react with another substance to form a new, third substance. Chemical properties of matter determine whether one material will react with another to form a new material. Substances with similar physical properties may not have similar chemical properties. The chemical properties of matter allow us to use different materials in different ways.

If you leave your bike out in the rain long enough, it will rust. The rusted metal on your bike is not the same chemical as the nonrusted metal. Rust is a substance that forms because of the chemical properties of iron, water, and oxygen. In the presence of water in the rain, oxygen chemically interacts with the iron in your bike. A new chemical is formed. It is iron oxide. The chemical process that occurs when oxygen is involved is oxidation.

If a material fails to interact with another material, that is also a chemical property. Zinc does not interact with oxygen and water. Iron pipes used in plumbing are sometimes coated with zinc. The zinc protects the iron in the pipes from oxidation. Without the zinc coating, the chemical properties of the iron would cause the pipes to rust. The iron in the pipes would become iron oxide.

Iron oxide has different physical properties from iron. Iron is a hard solid. It has a high density. Iron oxide is a softer solid. Its density is lower. Iron oxide breaks easily. It will not support a structure, like your bike frame, or hold liquids, like the plumbing pipes.

Houses, cars, and ships are painted to protect their surfaces from rotting or rusting. The paint does not change the physical properties of the wood or metal. Wood is still wood after it has been painted. Metal is still metal after it has been painted. Exposure to rain, road salts, and seawater can cause wood and metal to react and form different materials. The paint provides a physical barrier between the wood or metal and the environment.

This rusted chain is an example of what happens when water and oxygen chemically interact with iron to form iron oxide.

Chemical Reactions

The formation of new substances as a result of chemical changes between substances is called a chemical reaction. Chemical reactions can break down substances or allow them to combine into new substances. What happens to substances when they undergo chemical reactions? The substances are not destroyed. Burning paper creates ash and gases. The amounts of ash and gases created equal the amount of paper that was burned. The amounts of ingredients in cake batter equal the amount of cake that is made.

This principle of conservation of mass applies in all chemical reactions. It is a physical law. The law of conservation of mass states that mass is neither created nor destroyed in a chemical reaction. All the mass present in the substances before a chemical reaction is still present after the chemical reaction. The new substance has the same total amount of mass as the old substances that formed it did.

In all chemical changes, energy is involved. Energy is either released during a chemical reaction or absorbed during a chemical reaction. The energy may be in the form of heat, light, or electricity.

The Atom

We can explain the chemical and physical changes that occur in matter by the parts that make up matter. You may recall that all matter is made of atoms. An **atom** is the smallest unit of matter that cannot be broken down chemically. Atoms are not directly visible. They are extremely small. If you could lay atoms in a straight line, side by side, it would take about ten million atoms to extend 1 mm. That's about the size of a dot you make with a pencil. Even though atoms are very tiny, some advanced types of microscopes can detect their presence. Scientists have also discovered even smaller units that make up atoms.

The idea of the atom may have come indirectly from the ancient Chinese view of matter. In about 1700 B.C., Shu Ching proposed that all matter consisted of combinations of five elements—earth, metal, air, fire, and water. In 444 B.C., the Greek philosopher Empedocles (em pe′ də klēz) proposed that all matter consisted of only four elements—earth, air, fire, and water.

However, another Greek philosopher, Democritus (də mä′ kri təs), challenged this view. He was curious about what would happen if a piece of iron was cut into smaller and smaller pieces. His hypothesis was that eventually you would end up with such a small piece that it could no longer be cut. Democritus was describing atoms. He made up the word *atomos* for these small pieces. *Atomos* is the Greek word for "uncut." Democritus believed that these small pieces, which could not be cut, were the smallest particles of matter.

About 1300 years ago, scientists in India had a different view. They accepted the idea that all matter was created from just a few elements. They also developed an atomic theory. They suggested that each type of element had its own class of atoms that could not be divided into smaller units. This atomic theory was the first one that tried to explain the way different types of matter react with each other.

For the past 200 years, modern science has worked to develop tools to test the theory that different types of atoms make up matter. In 1803, the English chemist John Dalton restated the atomic theory. He proposed that matter is composed of atoms. Dalton thought that atoms of the same element were identical, but atoms of different elements were not alike. He also suggested that atoms combine to form compounds. This is still the current theory.

Greek symbols for earth, air, fire, and water

Inside the Atom

It took nearly 100 years before scientists learned that the atom is not the smallest particle making up matter. Sir Joseph John Thomson and other scientists conducting experiments with static electricity in the late 1800s discovered a particle of an atom. These were very small, negatively charged particles. These particles are called **electrons.** The experiments led to the production of electricity. You know that electricity is the movement of electrons. When electrons flow through wires, they make electric current.

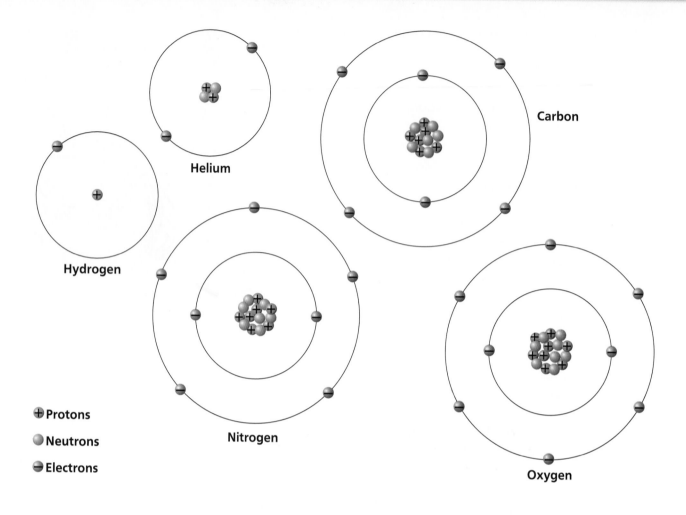

Helium

Carbon

Hydrogen

Nitrogen

Oxygen

⊕ Protons

◯ Neutrons

⊖ Electrons

About the same time that electrons were discovered, the scientist Ernest Rutherford found that atoms also contain a positively charged center. He called the tiny, very dense center of the atom a **nucleus.** He suggested that the negatively charged electrons travel around the positively charged nucleus. Rutherford also discovered that the nucleus had protons and neutrons. A **proton** is the positively charged part of the nucleus. A **neutron** has no charge—it is neutral. The chemical and physical changes that occur in matter can be explained in terms of these three units—electrons, protons, and neutrons.

Ernest Rutherford and another scientist, Niels Bohr, designed a model for atoms in 1911. Their model had protons held tightly in a small, positively charged nucleus. The electrons in their model were pictured as small, negatively charged particles in orbit around the nucleus.

These models help us understand the physical and chemical properties of matter. The number of protons in the nucleus determines the identity of the atom. The atomic number of an atom is the number of protons the atom has in its nucleus. Every atom can be identified by its atomic number. Hydrogen has only one proton in its nucleus, so its atomic number is 1. Oxygen, on the other hand, has an atomic number of 8. No two elements have the same atomic number. Just like people can be identified by their fingerprints, atoms are identified by their numbers of protons. Can you identify the atomic number of the elements pictured on page C84?

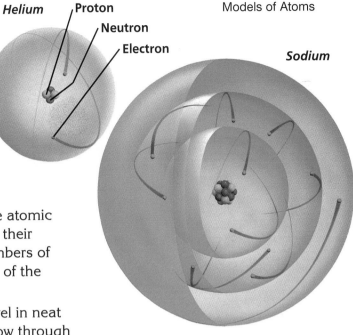

Helium **Proton**
Neutron
Electron
Models of Atoms
Sodium

Today, we know that electrons do not travel in neat orbits. They move from place to place and flow through wires. We also know that positive particles do not do this. Scientists believe that electrons are loosely held in the atom. They also believe that protons stay in the nucleus. The illustration on this page shows a current view of what scientists think an atom looks like.

Over time, scientists will continue to develop theories to explain the structure and behavior of the atom. They have already discovered that there are other parts of the atom besides electrons, neutrons, and protons. Some of the largest and most expensive scientific equipment on Earth is used to study the parts of atoms. These machines can accelerate atoms to incredibly high speeds. The machines let scientists observe the properties of the particles inside the atom.

Subatomic particles are studied in huge machines buried deep within the ground. The Fermi National Accelerator Lab in Batavia, Illinois, is one place where scientists can observe what's inside the atom.

CHECKPOINT

1. What are physical properties of matter?
2. Explain the difference between the physical and chemical properties of matter.
3. What are some of the parts in an atom?

 How do physical and chemical properties help us identify different kinds of matter?

ACTIVITY

Changing Water

Find Out

Do this activity to learn about some chemical properties of matter.

Process Skills

Measuring
Observing
Experimenting
Inferring

WHAT YOU NEED

three test tubes

apron

three droppers

5 mL water

5 cc each of baking powder, baking soda, cornstarch, and baby powder

marking pen

5 mL iodine solution

Activity Journal

5 mL vinegar

measuring spoon

safety goggles

masking tape

WHAT TO DO

1. Label your test tubes "Water," "Vinegar," and "Iodine."

2. Select the appropriate tool to measure about 1.25 cc of baking powder into each test tube. To the first test tube, add a dropper of water. Observe and record what happens.

3. To the second test tube, add a dropper of vinegar. Again, record your observations.

 **Wear your goggles and an apron. Be careful not to touch or spill the iodine solution. Wash your hands if you get iodine on them.**

4. To the third test tube, add a drop of iodine solution. Record your observations.

5. Rinse out the test tubes with water in an approved location. Repeat Steps 2–4, using baking soda, then cornstarch, and then baby powder instead of the baking powder.

6. Your teacher will give you an "unknown" sample to test. Experiment to determine what it is. Add it to the water, vinegar, or iodine solutions. Referring to your observation chart, try to identify this "unknown" sample. Record your observations.

CONCLUSIONS

1. What happened when you mixed the known substances with water, vinegar, or iodine solution? Were these combinations alike in any ways?

2. What is the identity of the "unknown" substance?

ASKING NEW QUESTIONS

1. What happened when you mixed the iodine with the baking powder?

2. What do you think might be in the baking powder?

SCIENTIFIC METHODS SELF CHECK

✔ Did I **measure** the substances correctly?

✔ Did I **observe** physical and chemical changes?

✔ Did I **experiment** to identify the unknown sample?

✔ Did I **infer** the identity of the unknown sample based on my results?

Ionic and Covalent Compounds

The Big QUESTION

What are ionic and covalent compounds?

Chemicals and chemical reactions are everywhere. At home, at school, in the grocery store, and at the movies, chemicals surround us. You know that iron rusts when it is exposed to oxygen and water. This new substance, rust, is actually the chemical iron oxide. This chemical has properties of its own that may be quite different from the elements that formed it.

Elements

You can identify matter by observing its physical properties. You can also observe the chemical properties of matter. When two substances react with each other and their chemical properties form a new substance, it is called a **compound.** A compound is a substance formed by two or more elements. Plastics, rubber, and nylon are compounds we use each day.

In the last lesson, you examined some line-drawing models of different types of atoms. You learned that the number of protons in the nucleus determines the identity of an atom. Every type of atom can be identified by its atomic number. Substances made up of only one type of atom are called **elements.** An element is a substance that cannot be broken down by physical or chemical means into a simpler substance. Each element is chemically unique. Research of more than a century has shown this comes from two factors. One of the factors is the atomic number of the atoms in the element. The other factor is the way the electrons are arranged in the atoms of the element.

You can classify elements by their atomic number. One kind of classification is the periodic table of the elements, as shown on pages C90 and C91. This table is based on patterns in the properties of the elements. These patterns were first recognized by Dmitry Mendeleyev (men də lā′ əf) and Lothar Meyer around 1870.

Substances made of one type of atom, like gold, copper, or sulfur, are elements.

The columns of elements in the periodic table of the elements have similar properties. The vertical columns are groups, or families, of elements. The rows that run across, from left to right, are periods. The properties of elements gradually change across a period.

Look at column 2 of the periodic table of the elements on page C90. The name of each element is written at the top of the block. The letters are symbols, or abbreviations, for each element. Find the elements beryllium, magnesium, calcium, strontium, barium, and radium. These are metallic elements. They will conduct electricity. Now, look at column 16 on page C91. Find the elements oxygen, sulfur, selenium, tellurium, and polonium. These elements are nonmetals. Most nonmetals do not conduct electricity.

Atoms of the same element can combine to form a molecule. Molecules of oxygen are in the air you breathe. Two oxygen atoms join to form one molecule of oxygen. Oxygen molecules have only oxygen atoms in them.

The Periodic Table of Elements

Key:

element name
atomic number
element symbol
1995 atomic mass

	1	2	3	4	5	6	7	8	9
1	hydrogen 1 **H** 1.008								
2	lithium 3 **Li** 6.941	beryllium 4 **Be** 9.012							
3	sodium 11 **Na** 22.990	magnesium 12 **Mg** 24.305							
4	potassium 19 **K** 39.098	calcium 20 **Ca** 40.078	scandium 21 **Sc** 44.956	titanium 22 **Ti** 47.88	vanadium 23 **V** 50.942	chromium 24 **Cr** 51.996	manganese 25 **Mn** 54.9380	iron 26 **Fe** 55.847	cobalt 27 **Co** 58.933
5	rubidium 37 **Rb** 85.468	strontium 38 **Sr** 87.62	yttrium 39 **Y** 88.906	zirconium 40 **Zr** 91.224	niobium 41 **Nb** 92.906	molybdenum 42 **Mo** 95.94	technetium 43 **Tc** 97.907	ruthenium 44 **Ru** 101.07	rhodium 45 **Rh** 102.906
6	cesium 55 **Cs** 132.905	barium 56 **Ba** 137.327	lanthanum 57 **La** 138.906	hafnium 72 **Hf** 178.49	tantalum 73 **Ta** 180.948	tungsten 74 **W** 183.85	rhenium 75 **Re** 186.207	osmium 76 **Os** 190.2	iridium 77 **Ir** 192.22
7	francium 87 **Fr** 223.02	radium 88 **Ra** 226.025	actinium 89 **Ac** 227.028	rutherfordium 104 **Rf** 261	dubnium 105 **Db** 262	seaborgium 106 **Sg** 263	bohrium 107 **Bh** 264	hassium 108 **Hs** 265	meitnerium 109 **Mt** 266

Properties of elements help us to classify them by their atomic number.

Lanthanide series

cerium 58 **Ce** 140.115	praseodymium 59 **Pr** 140.908	neodymium 60 **Nd** 144.24	promethium 61 **Pm** 144.913	samarium 62 **Sm** 150.36	europium 63 **Eu** 151.965

Actinide series

thorium 90 **Th** 232.038	protactinium 91 **Pa** 231.036	uranium 92 **U** 238.029	neptunium 93 **Np** 237.048	plutonium 94 **Pu** 244.064	americium 95 **Am** 243.061

10	11	12	13	14	15	16	17	18
								helium 2 **He** 4.003
			boron 5 **B** 10.811	carbon 6 **C** 12.011	nitrogen 7 **N** 14.007	oxygen 8 **O** 15.999	fluorine 9 **F** 18.998	neon 10 **Ne** 20.180
			aluminum 13 **Al** 26.982	silicon 14 **Si** 28.086	phosphorus 15 **P** 30.974	sulfur 16 **S** 32.066	chlorine 17 **Cl** 35.453	argon 18 **Ar** 39.948
nickel 28 **Ni** 58.693	copper 29 **Cu** 63.546	zinc 30 **Zn** 65.39	gallium 31 **Ga** 69.723	germanium 32 **Ge** 72.61	arsenic 33 **As** 74.922	selenium 34 **Se** 78.96	bromine 35 **Br** 79.904	krypton 36 **Kr** 83.80
palladium 46 **Pd** 106.42	silver 47 **Ag** 107.868	cadmium 48 **Cd** 112.411	indium 49 **In** 114.82	tin 50 **Sn** 118.710	antimony 51 **Sb** 121.757	tellurium 52 **Te** 127.60	iodine 53 **I** 126.904	xenon 54 **Xe** 131.290
platinum 78 **Pt** 195.08	gold 79 **Au** 196.967	mercury 80 **Hg** 200.59	thallium 81 **Tl** 204.383	lead 82 **Pb** 207.2	bismuth 83 **Bi** 208.980	polonium 84 **Po** 208.982	astatine 85 **At** 209.987	radon 86 **Rn** 222.018
(unnamed) 110 **Uun**	(unnamed) 111 **Uuu**	(unnamed) 112 **Uub**						

gadolinium 64 **Gd** 157.25	terbium 65 **Tb** 158.925	dysprosium 66 **Dy** 162.50	holmium 67 **Ho** 164.930	erbium 68 **Er** 167.26	thulium 69 **Tm** 168.934	ytterbium 70 **Yb** 173.04	lutetium 71 **Lu** 174.967
curium 96 **Cm** 247.070	berkelium 97 **Bk** 247.070	californium 98 **Cf** 251.080	einsteinium 99 **Es** 252.083	fermium 100 **Fm** 257.095	mendelevium 101 **Md** 258.099	nobelium 102 **No** 259.101	lawrencium 103 **Lr** 260.105

Compounds

Common table salt is formed when sodium atoms and chlorine atoms combine. Note that the ionic bond is the transfer of an electron from sodium to chlorine.

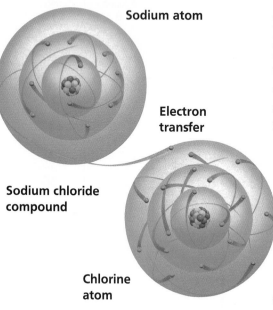

Sodium atom

Electron transfer

Sodium chloride compound

Chlorine atom

Chlorine molecule

Neutron

Electron

Proton

Covalent bonds form when atoms share electrons. Chlorine molecules form from covalent bonds between atoms of chlorine.

When two or more elements combine chemically, they form compounds. Compounds have more than one kind of atom in them. They contain atoms from all of the elements that are in the compound. Compounds form during chemical reactions because of the chemical activity of the elements that are involved.

Think about how many letters there are in the alphabet. Now think about the number of words you know. You know more than 26 words. You probably know many thousands of words! Just as the letters of the alphabet combine to form words, elements can combine to form compounds. How many compounds do you think there are? Scientists have discovered over thirteen million of them. As they continue to discover new elements, they also continue to find more compounds.

How do compounds form? You know that electrons are loose, movable particles that travel around the nucleus of atoms. The ability of an element to form compounds comes from how easily it gains or loses electrons. Metals tend to lose electrons when they react with other elements. On the other hand, nonmetals tend to gain electrons when they react with other elements.

A charged particle called an **ion** is formed when atoms gain or lose electrons. When ions bond or attach, this is **ionic bonding.** Compounds with high melting points usually have ionic bonds. They are usually hard solids with well-defined crystals, and they do not conduct electricity. Ionic compounds tend to easily dissolve in water.

Atoms can share electrons instead of transferring them to each other. When one or more pairs of electrons are shared between two atoms, a **covalent bond** is formed. Covalent compounds are often gases, liquids, or solids with low melting points. Some covalent compounds conduct electricity but do not dissolve easily in water.

Chemical Formulas

We identify elements by their symbols. These symbols can be used instead of writing out the whole name of the chemical. Compounds can also be written with the symbols of the elements in them. When the symbols are written in a certain way, they show the elements in the compound. These are chemical formulas.

Scientists use specific rules for writing chemical formulas. An easy formula is the one for water. The formula is H_2O. H is the symbol for hydrogen. The small number 2 after the H means that there are two hydrogen atoms in a molecule of water. O is the symbol for oxygen. Notice that the O has no number after it. This means that there is only one atom of oxygen in a water molecule. The number 1 is not written in chemical formulas. The formula for water—H_2O—says that in a molecule of water there are two hydrogen atoms and one atom of oxygen.

A different combination of hydrogen and oxygen atoms will make a different compound. The formula for hydrogen peroxide is H_2O_2. Hydrogen peroxide is used as a disinfectant. Unlike water, it is not safe to drink. How is the formula for hydrogen peroxide different from the formula for water?

Compounds with more than two elements in them can also be shown as chemical formulas. A good example is sugar. All sugars are made of the three elements oxygen, carbon, and hydrogen. Sugars form when atoms of oxygen, hydrogen, and carbon join in different ways. The formula for common table sugar is $C_{12}H_{22}O_{11}$.

A molecule is the smallest amount of a compound that still has all of the physical and chemical properties of the compound. For sugar to be sugar, at least one molecule of sugar has to be present. Chemical reactions can separate sugar molecules into the elements oxygen, hydrogen, and carbon. These elements do not have the same properties as sugar. At room temperature, oxygen and hydrogen are gases. They are odorless and colorless. Carbon is a solid. It is usually black, like charcoal.

The chemical formula for table salt is NaCl.

Common table sugar forms when 11 atoms of oxygen, 22 atoms of hydrogen, and 12 atoms of carbon join. How are the properties of sugar different from the properties of its elements?

Chemical Equations

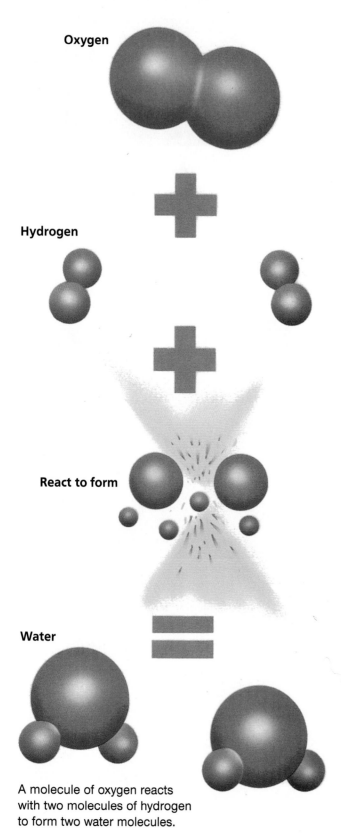

Oxygen

Hydrogen

React to form

Water

A molecule of oxygen reacts with two molecules of hydrogen to form two water molecules.

You know that matter cannot be created or destroyed. When matter changes, only its form changes. The total mass of matter stays the same. This helps us write a chemical formula. It also helps us write out chemical reactions. We put chemical reactions in equation form, just like in math.

Equations of chemical reactions are written by following rules. Chemical equations must show that matter has not been created or destroyed during the chemical reaction. A chemical-reaction equation is balanced. It has the same number of each kind of atom on both sides of the equal sign. The left side of the equation represents the amount of each substance in its original form. The right side of the equation represents the same atoms after the reaction.

For instance, look at the diagram here. It shows how oxygen and hydrogen molecules combine to form water. The chemical equation for the formation of water is written:

$$2H_2 + O_2 \rightarrow 2H_2O.$$

The numbers in front of the hydrogen symbol tell us that two molecules of two hydrogen atoms go into making two molecules of water. Just as in chemical formulas, the number 1 is not written in the equation. There is one molecule of two oxygen atoms that go into making two molecules of water.

Equation for the Formation of Water

There are almost as many chemical reactions as there are compounds. Most of these are of four general types. Reactions that form new compounds from one or more elements are synthesis reactions. *Synthesis* means "to put together" or "to form." You are familiar with a synthesis reaction. Photosynthesis is the process that combines water and carbon dioxide in the presence of sunlight to form sugars. You know the formula for water and one of the formulas for sugar. Do you recognize the formula CO_2?

Decomposition chemical reactions are reactions that take apart, or break down, compounds and substances. For example, your body's cells decompose, or break down, sugar. Your cells turn the complex molecule of sugar into its three elements— hydrogen, oxygen, and carbon.

The other two types of chemical reactions are displacement reactions. When something is displaced, it is removed and another thing takes its place. In displacement reactions, one or more of the elements in a compound are replaced by other elements. There are single-displacement reactions and double-displacement reactions. Single displacements, as their name suggests, are chemical reactions in which one element replaces another element. Double-displacement reactions are more complicated. In them, elements in two compounds react to form two new compounds.

CHECKPOINT

1. What is the periodic table of the elements?
2. What is a compound?
3. How are chemical formulas written?
4. Why must chemical equations balance?
 What are ionic and covalent compounds?

ACTIVITY

Making a New Material

Find Out

Do this activity to learn how chemical changes occur.

Process Skills

Observing
Communicating
Predicting
Designing an Investigation
Experimenting
Inferring

WHAT YOU NEED

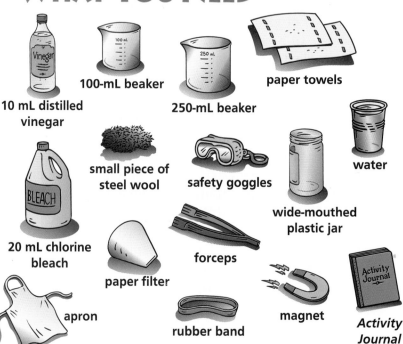

10 mL distilled vinegar

100-mL beaker

250-mL beaker

paper towels

20 mL chlorine bleach

small piece of steel wool

safety goggles

water

wide-mouthed plastic jar

apron

paper filter

forceps

magnet

rubber band

Activity Journal

WHAT TO DO

Safety! *Be sure to wear your safety goggles and an apron throughout this activity. Wash any spills and rinse your skin thoroughly with plenty of water.*

1. Pour 125 mL of water into a 250-mL beaker. Add 10 mL of distilled vinegar and 20 mL of chlorine bleach to the water.

2. Take a small piece of steel wool and hold it in one hand. With the other hand, hold the magnet near the wool. Record what happens.

3. Drop the steel wool into the water-vinegar-bleach solution. Observe what happens. Record the changes every 4 minutes for 24 minutes.

4. While the steel wool is reacting in the beaker, prepare a device for filtering. Place the filter paper into the mouth of the wide-mouthed jar. Use the rubber band to attach the filter to the top of the jar so that the filter hangs into the jar.

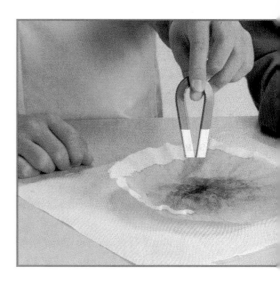

5. After your final observation of the water-vinegar-bleach solution, slowly pour the steel wool and solution into the filter paper. Let the liquid drain through. Add a little water to the beaker to rinse it and pour this into the filter as well. Use forceps to pick up the steel wool, hold it over the filter, and rinse it off with a small amount of water. Then, set the steel wool aside as your teacher directs.

6. When all the water has drained through the filter, carefully remove it from the top of the jar. Place the filter on several thicknesses of paper towels. Once the material in the filter is dry, observe it carefully. Hold the magnet near the material and record what happens.

CONCLUSIONS

1. What chemical changes took place during the experiment?
2. What can you infer about the type of material produced in the reaction?

ASKING NEW QUESTIONS

1. Predict whether steel wool in water would undergo the same reaction.
2. What type of investigation would you design to test your prediction?

SCIENTIFIC METHODS SELF CHECK

✔ Did I **observe** chemical changes?

✔ Did I **design an investigation** to test my **prediction?**

✔ Did I use the results of my **experiment** to **infer** what type of material was produced?

Acids, Bases, and Salts

Find Out

- What an acid is
- What a base is
- How an indicator is used
- What a salt is

Vocabulary

acid
base
indicator
neutral
salt

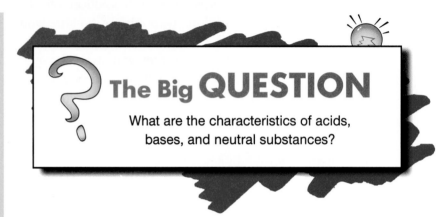

The Big QUESTION

What are the characteristics of acids, bases, and neutral substances?

The recipe for a chocolate cake calls for baking soda. Without this ingredient, the cake will look flat, like a brownie. The batter will not rise in the pan during baking. The baker who makes this cake uses chemistry—knowledge of the behavior of specific compounds. You can use chemistry too. Knowing how compounds react with each other can make things taste better. Sometimes, dangerous compounds can form. Some compounds should never be allowed to mix.

Acids

You know that elements have different physical and chemical properties. Did you know that compounds made from elements also have different physical and chemical properties? Those properties are the ways that compounds behave. The physical and chemical properties of compounds help us to classify them.

Scientists use many ways to classify compounds. Sometimes compounds are classified by the elements in them. For example, most compounds with the element carbon in them are organic compounds. Other times compounds are classified by how they react in the presence of oxygen. How compounds react with water can also be used to classify them. The new compounds formed when they are placed in water are either acids, bases, or salts.

A substance that forms hydrogen ions as it dissolves in water is an **acid.** The formula for a hydrogen ion is H^+. Hydrogen ions give all acids many of the same properties. Water molecules attract the hydrogen ions and form hydronium ions. The strength of an acid depends on its concentration of hydronium ions. Strong acids have more hydronium ions than weak acids do.

Acids and bases are found in many common household products. Cleaners, soaps, antacids, and deodorants are bases. Many foods, such as yogurt, citrus fruits, carbonated water, and vinegar, are acids.

Acids conduct electricity when dissolved in water. One chemical property of some acids is that they react with many metals. When acids react with metals, they produce hydrogen gas. The table at the bottom of page C101 lists some common acids.

Some acids are poisonous. Strong acids can cause burns on your skin or destroy fabrics. If you have ever seen blue jeans with big white spots on them, you know that too much bleach was used to clean them.

Some foods taste sour because they contain weak acids. For example, vinegar owes its sour taste to acetic acid. Oranges, lemons, and limes have citric acid in them. Many foods, like tomatoes and pickles, have different weak acids in them.

Many of your body fluids contain acids. Stomach acid aids food digestion. Many soft drinks contain carbonic acid. Soft drinks taste sweet, not sour. That's because most soft drinks also contain sugar or other sweeteners. Carbonic acid is also present in ocean water and in blood.

Stinging animals often have acids in their stingers or mouth parts. Wasps and red ants inject formic acid when they sting an animal. Some plants grow better in soils that are more acidic. Cranberries and conifers are two examples of plants that grow best in acidic soils. Some plants grow differently in soils that are more acidic.

You should *never* taste or touch a substance to find out if it is an acid. If you work with acids, you should always wear safety glasses.

Some foods, like tomatoes, have acids in them. Your stomach makes acid that helps you digest your food.

Debarked logs

Reels of finished paper

The photographs show steps in the production of paper. The bleaching action of the acid chlorine dioxide turns paper fibers white in the pulp washer.

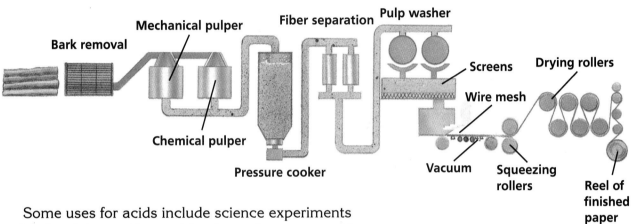

Some uses for acids include science experiments and industrial use. Along with other substances, acids are used to make paints and fertilizers. Acids are used to clean metals and concrete. The process of making paper relies heavily on the use of bleach.

Common Acids

Name	Formula	Common Occurrence
Acetic	CH_3COOH	vinegar
Boric	H_3BO_3	eye drops
Carbonic	H_2CO_3	carbonated beverages, also produced in body when carbon dioxide dissolves in blood
Citric	$C_6H_8O_7$	citrus fruits (limes, lemons, oranges, etc.)
Hydrochloric	HCl	stomach acids, industrial and home cleaning agents
Lactic	$C_3H_6O_3$	sour milk, yogurt, also produced in the muscles during contraction
Nitric	HNO_3	manufacturing agent in dyes and explosives, also used in urine test for protein
Phosphoric	H_3PO_4	cola soft drinks, also used in making of fertilizers
Sulfuric	H_2SO_4	automobile batteries, also used in the manufacturing of fertilizers and other items

Bases

A **base** is a substance that dissolves in water and forms hydroxide ions. A hydroxide ion is a unit of hydrogen and oxygen. Its formula is OH^-. The number of hydroxide ions determines the strength of a base. More hydroxide ions make stronger bases. Bases dissolved in water conduct electricity.

Like acids, bases have important uses, but can be dangerous. Strong bases cause burns to the skin. Bases are especially harmful if they get in or near the eye. The table on this page lists some common bases.

Always wear safety goggles when working with acids or bases. You should *never* taste or touch a substance to find out if it is an acid or a base. Bases have a bitter taste and many feel slippery. Some weak bases include baking soda and over-the-counter antacids. You may be familiar with a product that contains the base aluminum hydroxide. That's the active ingredient in many deodorants.

Many household chemicals are also bases. Ammonia is a base. It is used by itself or in other compounds for cleaning floors and windows. It has a distinctive odor and may cause your eyes to water.

Some soaps and detergents contain sodium hydroxide. Look at the chart on this page to find the chemical formula for sodium hydroxide. Compare this to the formula you learned for hydrogen peroxide in the last lesson. Sodium hydroxide is also called lye. It is a very strong base. If it touches your skin, it can cause a burn. Sodium hydroxide is also used in drain cleaners and oven cleaners. Like most bases, it will dissolve fats and oils.

Common Bases		
Name	Formula	Common Occurrence
Aluminum Hydroxide	$Al(OH)_3$	deodorant
Sodium Hydroxide	$NaOH$	oven cleaner, drain cleaner
Magnesium Hydroxide	$Mg(OH)_2$	milk of magnesia (antacid)
Ammonia	NH_3	household cleaner
Calcium Hydroxide	$Ca(OH)_2$	used in the making of plaster and mortar

Acid and Base Indicators

Scientists never taste or touch a substance to find out if it is an acid or a base. That would be dangerous. Instead, they use an indicator (in′ də kāt ər). An **indicator** is a compound that will change color when it is in contact with an acid or a base. Most indicators change colors when added to either acidic or basic solutions.

Hydrangea plants develop blue flowers when grown in acidic soils. When grown in basic soils, they develop pink flowers. The hydrangea plant is a natural indicator.

Litmus is an acid-base indicator. It comes from lichens. Litmus paper can be blue or red. Blue litmus paper will turn red when dipped in an acid. Red litmus paper will turn blue when dipped in a base.

Scientists use a scale called the pH scale to indicate the strength of acids and bases. The pH scale ranges between 0 and 14. The pH value of a substance is an indicator of the concentration of an acid or a base in a water solution. A pH reading of 7 indicates that a solution is neutral. **Neutral** means that a solution is neither an acid nor a base. Distilled water has a pH of 7.

A pH value of less than 7 means the solution is an acid. A pH higher than 7 indicates the solution is a base. The farther away from 7 the pH of the solution is, the stronger it is. A very strong acid would have a low pH value. A very strong base would have a high pH value.

Hydrangeas are natural indicators. They develop pink flowers when they grow in basic soils and blue flowers when the soil is acidic.

Salts

People often use the term *salt* to mean common table salt, or sodium chloride. Sodium chloride is a chemical salt as well. When an acid and a base combine in a chemical reaction, the result is water and a salt. This type of **salt** is a chemical compound that contains a positive ion from a base and a negative ion from an acid.

You know that water is neutral. A salt may also be neutral. Neutralization is a chemical process in which the hydronium ions from an acid combine with the hydroxide ions from a base to form water and a salt. This type of reaction is a double-displacement reaction.

The salt formed from this reaction has different properties from those of either the acid or the base. It is a completely different compound. Most salts contain two elements, a metal and a nonmetal. Different combinations of acids and bases can make different salts.

Some salts are common household items. You already know about sodium chloride (NaCl). It is the salt most often used to flavor food. A "salt substitute" for table salt is potassium chloride (KCl). Baking soda is another salt. It is sodium bicarbonate ($NaHCO_3$). Many toothpastes contain the salt stannous fluoride (SnF_2). Other toothpastes contain sodium fluoride (NaF).

Sodium chloride is the salt most often used to flavor food.

Toothpastes are usually made from salts containing fluorine.

Two other salts you may have seen are calcium carbonate ($CaCO_3$) and calcium chloride ($CaCl_2$). One form of calcium carbonate is chalk. Calcium chloride is used to melt snow and ice on streets and sidewalks. Sodium chloride can also be used for this purpose. When these salts mix with ice, the freezing point of water is lowered. The ice or snow becomes liquid salt water. You know that pure water turns to ice at 0 °C. When water is mixed with salt, its freezing point is lower. The salt will turn ice to liquid down to about −10 °C. At temperatures below that, salt no longer melts ice.

There are many other practical uses for different kinds of salt. Calcium chloride will melt snow. Calcium carbonate is chalk.

CHECKPOINT

1. What is an acid?
2. What is a base?
3. How is an indicator used?
4. What is a salt?

 What are the characteristics of acids, bases, and neutral substances?

ACTIVITY
Finding pH Values

Find Out

Do this activity to learn some pH values of common materials.

Process Skills

Observing
Communicating
Experimenting
Interpreting Data
Inferring
Defining Operationally

WHAT YOU NEED

safety goggles

red and blue litmus paper

household solutions

small test tube with rubber stopper

apron

droppers

paper towels

wide-range indicator paper

Activity Journal

WHAT TO DO

Safety! *Wear your safety goggles and an apron. Never taste, touch, or mix the substances. Handle all substances carefully. Rinse any spills with plenty of water.*

1. At your first station, lay a paper towel down on the table. Place one strip each of red and blue litmus paper and a wide-range indicator on the paper towel. Place one drop of vinegar on each of the strips.

2. Observe and record the colors. Also, record the pH shown by the color of the wide-range indicator paper. Dispose of all materials as your teacher directs.

3. Repeat Steps 1 and 2 with the other solutions. Record the results in a table.

CONCLUSIONS

1. Detergent is a base. Vinegar is an acid. Compared to these materials, which tested substances were acids?

2. Using the pH values in your table, determine which values indicate an acid.

3. Using the pH values in your table, determine which indicate a base.

ASKING NEW QUESTIONS

1. Do all acids or all bases have the same pH value?

2. How does knowing the pH values of solutions help you?

SCIENTIFIC METHODS SELF CHECK

✔ Did I **observe** indicators of acids and bases?

✔ Did I **experiment** to determine the pH values of food and nonfood items?

✔ Did I **interpret** the litmus paper color changes correctly?

✔ Did I **infer** the interactions between acids and bases?

✔ Did I **operationally define** what a pH value is?

Review

Reviewing Vocabulary and Concepts

Write the letter that best completes each sentence.

1. A ___ describes how a substance can react with another substance to form a new, third substance.
   - **a.** mechanical property
   - **b.** electrical property
   - **c.** chemical property
   - **d.** physical property

2. The smallest units of matter that cannot be broken down chemically are called ___.
   - **a.** compounds
   - **b.** atoms
   - **c.** reactions
   - **d.** molecules

3. The tiny, very dense center of an atom is called the ___.
   - **a.** proton
   - **b.** neutron
   - **c.** electron
   - **d.** nucleus

4. With the protons, ___ contribute to the mass of an atom.
   - **a.** neutrons
   - **b.** electrons
   - **c.** elements
   - **d.** molecules

5. ___ form when two or more elements combine chemically.
   - **a.** Atoms
   - **b.** Neutrons
   - **c.** Protons
   - **d.** Compounds

6. Charged particles that form when atoms gain or lose one or more electrons are called ___.
   - **a.** salts
   - **b.** bases
   - **c.** acids
   - **d.** ions

7. When molecules form between atoms by sharing electrons, a ___ bond is formed.
   - **a.** covalent
   - **b.** ionic
   - **c.** base
   - **d.** acid

8. ___ are substances that dissolve in water and form hydroxide ions.
   - **a.** Elements
   - **b.** Acids
   - **c.** Bases
   - **d.** Protons

9. When a solution is neither acidic nor basic, it is ___.
   - **a.** neutron
   - **b.** normal
   - **c.** neutral
   - **d.** negative

10. When an acid and a base combine in a chemical reaction, the result is water and a(n) ___.
    - **a.** salt
    - **b.** base
    - **c.** acid
    - **d.** compound

Understanding What You Learned

1. What holds the compound sodium chloride, also called table salt, together?

2. How does an element differ from a compound?

3. What are the meanings of the symbols and numbers in the formula for sulfuric acid, H_2SO_4?

4. What does a chemical formula represent?

5. What happens when an acid and a base combine?

Applying What You Learned

1. The wax in a candle first melts and then burns. Describe what type of properties melting and burning are.

2. Compare and contrast ionic and covalent compounds.

3. Explain what a chemical equation is and why it needs to be balanced.

4. If you were given an unknown liquid, how would you determine whether it was an acid or a base?

5. Explain how we can figure out how different types of matter interact with each other.

For Your Portfolio

Make a chart of several everyday examples of physical and chemical changes. Include a section that explains each change. For example, changes in size, shape, or state are physical changes. Rust on metal, fading colors on paper, and the formation of a new substance are chemical changes.

Unit Review

Concept Review

1. Describe what happens once radiant energy from the sun reaches Earth.

2. Describe the various ways that energy can be transferred and give an example of each.

3. Explain the periodic table and one way it can be useful to scientists or to someone who does not know about it.

Problem Solving

1. What determines an object's color?

2. Imagine you are picnicking on a hot day at the sandy shore of an icy lake. Devise and write plans to warm a baby's bottle by conduction and radiation. Also plan a way to cool off after playing volleyball without going into the water.

3. You should have a good idea of what matter is. Draw a line down the center of a piece of paper. Label one column "Matter" and the other column "Not Matter." List what you observe in the classroom in one column or the other. Think about what all the things you listed as "matter" have in common. For example, do they have mass and take up space? What about things you listed as "Not Matter?" What do they have in common?

Something to Do

So far you have studied matter as it exists—with familiar forms, familiar properties, and in a familiar environment. Do you think matter and its properties might change in a more unusual environment, such as in the zero gravity of outer space? Picture yourself as a scientist in an orbiting laboratory. Imagine what you could do to develop new materials, or encourage new properties and uses in existing substances. How would you expect mixtures to act in a weightless environment? What experiments would you conduct? Make a list. Write a brief television news bulletin describing one of your imaginary scientific breakthroughs.

THE NERVOUS SYSTEM

Computers can do many things humans cannot. However, these amazing machines have limits. For instance, if the room gets too hot for the computer to work efficiently, it can't move itself to another room.

You have an even more amazing control system in your body—your nervous system. Unlike a computer that can be turned off, your nervous system controls your body whether you are awake or asleep. It can do more than any computer too. How do you know when you are hungry, sleepy, or too hot or cold? Your nervous system tells you. What keeps your heart beating and your lungs breathing? Your nervous system does. If you want to dance, play guitar, or write answers to math problems, what controls your muscles and your memory? Your nervous system does.

The Big IDEA

The nervous system is the master control center of the body.

CHAPTER SCIENCE INVESTIGATION

Remember what your brain does while you sleep. Find out how in your *Activity Journal.*

D3

The Body's Nervous Systems

Find Out

- What role neurons, the brain, and the spinal cord have in the central nervous system
- How the peripheral nervous system works

Vocabulary

neurons
dendrites
axon
synapse
brain
spinal column
spinal cord

The Big QUESTION

How does the nervous system control the body?

*T*he complex nervous system of humans is one thing that separates them from other animals. It allows humans to think and reason. It gives them the ability to communicate by using written and spoken languages. If the nervous system is damaged, it doesn't heal the same way other body systems do. Although scientists know a lot about the human nervous system, doctors and other scientists continue to explore its structures and functions.

The Central Nervous System

The nervous system is the command-and-control center of the body. The human nervous system consists of neurons, or nerve cells, the spinal cord, and the brain. The nervous system is divided into two main parts: the central nervous system and the peripheral nervous system.

The central nervous system is made up of two parts, the brain and the spinal cord. The central nervous system is protected by bone and wrapped in protective membranes. The peripheral nervous system contains all the other nerves in the body.

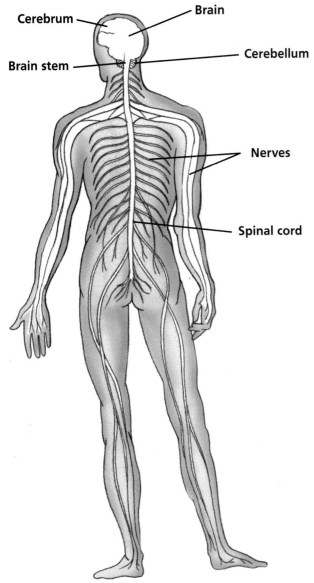

Cerebrum

Brain

Cerebellum

Brain stem

Nerves

Spinal cord

The spinal cord is an extension of the brain stem. It is made up of nerve cells that carry impulses from all parts of the body to the brain and back. It is about 43 cm long. The nerves of the spinal cord are protected by your vertebrae. There is a hole in each vertebra through which the nerves of your spinal cord pass. The nerves go into your arms, legs, and trunk and form part of the peripheral nervous system.

The human nervous system allows us to think and communicate.

How Neurons Do Their Job

Your body contains many different types of cells. Eye cells are not the same as stomach cells; muscle cells are different from hair cells. The cells that make up the nervous system are different from skin cells, bone cells, or any other type of cell.

Nervous-system cells, or nerve cells, are also called **neurons.** They are like other cells in some ways and different in other important ways. The main part of the neuron, called the cell body, isn't a lot different from other cell bodies. It has most of the same structures as other cells, such as a nucleus and a cell membrane.

A neuron is different from other cells in that it has lots of thin, hairlike structures around the edge of its cell body. Under a microscope, they look like tiny hairs or spider legs. These hairlike structures are **dendrites** (den′ drīts). They help the neurons receive impulses.

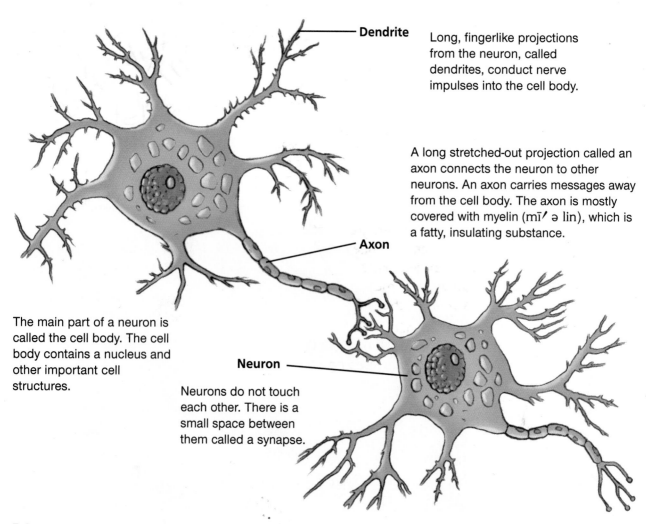

Dendrite

Long, fingerlike projections from the neuron, called dendrites, conduct nerve impulses into the cell body.

A long stretched-out projection called an axon connects the neuron to other neurons. An axon carries messages away from the cell body. The axon is mostly covered with myelin (mī′ ə lin), which is a fatty, insulating substance.

Axon

The main part of a neuron is called the cell body. The cell body contains a nucleus and other important cell structures.

Neuron

Neurons do not touch each other. There is a small space between them called a synapse.

At one end of the neuron is another structure, a longer, thicker fiber that looks something like a tail. It is an **axon.** Axons send messages to the next neuron. Axons and dendrites carry very small pulses of chemical energy. The pulses of this energy in the body are nerve impulses.

The dendrites pick up these tiny nerve impulses from other nerve cells and then pass them on to the axon. The axon carries the impulse out of the cell to the dendrites of the next nerve cell by means of chemicals.

Impulses move along neurons at a rate of 0.5 to 100 m/s. Impulses move across the space between neurons, or **synapse** (sin′ aps), with the help of a chemical produced by the neurons.

The Human Brain

The **brain** is the main organ of the central nervous system. It is in charge of a huge variety of functions. Located within the skull, the brain is made up of billions of individual nerve cells. Nerve tissues are gray cell bodies (called gray matter) and white, myelin-covered cells (called white matter). The tissues of the brain are arranged in many folds and wrinkles. If you could spread out a human brain, it would be nearly as large as your teacher's desk.

The brain controls things you think about doing: running, jumping, or petting your dog. It also controls the things you don't think about doing: keeping your heart beating, making sure your lungs work, and blinking your eyes.

Your brain also controls your emotions. It stores your memories, lets you read words on this page, and enables you to remember that 6 × 6 = 36. You will learn more about brain structures and functions in the next lesson.

Different parts of the human brain control specific body functions and activities.

The cerebrum (sə rē′ brəm) is the part of the brain in which thinking, sensory perception, memory, and control of voluntary muscles occur.

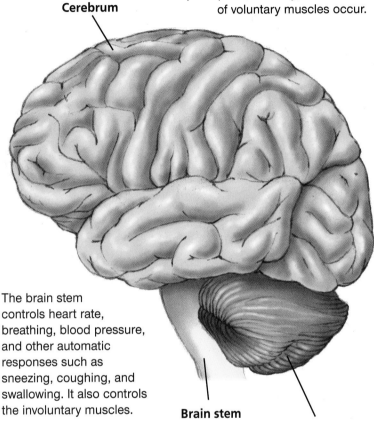

Cerebrum

The brain stem controls heart rate, breathing, blood pressure, and other automatic responses such as sneezing, coughing, and swallowing. It also controls the involuntary muscles.

Brain stem

Cerebellum

The cerebellum (ser ə bel′ əm) controls coordination of skeletal muscle contractions to maintain balance and muscle tone. It also processes the cerebral messages for voluntary muscle control.

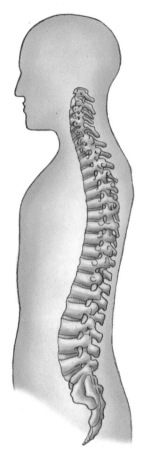

The spinal cord is protected by the meninges, or protective coverings, and vertebrae.

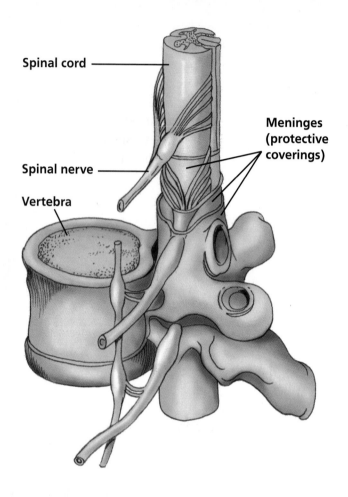

Spinal cord

Spinal nerve

Vertebra

Meninges (protective coverings)

The Spinal Cord

You can easily feel your **spinal column.** It is the set of bones in the middle of your back. The spinal column is made of 33 hollow bones called vertebrae (vert′ ə brā) that are stacked on top of one another like hollow blocks in a tower. There are disks of cartilage between each bone. The cartilage allows the spine to be flexible.

The **spinal cord** is located inside the vertebrae. It is the vital link between the body and brain. It is composed of gray and white matter, just as the brain is. The gray matter, located on the inside of the spinal cord, conducts chemical messages that go to the body's muscles. The white matter wraps around the gray matter. It conducts signals to and from the brain.

The spinal column and spinal cord are important to movement and feeling. If either one is badly damaged in an accident, a person may be unable to move. Which parts of the body are paralyzed and which can still move depends on how high on the spinal cord the damage occurred.

A nerve is a bundle of neurons with axons that all go to the same place in the nervous system. There are 12 pairs of cranial nerves and 31 pairs of spinal nerves that branch out from the spinal cord. Their function relates to their position on the spine. Nerves in the neck and head control functions in the throat and head. Nerves of the chest control the lungs and heart. Those farther down control the stomach, intestines, arms, hands, legs, and feet.

The Peripheral Nervous System

The peripheral nervous system is made up of all the other nerves in the body, the ones that don't run through the spinal cord. The word *peripheral* means "located away from the center." The peripheral nervous system has two parts—the somatic system and the autonomic system.

The Somatic System

Nerves in the somatic (sō mat′ ik) system link the body's sense organs—eyes, ears, nose, tongue, and skin—with the brain and spinal cord. They also send messages to the muscles. Your somatic system is functioning when you respond to the sensations of seeing, hearing, smelling, tasting, and touching.

There are three basic types of neurons: motor neurons, sensory neurons, and connecting neurons. The somatic nerves that carry messages of sensation are made of sensory neurons. Those nerves carrying messages that move the muscles are made of motor neurons. Connecting neurons relay messages between the sensory and motor neurons. Some nerves are a combination of both sensory and motor neurons and are called mixed nerves. They serve both functions. The somatic nerves usually start out from spinal or cranial nerves and then split off into smaller and smaller nerves—much like branches of a tree—until every area of the body is covered.

The somatic system allows you to engage in activities, such as riding a bike, by sending messages to and from your brain to tell your body what to do.

The Autonomic System

The autonomic (ô tō nom′ ik) system of the peripheral nervous system takes care of functions in your body that you do not willfully control. Just imagine if you had to control your heart beating, your lungs breathing, and your stomach digesting food by thinking. You could not possibly remember it all!

And you could not sleep. You would have to stay awake all the time to make sure your heart didn't stop or you didn't quit breathing. Fortunately, you do not have to do all that; the autonomic system does it for you automatically. The autonomic system does many things:

- It controls how fast and how strongly your heart beats, including speeding it up when you run.

- It controls your blood pressure—how hard the blood pushes against the veins and arteries it flows through.

- It controls how often and how deeply you breathe. It lets you breathe slowly and shallowly when you are asleep, and fast and hard when you are running or working hard.

- It controls how your kidneys work so waste can be removed from your body.

- It keeps the levels of salts, minerals, and other chemicals in your body in balance. Without that balance, your body would not work correctly.

- It controls your body's hormones. Hormones are chemical messengers that tell organs what to do. The autonomic system regulates hormone levels.

The autonomic system has one additional function that is very important: it controls your reflexes. If you step on a sharp rock, you pull your foot back without thinking, "That's sharp. I had better not step on it!"

The autonomic system makes sure you breathe regularly, whether you are awake or asleep.

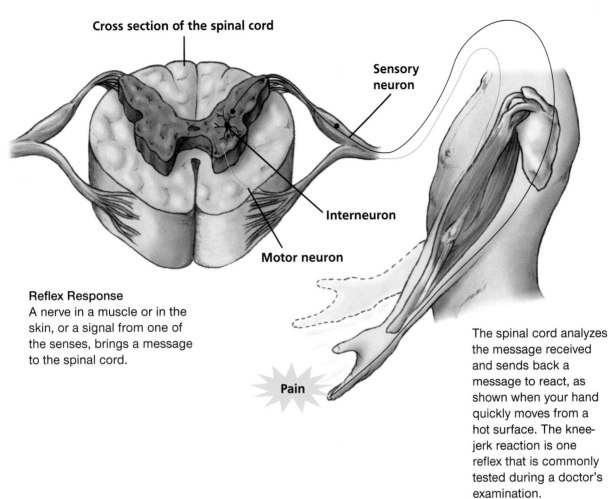

Cross section of the spinal cord

Sensory neuron

Interneuron

Motor neuron

Reflex Response
A nerve in a muscle or in the skin, or a signal from one of the senses, brings a message to the spinal cord.

Pain

The spinal cord analyzes the message received and sends back a message to react, as shown when your hand quickly moves from a hot surface. The knee-jerk reaction is one reflex that is commonly tested during a doctor's examination.

These reactions are reflexes. A reflex happens when the nervous system gets a signal, such as "The rock in the driveway is sharp," and signals your foot to pull away.

By the time the thinking part of your brain realizes what is happening, your foot has already pulled away from the rock, and the danger is past. Without reflexes, it would be much easier to get hurt. The autonomic system can send impulses to your muscles just like the somatic system does.

CHECKPOINT

1. What are the roles of the brain and the spinal cord in the central nervous system?

2. What are the roles of the somatic system and autonomic system in the peripheral nervous system?

 How does the nervous system control the body?

ACTIVITY
Modeling Neurons

Find Out

Do this activity to learn how to model two neurons and understand their structure and function.

Process Skills

Constructing Models
Defining Operationally
Communicating

WHAT YOU NEED

construction paper in various colors

glue

thin silver wire

black felt marker

yellow felt marker

Activity Journal

scissors

a large sheet of cardboard or heavy paper

WHAT TO DO

1. Look at the drawing of neurons on page D6 of your textbook. Choose a sheet of colored construction paper to represent the cell bodies of two neurons.

2. Cut out two oblong shapes, using the drawing on page D6 as a guide.

3. Glue the two cell bodies to the large sheet of cardboard or heavy paper, leaving at least 8 cm between them.

4. Cut 8-cm lengths of silver wire. Use the glue to attach the wires around the outside of each cell body to represent dendrites.

5. Braid several lengths of wire together to create a thicker wire representing the axon. Make one for each cell.

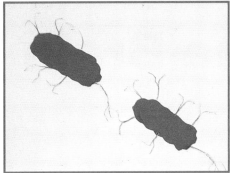

6. Glue the wire axon to the bottom of each cell. Make sure the axon of one cell does NOT quite touch the dendrites of the other cell.

7. With the black felt marker, draw arrows to show the direction messages flow through the neuron (in the dendrites and out the axon).

8. Use the yellow felt marker to represent the fluid that bridges the gap between the axon of one cell and the dendrites of the other cell. Use what you have made to explain how neurons work.

CONCLUSIONS

1. How do dendrites function in the neuron?
2. How does the fluid help send messages to the brain?

ASKING NEW QUESTIONS

1. What would happen if the fluid was somehow damaged?
2. Where do you think the impulses eventually go as they travel from neuron to neuron?

SCIENTIFIC METHODS SELF CHECK

✔ Does my **model** show how neurons work?

✔ Did I **operationally define** how neurons work?

✔ Did I clearly **explain** how neurons work to my classmates?

The Brain

Find Out

- What the different parts of the brain are
- How the brain gets its blood supply
- How to protect the brain

Vocabulary

cerebrum
cerebellum
brain stem
meninges
hemispheres

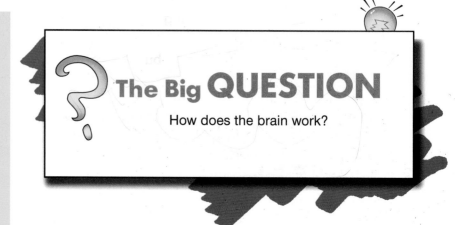

The Big QUESTION

How does the brain work?

In the last lesson, you learned that the brain is the largest and most complex part of the nervous system. It helps you think and coordinates the movement of your muscles. In this lesson, you will look more closely at the brain to learn more about how it is put together and how it works.

Brain Structures

The human brain contains 50 billion nerve cells. It's about as heavy as a thick textbook and is very sophisticated. The brain makes us who we are. There are three main parts of the brain: the cerebrum, the cerebellum, and the brain stem.

The **cerebrum** (sə rē′ brəm) is the largest part. It covers the top and front of the brain. It controls every intentional move, such as walking and eating. It is also the location of thoughts and memories. The cerebrum is divided into left and right halves, which are connected by nerve fibers. The outer layer of the cerebrum is the cortex. The cortex is made up of gray matter and is the area where memory and intelligence are located. Underneath the cortex is an area of white matter that controls the voluntary muscle system.

The **cerebellum** (sâr ə bel′ əm) is at the back of the brain. It coordinates movement and allows you to keep your balance. The **brain stem** at the back of the skull connects the brain and spinal cord. It contains the medulla (mə dōō′ lə), which controls what your body does without your thinking: maintaining your heartbeat, digesting food, and breathing.

The fragile brain is well protected, but a hard blow can bruise it badly. The bones of the skull are hard and thick and can prevent many injuries. The brain itself is wrapped in the **meninges.** The meninges are three layers of protective membrane that also wrap around the spinal cord. The meninges are separated by fluids that act as shock absorbers. They keep the brain from bouncing off the skull bones during normal movement. The meninges and bones, however, cannot always protect the brain from sudden or strong impacts.

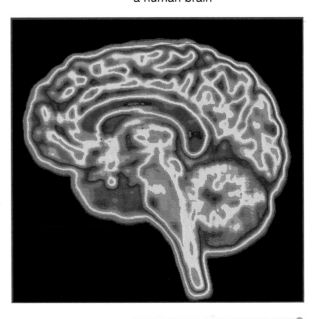

Computer-generated image of a human brain

The cerebrum is the part of the brain in which thinking, sensory perception, memory, and control of voluntary muscles occur. The cerebrum is divided into two hemispheres—the right and the left. The right side of the brain controls the left side of the body and the left side of the brain controls the right side of the body. Each hemisphere has five lobes, four of which are visible at the surface. Each lobe has control centers for different body functions.

The frontal lobe is important for translating thought into speech. It also controls the voluntary muscles, memory, emotions, and reasoning.

The parietal (pe ri′ ə təl) lobe controls the sense of touch. It seems to be important in understanding speech.

The temporal (tem′ pər əl) lobe controls hearing and seems to be involved in memory.

The occipital (ok sip′ ə təl) lobe processes stimuli into visual images.

The brain stem controls heart rate, breathing, blood pressure, and other automatic responses such as sneezing, coughing, and swallowing. It also controls the involuntary muscles.

The cerebellum controls coordination of skeletal muscle contractions to maintain balance and muscle tone. It also processes the cerebral messages for voluntary muscle control.

D15

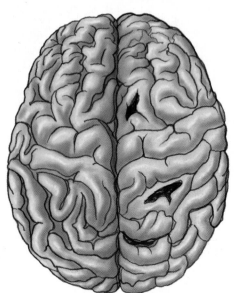

The cerebrum is divided into two hemispheres—the right and the left. Each hemisphere looks the same.

Left side of the cerebrum   **Right side of the cerebrum**

Top view

Why the Brain Has Two Sides

If you looked down on your brain from above, the two sides, or **hemispheres,** of the cerebrum would look the same. Although the hemispheres look alike, they work somewhat differently and are in charge of different things.

Whatever your body is doing, both hemispheres are at work. But one side is likely to be more active than the other, depending on the task. The left side of the brain is more active, or dominant, in talking, writing, reading, and doing math. The right side tends to take over when you are dealing with big concepts or when you are being creative, such as painting a picture or composing music.

The left side of the brain controls the right side of the body, including the right hand; the right side of the brain controls the left side of the body. For most people, the right hand, controlled by the left side of the brain, is easier to use. We say those people are right-handed. But about 11 percent of the population is left-handed. These people find it easier to use their left hand, which is controlled by the right side of the brain. We do not know why that is, but we do know a left-handed person's brain is not reversed. The right side is still the creative side and the left side is the task side. All brains, no matter which hand is dominant, look the same.

The left side of the cerebrum also contains the primary area that controls speech. If that side is damaged, the right side can eventually take over the speech function. However, the injured person must relearn how to speak.

Getting Blood to the Brain

You know that every part of your body needs blood. No matter where you cut yourself—finger, forehead, or shin—blood oozes out. Blood brings oxygen and nutrients to the body's cells and takes away waste products. Without a blood supply, a body organ would die.

The brain is no different. It needs a constant supply of blood. In fact, it needs about 710 mL of blood a minute, more than any other organ. An adult's brain is only one-fiftieth of his or her total body mass, but it uses about a fifth of the oxygen and nutrients in the blood

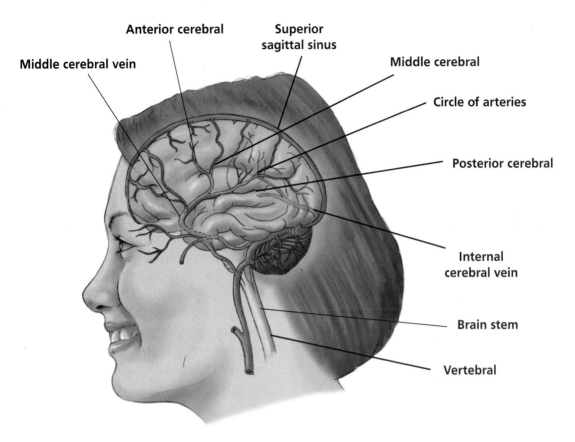

Middle cerebral vein

Anterior cerebral

Superior sagittal sinus

Middle cerebral

Circle of arteries

Posterior cerebral

Internal cerebral vein

Brain stem

Vertebral

The brain uses ten times the amount of blood found in any other part of the body.

supply available to the whole body. The brain uses ten times the amount of blood used by other parts of the body.

The brain gets its blood from several pairs of arteries that lead directly from the heart to the brain. They run up the sides of the neck and next to the spinal column. Once in the brain, they branch out, just like the arteries in every other part of the body. This way, oxygen and nutrients can get to each brain cell. Veins in the brain carry away waste products.

Blood vessels going to the brain get help from cerebrospinal (sə rē′ brō spī′ nəl) fluid. This yellow fluid bathes the folds of the brain and runs between the meninges. Cerebrospinal fluid also functions as a shock absorber, helps deliver oxygen and nutrients, and eliminates wastes.

Brain Functions

An important function of the brain is to do your thinking. The cerebrum, your "thinking machine," is in charge of that. Its two hemispheres produce thoughts and ideas, as well as generate emotions and store memories.

Between the two halves of the cerebrum is a "bridge" made of specialized nerve fibers that allow the two halves of the brain to communicate with each other.

In the brain stem, near the cerebrum, are two special structures. One is the thalamus (thal′ ə məs), sometimes called the "gateway to the brain." Nerve signals go through the thalamus. It sorts them and sends them to their proper place. The second is the hypothalamus (hī′ pō thal′ ə məs). This bean-shaped organ is one of the body's master control centers. The hypothalamus is linked to the autonomic system of the medulla. The hypothalamus is in charge of breathing, heartbeat, digestion, body temperature, hunger, thirst, and sleep.

The brain also controls memory. Memory is not in just one location in the brain. It seems to be spread out. There are two types of memory: short-term and long-term. If you look up a phone number, you might remember it long enough to make a phone call. An hour later, you probably will have forgotten it, because it was stored in your short-term memory. When you did not need it anymore, you forgot it.

However, you probably will never forget the date you were born, your best friend's name, or that 1 + 1 = 2. These facts are stored in your long-term memory. Scientists think a structure called the hippocampus, buried deep in the brain, is responsible in part for converting short-term memories into long-term ones.

Another important function of the brain is to control movement. If you study the violin, drawing the bow across the strings is hard at first; the sounds you make usually sound more like squawks than music! If you have been taking regular lessons, you probably do not need to think about the motions of the bow anymore. After doing any activity many times, the motions involved become automatic.

Your short-term memory allows you to remember a new phone number long enough to make a call. Your long-term memory stores knowledge you use over and over or that you need to recall over a long time.

The cerebellum controls any kind of coordinated movements you want your body to do. *Cerebellum* means "little brain" in Latin. It looks like the cerebrum directly above it. It is the second-largest part of the brain, although it accounts for only about one-tenth of the brain's total mass.

When you direct your body to move, the cerebellum sends nerve signals to your muscles. It controls what the muscles do. Sensors in the skin and muscles send impulses back to the cerebellum on how the movement is going.

When everything is working correctly, which it does in most people most of the time, the impulses go back and forth in a fraction of a second. Your body responds with smooth movements and good balance. If there is a problem, the body may respond in a jerky or uncoordinated way.

The cerebellum coordinates movements you direct your body to do.

Problems of the Brain

Because the brain is such a complex organ and does so many things, it is not surprising that a lot of things can go wrong with it. Problems can be caused by muscle contractions, disease, or injury.

Headaches are the most common brain problem. A headache is not a disease by itself, but is a symptom of something else that is wrong. It usually is the result of tension in the head muscles. Problems with the blood vessels in the head or chemical imbalances are rare. However, a person who has a lot of headaches should see a doctor to have the problem diagnosed.

A stroke happens when a blood vessel inside the brain either bursts or becomes blocked so blood cannot get through. Depending on what part of the brain is affected, the person may lose the ability to talk or may become paralyzed in some part of the body.

Technology can help people with disabilities do many things.

Meningitis is a disease in which the meninges covering the brain or spinal cord become infected. This serious disease causes bad headaches, a stiff neck, sensitivity to light, and an upset stomach. Certain kinds of meningitis can be cured with antibiotics, but sometimes the disease is fatal.

Other problems result from head injuries or other medical conditions. Epilepsy is a disease that causes a person to lose consciousness. These periods of unconsciousness are seizures. For many years, brain surgery was the only remedy for epilepsy. Now, many medicines are available to reduce or stop the seizures. Other diseases, such as diabetes or arthritis, can damage the connections between the peripheral nervous system and the brain. These diseases lead to loss of motor and sensory function in the arms, hands, fingers, legs, feet, and toes. Memory loss and other diseases are areas of current medical research.

The brain has several built-in shock absorbers that protect it from normal movement. These shock absorbers do not protect the brain from damage caused by trauma, or sudden impact or injury. Every year, more than 90,000 people in the U.S. suffer moderate to severe brain injury. Some injuries even cause death.

You can protect your brain from injury by obeying some simple safety rules when you walk, ride, and play. By paying attention to traffic signs and signals, you know when it's safe to cross a street, an intersection, or a railroad crossing. By always wearing a safety belt when riding in a vehicle, you keep your head from being banged up. Safety belts keep you from being tossed around a vehicle if it's in an accident. When swimming, you should always check the water depth before diving. When riding your bike, skating, or playing any contact sport, you can protect your brain from injury by wearing a helmet. If you do get a blow to the head, for any reason, you should get medical attention immediately. These safety precautions can help you protect one of the most delicate, but most important, organs in your body.

Wearing a helmet when riding or playing sports can protect your brain from injury.

CHECKPOINT

1. Name the main parts of the brain.
2. How does the brain gets its blood supply?
3. What things can you do to protect your brain?

 How does the brain work?

ACTIVITY

Testing Short-Term Memory

Find Out

Do this activity to learn how short-term memory and your autonomic nervous system are linked.

Process Skills

Experimenting
Observing
Communicating
Using Numbers
Classifying

WHAT YOU NEED

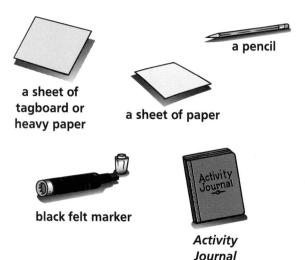

a sheet of tagboard or heavy paper

a sheet of paper

a pencil

black felt marker

Activity Journal

WHAT TO DO

1. Cut the heavy paper or tagboard into 30 rectangles, each about 10 cm by 15 cm.

2. Use the felt marker to print numbers from 1 to 30 on the rectangles.

3. Work with another student. Have one person be the tester and the other take the "test." Have the tester show a numbered rectangle to the person taking the test, then turn it upside down. The person taking the test should say the number aloud. As each number is shown, the person taking the test must repeat all the numbers that came before, then add the new number.

4. The tester should record how many numbers the person taking the test gets right before he or she makes a mistake. This will be how many numbers the person can put into his or her short-term memory before he or she begins to forget.

5. Reverse roles and let the tester take the test. Be sure to change the order of the numbers before testing.

6. Fifteen minutes later, try to recall the sequence of the numbers. See how much remains in your short-term memory.

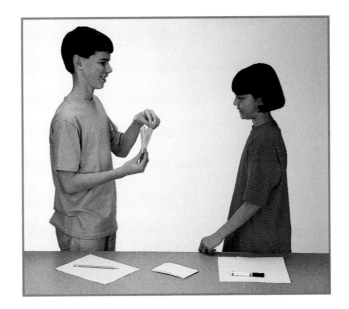

CONCLUSIONS

1. Compare your results with your partner's results.

2. Who remembered the most numbers?

3. Who has the longest short-term memory?

ASKING NEW QUESTIONS

1. Do you think testing your short-term memory on a regular basis would improve it?

2. On an everyday basis, when do you need to use short-term memory?

SCIENTIFIC METHODS SELF CHECK

✔ Did I **observe** my partner's short-term memory skills?

✔ Did I **record** the results of the test?

✔ Did I set up a **sequence** of numbers for the **experiment?**

✔ Did I **identify** who has the longest short-term memory?

Review

Reviewing Vocabulary and Concepts

Write the letter of the answer that completes each sentence.

1. Nerve cells in the human nervous system are called ___.
   - **a.** meninges
   - **b.** dendrites
   - **c.** neurons
   - **d.** axons

2. The link between the body and the brain that conducts signals to and from the brain is the ___.
   - **a.** vertebra
   - **b.** spinal column
   - **c.** brain stem
   - **d.** spinal cord

3. The largest part of the brain is the ___.
   - **a.** cerebrum
   - **b.** brain stem
   - **c.** cerebellum
   - **d.** hypothalamus

4. A three-layer membrane that protects the brain and the spinal cord is the ___.
   - **a.** white matter
   - **b.** concussion
   - **c.** reflex
   - **d.** meninges

5. The two sides of the brain are called ___.
   - **a.** hemispheres
   - **b.** seizures
   - **c.** nerves
   - **d.** folds

Match the definition on the left with the correct term.

6. carries nerve impulses into the neuron
7. carries nerve impulses away from the neuron
8. the space between neurons
9. made up of 33 vertebrae
10. an extension of the brain stem
11. largest part of the brain, believed to control emotions and memory
12. coordinates movement and allows you to keep your balance
13. connects the brain and spinal cord
14. three layers of protective membrane that wrap around the brain and the spinal cord
15. one of two sides of the cerebrum

- **a.** cerebellum
- **b.** spinal column
- **c.** meninges
- **d.** dendrite
- **e.** synapse
- **f.** hemisphere
- **g.** axon
- **h.** cerebrum
- **i.** spinal cord
- **j.** brain stem

Understanding What You Learned

1. Briefly describe the two main parts of the human nervous system.
2. Describe how nerve impulses travel through the body to the brain.
3. If your autonomic system did not work, what parts of your body would stop functioning?
4. Which things does the dominant hemisphere of the brain usually control?
5. How does the brain get the oxygen and nutrients it needs?

Applying What You Learned

1. Why are injuries to the spine so serious?
2. Why are reflexes important?
3. Which part of your brain do you use when you are being creative?
4. Your birth date and your name are examples of information stored in long-term memory. What are some other examples?

5. What makes your nervous system the master control center of your body?

For Your **Portfolio**

Think about all you've learned about the nervous system and why taking care of it is so important. Then choose a way to communicate this information. You could make up a safety song. You could write a short play about wearing a helmet. You might draw pictures of ways to protect different parts of the nervous system. You could make a safety poster promoting some ways to protect your nervous system.

Global Health

During most of human history, people have lived in isolated groups. Cities were far away from each other. People rarely traveled between them. Interaction among different groups took a major effort. Any infectious diseases in one area would spread only among people in that area. Epidemics, the rapid spread of disease among large numbers of people, were rare. Only when different groups of people met others through trade, exploration, or war would epidemics spread to other geographic regions.

In today's world cars, trucks, trains, and airplanes have replaced slower-moving ships and caravans of the past. Now diseases as well as people move at remarkable speeds. An outbreak of a disease anywhere in the world could cross into other continents within days. As a result, epidemics happen more easily. Individuals and communities must protect themselves against disease by fighting disease globally.

The Big IDEA

Preventing the spread of disease is a global concern.

案内所
INFORMATION

両替
MONEY EXCHANGE

旅行傷害保険
TRAVELLER'S INSURANCE

CHAPTER **SCIENCE** **INVESTIGATION**

Investigate the spread of an infectious disease. Find out how in your *Activity Journal.*

Communicable Diseases

Find Out

- What causes communicable diseases
- How germs are spread
- What agents of disease are
- About the body's defense systems

Vocabulary

communicable disease
infectious
viruses
toxins
immune system
lymphatic system
immunity

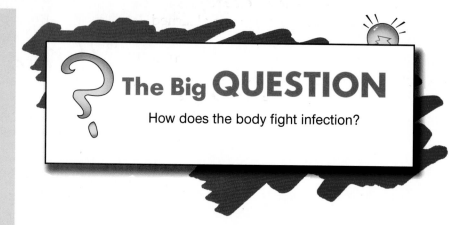

The Big QUESTION

How does the body fight infection?

*T*wo days ago, you were playing in the park with your best friend. You felt fine, but your friend was sneezing every ten minutes. Today, you woke up with a scratchy throat and runny nose. Your muscles don't ache and you don't have a fever. It sounds like you have a cold. Did your friend make you sick?

Communicable Diseases

When you have a cold or the flu, you are a victim of a **communicable** (kə myōō′ ni kə bəl) **disease.** Communicable diseases are illnesses that spread from person to person. Some, such as the common cold, are relatively harmless. Others, such as influenza and tuberculosis, have killed millions of people.

You can develop healthful habits to slow down or stop the spread of communicable diseases. If you're sick, you can avoid infecting others. By living a healthful lifestyle, you can avoid getting sick yourself.

When you cough or sneeze, you spray germs into the air. If these germs infect other people, chances are they will come down with your illness. Colds and influenza are examples of **infectious** (in fek′ shəs) diseases, diseases you get from a germ that invades or infects your body.

Germs are agents of disease. The main agents of disease are bacteria, fungi, protozoa, and viruses. You learned about bacteria, fungi, and protozoa in the Life Science unit. **Viruses** are small, nonliving bits of nucleic acid and protein. They can cause disease when they invade living cells.

Germs that cause infectious disease can be passed from person to person.

How Germs Are Spread

Germs that cause diseases are spread in several ways. Most germs are spread through direct contact. When you open a door or pick up someone's pencil, you may pick up germs from an infected person on your hands. If you touch your nose, mouth, or eyes, you give the germs an opportunity to enter your body. Sharing food, food implements, or a drinking glass with someone else also gives germs a chance to infect your body. You can also get sick from contact with an infected person's body fluids. Diseases easily passed by direct contact include measles, mumps, chicken pox, and the common cold.

Some germs are spread through the air. When someone who is sick sneezes, droplets of their mucus enter the air. Other people can inhale the germs. Airborne diseases include colds, influenza (the flu), tuberculosis, and mononucleosis.

Animals also spread disease. Mosquitoes, fleas, ticks, and other biting insects spread some of the most dangerous diseases. Mosquitoes spread encephalitis, malaria, and yellow fever. Fleas can carry the plague and head lice can transfer typhus. Ticks also spread typhus, as well as Lyme disease and Rocky Mountain spotted fever.

When you sneeze or cough, germs can be blown into the air.

In areas where food and water sources are polluted, disease-carrying microorganisms and viruses can pass to many people through drinking water. Flies and other insects that land on polluted water and then land on food can also spread disease. Polio, cholera, and typhoid are diseases that can spread through water.

Agents of Disease

The smallest germs are viruses. Millions of viruses might cover the head of a straight pin. Only special electron microscopes magnify viruses enough for them to be seen.

Viruses are not alive and can only exist inside a host cell. The virus hijacks its host cell's materials to make more viruses. Viruses cause the common cold, influenza, mumps, mononucleosis, chicken pox, measles, and HIV (human immunodeficiency virus), which can lead to AIDS (acquired immune deficiency syndrome). There are no cures for diseases caused by viruses.

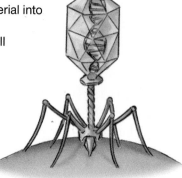

Viruses can inject their genetic material into living cells and begin to reproduce. As viruses reproduce they fill the cell until it bursts, killing the cell and spilling virus particles into the blood and lymph.

Germs that are a bit larger than viruses are bacteria. Bacteria are single-celled organisms too small to be seen without high-powered microscopes. They can damage the body by producing **toxins.** Toxins are poisons that kill cells or interfere with the way they work. Not all bacteria cause disease. Your intestines hold bacteria that help digest your food and combat disease. Other bacteria, in your mouth and on your skin, also help protect your body from disease.

Bacteria are responsible for many infectious diseases. Tuberculosis (tə bur kyōō lō′ sis) is a disease that infects the lungs. Typhoid fever is a deadly disease that causes red rashes, high fever, and bleeding in the intestines. Rheumatic (rōō mat′ ik) fever is a disease that mostly affects children. It causes painful swelling of the joints and damages the heart.

Strep throat is caused by a streptococcus bacterium (strep, for short) that is highly infectious. Did you ever wonder why it seems everyone gets strep throat at the same time? The infection starts before anyone feels sick. The strep bacteria pass from person to person before any symptoms of illness are present. So one person with strep throat can infect many people before the person realizes that he or she is infectious.

The most poisonous bacterial toxin is botulin. It is so poisonous that less than 5 mL of this toxin is enough to kill 10 million people. That's more people than live in most cities. Bacteria that make botulin only grow in places where there is no oxygen, such as in canned foods. As they grow, the bacteria produce gas and botulin. You should never eat food from a can with a dent or a bulge in it, because it may contain this poison.

Some diseases are caused by parasites. These organisms obtain food by breaking down body tissues or by absorbing predigested food from the intestines. These invaders can live in muscle, blood, or digestive-system tissues. They create problems by giving off wastes foreign to the body and consuming nutrients meant for the body's cells.

Fungi, protozoa, flatworms, and roundworms are parasites that often cause disease. Fungi can cause athlete's foot, brain inflammation, and lung disease. Protozoa cause malaria, the most widespread disease in the world. Protozoa also cause amoebic dysentery, an infection of the intestines, and African sleeping

Streptococcus pyogenes

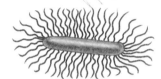

Bacillus proteus

Theospirillum

Bacteria and other foreign particles can also cause cell destruction. Bacteria can reproduce outside living cells. During this process, bacteria produce poisons called toxins. Toxins can either kill cells or interfere with their normal cellular processes.

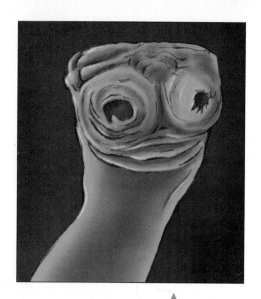

Parasites are organisms bigger than viruses and bacteria that can live within muscle tissue, the bloodstream, or the digestive system. Parasites give off wastes and consume nutrients meant for the body's cells. The tapeworm shown here is just one kind of parasite.

sickness, a fatal disease. Worm parasites can invade the body in many ways. Tapeworms can live in the human digestive tract and consume nutrients meant for the body. Flatworms can live in many different body systems and can cause disease.

Your Body's Defense Systems

Coming in contact with germs does not instantly make you get sick. In fact, the vast majority of airborne germs do not even get inside your body.

Your body has natural defenses that keep out germs. First, your skin forms a nearly germ-proof barrier around your body. It keeps out many germs that touch you. As long as you do not have an open wound where germs can get in, your skin protects you from disease. One of the best ways to help your skin is to keep your hands clean. Using soap and hot water to wash your hands helps keep disease away.

What happens if agents of disease get past the skin? Mucous (myoo′ kəs) membranes lining the nose, reproductive tract, and respiratory tract produce mucus, which is a sticky substance. Germs that come into contact with the mucus stick to it. They are removed when the mucus is pushed out of the body.

In the throat, tiny hairs called cilia move the mucus toward the mouth, where it is either swallowed or spit out. This can sometimes be accompanied by coughing, which also helps to remove mucus.

The Immune System

If germs manage to get past this second line of defense, the body has an elaborate system to fight off foreign particles such as bacteria, fungi, and viruses. The **immune** (i myoon′) **system** functions to fight off invaders.

Fever is another way that your body's immune system fights off disease. Fever causes the immune system to speed up and work harder.

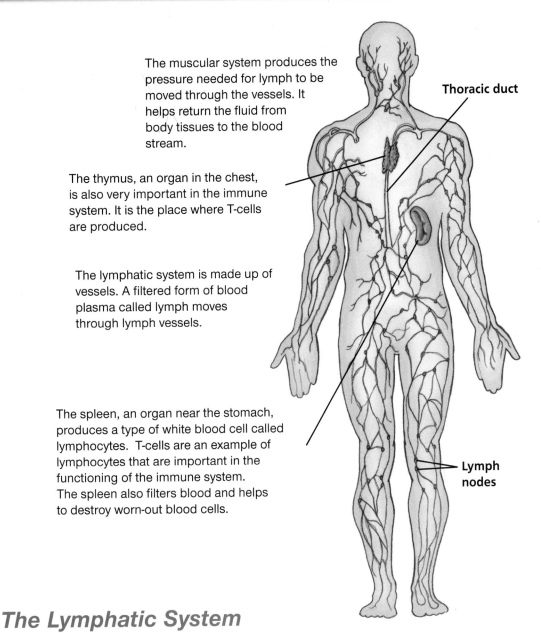

The muscular system produces the pressure needed for lymph to be moved through the vessels. It helps return the fluid from body tissues to the blood stream.

The thymus, an organ in the chest, is also very important in the immune system. It is the place where T-cells are produced.

The lymphatic system is made up of vessels. A filtered form of blood plasma called lymph moves through lymph vessels.

The spleen, an organ near the stomach, produces a type of white blood cell called lymphocytes. T-cells are an example of lymphocytes that are important in the functioning of the immune system. The spleen also filters blood and helps to destroy worn-out blood cells.

Thoracic duct

Lymph nodes

The Lymphatic System

One of the important parts of the immune system is the **lymphatic** (lim fat′ ik) **system.** The lymphatic system transports nutrients too large to enter the bloodstream, such as some large fat molecules, and removes waste. The fluid in the lymphatic system is lymph. Lymph and blood interact to form an incredibly complex defense against foreign particles. The illustrations on the next page show the roles of different immune-system cells that fight disease in your body.

The response of the immune system to foreign particles is quite complex. This system is an interwoven system of cells and chemicals that help the body fight off infection. Lymphocytes are white blood cells that produce antibodies. Macrophages are lymph cells that "swallow up" foreign particles.

Immune System Cells

B-cell

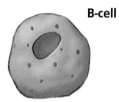

B-cell: B-cells are white blood cells that mark foreign particles with proteins called antibodies. The antibodies cause other proteins to move in and destroy the foreign particles.

Killer T-cell

Killer T-cell: T-cells come in many varieties. They destroy cells infected with foreign particles.

Helper T-cell

Helper T-cell: Helper T-cells help B-cells fight off invaders.

T-suppressor cell

T-suppressor cell: T-suppressor cells alert the body that the foreign particles have been destroyed and the body's defenses can relax.

Your immune system responds to foreign particles with the following steps:

- Viruses, bacteria, or parasites enter the bloodstream. The body recognizes these as foreign particles.
- Phagocytes, or white blood cells, respond to the invasion and alert helper T-cells.
- Helper T-cells multiply and alert the B-cells, another kind of white blood cell.
- B-cells produce antibodies, or types of proteins. These antibodies attach to the invading cells and disarm them.
- Blood proteins recognize the antibodies and surround the foreign particles with antibodies attached to them.
- The blood proteins destroy the foreign particles.
- T-suppressor cells move in and alert the body when the foreign particle is destroyed. At that point, the body's defense system relaxes.

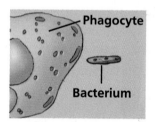
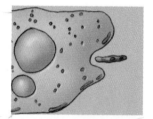
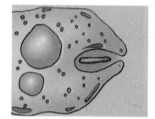
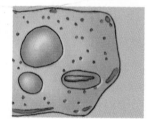

Phagocyte

Bacterium

Phagocytes (fā′ gə sīts), a type of white blood cell, swallow up foreign particles in much the same way an amoeba engulfs its food. The liver has a large number of phagocytes that remain in place. As the blood is filtered through the liver, the phagocytes remove almost all foreign particles.

It's important to remember that the immune system responds to invaders. It responds more quickly to invaders that it remembers. In fact, sometimes the immune system reacts so swiftly to a foreign invader that you do not come down with the disease. You are immune! **Immunity** is the body's resistance to disease.

There are no cures for diseases caused by viruses. For most viral diseases, like mononucleosis, colds, and HIV, there are no vaccines. However, scientists have developed some vaccines to help the body fight certain viral diseases. Vaccines introduce a little bit of dead or weak virus into the body, allowing the body to learn how to fight it off. The body then develops an immunity to that virus. As a young child, you were most likely vaccinated against many viral and bacterial diseases.

The most common childhood vaccinations are for diphtheria, tetanus and pertussis (DPT), measles, mumps, and rubella (MMR), and poliomyelitis (OPV). More recent childhood vaccinations include hepatitis B (HEP B) and hemophilus influenza, type B (HIB). Sometimes, repeated vaccinations are necessary. Diphtheria and tetanus boosters are generally given at age 14 and repeated every ten years thereafter.

Sometimes the body's defense systems do not work properly. Serious diseases or drugs can weaken or destroy the immune system. Usually, but not always, the body can rebuild its immune system. Until then, when someone's immune system is not working properly, he or she needs to take extra precautions against communicable diseases.

CHECKPOINT

1. What is a communicable disease?
2. How can germs spread from person to person?
3. Describe some diseases caused by bacteria, viruses, and parasites.
4. What are your body's defense systems?

 How does the body fight infection?

ACTIVITY

Virus Modeling

Find Out

Do this activity to see how to formulate a model of a virus.

Process Skills

Constructing Models
Measuring
Interpreting Data
Using Numbers
Communicating
Inferring
Hypothesizing

WHAT YOU NEED

1–2 sheets of construction paper

manila folder or cardboard

small balloon

5-cm foam ball

pencil

straw

scissors

glue

transparent tape

five craft pipe cleaners

Activity Journal

metric ruler

WHAT TO DO

1. Look carefully at the photos on the next page. This is a T-4 virus that has been observed by scientists through an electron microscope. You can learn more about this virus by making a three-dimensional model of it. First, make a list of the parts you can see. Measure each part.

2. Using the materials provided, or any others that you think would work better, design a model of this virus. Before you start to work, list the materials you plan to use to construct it. Make sure the proportions of the model are accurate. Then, build your model. You can change your plans as you go along.

 Safety! *Use care with scissors.*

Conclusions

1. Compare your finished model with the photo and computer-generated model. Describe how your model is different from them and how it is the same.

2. Compare your model with your classmates' models. Is there one that is more similar to the photo and computer-generated model than yours? How is yours better? Describe ways you could improve your model.

3. List ways your model is not like a real virus.

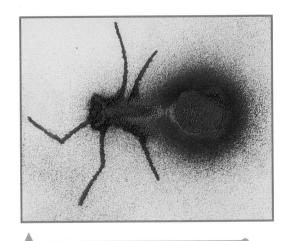

A simple electron micrograph of a T-4 virus, magnified 94,000×.

Asking New Questions

Computer-generated model of a T-4 virus.

1. Compare your model of a virus to a typical animal cell. List the differences between them.

2. Do any structures on your virus model remind you of structures in cells? Make inferences about what you think the different parts of the virus do.

3. Do you think a virus could reproduce, digest or produce food, or move? Use what you know about viruses to develop a hypothesis about what a virus is. Don't worry about being wrong. Scientists make predictions based on the information they have at the moment and then change their ideas as they get new information.

4. Write two or three problem statements or questions about viruses that you would like to be able to answer.

SCIENTIFIC METHODS SELF CHECK

✔ Did I **interpret** my **measurements** to **design** my **model?**

✔ Did I **compare** models with the photos and my classmates' models?

✔ Did I **describe** or **list** the differences between the model and the photos?

✔ Did I make **inferences** about what parts of a virus do?

✔ Did I **hypothesize** about what a virus is?

Environment and Health

Find Out

- How Earth is an interdependent ecosystem
- What a clean environment is
- What impact humans have on the environment
- What you can do to protect the environment

Vocabulary

pollution
reduce
reuse
recycle

The Big QUESTION

How does your environment affect your health?

One of the most obvious effects of pollution is that it makes the surroundings ugly. Few people like to look at trash along a roadside or in the water at a harbor. Pollution in the air can obscure the sunlight. Pollution is ugly. If it were only ugly, you could probably live with it. But pollution can cause breathing problems. It can lead to sunburn. It can cause disease. Pollution is not only ugly—in many cases, it is also dangerous to your health.

Planet Earth as an Ecosystem

Air, soil, and water are among the resources people have always taken for granted. Even in ancient times, people abused these resources, burning fires that put smoke into the air, purposely ruining the soil by sowing salt in the fields of military enemies, and dumping wastes into rivers, lakes, and oceans. With the world's large human population, we can no longer afford to take any of our natural resources for granted. People are mounting worldwide campaigns to protect the atmosphere, clean up our waterways, and save the soil.

Among the dangerous problems facing our world is the destruction of the environment because of misuses of resources. We make the air dirty with greenhouse gases, including carbon dioxide, nitrogen oxides, and methane. Because of this, the planet could be warming up at an unprecedented rate. Many of our waterways have become toxic dumping grounds. The toxins, including lead and cadmium, find their way into the food chain, harming thousands of species of animals. Overclearing land in different parts of the world has led to destruction of the soil. Many once-fertile places have turned into desert because of this abuse.

Your environment is an ecosystem. Everything in it is interdependent.

Everything on Earth is interdependent. That's because Earth is an ecosystem. An ecosystem is all the living and nonliving things in an area that work in relation to each other.

In an ecosystem, sunlight and CO_2 provide energy for plants. Plants, in turn, provide food for animals. Animals, plants, and other living things depend on sunlight, water, soil, and air. Decomposers return nutrients to the soil.

How healthy an ecosystem is depends on the health of all of its parts. Your health depends on the health of the ecosystem in which you live.

Air pollution can be visible, but it may also be an invisible health hazard.

A Clean Environment

The condition of the environment greatly affects the health of all living things. For living things to be healthy, the air, water, and soil in the environment must be clean.

Clean Air

Earth's atmosphere has several layers. The energy absorbed by Earth warms the atmosphere above it. Temperatures in the atmosphere vary according to altitude. The air in Earth's atmosphere contains a mixture of gases, liquids, and solids. Of the gases, nitrogen makes up about 78 percent of our air, and oxygen makes up about 21 percent. The remainder is tiny amounts of other gases, including carbon dioxide and water vapor.

The air and atmosphere are great protectors of life on Earth. We depend on clean air so that we can breathe. We depend on a clean atmosphere to protect us from harmful solar radiation.

Clean Water

Nearly 75 percent of Earth's surface is water. Although water cycles around the planet, there is only a limited amount that is useable. Humans and other organisms depend on Earth's water. People use water for drinking, washing, and bathing. They also use it for manufacturing, farming, or household activities. Our water supply comes from groundwater, rivers, or lakes. Many communities collect, treat, and distribute water for their populations. In other areas, people get their water from private wells. Wherever it comes from, people expect their water to be free of chemical or microorganism contamination. If water is contaminated, it must be cleaned before we use it or it can make us sick.

Clean Soil

One fourth of Earth's surface is land. Like water, Earth's soil is a limited resource. Plants and microorganisms depend on soil for nutrients. Therefore, clean soil is necessary for the health and growth of most organisms. Not all land on Earth has soil capable of supporting life. Keeping soil clean and fertile is critical to our health and well being.

A clean environment is important to your health.

Human Impact on the Environment

In today's society, humans are dependent on the use of air, water, and soil. Unfortunately, there are limited amounts of these resources. Our lives are at risk if any of these resources disappear. One of the ways these resources can disappear is through pollution. **Pollution** is the introduction of substances that cause harmful changes in the environment. It's important to learn how pollution happens and how to prevent or repair pollution damage.

Air Pollution

Air quality is important for our health and welfare. However, many human activities contribute to air pollution. Humans burn fuels—coal, oil, gas, and wood—for various reasons. Burned fuels cause oxides of carbon, nitrogen, and sulfur to form in the air. The reactive nature of oxygen creates these atmospheric pollutants.

One result of increased oxide levels could be an increase in the spread of disease. Some scientists estimate that carbon dioxide levels in the air could double over the next 100 years. This in turn will increase temperatures on Earth and could melt some of the water in the polar ice caps. This could raise sea levels by 15–90 cm. Increased water levels would favor the life cycle of mosquitoes. Mosquito-borne diseases, like malaria and encephalitis, are among the most dangerous to worldwide public health.

Air pollution from industrial manufacturing and power plants is largely responsible for the oxides of nitrogen and sulfur in our air. Scientists have found that increased levels of nitrogen oxides in the air are responsible for lower respiratory tract symptoms. Increased levels of atmospheric sulfur dioxide will cause bronchitis in children. Communities that monitor air pollution may issue a smog alert when air pollution gets too high.

When air pollution gets too high, a smog alert can happen. This is a warning for sick and elderly people to stay indoors.

Atmospheric Pollution

Humans depend on the ozone layer of Earth's atmosphere to filter ultraviolet radiation from the sun. Ultraviolet radiation burns the cells of living things. Radiation can also disrupt cellular processes involving the genetic material DNA. Have you ever had a sunburn? A sunburn results from your skin cells being burned by ultraviolet rays.

Chlorofluorocarbons (CFCs) are gases that were used in refrigerators, air conditioners, water purification, some aerosol sprays, and other devices before the year 2000. When these compounds escape into the atmosphere, ultraviolet rays break them down. The chemical chlorine is released as a gas. Chlorine gas breaks down ozone. One scientific estimate suggests that as much as 25 percent of the ozone layer over the northern hemisphere was destroyed between 1979 and 1996. A hole in the ozone layer has already developed in the southern hemisphere. Chlorofluorocarbons were banned internationally beginning in the year 2000. It is possible that some products made before then are still in use today. Hopefully, the international ban on the use of these compounds will allow the ozone layer to return to its pre-1979 levels.

Water Pollution

Chemicals on the ground can lead to water pollution. Think of a hard midwestern rain falling on a large wheat farm in Kansas in late August. The dry, dusty soil gets soaked. Eventually, if the rain falls long enough and hard enough, some of the soil erodes into a nearby stream. This agricultural runoff carries more than farm soil. It also carries some of the agricultural chemicals used on the farm. Once these chemicals enter the groundwater, the water is no longer clean. Before contaminated water is safe to use, it has to be treated.

Another source of water contamination is large, transcontinental cargo ships. These large ships draw water for ballast from one port and release it in another. Ballast water is one way foreign organisms can be transported around the world. It may also carry harmful algae, bacteria, or viruses. It is believed that ballast water released from a Chinese freighter at a port in Lima, Peru, caused a deadly outbreak of cholera in 1991. The water supply in Lima comes from the port. The water was not treated after the discharge, and an

This lake in Pitman, New Jersey, is so polluted that swimming in it or eating fish from it could make you sick.

epidemic of cholera broke out. More than 300,000 people got sick and more than 3500 people died in this epidemic.

Land Pollution

Americans generate almost 373,000,000 kg of trash every day. One estimate of typical American household garbage puts the contents at 10 percent unused food and 60 percent paper. About one percent of landfill waste comes from fast food packaging. Before the Clean Air Act in the 1970s, people burned their trash. After that law, trash burning was banned in many communities. Now, most residential and business trash is hauled to sanitary landfills. Sanitary landfills are places where trash is dumped and buried between layers of soil. However, many landfills are already full. You can see that trash disposal is a real concern. It is also a major contributor to the pollution of our land resources.

We are running out of places to put our trash.

Some products are not allowed to be buried in sanitary landfills. Products such as batteries and tires, many chemicals, and nuclear or radioactive materials are hazardous wastes. Hazardous wastes are dangerous to people and the environment. Laws control the disposal of hazardous wastes.

Environmental problems can occur from buried hazardous waste. Often, water seepage moves toxic chemicals from landfills into groundwater. Sometimes, these toxic chemicals remain in the water after treatment. Other times, landfill ground becomes so toxic that nothing grows on or near these landfills. In 1980, the U.S. Congress gave the Environmental Protection Agency (EPA) authority to recover money from businesses and people who illegally dump toxic materials. The EPA then uses the money to clean up toxic places.

Hazardous wastes cause human health problems too. Increased numbers of cases of serious disease, such as childhood leukemia and other cancers, sometimes occur in areas near hazardous waste dump sites.

What You Can Do

Human health and welfare depend on the quality of the air, water, and soil in the environment. Caring for the environment is everyone's responsibility. Your generation will inherit a variety of environmental issues. It will be important for you to contribute ways to address these issues in society. You can start now by learning to reduce, reuse, and recycle. When you **reduce,** you use less. When you **reuse,** you use things more than once. When you **recycle,** you find a different way for the material to be used again.

Reduce the amount of trash you make.

- Pay attention to the type of packaging and containers of products you buy. Avoid buying items that are overpackaged. Choose products with packages that can go to a recycling center.

- Read product labels. Many products contain chemicals that should not go in a landfill. Some of these include computer disks and things you use to care for your pet or your hair. Use and discard all products as directed. On the other hand, you can select environmentally safer alternatives.

Don't be an overconsumer. Find ways to reduce, reuse, and recycle rather than creating trash.

You can make a difference in the health of your environment.

Reuse items before disposing of them.

- Find four different ways to reuse every item before you throw it away. For example, if you buy a new pair of jeans, you can wear them as new jeans for a while. Then, they can be your old jeans. Then, you can cut the legs off and make a pair of shorts. You can use the legs as rags or cut them into patches for other clothes.

Recycle items instead of throwing them away.

- Learn what kinds of items go to your recycling center. Most communities have recycling centers, which accept a variety of materials. Metals and paper are good candidates for recycling. Many plastics can also be recycled. Find out if stores and businesses recycle their products or if they use recycled products.

- Make compost. Start your own pile or begin one for your community. Grass and lawn trimmings are excellent sources for making compost. Certain food wastes can go into a compost pile as well. You can use compost in gardening projects.

CHECKPOINT

1. How is everything on Earth interdependent?
2. What is a clean environment?
3. How do humans impact their environment?
4. What can you do to help care for your environment?

 How does your environment affect your health?

ACTIVITY

Measuring Soil Seepage

Find Out

Do this activity to learn how different soils affect seepage.

Process Skills

Observing
Measuring
Communicating
Predicting
Experimenting
Controlling Variables
Using Numbers
Interpreting Data
Defining Operationally
Inferring

WHAT YOU NEED

two large coffee cans

small wooden board

500 mL water

trowel

watch or clock with second hand

masking tape

hammer

Activity Journal

metric ruler

Activity Journal

WHAT TO DO

1. Find a place in the schoolyard or lawn where plants don't grow very well. Find another spot where the grass is thick and green. Use a trowel to remove a section of sod from the grassy spot. Try to poke your pencil into the soil at each spot. Observe which soil seems harder. Describe any difference in appearance.

2. Using a ruler, measure and mark the outside of each coffee can 5 cm from one end. Place a can at each location. Put the board on top of each can and have one person hold the board while another person hammers on the wood to push the can into the soil down to the 5 cm mark.

Safety! *Use the hammer carefully. Keep your hands and fingers out of the way.*

3. Predict which soil will absorb water the fastest.

4. Pour 250 mL water into each can and time how long it takes the water to soak into the ground. Record the soaking time at each location.

5. Make a bar graph to compare the soaking times at each location.

CONCLUSIONS

1. At which location was water absorbed more quickly?

2. Recall the results from poking the soil at each spot with your pencil. Do you think there is a relationship between soil hardness and soaking rate?

ASKING NEW QUESTIONS

1. Use your findings to infer which kind of soil would be a better choice for landfill soil.

2. Why would soil that allows greater water seepage not be good for a landfill?

SCIENTIFIC METHODS SELF CHECK

✔ Did I **record** my **observations** about the types of soil?

✔ Did I **predict** which soil type would have faster drainage?

✔ Did I **experiment** to test my prediction?

✔ Did I **control the variables** so that only soil type changed?

✔ Did I **measure** the amounts of water and soaking times accurately?

✔ Did I **graph** my observations?

✔ Did I **interpret the data** about different soil types?

✔ Did I **operationally define** seepage?

✔ Did I **infer** which soil would be better in landfills?

D47

· LESSON 3

World Health

Find Out

- How countries fight disease locally
- What some worldwide health organizations are
- What stops epidemics from starting

Vocabulary

volunteer
Centers for Disease Control
National Institutes of Health
World Health Organization
quarantine

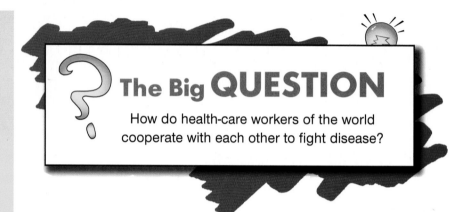

The Big QUESTION

How do health-care workers of the world cooperate with each other to fight disease?

*D*iseases know no borders. That's why a global approach to disease control is necessary. Organizations such as the World Health Organization (WHO) and the Centers for Disease Control (CDC) fight against disease all over the world. Organizations like SHARE, the Red Cross, Project Hope, and Doctors Without Borders also contribute to the effort.

Government Health Agencies

Communities and nations do many things to prevent the spread of disease. Communities regularly check their water sources to make sure the water supply is pure. Local and state governments make and enforce laws so that trash and other wastes are properly discarded. There are local and national inspections of the food you buy at the store or in a restaurant.

Many communities offer health services to the public. Low-cost immunization programs for children prevent diseases. Health and wellness testing for children of all ages help detect diseases early. All of these are ways to protect people in the community from illnesses such as typhoid fever, cholera, and dysentery. All of these community activities help prevent disease.

Health care worker doing field work in Kenya

Countries also work to stop the spread of disease. Doctors report cases of communicable illnesses to the government and to their professional organizations. Doctors also report other disease and injury information to government agencies. Sometimes, they are required to report diseases. Other times, they **volunteer** the information. To volunteer means to give freely.

United States agencies, such as the **Centers for Disease Control** (CDC) in Atlanta, Georgia, and the **National Institutes of Health** (NIH), a government health service agency in Maryland, conduct research and collect medical data and information from doctors, schools, and research groups. The United States government supports disease research and prevention efforts in a variety of ways.

For instance, the surgeon general of the United States warns the general public about threats to health. For example, every pack of cigarettes carries a surgeon general's warning. Scientists know cigarettes cause cancer, heart disease, and other illnesses. This information was collected, analyzed, and published by the NIH.

Because disease is a worldwide problem, it must be addressed by people all over the world. As a result, nations and private organizations work together to prevent, control, or eliminate diseases.

A government food inspector helps insure the food is safe to eat.

Global Health Organizations

The **World Health Organization** (WHO) is the leading organization through which different countries work together to prevent disease. It was founded in 1948 by the United Nations and is headquartered in Geneva, Switzerland. The WHO provides a way for many countries to share information about disease and to alert others of serious outbreaks.

In its first 30 years, the WHO concentrated on eliminating major diseases such as malaria, tuberculosis, leprosy, and smallpox. By acting as a global health service, it provided vaccines and treatment for these diseases throughout the world. It helped eliminate smallpox and greatly reduced the number of cases of leprosy. Malaria and tuberculosis are still concerns of the WHO.

The World Health Organization was founded in 1948 by the United Nations.

United Nations medical worker examining a child in Cambodia

The WHO started providing wellness checkups and immunizations in many places in 1978. The WHO believes that educating people about hygiene and providing essential drugs, sanitation, and nutrition improves the world's health.

In 1998, the WHO picked several diseases as major world health threats. Malaria, tuberculosis, and AIDS and human immunodeficiency virus (HIV) top their list. After 50 years of international efforts to rid the world of malaria and tuberculosis, there are still many cases of these diseases. HIV is the virus that causes AIDS. HIV is a major concern because about 15,000 people are infected every day. The WHO is looking for vaccines for all of these diseases and provides clinics for people with these diseases.

The WHO's goal is to work toward the health of all people. It believes that all people deserve equal access to health services to enable them to lead healthy and meaningful lives.

Other Health Organizations

A number of other international organizations work to rid the world of disease. Most of them work in cooperation with the WHO or their national governments.

Nations in the western hemisphere founded the Pan American Health Organization in 1902. An organization like the WHO, the Pan American Health Organization aims to improve physical and mental health in the Americas. It is a health information exchange. It supports educational programs and disaster relief activities.

SHARE—Services for Health in Asian and African Regions—is a medical association. SHARE is headquartered in Tokyo, Japan. Health professionals provide health care for people living in developing areas of Africa and Asia.

There are many international organizations to fight disease. Here *Doctors Without Borders* provides medical care in Sierra Leone.

Many volunteer organizations contribute to the fight against disease. The fast response of relief organizations to disasters helps stop the spread of disease. Disasters, such as floods and hurricanes, often lead to a lack of safe drinking water. After a disaster, water supplies usually get contaminated by disease-carrying microorganisms. Volunteers bring water and other aid to disaster victims. Without volunteers, many natural disasters could become worldwide epidemics.

The International Federations of the Red Cross and the Red Crescent are two of the world's largest relief organizations. Disease control is only one of the many ways they help victims of disasters. The American Red Cross also tests donated blood to be certain it is free of disease. That effort helps prevent the spread of disease to people who need blood.

Doctors Without Borders, founded in 1971, is a volunteer organization of medical professionals who assist victims of wars and natural disasters. Another notable volunteer organization is Project Hope. It provides immunizations and reliable health-care services in many regions of the world that need them.

Without volunteer organizations many natural disasters could become worldwide health problems. Here volunteers from the American Federation of the International Red Cross are bringing water to victims of the 1994 earthquake in Los Angeles.

Preventing Epidemics

The two most effective ways to keep diseases from becoming epidemics are vaccinating and quarantining. A **quarantine** is the separation of people with a highly contagious communicable disease from other people.

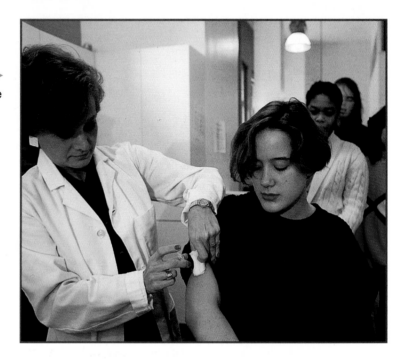

A vaccination campaign rid the world of smallpox by 1979.

Vaccines are made from dead or weakened germs that stimulate the body's natural immune system. Vaccines are one of the safest and least expensive weapons for fighting infectious disease. There are about 20 different vaccines in worldwide use today. They prevent millions of deaths every year.

By 1979, for example, vaccines helped rid the world of smallpox, a highly infectious, deadly disease. The WHO estimates that delivering all of the smallpox vaccines costs about $330 million. They believe the world saves $1 billion annually by not having to treat people for smallpox illness.

Quarantines are another effective tool in controlling the spread of airborne and waterborne diseases. Quarantines work by stopping people from traveling. If people in a region are suspected of having a highly contagious, deadly disease, they are put in isolation, or quarantine. The quarantine usually ends when doctors are sure no one in the region is still infectious.

The WHO helped set up the quarantine laws in most countries of the world. These laws help prevent deadly infectious diseases from entering a country. Quarantine laws around the world apply to anyone who has been exposed to cholera, plague, relapsing fever, typhus, or yellow fever.

Also, new situations sometimes require quarantines. Astronauts who traveled to the moon in the 1960s were placed in quarantine upon their return to Earth. Doctors wanted to be sure the astronauts were not bringing any germs or diseases back with them.

Apollo astronauts were quarantined to ensure they would not introduce new diseases to Earth.

What Still Needs to Be Done

With the high rate of travel between countries, the threat of worldwide epidemics is real. Disease can spread more quickly than ever before. An outbreak of a disease in any part of the world can reach your neighborhood in a matter of days. Sometimes, diseases don't make people sick right away. People can be infected but not show symptoms. By the time they have symptoms, or feel sick, they may have already infected many other people. These others then go through the same cycle. Scientists and doctors want a better warning and surveillance program for this kind of disease.

CHECKPOINT

1. How do countries fight disease on a local basis?
2. Name some of the global health organizations engaged in the fight against communicable diseases.
3. What can stop epidemics from starting?
 How do health-care workers of the world cooperate to fight disease?

ACTIVITY

Finding Out About Diseases

Find Out

Do this activity to see what kind of information is in a Centers for Disease Control report.

Process Skills

Observing
Classifying
Using Numbers
Interpreting Data
Inferring

WHAT YOU NEED

paper

copy of the Morbidity and Mortality Weekly Report

calculator

pencil or pen

Activity Journal

WHAT TO DO

1. Visually inspect your copy of the MMWR. What kinds of information does it contain?

2. How is the report organized? Can you identify the system of classification that is used?

3. Find Table I. Which disease has the greatest number of reported cases this year? How many diseases had no reported cases this year? What is the difference?

4. Find Table II. Which region of the United States had the greatest number of reported cases last year? Which region has the greatest number of cases reported this year? Compare the locations of these regions. Are they close to each other?

5. Which region of the United States had the fewest reported cases this year? Calculate the percentage difference between that region's reported cases from last year and this year.

6. Which table shows numbers of cases of diseases for which there are vaccines?

7. Find Table III. What is the most common disease among the children in the United States? Calculate what percentage of children in the United States with that disease come from your region and your state.

8. Find Table IV. How does the time period of this table differ from the other tables? How is it the same?

9. How many cases of pneumonia and influenza were reported for your region? How many for the largest city near where you live? Which region had the most reported cases of pneumonia and influenza? Which region had the least so far this year?

10. Did any region have fewer deaths from all causes in the over 65 age category than in any of the other age groups?

CONCLUSIONS

1. Were the data only from each state of the United States? If not, what other places were included?

2. Where do the data come from?

ASKING NEW QUESTIONS

1. What other information or reports would help public health officials prevent disease?

2. How would this report be useful to your doctor?

SCIENTIFIC METHODS SELF CHECK

✔ Did I **observe** the tables?

✔ Did I discover the way the information was organized and **classified?**

✔ Did I use my **math** skills to get more data?

✔ Did I **interpret the data** to get more information from the tables?

✔ Did I **infer** the usefulness of reporting diseases to prevent the spread of disease?

Review

Reviewing Vocabulary and Concepts

Write the letter of the answer that best completes each sentence.

1. We describe diseases that can spread from person to person as ____.
   - **a.** toxins
   - **b.** common diseases
   - **c.** carriers
   - **d.** communicable diseases

2. Nonliving bits of nucleic acid and protein that can cause disease are called ____.
   - **a.** fungi
   - **b.** viruses
   - **c.** bacteria
   - **d.** parasites

3. When you avoid buying items that are overpackaged, you ____.
   - **a.** reduce
   - **b.** repair
   - **c.** recycle
   - **d.** reuse

4. When you find new things to do with old items you own, you ____.
   - **a.** recycle
   - **b.** reduce
   - **c.** repair
   - **d.** reuse

5. When you make compost from grass and food waste, you ____.
   - **a.** reduce
   - **b.** reuse
   - **c.** recycle
   - **d.** repair

Match the definition on the left with the correct term on the right.

6. a germd that invades your body   **a.** National Institutes of Health

7. poisons that kill cells or interfere with their function   **b.** Centers for Disease Control

8. the body's system that fights off foreign particles   **c.** immunity

9. the body's resistance to disease   **d.** quarantine

10. introduction of substances that cause harmful changes in the environment   **e.** infectious

11. to give freely   **f.** toxins

12. public health service agency with headquarters in Georgia   **g.** pollution

13. public health service agency with headquarters in Maryland   **h.** immune system

14. global health agency with headquarters in Switzerland that helps countries share information about disease   **i.** volunteer

15. separation of people with serious contagious disease   **j.** World Health Organization

Understanding What You Learned

1. You come in contact with germs every day. What things prevent you from always being sick?

2. What things in the environment must be kept free of pollution for living things to remain healthy?

3. What do government health agencies do to prevent the spread of disease?

4. What do world organizations do to promote health?

5. How can quarantines and vaccines prevent an epidemic?

Applying What You Learned

1. Bacteria cause many infectious diseases, such as strep throat. Would being able to destroy all the bacteria in the world be a good idea? Why?

2. How can you tell your immune system is healthy and working efficiently?

3. What are some ways that large industries can help to reduce pollution?

4. What have you done at school or home in the past three weeks to help prevent pollution?

 5. Why is preventing disease a global concern?

For Your **Portfolio**

The response of the immune system to foreign particles is quite complex. Sometimes, acting out a process can help you understand it better. Use the information in the text and any other information you can find to write and act out a play in which the immune system responds to a bacterial infection. A couple of members of your group might write the dialogue that will explain the actions. One or two may design costumes or sets. Others can work on casting and staging the play. When you are finished, perform the play for another class to explain the functioning of the immune system.

CHAPTER 3

NUTRITION

Why do you eat the foods you eat? Do you eat what's put on your plate? Or do you just pick out the things that taste good to you? Would you eat only brownies, ice cream, apple pie, and chocolate cake if you were allowed to? Or do you try to eat fruits and vegetables too?

What you choose to eat is your diet. A diet is all the food and drink a person regularly consumes. To stay healthy, you need to choose foods that give you good nutrition. People around the world make different food choices, just like you do. In fact, new technologies have increased the world's food supply. There are many ways to meet the body's need for healthful foods.

The Big IDEA

A variety of foods is important for a healthful diet.

SCIENCE INVESTIGATION

Investigate diets from around the world. Find out how in your *Activity Journal.*

Diets for Good Health

Find Out

- What your body gets from food
- What micronutrients are
- What macronutrients are

Vocabulary

nutrients
minerals
vitamins
carbohydrates
proteins
fats

The Big QUESTION

What's in a healthful diet?

The cells in your body get their energy from food. Food builds and maintains all of your body's systems. The number of Calories in a food is a measure of that food's energy. How many Calories you need to consume depends on several things: your age, gender, body size, and daily activities.

Energy from Food

The source of energy for the cells in your body is the food you eat. Food builds and maintains all of your body's systems. The number of Calories food contains is a measure of its energy. How many Calories you need to eat depends on several things. The right amount for you depends on your age, gender, body size, and your daily activities. A good diet provides you with the correct number of Calories. A 2200-Calorie diet is recommended for most children and teenage girls. Teenage boys need about 600 more Calories per day in their diet, or 2800 Calories. If you don't eat enough Calories, your body may not grow properly. If your diet has too many Calories, your body stores the extra ones as fat.

Micronutrients

Calories aren't the only part of a healthful diet. Your body needs many types of **nutrients** (nōō′ trē əntz). Nutrients are substances that living things need for their survival. The most important nutrient you need is water. Without water, your body would not work at all. Water carries other nutrients through your body. It helps your digestion system and has a major role in keeping your body at the right temperature.

Micronutrients are chemicals and compounds in the diet that your body needs in small amounts. Two classes of micronutrients are minerals and vitamins. **Minerals** are chemical elements that help your bones, blood, and tissues. Your body needs many different minerals. Different body systems need different minerals. Minerals like calcium and phosphorous are important in bone growth and development. Calcium and phosphorous come from nuts, fish, and vegetables. Calcium is most abundant in milk. Iodine controls the body's metabolism. Iodine is in onions and dairy products. Most Americans get iodine from table salt that has iodine added to it. Potassium, sodium, and chlorine keep your blood at the proper pH. Potassium comes from nuts, fruits, and grains. You get sodium and chlorine from salt. Iron is the main mineral in human blood. You get iron from meat, fish, beans, and grains.

Vitamins are chemical compounds that help your cells function. Some vitamins are stored in your body tissues. The body uses or excretes the other vitamins. Vitamins that stay in your body for a long time include vitamins A, D, E, and K. You need only very small amounts of these vitamins every day. Because your body stores them, people who eat healthful diets do not need to take vitamin supplements for these vitamins. In fact, too much of these vitamins can make you sick.

Vitamin A comes from yellow and orange vegetables like carrots and squash. It builds your bones and skin and helps your eyes work. Vitamin D comes from fish and dairy products. It helps your body use vitamin A and calcium. Vitamin E comes from vegetable oils, beans, nuts, and rice. The nervous and immune systems need vitamin E. Vitamin K comes from brocolli, cabbage, and other similar cruciferous (krū sif′ ər əs) vegetables.

Every day you need to eat foods that contain the vitamins your body doesn't store. These include vitamin C, biotin, and the B-group vitamins (thiamine, riboflavin, niacin, folic acid, B_6, and B_{12}). Vitamin C comes from berries, citrus fruits, and most green vegetables. Your body's tissues need vitamin C. Biotin comes from nuts, grains, milk, and fruits. It helps your body use vitamin C. Many B-group vitamins come from leafy vegetables and other foods. Your blood cells and vascular tissues need the B-group vitamins to work properly.

Macronutrients

A good diet must include the right types of food for you. Nutrients your body needs in large amounts are macronutrients. The Food Guide Pyramid is the current best estimate of the macronutrients needed in a healthful diet. This food guide was developed by the

The Food Guide Pyramid

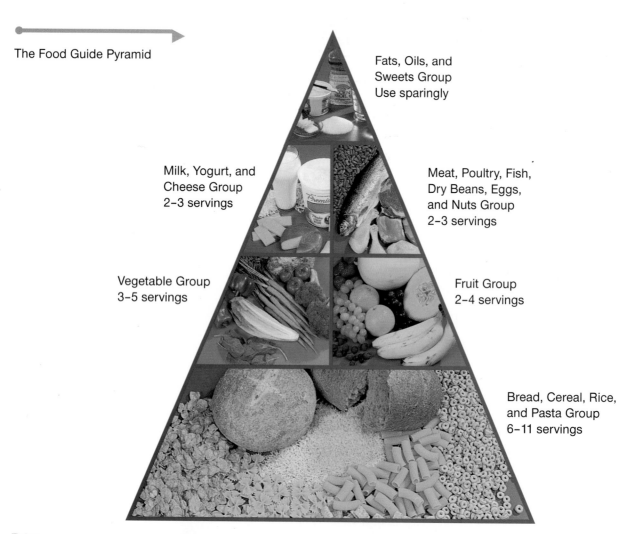

Fats, Oils, and
Sweets Group
Use sparingly

Milk, Yogurt, and
Cheese Group
2–3 servings

Meat, Poultry, Fish,
Dry Beans, Eggs,
and Nuts Group
2–3 servings

Vegetable Group
3–5 servings

Fruit Group
2–4 servings

Bread, Cereal, Rice,
and Pasta Group
6–11 servings

U.S. Department of Agriculture, the International Food Information Council Foundation, and the Food Marketing Institute.

At the base of the pyramid is the bread, cereal, rice, and pasta group. These foods contain complex **carbohydrates** (kär′ bō hī′ dr āts). They are the main source of your body's energy. The body's digestive system turns these foods into usable sugar. Foods in this group include starches, such as potatoes, and grains, such as rice, wheat, and corn. Products made from grains, such as crackers, cereal, bread, and pasta, are also in this group. These foods provide fiber. A good diet will include 6–11 servings of bread, cereal, rice, and pasta group foods.

In the next level up the pyramid are two groups—the fruit group and the vegetable group. These food groups also are high in fiber. Foods in the fruit group are high-energy foods. Apples, oranges, berries, bananas, and grapes belong in the fruit group. Foods in the vegetable group are the primary sources of vitamins and minerals in our diets. Green leafy vegetables, broccoli, carrots, and radishes are examples of foods in the vegetable group. Good diets include less servings of fruits and vegetables than bread group foods. Because of the sugar content in fruits, it is recommended that diets should have slightly less fruits and more vegetable servings.

Near the top of the pyramid are the meat, poultry, fish, dry beans, eggs, and nuts group and the milk, yogurt, and cheese group. The foods in the meat, poultry, fish, dry beans, eggs, and nuts group are high in proteins. **Proteins** (prō′ tēnz) are nutrients made of amino acids, which are the building blocks of protein and are necessary for growth and repair of the body's cells. Beans and nuts are in this group because they contain more amino acids than other vegetables do. Foods from one plant group do not have all the amino acids humans need. Plants have incomplete proteins. It is still possible to get all the necessary amino acids in a meat-free diet by combining different plant foods, like beans and rice, to get all the proteins your body needs. Foods from animals are complete proteins. They contain all the amino acids the body needs.

The other group at this level in the pyramid contains dairy products. They provide minerals and some fat in the diet. Healthful diets have fewer servings of proteins and dairy foods than foods from the vegetable and fruit groups.

At the top of the pyramid is the fats, oils, and sweets group. **Fats** are high-energy, high-Calorie foods. Although there are no recommended number of fat servings, fats are important. Fats help growing bodies develop properly. Your body uses fat for energy storage and to regulate its temperature. Children and teenagers should have a diet with about one third of their Calories coming from fat. Most diets have some fat in them. If you eat protein-rich foods you are also eating some fat. Butter, margarine, oil,

Fat Group (approximately 110 Calories per serving)

    1 tsp. butter

    1 tsp. vegetable oil

    1 tbsp. sugar

    $\frac{1}{2}$ doughnut

    6 oz. soft drink

    1 piece of bubble gum

Milk, Yogurt, and Cheese Group (approximately 120 Calories per serving)

    1 cup of milk or yogurt**

    $1\frac{1}{2}$ oz. natural cheese

    2 oz. processed cheese

Meat, Poultry, Fish, Dry Beans, Eggs, and Nuts Group (approximately 250–350 Calories per serving)

    2–3 oz. cooked lean meat, poultry, or fish*

    $\frac{1}{2}$ cup cooked dry beans

    1 egg

    2 tbsp. peanut butter

    $\frac{1}{3}$ cup nuts

*Calories depend on fat content.

**Calories depend on whether nonfat, low-fat, or whole milk is used.

and cream are fats. Foods made with fats include gravies, salad dressings, processed meats, and sweets. Pure sugar, a simple carbohydrate, is also in the fats, oils, and sweets group. Sugar has little nutrient value but is high in Calories. Soft drinks are mostly sugared water and are also classified in this group. Pure fat and pure sugar provide "empty" Calories. Empty Calories have little other nutritional value than being a Calorie.

Vegetable Group (approximately 25 Calories per serving)

1 cup raw, leafy vegetable

$\frac{1}{2}$ cup cooked or chopped raw vegetables

$\frac{3}{4}$ cup vegetable juice

Fruit Group (approximately 60 Calories per serving)

1 piece of medium fruit

$\frac{1}{2}$ cup chopped, cooked, or canned fruit

$\frac{3}{4}$ cup fruit juice

Bread, Cereal, Rice, and Pasta Group
(approximately 80 Calories per serving)

1 slice of bread

1 oz. of ready-to-eat cereal

$\frac{1}{2}$ cup of cooked cereal, rice or pasta

$\frac{1}{2}$ bagel or English muffin

5–6 small crackers

$\frac{1}{2}$ cup cooked noodles

Serving Size

To get the right amount of nutrients in your diet, you need to eat several servings from each food group each day. The Food Guide Pyramid recommends a range of servings of each food group.

The Food Guide Pyramid is a practical way for you to make nutritious food choices. Build your diet from the bottom up. Think of your plate and fill three sections with plenty of breads, fruits, and vegetables. Fill the fourth section of your plate with food from the meat, poultry, fish, dry beans, eggs, and nuts group and put a glass of milk next to your plate. Your meal will be complete and full of good nutrition.

There are many ways to create a healthful diet.

Sometimes, people don't eat just simple food servings. They eat food mixtures, or foods combined with other foods. Food mixtures belong in more than one food group. Pizza, burritos, sandwiches, chicken stir-fry, and omelets are all food mixtures. Consider a small bean burrito. The beans count as a protein serving at 250 Calories. The tortilla counts as a bread serving at 80 Calories. The cheese is one half of a milk, yogurt, and cheese group serving at 60 Calories. The tomato and lettuce are a vegetable-group serving at 25 Calories. With no toppings, this is a 415-Calorie meal. If you add salsa, guacamole, and sour cream, then you must count one vegetable and two fats, oils, and sweets group servings, or another 245 Calories. With toppings, this is a 660-Calorie meal.

To make the Food Guide Pyramid work for you, you have to balance your daily food choices with your lifestyle and the amount of Calories you need.

It is important to count all of the servings of all the foods present in food mixtures.

CHECKPOINT

1. What does your body get from food?
2. Describe the role of micronutrients in a healthful diet.
3. What nutrients are in macronutrients?

 What's in a healthful diet?

ACTIVITY

Balancing Act

Find Out

Do this activity to learn how to plan a healthful menu for one day.

Process Skills

Classifying
Communicating
Defining Operationally

WHAT YOU NEED

Food Guide Pyramid

vitamins and minerals chart

colored markers

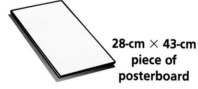

28-cm × 43-cm piece of posterboard

Activity Journal

WHAT TO DO

1. Carefully examine the charts your teacher provides. Use the information on the charts to plan a menu, including any snacks, for a single day.

2. Consider how you will get all of the allowances of different food groups, vitamins, and minerals. Plan and record a menu for one day that includes the proper balance of foods from each food group.

3. Check to see that as many vitamins and minerals as possible are present. For comparison, write down what you ate yesterday.

4. Once you have planned the menu, make a poster on your posterboard that illustrates your suggested meals.

CONCLUSIONS

1. Which food group provides the most Calories for the day?
2. Which food group provides the most servings for the day?
3. Which food group provides the fewest Calories for the day?
4. Which food group provides the fewest servings for the day?
5. How healthful are the choices you made for the day's meals?

ASKING NEW QUESTIONS

1. Compare your menu with your diet of the day before. How healthful is your normal diet?
2. Share your poster with other class members to see if you can come up with a week or more of healthful meals.

SCIENTIFIC METHODS SELF CHECK

✔ Did I **classify** foods into their proper food groups?

✔ Did I remember to **classify** combination foods?

✔ Did I **operationally define** a healthful and balanced diet?

✔ Did I **communicate** my results to others with my poster?

Threats to Good Health

Find Out

- How your body obtains nutrients
- What your heart does
- What the circulatory system does
- What role fat plays in heart disease

Vocabulary

circulatory system
arteries
veins
atherosclerosis
blood pressure

The Big QUESTION

How does your diet affect your blood vessels and heart?

Your body systems keep your internal environment stable. To perform your daily activities, your body takes in oxygen, food, and water and delivers them to the cells, where energy is released from food. Your body also removes carbon dioxide and other wastes from your system. These functions allow your body to respond to your needs and choices throughout the day. You make choices about how you treat your body. Good choices keep your body systems healthy. If you make unhealthful choices, different parts of your body will have trouble working together.

Turning Nutrients into Energy

Your body needs food as its source of energy and as a source of materials for maintaining healthy body systems. Proper nutrition is an important part of keeping your entire body functioning as it should. Proper nutrition, as you learned in Lesson 1, includes a balanced diet of proteins, carbohydrates, fats, vitamins, minerals, and water.

Your body's digestive system works to provide your body's cells with nutrients from food. Digestion begins in the mouth. There, food is physically broken down by chewing. At the same time, the food is mixed with saliva (sə līˈvə), a clear fluid secreted by glands in your mouth. Saliva contains digestive enzymes (enˈzīmz), which are chemical compounds that speed up digestion.

Once your food is thoroughly chewed, it passes down the esophagus (i sofˈə gəs) to the stomach. The stomach continues the physical and chemical breakdown of food. As the muscles of the stomach contract, gastric juices are secreted into the stomach. Gastric juices help break down food into smaller particles. From the stomach, food is passed into the small intestine where digestion is completed. The digested food passes through the walls of the small intestine and enters either the lymphatic system or the bloodstream, and is eventually delivered to the body's cells.

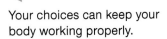

Your choices can keep your body working properly.

The Respiratory System

The respiratory system is another important body system. It is responsible for delivering oxygen to the blood and removing carbon dioxide from it. Air containing oxygen enters the body through the mouth or the nose. It passes down the throat to the trachea (trā′ kē ə), or windpipe. The trachea divides into two branches, or bronchi (bron′ kī). One bronchial tube enters each lung. In the lung, the branching continues to form smaller passageways. These passages are the bronchioles. Alveoli are cup-shaped pouches protruding from the walls of the bronchioles. Oxygen from the air and carbon dioxide in the blood are exchanged in the alveoli.

Oxygen enters your body through your mouth or nose.

The respiratory system delivers oxygen to the blood and removes carbon dioxide from it.

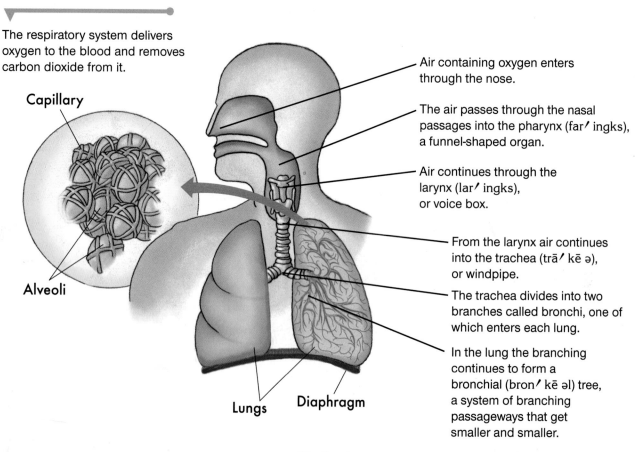

Capillary

Alveoli

Lungs

Diaphragm

Air containing oxygen enters through the nose.

The air passes through the nasal passages into the pharynx (far′ ingks), a funnel-shaped organ.

Air continues through the larynx (lar′ ingks), or voice box.

From the larynx air continues into the trachea (trā′ kē ə), or windpipe.

The trachea divides into two branches called bronchi, one of which enters each lung.

In the lung the branching continues to form a bronchial (bron′ kē əl) tree, a system of branching passageways that get smaller and smaller.

Finally, air enters the alveoli (al vē′ ə lī), where gas exchange takes place in the blood.

The Heart

In order for blood to carry digested nutrients and oxygen to the body's cells and get rid of carbon dioxide and other wastes, it must move through the body. This is the job of the **circulatory** (sûr´ kyo͞o lə tor´ ē) **system.** The circulatory system moves the blood through the body. How does the blood move?

The heart is the main organ of the circulatory system. It pumps the blood. The heart is a big muscle, about the size of your fist. It is composed of special cardiac (kär´ dē ak) muscle, which contracts rhythmically under the control of the nervous system. The heart itself is the core of the pumping process. Examine the diagram on this page to understand how blood moves through the heart.

The heart is the main organ of the circulatory system.

4. Blood is then pumped from the heart through the pulmonary (pul´ mə ner´ ē) artery. The word *pulmonary* is related to the lungs. The blood is leaving the heart and going to the lungs.

1. Blood enters the heart through the inferior (or lower) and superior (or upper) **vena cava** (vē´ nə kā´ və). These blood vessels return blood from the lower and upper body. The blood that enters the heart has already circulated around the body, delivering oxygen to cells and picking up carbon dioxide and waste materials. It is oxygen poor as it enters the heart.

5. When blood enters the lungs, it gives off carbon dioxide that the lungs expel from the body by exhaling. The blood also picks up oxygen that has been inhaled.

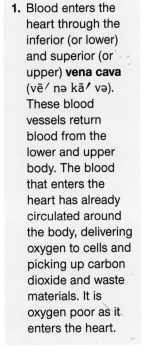
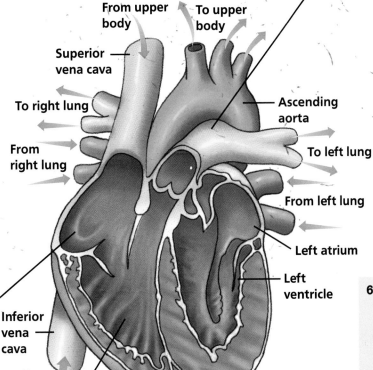

From upper body — To upper body

Superior vena cava

To right lung

From right lung

Ascending aorta

To left lung

From left lung

Left atrium

Left ventricle

2. Blood first enters the right **atrium,** or right upper chamber of the heart.

Inferior vena cava

From lower body

To lower body

Descending aorta

6. Blood, now oxygen-rich, returns to the heart through the pulmonary vein and enters the left atrium. It is pumped into the left ventricle. From there it is pumped out to the body through the **aorta** (ā ôr´ tə), or main artery of the body.

3. It is pumped out of the right atrium into the right **ventricle,** or right lower chamber of the heart.

The Circulatory System

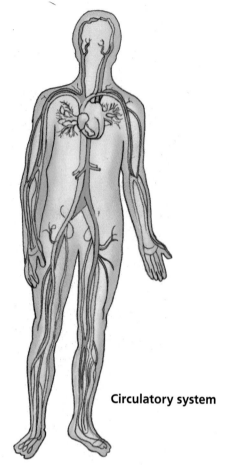

Circulatory system

The heart and the blood vessels make up the circulatory system.

The circulatory system includes a network of blood vessels that move blood throughout the body. The vessels through which blood is pumped away from the heart are called **arteries.** The vessels through which blood returns to the heart are called **veins.** Between the arteries and veins are the capillaries.

Each cell in the body is connected to the circulatory system. The capillaries are the extremely small and narrow vessels that exchange gases, nutrients, and wastes with the body's cells. The capillaries carry nutrients and oxygen to the cells and remove wastes and carbon dioxide from them.

You know that the lungs are where oxygen and carbon dioxide are exchanged. The excretory system removes the other wastes that the body's cells produce. The major organs of the excretory system are the liver, kidneys, and bladder. The kidneys remove the wastes and return most of the water to the blood. Your kidneys process your entire blood supply once every 40 minutes.

Blood travels through the body in about one minute. Your heart averages about 70 beats a minute. Sometimes, perhaps after a lot of exercise, you can feel your heart beating much faster. After a while, your heart slows down to its normal rate. When you are not active for long periods, such as when you are sleeping, your heartbeats slow down even more.

The body controls the amount of oxygen and carbon dioxide in the blood. When you exercise, your cells use more oxygen and create more carbon dioxide. When the carbon dioxide level in the blood increases, your nervous system causes you to increase your breathing. You inhale and exhale more often. You also take deeper breaths than normal. This deep breathing lowers the amount of carbon dioxide in your blood. It also keeps your cells supplied with oxygen.

When you exercise, you inhale and exhale more often.

Diseases and Disorders

Some diseases and disorders affect the regulatory systems of the body. For instance, diseases of the arteries can cause the circulatory system to stop working. If there is not enough oxygen in the arteries, the cells of the body may stop working. When the cells of the brain stop working, a person suffers a stroke. When the cells of the heart stop working, the person suffers a heart attack. What causes diseases of the arteries?

A poor diet can contribute to problems with the arteries. In the last lesson, you learned that fats are nutrients. There are two kinds of fat. Unsaturated fats are liquid at room temperature. Saturated fats are solid at room temperature. Cholesterol (kə les′ tə rol) is a compound that comes from the saturated fats found in foods made from animals. It is not found in plant tissues. Even though peanut butter contains saturated fat, it has no cholesterol. Eggs, meat, butter, and cheese all contain cholesterol. Some cholesterol is needed by the body to work properly.

How does cholesterol cause disease? Think about pumping muddy water through a garden hose. If you put more mud and less water through the hose, the mud builds up inside it. The opening in the hose becomes narrower and narrower, until no water can go through. Your arteries are like the hose. They can get clogged with cholesterol.

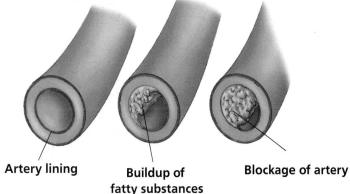

Artery lining   **Buildup of fatty substances**   **Blockage of artery**

Buildup of fatty material in blood vessels can lead to blockages that result in poor circulation, blood clots, and sometimes heart attacks.

Human body cells, like other animal cells, make cholesterol naturally. When people eat too much cholesterol, however, some of it sticks to the inside of their arteries. After a while, the arteries fill up and become narrower. **Atherosclerosis** (ath ûr ō⁄ sklə rō⁄ sis) is a disease that results from a diet high in fat and deposits of cholesterol in the arteries. Atherosclerosis can lead to blockages of the arteries in the heart and neck. Blood clots, heart attacks, and strokes are possible results. Usually, atherosclerosis does not occur until a person is older. But, layers of cholesterol can start to build up in childhood.

Another result of narrow arteries is high blood pressure. Everybody has **blood pressure.** Your blood pressure is the force of your blood pushing against the walls of the blood vessels. If the blood vessels are too narrow, the heart must pump harder and more often to move the blood through the vessels. If the force of the blood pushing on the walls of the blood vessels is too high, hypertension (hī pûr ten⁄ shən) occurs. Being overweight, diets high in fats, and even stress can cause hypertension. When the heart is pumping harder and more often, its cells are also working harder. This puts the heart muscle under a lot of strain. Sometimes, it stops working as a result. This is called heart failure.

Having your blood pressure checked is a good way to monitor the health of your circulatory system.

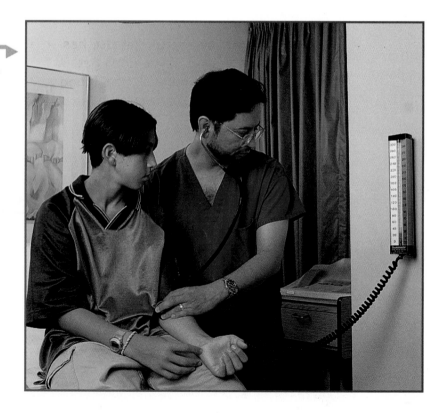

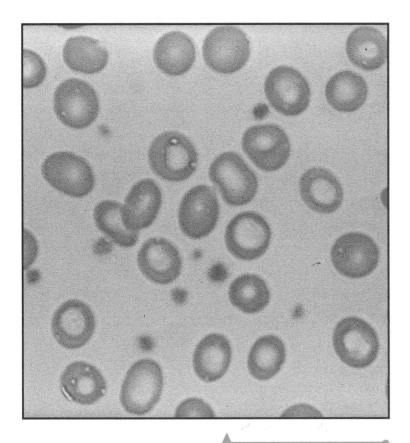

Without enough iron, your blood cells can lose their ability to carry oxygen.

The amount of iron you get from your diet also has an effect on your circulatory system. If you don't get enough iron, which is an important mineral, your blood can lose its ability to carry oxygen. This results in anemia (ə nē′ mē ə).

CHECKPOINT

1. What happens to food in the body?
2. What does your heart do?
3. What does the circulatory system do?
4. What role does fat play in heart disease?

 How does your diet affect your blood vessels and heart?

ACTIVITY

Finding Fat, Salt, and Sugar in Your Food

Find Out

Do this activity to see where unhealthful things in your diet come from.

Process Skills

Measuring
Communicating
Inferring

WHAT YOU NEED

 felt marker

nutrition labels from packages of cereal, crackers, cookies, catsup, pickles, ice cream, frozen dinners

 glue

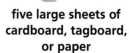

five large sheets of cardboard, tagboard, or paper

Activity Journal

WHAT TO DO

1. Collect all the food labels that list saturated fat as an ingredient. Stack them in order of amount of fat from most to least. Glue them to one of the sheets of cardboard beginning with the highest fat content down to the lowest. Use the felt marker to write the name of the food and the amount of fat it contains next to each label.

2. Do the same thing with three more nutrients on three more sheets of cardboard: unsaturated fat, sodium, and sugar. Use photocopies of the food labels if you need them in more than one category.

3. Compare the foods. Use the fifth sheet of cardboard to make a summary of what you have learned. Record your results.

4. Infer which foods are more healthful. Rank the foods you have studied from most healthful to least healthful.

CONCLUSIONS

1. Which foods contained the most saturated fat?

2. Which foods contained the most unsaturated fat?

3. Which foods contained the most sodium and sugar?

4. Were foods with high amounts of fat, sodium, and sugar in the least healthful part of your list?

ASKING NEW QUESTIONS

1. How did your food rankings compare with your classmates' rankings?

2. Why do you think some products contain large amounts of salt and sugar?

SCIENTIFIC METHODS SELF CHECK

✔ Did I **compare** different food labels?

✔ Did I **record** my results?

✔ Did I **infer** which foods were more healthful?

LESSON 3

Feeding the World's Population

Find Out

- What malnutrition is
- How to protect soil from erosion
- What some new and different ways to raise food are

Vocabulary

organic
arable
agriculture
fertilizer
aquaculture
hydroponics

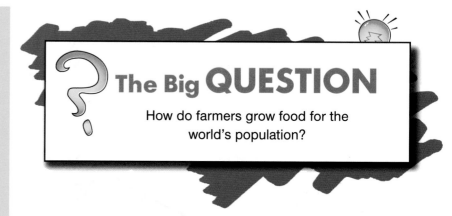

The Big QUESTION

How do farmers grow food for the world's population?

There is only so much land on Earth. The amount of soil that can grow crops is not increasing. On the other hand, the world's population is growing. The world's population grew by about 3,000,000,000 people from 1950 to 1990. In fact, the world's population increases by nearly 90 million people each year. Yet most people in the world do not go hungry. New ways of farming make each square kilometer of land more productive. Simply put, we can feed more people with less land.

World Nutrition

To stay healthy, an average adult should consume between 2000 to 2400 Calories a day. A diet with less than the minimum number of Calories causes health problems. Malnutrition is the lack of enough Calories in the diet to keep the body healthy. Diets with less than the recommended amounts of other nutrients, such as vitamins or minerals, cause people to be undernourished.

The world's population increases every year. Cities like Bangkok, Thailand, become more crowded and congested every year.

People in the United States and other developed countries eat about 3300 Calories per day, or about 1000 Calories more per day than people in developing countries do. About 20 percent of the people in the world (about 800 million people) are undernourished. Before 1960, more than 40 percent of the world's population was malnourished.

The amazing thing about the drop in the proportion of undernourished and malnourished people in the world is that the world's population increased by about 3 billion people in that same time. Yet most of the world's population gets enough food. Clearly, the world's food supply increased. In fact, enough food is produced each year to provide every person in the world with an adequate diet. There are many social reasons why some people do not get enough food. Scientists and others are working on ways to provide enough food for everyone.

Soil Conservation

To make food. we need soil. Soil contains both inorganic and organic material. The inorganic materials are mostly rock and mineral particles. Water and air are the other inorganic materials present in soil. The **organic** part of the soil includes plants and other organisms that are alive or were once alive.

In soil, the organic material is called humus (hy$\overline{oo}$′ məs). Most soils have three basic layers. The depth and color of the layers and what is in them may differ from place to place. The layers form a soil profile, as shown in the diagram on this page. A soil profile includes the topsoil, the subsoil, and a layer of parent material. The parent material contains large rocks and materials that allow soil to form. The subsoil contains clay and other materials. The top layer of soil is called topsoil. It has the most humus. Humus is rich in nutrients and helps hold water in the ground.

Fertile soils, where food can grow, only cover a small portion of the world's total land area. Soils vary across Earth's land surfaces. About one third of Earth's land surface supports little or no plant growth. The continent of Antarctica is a good example of a region of Earth that has little or no plant growth. The frozen ground there does not allow plants to grow. But did you realize that your own town could also be an example of land that is not good for growing food? Cities and urban areas are not good for growing food because large areas are paved over or have buildings on them. Deserts, forests, mountains, or mining sites are not good food-growing sites either. In fact, only about 30 percent of the world's total land area is **arable** land. Arable land is where the soil is good for growing food. Almost all of Earth's arable land has been in use for many years. Yet, the amount of food we get from the world's soil has been going up.

This increase in the world's food production is called the "green revolution." It has been taking place over the past 40 years. It is a result of scientists' continuing to find new ways to increase the amount of food that comes from each square kilometer of arable land. The science of producing food is **agriculture** (ag′ ri kul chər). Agriculture is commonly known as farming and ranching.

Topsoil

Subsoil

Parent material

The amount of each of the three different layers of soil form a soil profile. Fertile soil has a thick topsoil layer.

Topsoil is very important in agriculture. It is the layer of soil where crops and grazing plants grow best. Because it is usually a very thin layer, topsoil can erode easily. Erosion is the removal of topsoil by wind, water, ice, or gravity. Wind and rain erode bare topsoil very easily. Plants help stop erosion by holding the soil in place, keeping it moist, and reducing the effects of strong winds and rainfall on the top layer of soil.

It is important to prevent soil erosion when raising food. There are different ways to conserve soil. One way is knowing how to plant crops. One type of soil management is planting a cover crop. A cover crop is a fast-growing plant with many shallow roots. Alfalfa and clover are good cover crops. Many farmers plant cover crops after their autumn harvest. These crops protect the topsoil during winter. They also add nutrients to the soil and can be used as feed for farm animals, such as cattle.

Another way to prevent erosion is to plant more than one crop in a field. Strip cropping is the planting of several rows of cover crop between rows of a main crop. A farmer may plant a strip of corn, then a strip of clover, then another strip of corn, and so on. The cover crop holds water in the soil. The water kept in the soil helps the main crop grow better.

Good soil management helps prevent soil erosion.

Other ways of preventing erosion are windbreaks, contour planting, and conservation farming. Windbreaks are trees or shrubs planted along the side of a field. Windbreaks prevent wind from blowing soil away. In winter, windbreaks also keep snow from blowing off a field. When the snow melts, it adds moisture to the soil.

Contour planting is planting crops in rows that follow the shape, or contour, of the land. Straight rows of crops on uneven land allow rain to carry topsoil and nutrients away from the plants at the top and give too much water and nutrients to the plants at the bottom. Sometimes, on very steep hillsides, farmers will put in terraces, or land steps. The terraces prevent the soil from washing away.

Plowing turns over the top part of soil in a field. It puts old plant growth and weeds under the soil. Tilling breaks up the land before seeds are planted. Plowing and tilling cause soil erosion. On some farms, seeds and other nutrients are added directly to a field at tilling time without plowing first. This conservation farming method reduces soil erosion as well as the amount of water and energy needed to raise crops. No-till farming is another way to reduce soil erosion. With no-till farming, seeds and other nutrients are added directly to the unplowed, untilled field.

Feeding the Soil

If the soil is too dry, food plants do not grow well. Adding water to soil for plant growth is irrigation. Have you ever watered your lawn? If so, you were practicing irrigation! Irrigation makes it possible to grow crops in places that do not have much rainfall. However, some scientists believe that using water for agriculture can deplete our world's water supply and add salt to Earth's soil. When soil is too salty, plants are not able to grow in it.

Stopping soil erosion is good, but we also need to make sure the soil will support plant growth. Plants remove nutrients, such as nitrogen and phosphorous, from the soil when they grow. To allow more crops to grow in soil, we need to replace the nutrients they use.

Different crops take different nutrients out of the soil when they grow. Some crops, like legumes, put nitrogen into the soil. Other crops use more nitrogen. One way to replace nutrients in soil is to switch the crops planted in a field every season. This crop rotation gives the soil a chance to rest. For example, alfalfa plants are legumes which add nitrogen to the soil. Wheat plants take a lot of nitrogen out of the soil. To even out the use of soil nitrogen, farmers can plant alfalfa one season, then plant wheat the next season, then plant alfalfa the next, and so on. By rotating their crops, farmers can maintain fertile soil.

One of the biggest contributors to the "green revolution" was the invention of **fertilizer.** All fertilizers add nutrients to the soil. Fertilizers help crops grow better and faster. When fertilizers are used, the food

This wheat farm in the United States helps feed the world's population.

supply goes up. Fertilizers can be natural or synthetic. Natural fertilizers contain only organic matter, such as dead plants and animal wastes, or manure. They are a way to increase the amount of humus in the topsoil. Some farmers specialize in organic farming. These farmers use only organic fertilizers and add no other chemicals to their land. Synthetic fertilizers are made from fossil fuels, hydrogen, and air. Even though synthetic fertilizers have helped increase the world's food supply, some scientists believe that the amount of energy and fossil fuels needed to make synthetic fertilizers are bad for the environment. They are looking for ways to reduce the use of synthetic fertilizers and still get more food from the land.

Other Food Technologies

Keeping and improving soil are good ways to grow food. That is not enough to grow all the food we need from our limited land resources. Some other ways to increase the world's food supply are selective breeding of plants and animals, use of computers and satellites, food transportation, aquaculture, and hydroponics.

If plants could be made to produce more grain, and if animals could be raised to provide more meat or milk, then we could feed more people with fewer plants and animals. Scientists use selective (sə lek′ tiv) breeding to develop high-yield plants. A yield is the amount of usable crop produced per square kilometer. By pollinating plants for certain traits, scientists have created new plant varieties. Many common crops, such as rice, corn, wheat, beans, and sorghum, have much higher yields than they did 40 years ago. Some new plant varieties do not need as much water as the original plants did. Other selectively bred plants make new chemicals in their structures. These chemicals keep insects and other pests away from the plants and allow them to grow better.

Through the same kind of selective process, animals have been developed that yield more meat, more milk, or are more immune to disease. Scientists also use selective breeding to create better pastures for livestock. Some of the new pasture plant varieties reduce the amount of water needed or give the animals

Precision farming uses satellite information to help farmers grow food.

more nutrients. Other ways of improving pastures include selecting animals that eat only plant tops. This gives the plant roots a chance to regrow quickly and helps stop soil erosion in pastures.

Many farmers today use their computers as well as their tractors. Crop farmers can keep track of planting, fertilizing, and harvesting schedules. Livestock farmers can keep track of breeding, feeding, and transportation schedules.

Precision farming is a new technology that combines computers and the Global Positioning Satellite System, or GPS. The satellites survey farm lands as small as 120 square meters. The survey includes data about soil, water, and nutrient content as well as data about expected yields from crops. The data are sent to the farmer's computer. The farmer then analyzes the data and makes decisions about what to plant, where to plant, and when to harvest.

Farmers can produce more food without waste too. If they know the food they make will be used, they may plant extra crops or raise extra livestock. Seasons vary across different parts of the world, so it's easy to see that somewhere in the world, it's growing season. Plus, it's easy to ship food quickly to any place in the world. Apples grow in Brazil and America. When Americans want apples in January, they can eat Brazilian apples. When Brazilians want apples in August, they can eat American apples. Other ways of packaging and shipping food include canning and freezing.

The use of soil is not our only source of food production. A large percentage of the world's food comes from our water environments. People in almost every country eat fish. In fact, the world's demand for fresh fish is reducing the stock of fish in the world's oceans and lakes. Water farming, or **aquaculture,** is a way to raise fish as food in a controlled environment without depleting the world's oceans and lakes.

Asia is the largest aquaculture farming region. Nearly 80 percent of the world's farmed fish, shrimp, and shellfish are raised in Asia. In China, carp are the biggest fish crop. Carp are herbivores and easy to grow. In America, catfish and trout farms are popular. Other common aquaculture crops include salmon, tilapia, shrimp, oysters, and different types of seaweed.

Plants can also be grown without soil. Thousands of years ago, people in China grew plants in water without soil. By 1937, the scientist William Gericke had coined the word **hydroponics** to mean growing plants without soil. Hydroponic farming is a useful way to grow food where there is little or no arable soil. Hydroponic farming was even used to grow food in space.

Usually, hydroponic plants are grown in water to which nutrients, such as nitrogen, phosphorus, and potassium, have been added. Sometimes gravel is used to support the plants' root systems. Hydroponic farms are usually built in greenhouses, which keep away insects and allow a year-long growing season. Strawberries and tomatoes are among the many fruits and vegetables grown hydroponically.

All of these technologies give us the world's food supply. In fact, as scientists find new ways of producing food, we can expect the world's food supply to continue to increase. What we do not know is whether these increases will be enough to feed the world's population in the future.

CHECKPOINT

1. What is malnutrition?
2. How can soil be protected from erosion?
3. What are some new and different ways to raise food?

 How do farmers grow food for the world's population?

ACTIVITY

Watering Soil

Find Out

Do this activity to see how different soil types hold water.

Process Skills

Measuring
Communicating
Interpreting Data
Controlling Variables
Inferring

WHAT YOU NEED

two plastic bottles

two funnels

stopwatch

two pieces of filter paper

250 mL water

safety goggles

sand

topsoil

graduated measuring beaker

Activity Journal

WHAT TO DO

1. Put on your safety goggles.

2. Put a piece of filter paper inside one of the funnels. Then place the funnel in one of the plastic bottles.

3. Select the appropriate tool to measure 1 cup of sand into the filter. Slowly pour 125 mL of water over the sand. Be sure to pour slowly and wet all of the sand. Wait two minutes. Recycle the filter paper and the sand in it.

 Be careful when handling sand.

4. Select the appropriate tool to measure the amount of water that drained from the sand into the plastic bottle. Record this amount.

5. Put the second filter paper inside the other funnel. Place the funnel in the second bottle.

6. Select the appropriate tool to measure 1 cup of topsoil into the filter. Slowly and carefully pour 125 mL of water over the topsoil to wet all of the soil. Wait two minutes. Recycle the filter paper and the soil in it.

7. Select the appropriate tool to measure the amount of water that drained from the soil into the plastic bottle. Record this amount.

8. Compare the different amounts.

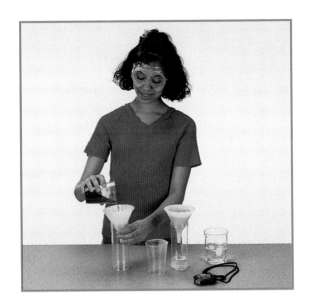

CONCLUSIONS

1. Which material had more water in the bottle after two minutes? Explain why more water passed through that material.

2. Infer which material would be better for plants to grow in.

ASKING NEW QUESTIONS

1. What evidence did you use to infer which material was better for plant growth?

2. How could plant roots slow the flow of water through the soil or the sand?

3. What could be done to the sand to better allow plants to grow in it?

SCIENTIFIC METHODS SELF CHECK

✔ Did I **measure** the sand, soil, and water accurately?

✔ Did I **record** the amounts of water that flowed through the material?

✔ Did I **compare** the amounts of water from the two experiments?

✔ Did I **control the variables** by changing only the type of soil?

✔ Did I **infer** which material holds more water and is better for plants to grow in?

Review

Reviewing Vocabulary and Concepts

Write the letter of the answer that best completes each sentence.

1. ___ are chemical elements that help your bones, blood, and tissues.
   - **a.** Minerals
   - **b.** Vitamins
   - **c.** Hydroponics
   - **d.** Proteins

2. The main source of the body's energy are ___.
   - **a.** nutrients
   - **b.** hydroponics
   - **c.** carbohydrates
   - **d.** fertilizers

3. The job of the circulatory system is to ___.
   - **a.** deliver oxygen to the blood
   - **b.** move blood through the body
   - **c.** repair the body's cells
   - **d.** remove carbon dioxide from the body

4. Fish farming is called ___.
   - **a.** aquaculture
   - **b.** organic
   - **c.** hydroponics
   - **d.** arable

5. Growing plants in something other than soil is called ___.
   - **a.** agriculture
   - **b.** aquaculture
   - **c.** cholesterol
   - **d.** hydroponics

Match each definition on the left with the correct term.

6. substances that living things need for their survival

7. chemical compounds that help your cells function

8. made from amino acids

9. high-energy foods that are also high in Calories

10. only found in animals

11. a blockage of the arteries caused by a buildup of fatty deposits

12. force of blood on the walls of the blood vessels

13. soil that is good for growing food

14. the science of growing food

15. compound that adds nutrients to the soil

- **a.** arable
- **b.** proteins
- **c.** fats
- **d.** atherosclerosis
- **e.** agriculture
- **f.** vitamins
- **g.** cholesterol
- **h.** fertilizer
- **i.** nutrients
- **j.** blood pressure

Understanding What You Learned

1. What determines how many Calories you need to consume?
2. What are the differences between veins and arteries?
3. Where does cholesterol come from?
4. What is the "green revolution"?
5. What is organic farming?

Applying What You Learned

1. Foods from animals have complete proteins in them. If you do not eat food from animals, you need to combine different plant foods to make a meal with complete proteins in it. Using the combinations mentioned in the chapter as examples, make up some other plant food combinations that equal complete proteins. (Hint: combine grain products with beans, seeds, or nuts.)
2. List your top five favorite foods. For each one, list how many Calories are in your normal serving.
3. What can you do now to prevent heart disease later in your life?
4. A friend of yours decides to spend a year living with an uncle who owns a farm. What can you tell him about how to avoid erosion of the soil?

5. Why does a variety of foods make a healthful diet?

For Your **Portfolio**

The Food Guide Pyramid suggests how many servings of each type of food you need to eat each day to get all the nutrients your body needs. Create your own Food Guide Pyramid! Use pictures of foods you like that meet your daily requirements. You might discover that you like more vegetables than you thought! Count your pictures for each food group. Is your pyramid stable? Or will your pyramid tip over because there are too many pictures in the top categories?

Unit Review

Concept Review

1. Thinking of the nervous system as a control center, explain your reflexes.

2. Describe two ways you can stop the spread of disease.

3. How does the Food Guide Pyramid give you choices in creating a healthful diet?

Problem Solving

1. Explain how an injury to the brain can paralyze a muscle in a completely different part of your body.

2. What would happen if all bacteria were killed?

3. Describe how a country's geography and resources can influence the normal diet in that country.

Something to Do

Create a chart about diseases and disorders of two centuries: the 1500s and the 1900s. Use geography, history, and social studies books for your research. Also, use materials from the Internet or the CDC or the WHO. Decide what countries you want to include. Include major diseases—note if they were communicable or infectious or neither. Include any treatments such as vaccines and the date they were first used. Illustrate your chart and share it with your classmates.

Reference

Classifying Living Things

Did you know that about one and a half million different kinds of living things have been classified by scientists? Even so, scientists hypothesize that there are millions more living things that have yet to be discovered! The chart on these pages outlines some of the subsets of the five kingdom classifications.

   To call a group of organisms a species, the organisms must first pass two simple tests. First, all of the members must look similar. Second, all members of a species must be able to reproduce, making individuals that are able to reproduce too. We may be about halfway toward classifying the diversity of life on Earth!

KEY

Different colors show various classification groupings in this chart. Where numbers of species are given, they are approximate estimates. Divisions of the plant kingdom are equivalent to phyla in other kingdoms.

Kingdom	Sub-phylum
Division	Class
Phylum	Order

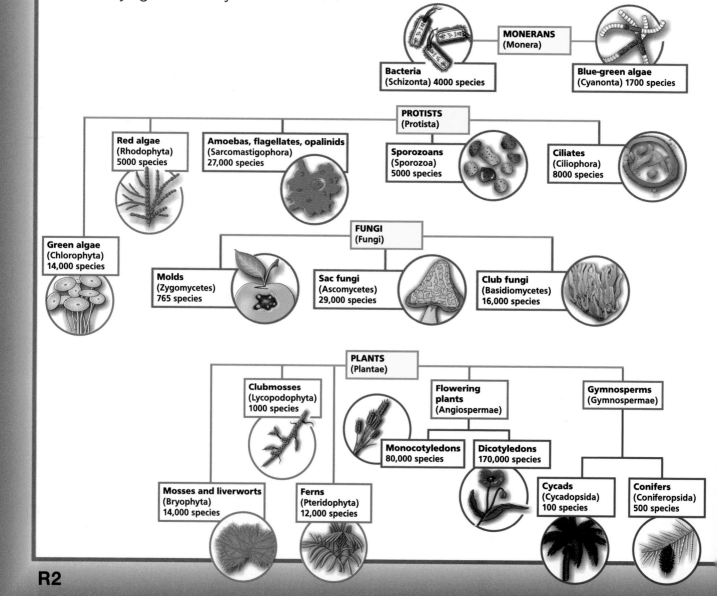

MONERANS
(Monera)

Bacteria
(Schizonta) 4000 species

Blue-green algae
(Cyanonta) 1700 species

PROTISTS
(Protista)

Red algae
(Rhodophyta)
5000 species

Amoebas, flagellates, opalinids
(Sarcomastigophora)
27,000 species

Sporozoans
(Sporozoa)
5000 species

Ciliates
(Ciliophora)
8000 species

Green algae
(Chlorophyta)
14,000 species

FUNGI
(Fungi)

Molds
(Zygomycetes)
765 species

Sac fungi
(Ascomycetes)
29,000 species

Club fungi
(Basidiomycetes)
16,000 species

PLANTS
(Plantae)

Clubmosses
(Lycopodophyta)
1000 species

Flowering plants
(Angiospermae)

Gymnosperms
(Gymnospermae)

Monocotyledons
80,000 species

Dicotyledons
170,000 species

Mosses and liverworts
(Bryophyta)
14,000 species

Ferns
(Pteridophyta)
12,000 species

Cycads
(Cycadopsida)
100 species

Conifers
(Coniferopsida)
500 species

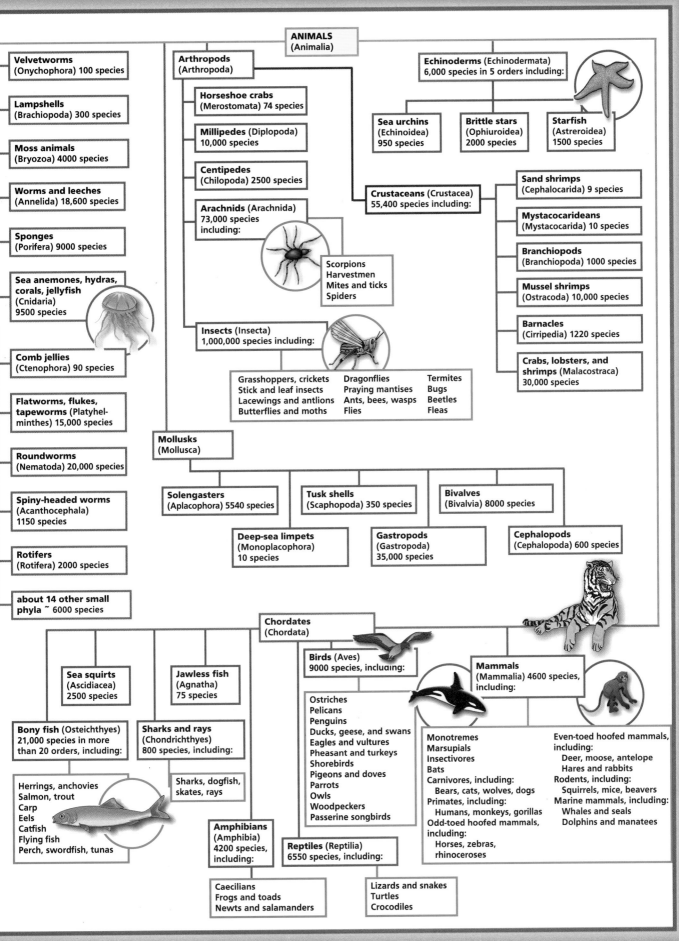

ANIMALS (Animalia)

Velvetworms (Onychophora) 100 species

Lampshells (Brachiopoda) 300 species

Moss animals (Bryozoa) 4000 species

Worms and leeches (Annelida) 18,600 species

Sponges (Porifera) 9000 species

Sea anemones, hydras, corals, jellyfish (Cnidaria) 9500 species

Comb jellies (Ctenophora) 90 species

Flatworms, flukes, tapeworms (Platyhelminthes) 15,000 species

Roundworms (Nematoda) 20,000 species

Spiny-headed worms (Acanthocephala) 1150 species

Rotifers (Rotifera) 2000 species

about 14 other small phyla ~ 6000 species

Arthropods (Arthropoda)

Horseshoe crabs (Merostomata) 74 species

Millipedes (Diplopoda) 10,000 species

Centipedes (Chilopoda) 2500 species

Arachnids (Arachnida) 73,000 species including:

Scorpions
Harvestmen
Mites and ticks
Spiders

Insects (Insecta) 1,000,000 species including:

Grasshoppers, crickets
Stick and leaf insects
Lacewings and antlions
Butterflies and moths
Dragonflies
Praying mantises
Ants, bees, wasps
Flies
Termites
Bugs
Beetles
Fleas

Crustaceans (Crustacea) 55,400 species including:

Sand shrimps (Cephalocarida) 9 species

Mystacocarideans (Mystacocarida) 10 species

Branchiopods (Branchiopoda) 1000 species

Mussel shrimps (Ostracoda) 10,000 species

Barnacles (Cirripedia) 1220 species

Crabs, lobsters, and shrimps (Malacostraca) 30,000 species

Echinoderms (Echinodermata) 6,000 species in 5 orders including:

Sea urchins (Echinoidea) 950 species

Brittle stars (Ophiuroidea) 2000 species

Starfish (Astreroidea) 1500 species

Mollusks (Mollusca)

Solengasters (Aplacophora) 5540 species

Tusk shells (Scaphopoda) 350 species

Bivalves (Bivalvia) 8000 species

Deep-sea limpets (Monoplacophora) 10 species

Gastropods (Gastropoda) 35,000 species

Cephalopods (Cephalopoda) 600 species

Chordates (Chordata)

Sea squirts (Ascidiacea) 2500 species

Jawless fish (Agnatha) 75 species

Bony fish (Osteichthyes) 21,000 species in more than 20 orders, including:

Herrings, anchovies
Salmon, trout
Carp
Eels
Catfish
Flying fish
Perch, swordfish, tunas

Sharks and rays (Chondrichthyes) 800 species, including:

Sharks, dogfish, skates, rays

Amphibians (Amphibia) 4200 species, including:

Caecilians
Frogs and toads
Newts and salamanders

Birds (Aves) 9000 species, including:

Ostriches
Pelicans
Penguins
Ducks, geese, and swans
Eagles and vultures
Pheasant and turkeys
Shorebirds
Pigeons and doves
Parrots
Owls
Woodpeckers
Passerine songbirds

Reptiles (Reptilia) 6550 species, including:

Lizards and snakes
Turtles
Crocodiles

Mammals (Mammalia) 4600 species, including:

Monotremes
Marsupials
Insectivores
Bats
Carnivores, including:
    Bears, cats, wolves, dogs
Primates, including:
    Humans, monkeys, gorillas
Odd-toed hoofed mammals, including:
    Horses, zebras, rhinoceroses

Even-toed hoofed mammals, including:
    Deer, moose, antelope
    Hares and rabbits
Rodents, including:
    Squirrels, mice, beavers
Marine mammals, including:
    Whales and seals
    Dolphins and manatees

Human Interactions with Animals

Humans care for and breed domestic animals. These include pets, like cats or dogs. It also includes the animals we raise for food, transportation, or sport. Humans also impact the environment of animals on Earth. Sometimes, human activity can ruin Earth's habitats, speeding up the disappearance of many plant and animal species. Other times, human activity can improve Earth's habitats, preventing the extinction of some species.

Animals Kept by Humans

Domesticated Animal Populations

Animal	World Total
Cattle	1,284,188,000
Chickens	11,279,000,000
Donkeys	44,270,000
Horses	60,843,000
Pigs	864,096,000
Sheep	1,138,363,000

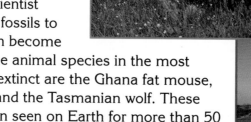

In the early 1800s, scientist Georges Cuvier used fossils to show that species can become extinct, or die out. The animal species in the most danger of becoming extinct are the Ghana fat mouse, the Halcon fruit bat, and the Tasmanian wolf. These animals have not been seen on Earth for more than 50 years. The Arabian oryx used to be an endangered species. They were not found in the wild, but some were living in captivity. Because of a successful breeding program, the Arabian oryx has been reintroduced into its natural habitat.

Most Threatened Animal Species

Animal Group	Species at Risk
Birds	880
Insects	875
Other Invertebrates	510
Mammals	500
Fish	270
Reptiles	170
Amphibians	60

Indian Tiger   Siberian Tiger

One group of mammals threatened by the loss of habitat is the tiger. The numbers of tigers and tiger species have declined because of poaching, or illegal hunting, and because of the destruction of their habitat. This map shows how the habitat of the tiger has shrunk over the past 100 years. It also shows where three extinct species of tigers—the Caspian tiger, the Balinese tiger, and the Javan tiger—used to be found. The numbers of individuals of each type of tiger are in parentheses below the name.

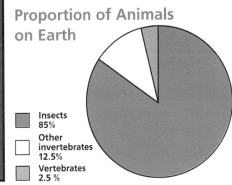

Sumatran Tiger

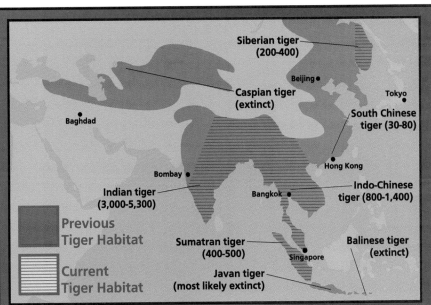

Siberian tiger (200-400)
Beijing
Tokyo
Caspian tiger (extinct)
Baghdad
South Chinese tiger (30-80)
Bombay
Hong Kong
Indian tiger (3,000-5,300)
Bangkok
Indo-Chinese tiger (800-1,400)
Previous Tiger Habitat
Sumatran tiger (400-500)
Singapore
Balinese tiger (extinct)
Current Tiger Habitat
Javan tiger (most likely extinct)

Proportion of Animals on Earth

- Insects 85%
- Other invertebrates 12.5%
- Vertebrates 2.5%

Fast Facts

Fast Animal Facts

- At an estimated 290,000 species, there are more kinds of beetles than any other kind of animal on Earth. There is only one species of human beings. However, humans affect the environment more than any other type of living thing.

- There are more species of plants and animals in the rain forest biome than in any other part of the world. Some scientists estimate that about half of all species of plants and animals live in the rain forest.

Energy from Nutrients

Composting works because of decomposers like fungi and bacteria. These organisms break down the materials in once-living things and return the nutrients back into the ecosystem for other organisms to use. Use this recipe to start your own compost pile.

Burning Calories

This chart shows the average number of Calories burned per hour by a person who weighs 150 pounds.

Compost Recipe

6 parts	dry leaves
3 parts	food scraps (no fat or meat products)
3 parts	fresh grass
1 part	manure

Sprinkle any of the following throughout the pile:
Finished compost	
Bone meal	1/2 shovelful
Fireplace ashes	1/2 shovelful
Packet of compost starter	shovelful

Add water until mixture is about as wet as a squeezed-out sponge. Mix as needed.

Activity	Calories burned per hour
Sleeping	1
Sitting	100
Walking (1.25 km/h)	150-240
Riding a bicycle (3 km/h)	210
Walking (2.5 km/h)	300-400
Playing volleyball	350
Walking (3.1 km/h)	420-480
Playing tennis	420-480
Playing football	500
Riding a bicycle (8 km/h)	660
Swimming	500-700

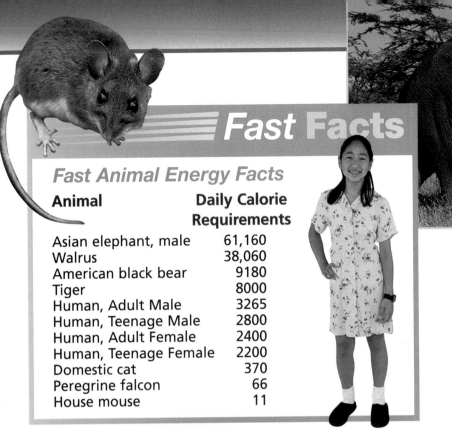

Fast Facts

Fast Animal Energy Facts

Animal	Daily Calorie Requirements
Asian elephant, male	61,160
Walrus	38,060
American black bear	9180
Tiger	8000
Human, Adult Male	3265
Human, Teenage Male	2800
Human, Adult Female	2400
Human, Teenage Female	2200
Domestic cat	370
Peregrine falcon	66
House mouse	11

Vitamin	Why We Need It	Where to Get It
A	Healthy eyes and skin growth, fights infection	liver, egg yolk, yellow and orange fruits, and vegetables
B1	Healthy nervous and digestive systems	whole-grain breads and pastas, brown rice, liver, beans, peas, nuts
B2	Keeps tissues healthy	milk, liver, cheese, eggs, green vegetables, lean meat
B3	Energy, healthy skin	liver, lean meat, poultry, fish, whole-grain breads and cereals, nuts, dried beans
B6	Producing red blood cells	liver, pork, poultry, fish, bananas, potatoes, most fruits and vegetables
C	Healthy skin, teeth, bones, and tissues; fighting disease	citrus fruits, strawberries, tomatoes, potatoes
D	Strong teeth and bones	salmon, liver, eggs
E	Producing red blood cells, protecting the lungs	lettuce, leafy green vegetables, whole-grain cereals, margarine, nuts

The Brain

The brain is the body's control center.

The **cerebrum** controls voluntary movement, speech, the senses, perception, decision making, learning, memory, thought, and reasoning.

The **cerebellum** controls muscle coordination and balance.

The **brain stem** controls automatic functions like breathing and heartbeat.

The **thalamus** sends incoming messages from the body to the appropriate area of the brain.

The **hypothalamus** is the control center for automatic functions like breathing and digestion.

The **pituitary gland** controls other glands and many of your body processes like growth. The hypothalamus controls the pituitary gland.

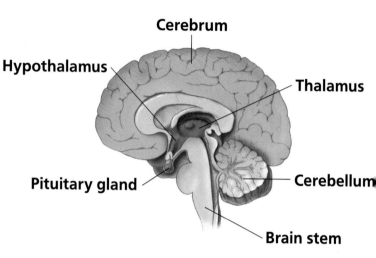

Cerebrum

Hypothalamus

Thalamus

Cerebellum

Pituitary gland

Brain stem

Brain Comparisons

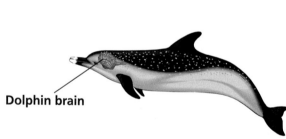

Dolphin brain

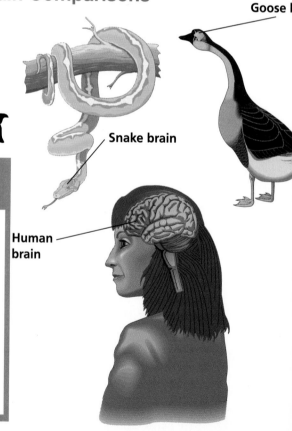

Goose

Snake brain

Human brain

Fast Facts

Fast Brain Facts

- An adult's brain mass is 1.4 kg.
- Blood travels through the brain at a rate of about 0.85 L/s.
- There are about 50 billion cells in a human brain.
- Some cells in your body live only three days. A brain cell can last your whole life.
- Neurons, or nerve cells, are the longest cells in the body. Some are more than 18 cm long.
- Nerve cells are the only cells in the body that do not divide.

The Eye and Light

Light rays reflect off images and travel to the eye. The light rays enter the eye through the cornea. The lens of the eye focuses the image and reflects it onto the retina. Because the light rays cross over behind the lens, the image on the retina is upside down. The image is transmitted to the brain along the optic nerve. The brain turns the image the right way up.

Clear jelly

Optic nerve

Retina

Iris

Lens

Pupil

Cornea

Suspending ligament

Muscle

Sight and Color Blindness

Cones are the cells in the eye that allow people to see color. Some people cannot see the colors red or green. Complete color blindness, where people only see shades of black and white, is a very rare condition in humans.

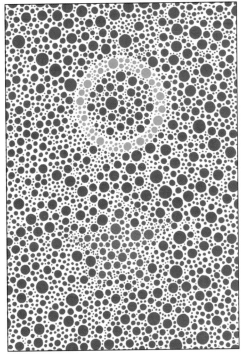

This is a representation of the Creamer Color Chart which is a screening tool for red-green color blindness.

Fast Facts

Fast Eye Facts

- Most people blink about once every 4 seconds.
- No one knows why humans cry, but the body makes excess tears during times of strong emotion. Extra tears drain down the tear ducts to the nose.
- To see better in the dark, you need Vitamin A. The light sensitive chemical in the rods comes from Vitamin A.
- Human eyes are about 1000 times more sensitive to colors and light than the best photographic film made.
- No machine is able to distinguish as many colors as the human eye can.
- Light travels about 300,000 m/s.

Different Measures

First adopted in France in 1795, the standard system of units that scientists throughout the world use is the Systeme Internationale d'Unites, or SI. Many of the units used in this decimal system of measurement have very specific standards. For instance, the standard second is measured by the radiation of the cesium[133] atom in a cesium clock, and the standard kilogram is measured by a specific amount of platinum. Other SI units measure length, volume, temperature, frequency, and energy.

Quantity	Unit	Symbol
Time	Second	s
Mass	Kilogram	Kg
Length	Meter	m
Volume	Liter	L
Temperature	Celsius	C
Frequency	Hertz	Hz
Energy	Joule	J

Fast Time Facts

- Time is usually measured in seconds or in minutes and hours.

- Since 1967, time has been measured by atomic clocks rather than by Earth's rotation.

- Cesium atoms vibrate at 9,192,631,770 times per second, exactly!

- Time kept by the standard atomic clock is officially called *Coordinated Universal Time.*

- Most calendar years are 365 days long. The longest year on record is 46 B.C., which was 445 days long. In order to align the calendar and the solar year, Roman officials added 90 days to the calendar that year.

- Earth's rotation around the sun is slowing down. In a few million years, leap years will not be needed.

- It takes 0.1 second for an Olympic sprinter to run 1m.

- It takes Saturn one billion seconds to complete an orbit around the sun.

- A flash of lightning lasts for about one millionth of a second.

To convert:	Into:	Multiply by:
Kilometers	Miles	0.6214
Miles	Kilometers	1.6093
Centimeters	Inches	0.3937
Inches	Centimeters	2.54
Kilograms	Pounds	2.2046
Pounds	Kilograms	0.4536
Liters	Pints	2.1138
Pints	Liters	0.4732
Liters	Gallons	0.2642
Gallons	Liters	3.7854

To convert:	Into:	Use the formula:
Celsius (°C)	Fahrenheit (°F)	°F = (°C × 1.8) + 32
Fahrenheit (°F)	Celsius (°C)	°C = (°F − 32) ÷ 1.8

Reading a Weather Chart

Charts can give you a picture of what the weather is going to be like for an area. Information about temperature, wind patterns, air pressure and precipitation can be read from a weather chart.

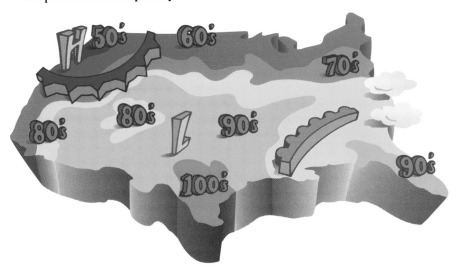

cold front

warm front

A line of triangles indicates a cold front. A line of semi-circles indicates a warm front. The symbols point in the direction the front is moving.

high pressure **low pressure**

A big H marks areas of high pressure. A big L marks areas of low pressure.

clouds

Wind and clouds move from high-pressure areas to low-pressure areas.

temperatures

100's 90's 80's 70's 60's 50's

Fast Facts

Fast Wind and Weather Facts

- Buffalo, New York, receives about 230 cm of snow per year. That's over 2 meters of snow!

- At 1909 meters, Mount Washington, New Hampshire, holds the world's record for the highest wind speed recorded on Earth. The recorded speed was 103.25 m/s.

- In a strong jet stream, a 727 airplane flying from Chicago to New York City can use up to 1892.7 fewer liters of fuel than it would if it were going in the opposite direction.

- The eastern Sahara gets unobstructed sunlight 97 percent of the time. It is the least cloudy place on Earth.

- At different temperatures, snowflakes have different shapes. The colder the air, the fluffier snowflakes tend to be. Fluffier snowflakes make snowfalls deeper.

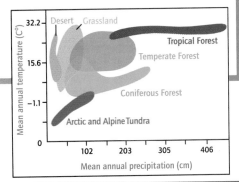

This climograph shows the annual mean temperatures and precipitation for several major North American biomes.

Our Solar System

Scientists have learned about our solar system through observation and from data gathered by different types of space probes. Much of what we know about our solar system, we know from our observation of Earth. We use Earth as a model when exploring other planets with telescopes and space probes.

INNER PLANETS
Diameter
Surface temperature range
Average distance from the s
Time taken to orbit the sun
Speed around sun
Time taken to rotate on its a
Number of Moons
Tilt

OUTER PLANETS	Jupiter	Saturn
Diameter	142,800 km	120,660 km
Surface temperature range	–148 °C	–178 °C
Average distance from the sun	483.6 million miles	887 million miles
Time taken to orbit the sun	11.86 Earth years	29.46 Earth years
Speed around sun	13 km per second	9.7 km per second
Time taken to rotate on its axis	10 Earth hours	10 Earth hours
Number of Moons	16	21
Tilt	3.08°	26.73°

(Art is not to scale.)

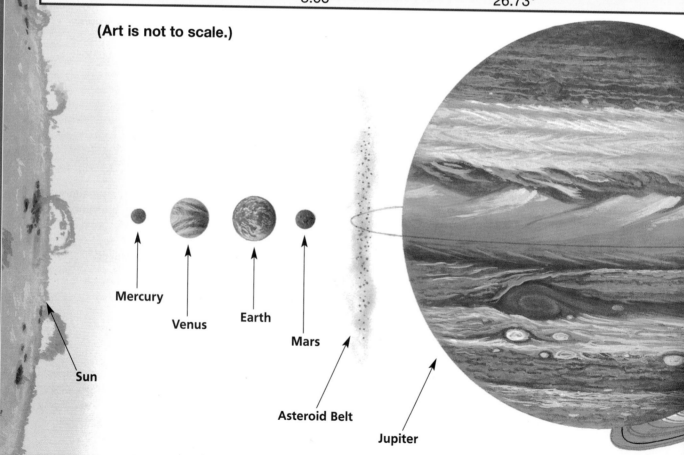

Sun

Mercury

Venus

Earth

Mars

Asteroid Belt

Jupiter

Mercury	Venus	Earth	Mars
878 km	12,104 km	12,756 km	6787 km
173 to +427 °C	462 °C	−89.6 to +58 °C	−143 to +17 °C
78.3 million km	1.43 billion km	2.87 billion km	4.5 billion km
8 Earth days	225 Earth days	365 Earth days	687 Earth days
8 km per second	35.4 km per second	30.5 km per second	24 km per second
9 Earth days	243 Earth days	1 Earth day	24.5 Earth hours
0	0	1	2
0°	178°	23.44°	23.98°

Uranus	Neptune	Pluto
51,000 km	49,500 km	2253 km
−216 °C	−214 °C	−233 to −223 °C
1,784 million miles	2,794 million miles	3,675 million miles
84.01 Earth years	164.79 Earth years	248.54 Earth years
6.4 km per second	4.8 km per second	4.8 km per second
17 Earth hours	16 Earth hours	6 Earth days, 9 hours
15	8	1
97.92°	28.80°	98.8°

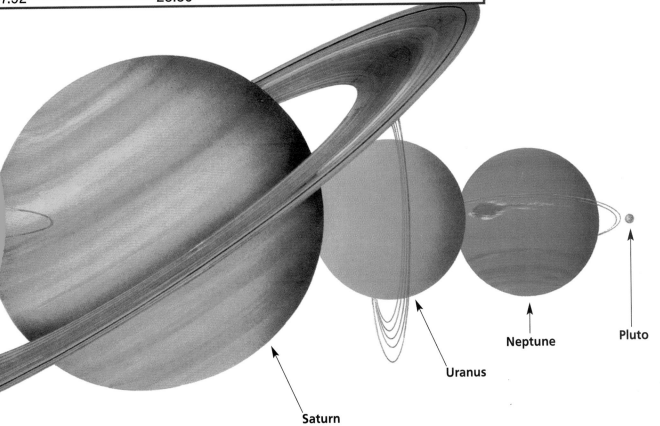

Saturn

Uranus

Neptune

Pluto

Glossary

A

abiotic nonliving

acid a substance that forms hydrogen ions as it dissolves in water

agriculture the science of producing food

air pressure the weight or density of air

amphibians cold-blooded animals with backbones; when young, they live in water and breathe with gills, and as adults, develop lungs and live on land

amplitude the height of a wave

angiosperm vascular plant that produces seeds inside fruits, which form from flowers

angle of incidence the angle at which the light ray from a source falls on a surface

aquaculture a way to raise fish without harming their natural environment; it is also called fish farming

arable land where soil is good for growing food

arteries the blood vessels through which blood is pumped away from the heart

arthropod an animal with a segmented body, an exoskeleton, and appendages

artificial satellite a satellite created by humans

asteroids thousands of minor planets in space

atherosclerosis a disease that can lead to blockages of the arteries in the heart and neck, resulting from a diet that is high in fat

atom the smallest unit of matter that cannot be broken down chemically

axon a long projection that connects a neuron to other neurons and carries messages away from the cell body

B

base a substance that dissolves in water and forms hydroxide ions

Big Bang theory a widely accepted theory about the origin of the universe; it states that 13 to 21 billion years ago, a fireball exploded, causing space, matter, and energy to spread apart

biodiversity the variety of plant and animal species that live in the same environment

biotic living

biomes stable communities of plants and animals in a particular geographic area with a distinct climate

birds warm-blooded vertebrates that have wings, a beak, two legs, and a feather-covered body; all birds lay eggs

black hole an object formed at the death of a large star; matter is condensed and its gravity field becomes so strong that light cannot escape

blood pressure the force of blood pushing against the walls of blood vessels

brain the main organ of the central nervous system; it is located inside the skull

brain stem a part of the brain that is located at the back of the skull and that connects the brain and the spinal cord; it contains the medulla, thalamic organs, and pons

C

canyon a narrow gorge or ravine with steep cliff walls; formed by a river or stream

carbohydrates substances in foods that break down into sugar and give the body energy

carbon cycle the continuous exchange of carbon dioxide and oxygen among producers, consumers, and the atmosphere

Glossary

carrying capacity the number of individuals and populations that can live in an environment

cell membrane outer covering of a cell

cell wall a structure in plants that surrounds the cell membrane and helps provide shape and support for the cell

Centers for Disease Control (CDC) a United States government agency that collects and reports on medical information from various groups

cerebellum the part of the brain that coordinates movement and helps keep balance; located at the back of the brain

cerebrum the largest part of the brain; it is where every intentional move is controlled and where thoughts and memories are located

chemical property a description of how a substance can react with another substance to form a new substance

chromosomes long, intertwined strands of chromatin, which hold the information for inherited traits

circulatory system the system that moves blood through the body

climate the typical weather in a place over a long period of time

cold front the boundary formed when a cold air mass moves into a region occupied by a warm air mass

comet a mass of frozen gases, dust, and rocky particles that orbits the sun

communicable disease an illness that spreads from person to person

community organisms sharing the same habitat

compound a substance formed by two or more elements

compression the process of squeezing together; one way mountains are formed

conduction when thermal energy flows from one body of matter to another through touch

conductors substances that conduct heat easily

conservation the planned use of natural resources to prevent their depletion, destruction, or neglect

consumers organisms that do not make their own food and eat other organisms

continental drift the theory that Earth's continents have moved over time

contraction when matter is cooled and its molecules take up less space

convection the transfer of thermal energy in a fluid

convergent boundary where two continental plates meet and converge or collide

cotyledons the parts of the plant seed that provide nutrients to the growing embryo

covalent bond when one or more pairs of electrons are shared between two atoms

crust the outermost layer of Earth

crustal movement the movement of the lithospheric pieces that causes the continents to shift

cytoplasm a clear, jelly-like substance on the inside of a cell

D

dendrites long projections from a neuron that conduct nerve impulses into the cell body

desalination the process in which salt water is changed into freshwater

dicot a plant seed with two cotyledons

discharge the amount of water running through a channel in a given period of time

diurnal tides when there is only one high tide and one low tide each day

Glossary

divergent boundary where two continental plates move away from one another

Doppler shift a change in wavelength frequency in electromagnetic waves, including light, sound, radio, and X rays

E

eclipse when one object passes into the shadow of another object

efficiency the percentage of energy that is converted into the desired form

electric power the rate at which electrical energy is used, measured in watts or joules of energy used in a second

electromagnetic waves waves composed of electric and magnetic fields that vibrate at right angles to each other

electrons negatively charged particles that move around the nucleus of an atom

elements substances made up of only one type of atom

ellipse an oval shape

environmental impact the effect of human activity on the total environment

epicenter the area on Earth's surface above the center of an earthquake

erosion the process by which weathered particles are carried away and redeposited through change

exosphere the part of Earth's atmosphere farthest from Earth's surface

expansion joints the spaces put between solid objects, such as sidewalk squares, to allow for expansion or contraction of the objects

F

fats high-energy, high-Calorie foods

fault place in Earth's crust where a rock mass has broken and moved in relation to another rock mass

fertilizer a chemical or organic substance that adds nutrients to soil

food web a series of interlinking food chains

fossil fuels fuels, including coal, oil, and natural gas, formed from once-living things decaying in the ground

frequency the number of wave crests that pass a point in one second

front the boundary between air masses

fungi a kingdom that includes plantlike organisms, such as mushrooms, molds, and yeast, that have no chlorophyll; they chemically break down other organic matter and absorb it as food

G

gene a group of DNA molecules on a chromosome

genus a category of living things that is smaller than a family and larger than a species

geologic eras major geologic time divisions

geothermal heat from Earth

glaciers large masses of moving ice

gymnosperms seed-bearing vascular plants that do not produce seeds in flowers and do not have fruits, but usually have cones

H

habitat the place and natural conditions, including biotic and abiotic factors, in which an animal or plant lives

heat the transfer of thermal energy between objects because of their difference in temperature

hemispheres the two halves of the brain

heredity the transfer of traits from one generation to the next

Glossary

hot spots areas where volcanoes form because of powerful pressures that push magma up through the crust

human immunodeficiency virus (HIV) the virus that causes AIDS

hurricanes cyclonic storms that develop at sea when warm, moist air rotates around a low-pressure center

hydrocarbons organic compounds containing carbon and hydrogen

hydroelectric power the production of energy by water power

hydroponics growing plants without soil

I

igneous rocks rocks that are created from cooled magma

immune system a complex body system that helps fight off invading germs

immunity the body's resistance to disease

indicator a compound that will change color when it is in contact with an acid or a base

inexhaustible resources resources that are always available, such as wind and solar power

infectious a kind of disease that is caused by a germ infecting or invading the body

infrared rays rays of energy that when absorbed by an object, warm the object

inorganic a kind of material formed from minerals, not from plant or animal material

insulators materials that slow down or prevent the flow of thermal energy

International Space Station a space station being constructed cooperatively by many nations

invertebrates animals without backbones

ion a charged particle formed when atoms gain or lose one or more electrons

ionic bonding bonding between atoms when electrons transfer from one atom to another

J

Jovian planets the large, outer planets made of gas—Jupiter, Saturn, Uranus, and Neptune

K

kingdom the largest and most general classification, or grouping, of living things

L

landslides movements of soil and rocks down hillsides

latitude distance measured in degrees north or south of the equator

lava magma that rises to Earth's surface

lithosphere the layer of Earth made up of the crust and the upper mantle; it is divided into seven large and several smaller pieces of rock

lymphatic system a part of the immune system that transports nutrients too large to enter the bloodstream and removes waste

M

magma molten rock inside Earth

mammals warm-blooded vertebrates with hair that produce milk for their young

mantle the middle layer of Earth; it is made up mostly of iron, magnesium, silicon, and oxygen

marine saltwater biome in the oceans, in which the salt content is around 3.5 percent

mechanical energy the energy of moving parts

Glossary

meiosis a type of cell division that produces cells that have half as many chromosomes as the parent cell

meninges three layers of protective membrane separated by fluid that are wrapped around the brain and spinal cord

mesosphere the layer of atmosphere that extends from about 50 km to 80 km above Earth's surface

metallic core the center of Earth; it is made up of iron and nickel

metallic minerals kinds of minerals that are a source of metals

metamorphic rocks rocks that form from other rocks that undergo a major change due to heat or pressure

meteors small chunks of orbiting matter that have reached Earth's atmosphere

minerals elements or compounds that occur in nature, are inorganic, and have their own crystalline shape; chemical elements that help your bones, blood, and tissues

mitochondria bean-shaped organelles in the cytoplasm of a cell that provide energy to the cell

mitosis the process in which a cell divides into two identical cells, each having the same number and type of chromosomes as the original cell

monera kingdom that includes one-celled organisms that lack a nucleus

monocot a plant seed with a single cotyledon

N

National Institutes of Health (NIH) a United States government agency based in Maryland that collects and reports on medical information from various groups

nebula a low-density cloud of gas and dust in space

neurons nerve cells

neutral describes a solution that is neither an acid nor a base

neutron a part of the nucleus of an atom that has no charge, or is neutral

nitrogen cycle the continuous movement of nitrogen in an ecosystem

nonmetallic minerals kinds of minerals that do not contain metal

nonrenewable resources resources that cannot be replenished within 30 years, such as oil and coal

nuclear membrane the outer covering of the nucleus of a cell

nucleus the tiny, very dense center of an atom that contains protons and neutrons; a small organelle inside a cell that contains most of the cell's hereditary material

nutrients materials that living things need for survival

O

occluded front a cold front that overtakes another cold front

opaque the characteristic of materials that light rays do not pass through

orbit a planet's path through space and around the sun

ores deposits of rocks and minerals large enough to be worth mining

organic having to do with or coming from living things

P

Pangaea the name given to the theoretical supercontinent that existed before the continental plates started to separate

parallax the difference in apparent direction of an object as seen from two different points

Glossary

phloem tissue in vascular plants that carries water, nutrients, and waste materials throughout the plant

phylum a category of living things that is smaller than a kingdom and larger than a class

planet one of the heavenly bodies circling the sun

plate tectonics theory the idea that Earth is made of continental and oceanic plates, which move

plates the large moving pieces of Earth's crust and mantle

polar zones areas above 60 °N and 60 °S latitudes that have low temperatures all year

pollution harmful materials, such as chemicals and exhaust, that contaminate Earth's air, water, and soil

population all the organisms of the same species that live in an area

producers organisms that produce their own food, especially green plants

proteins nutrients made of amino acids that are necessary for growth and repair of the body's cells

protista a kingdom that includes single-celled organisms that have nuclei and organelles

proton a positively charged part of the nucleus of an atom

Q

quarantine the separation of people with highly contagious communicable diseases from other people

R

radiant energy energy transferred by waves from warmer objects to cooler objects

radiation the transfer of thermal energy through air and space

radiation balance the balance maintained by Earth's receiving solar radiation and releasing an equal amount of energy

recycle to find a different way for material to be used again

red shift an indicator that a light source is moving away from an observer

reduce to use less of a material

reflection when light or other electromagnetic waves bounce off a surface

refraction the bending of a light wave as it enters a different medium

renewable resources resources that can be replenished within 30 years, such as wood and compost

reproduction the process through which a living thing produces new organisms like itself

reservoirs pockets of oil or natural gas formed over time in sediment

reuse to use a material more than once

ribosomes complex organelles in cytoplasm that produce proteins

Richter scale a scale for describing the measurement of the seismic waves of an earthquake

Ring of Fire zone that circles the Pacific Ocean where many volcanic eruptions occur

rock cycle the constant change of rocks caused by chemical and physical processes on and below Earth's surface

rockets tubes filled with fuel that can be launched into space by the force created when their fuel burns

rotation a spinning motion; Earth rotates on its axis

Glossary

S

salt a chemical compound that contains a positive ion from a base and a negative ion from an acid

sediment rocks, sand, or dirt that has been carried to a place by water, wind, or a glacier

sedimentary rocks rocks that form when sediment is pressed together over time

semidiurnal tides when an area has two high tides and two low tides daily

shuttle a reusable spacecraft

siltation when fine particles are deposited at the bottom of a lake or river

solar radiation energy released by the sun

solar system the planets that move around a star

space probes rocket-launched space vehicles loaded with instruments and cameras to gather data

species the specific group to which an organism is related; a group of similar organisms that can mate and produce offspring

spinal column the row of bones, called vertebrae, in the middle of the back that contains and protects the spinal cord

spinal cord the part of the central nervous system that links the body and the brain; located inside the spinal column

spiral galaxy a disk-shaped galaxy with arms that rotate around a dense center

stationary front a warm or cold front that stops moving for a period of time

stratosphere the layer of atmosphere that lies from 11 to 50 km above Earth's surface

strip mining stripping away layers of soil and rock overlaying mineral deposits near Earth's surface

subduction when one continental plate slips under the plate with which it is colliding

succession the process of plant and animal populations replacing other populations over time

supernova an explosion of a star

synapse the space between neurons

T

temperate zones areas between the tropics and the polar regions that have mild or moderate temperatures

temperature a measure of the average kinetic energy of the molecules within matter

terrestrial planets solid, rocklike, and dense planets; the inner planets— Mercury, Venus, Earth, and Mars

theory an organized set of observations, ideas, and experimental evidence designed to predict or explain an event

thermal energy the total kinetic energy in the molecules of a sample of matter

thermal expansion the transfer of thermal energy that makes molecules spread out

thermosphere the layer of atmosphere that begins 80 km above Earth's surface and extends to outer space

topography a detailed illustration of the physical features of an area of Earth's surface

tornadoes powerful winds that can form during storms and move in narrow paths over land

toxins poisons that kill cells or interfere with normal functioning

transform boundary where two plates slide past one another, or in the same direction, but at different speeds

Glossary

translucent the characteristic of a material that lets light rays pass through but scatters them so no clear image forms

transparent the characteristic of a material that light passes through easily

tropical zone the area north and south of the equator where the sun's rays fall most directly

troposphere the layer of atmosphere closest to Earth

tsunami a seismic sea wave

turbines wheels with blades powered by a fluid that convert steam energy to electrical energy

V

vacuoles the cell's reservoirs for water, minerals, and other nutrients

veins the blood vessels through which blood is pumped to the heart

vertebrates animals with backbones

viruses small, nonliving bits of nucleic acid and protein

vitamins chemical compounds that help the cells function

volunteer to give freely

W

warm front the boundary formed when a warm air mass overtakes a cold air mass

water cycle the continual movement of water from one place to another

wavelength the distance between a point on one wave and the identical point on the next wave

waves rhythmic disturbances that carry energy through matter and space

weathering the breaking down of rocks into smaller pieces through natural conditions, both physical and chemical

wind movement of air

windfarms windmills grouped together to produce electrical energy

World Health Organization (WHO) an international organization through which different countries work together to prevent disease

X

xylem tissue in vascular plants that carries water and nutrients up from the roots of the plant

Index

Index

Index

Index

Index

Index

M

macronutrients, D64
  carbohydrates, D65
  fats, D66
  proteins, D65
  vegetables, D65
magma, B49–B50, B102, B111
malaria, D29
malnutrition, D82
mammals, A31
mammary glands, A31
mantle, B90, B93
marine, A55
Mariner 10, B145
Mars, B144, B146
marsupials, A31
mass, C55–C56, C76
matter, C76–C85
  chemical properties, C80–C81, C86–C87, C98
  physical properties, C76–C80, C98
  states, C78
measles, D29, D35
mechanical energy, C29, C57
meiosis, A87–A88
melting point, C78
Mendeleyev, Dmitry, C89
meninges, D15
Mercury, B144, B145
mesosphere, B10
metallic core, B90
metallic elements, C89
metallic minerals, B67
metamorphic rocks, B49–B50
metamorphosis, A29
metaphase, A85–A87
meteoroids, B149
meteorologists, B28–B29, B31, B33
meteors, B149
methane, B12
micronutrients, D63

  minerals, D63
  vitamins, D63
Milky Way, B158–B159
minerals, B44–B47, B52–B53, B64, B66–B67, D63
mirrors, C16–C17
  concave, C17
  convex, C17
mitochondria, A74–A79
mitosis, A85–A86, A88, A90–A91
Mohs Scale of Mineral Hardness, B47
molecules, C47–C48, C89, C93
mollusks, A25–A26
molting, A27, A30
monera, A7, A78
monocot, A21
mononucleosis, D30
monotremes, A31
moon, B136–B139
mosses, A16
motor neurons, D9, D11
mountains
  compression, B104
  fault-block mountains, B105, B109
  folded mountains, B104
mucous membranes, D32
mumps, D29, D35
muscular system, D33
mushrooms, A11–A13
mycelium, A10
myelin, D6–D7

N

National Institutes of Health (NIH), D49
natural gas, B69, C67, C70
natural resources, B64–B75, C30, C66–C71
  fossil fuels, B64, B68–B71, C10, C30, C66–C71
  metallic minerals, B67
  minerals, B44–B47,

  B52–B53, B64, B66–B67, D63
  natural gas, B69, C67, C70
  nonmetallic minerals, B67
  ores, B67
  petroleum, B69
nearsighted, C23
nebula, B157
Neptune, B144, B147
nerve cells, D4–D5
  axon, D7
  dendrites, D6–D7
  myelin, D6–D7
  synapse, D6–D7
nerve impulses, D7
nerve tissues, D7
nervous system, A26, D4–D13
  central nervous system, D4–D9
  peripheral nervous system, D4–D5, D9–D11
neurons, D4, D6–D7, D9, D11–D13
  connecting neurons, D9
  motor neurons, D9, D11
  sensory neurons, D9, D11
neutral, C103–C104
neutrons, C84
neutron star, B157
Newton, Sir Isaac, B153
niche, A41
nitrogen cycle, A64
nonmetallic, B67
nonrenewable resources, B71, C30
nonvascular plants, A16
nuclear energy, B70, C57
nuclear membrane, A74, A77, A86

Index

Index

Index

Index

Credits

Photo Credits

Covers, Title Page, Unit Openers, Dave Schiefelbein/Tony Stone Images; **iv (t),** Victoria McCormick/Earth Scenes, **(b),** ©Tom & Pat Leeson/Photo Researchers, Inc.; **v,** T.A. Wiewandt/DRK Photo; **vi (b),** Thomas Schitt/The Image Bank, **(t),** Tom McCarthy/PhotoEdit; **vii (t),** Visuals Unlimited/©John Sohlden, **(b),** Stephen J. Krasemann/DRK Photo; **viii (t),** ©JISAS/Lockheed/Science Photo Library/Photo Researchers, Inc., **(b),** ©Alfred Pasieka/Science Photo Library/Photo Researchers, Inc.; **ix,** ©KS Studios; **x,** Richard Hutchings/PhotoEdit; **xi (t),** Michael Newman/PhotoEdit, **(b),** Ken Straiton/The Stock Market; **xii, xiii, xiv, xv,** Matt Meadows; **A2-A3,** Victoria McCormick/Earth Scenes; **A5 (t),** Wayne Lankinen/DRK Photo, **(c, b),** ©Stephen Dalton/Photo Researchers, Inc.; **A8 (tl),** Visuals Unlimited/©Michael Abbey, **(bl),** BioPhoto Associates/Photo Researchers, Inc., **(br),** ©Nuridsany et Perennou/Photo Researchers, Inc.; **A11,** ©KS Studios; **A12, A13,** ©Matt Meadows; **A15,** Corbis/Paul A. Souders; **A16,** BioPhoto Associates/Photo Researchers, Inc.; **A17,** Jane Grushow from Grant Heilman; **A23,** Studiohio; **A25 (tl),** I. Newman & A. Flowers/Photo Researchers, Inc., **(tr),** Neil McDaniel/Photo Researchers, Inc.; **A27 (t),** Runk/Schoenberger from Grant Heilman, **(ct),** Stanley Breeden/DRK Photo, **(cb),** Jone McDonald/DRK Photo, **(bl),** Stephen J. Krasemann/DRK Photo, **(br),** Norbert Wu/DRK Photo; **A28 (l),** Anthony Mercieca/Photo Researchers, Inc., **(r),** Steve Skjold/PhotoEdit; **A30 (t),** Robert H. Potts/Photo Researchers, Inc., **(b),** Corbis/Peggy Heard/Frank Lane Picture Agency; **A31 (t),** Fritz Prenzel/Animals Animals, **(c),** Pat & Tom Leeson/Photo Researchers, Inc., **(b),** Tom Brakefield/DRK Photo; **A32, A33,** ©Matt Meadows; **A36-A37,** Tom & Pat Leeson/Photo Researchers, Inc.; **A39,** Pat O'Hara/DRK Photo; **A40,** John Cancalosi/Tom Stack & Associates; **A41,** ©Isaac Geib from Grant Heilman; **A42 (t),** Jeffrey Hutcherson/DRK Photo, **(bl),** L. West/Photo Researchers, Inc., **(br),** Denise Tackett/Tom Stack & Associates; **A43 (tr),** John Shaw/Tom Stack & Associates, **(bl),** Rod Planck/Tom Stack & Associates, **(br),** ©Michael P. Gadomski/Photo Researchers, Inc.; **A46, A47,** ©David Young-Wolff/PhotoEdit; **A49,** Fred Bruemmer/DRK Photo; **A52 (t),** Tom Bean/DRK Photo, **(b),** Arthur C. Smith III from Grant Heilman Photography; **A53 (t),** Lynn M. Stone/DRK Photo, **(b),** Doug Sokell/Tom Stack & Associates; **A54 (t),** Jeremy Woodhouse/DRK Photo, **(b),** Tom Bean/DRK Photo; **A56, A57,** ©Matt Meadows; **A66, A67,** ©KS Studios; **A70-A71,** T.A. Wiewandt/DRK Photo; **A73,** Runk/Schoenberger from Grant Heilman; **A80, A81,** ©Matt Meadows; **A83,** ©Lawrence Migdale; **A85,** Runk/Schoenberger from Grant Heilman Photography; **A88 (t),** ©L. Willatt, East Anglian Regional Genetics Service/Science Photo Library/Photo Researchers, Inc., **(b),** ©Carolyn A. McKeone/Photo Researchers, Inc.; **A89,** Savage/The Stock Market; **A90, A91, A95,** ©Matt Meadows; **B2-B3,** Tom McCarthy/PhotoEdit; **B5 (t),** Nicolas Le Corre/Liaison Agency, **(b),** Christi Carter from Grant Heilman; **B6,** Brian Milne/Earth Scenes; **B8,** P. Baeza/Publiphoto/Photo Researchers, Inc.; **B10,** NASA/Peter Arnold; **B11,** Silver Image; **B12,** Winston Patnode/Photo Researchers, Inc.; **B13,** Wesley Bocxe/Photo Researchers, Inc.; **B14,** Grantpix/Photo Researchers, Inc.; **B16, B17,** ©KS Studios; **B19 (l),** David R. Frazier/Photo Researchers, Inc., **(r),** Maresa Pryor/Earth Scenes; **B20,** Ken Cole/Earth Scenes; **B22,** Gary Braasch and Dennis Wianko; **B26, B27,** ©Matt Meadows; **B31,** E.R. Degginger/Earth Scenes; **B32,** Jose L. Pelaez/The Stock Market; **B35,** Larry Miller/Photo Researchers, Inc; **B38,** ©KS Studios; **B42-B43,** Thomas Schitt/The Image Bank; **B45 (t),** Corbis, **(cl, bl),** ©Matt Meadows, **(cr),** ©KS Studios; **B46 (t),** Aaron Haupt/Photo Researchers, Inc., **(c),** Charles D. Winters/Photo Researchers, Inc., **(b),** J & L Weber/Peter Arnold, Inc.; **B47,** Brent Turner/BLT Productions; **B48,** Sylvain Grandadam/Photo Researchers, Inc.; **B49,** Joyce Photographics/Photo Researchers, Inc.; **B51,** Breck P. Kent/Earth Scenes; **B52,** ©Brent Turner/BLT Productions; **B55,** Corbis/Bettmann; **B57,** Tom Bean/DRK Photo; **B58,** Porterfield/Chickering/Photo Researchers, Inc.; **B59,** Jim Wark/Peter Arnold, Inc.; **B60,** **(t),** Visuals Unlimited/©McCutcheon, **(b),** Tom McHugh/Photo Researchers, Inc.; **B61 (t),** Stephen J. Krasemann/DRK Photo, **(b),** Visuals Unlimited/©James R. McCullagh; **B62, B63,** ©KS Studios; **B65,** Brownie Harris/The Stock Market; **B66,** **(t),** Harvey Lloyd/Peter Arnold, Inc, **(b),** ©David Young-Wolff/PhotoEdit; **B67,** Jeff Greenberg/The Image Works; **B68,** Kaj R. Svensson/Science Photo Library/Photo Researchers, Inc.; **B69,** Fred Busk III/Peter Arnold, Inc; **B70,** Daniele Pellegrini/Photo Researchers, Inc.; **B71,** Roy Morsch/The Stock Market; **B72, B73,** ©Matt Meadows; **B75 (t),** Grapes/Michaud/Photo Researchers, Inc., **(b),** David M. Dennis/Tom Stack & Associates; **B76,** Charles M. Falco/Photo Researchers, Inc.; **B77,** Corbis/Annie Griffiths Belt; **B79 (t),** ©Corbis/Bettmann, **(b),** ©Jim Baron/The Image Finders; **B80,** John Deeks/Photo Researchers, Inc; **B82, B83,** ©Matt Meadows; **B86-B87,** Visuals Unlimited/©John Sohlden; **B89 (l),** Doug Cheeseman/Peter Arnold, Inc., **(r),** Tamas Revesz/Peter Arnold, Inc.; **B94 (l),** M. Mastrorill/The Stock Market, **(r),** Ary Diesendruck/Tony Stone Images; **B100,** Lewis Kemper/DRK Photo; **B101,** Kevin Schafer/Peter Arnold, Inc.; **B103 (t),** Visuals Unlimited/©Peter Dunwiddie, **(b),** Stephen and Donna O'Meara/Photo Researchers, Inc.; **B104,** Bill O'Connor/Peter Arnold, Inc.; **B105,** Gunter Ziesler/Peter Arnold, Inc.; **B106, B107,** ©Matt Meadows; **B109,** K.D. McGraw from Rainbow; **B110,** John Kapreilian/Photo Researchers, Inc.; **B111,** M. Colbek/Earth Scenes; **B112,** Dr. Ken Macdonald/Science Photo Library/Photo Researchers, Inc.; **B113,** Ragnar Larusson/Photo Researchers, Inc.; **B116, B117,** ©Matt Meadows; **B119,** Stephen J. Krasemann/Photo Researchers, Inc.; **B122,** **(t),** Tom Bean/DRK Photo, **(b),** Larry Ulrich/DRK Photo; **B123,** US Geological Survey/Science Photo Library/Photo Researchers, Inc.; **B124,** Michael Fredericks/Earth Scenes; **B126, B127,** ©Matt Meadows; **B130-B131,** Stephen J. Krasemann/DRK Photo; **B133,** NASA; **B139,** Dr. Fred Espenak/Science Photo Library/Photo Researchers, Inc.; **B141,** ©Matt Meadows; **B143,** NASA/Science Photo Library/Photo Researchers, Inc.; **B144,** NASA/Photo Researchers, Inc.; **B145,** NASA; **B146 (t),** NASA, **(b),** NASA/Science Photo Library/Photo Researchers, Inc.; **B147 (t),** NASA/Photo Researchers, Inc., **(c),** NASA, **(b),** W. Kaufmann/JPL/Photo Researchers, Inc.; **B148 (t),** NASA, **(b),** Pekka Parviainen/Science Photo Library/Photo Researchers, Inc.; **B150,** ©Matt Meadows; **B153 (t),** ©NASA/Science Photo Library/Photo Researchers, Inc., **(b),** Space Telescope Science Institute/NASA/Science Photo, Library/Photo Researchers, Inc.; **B154,** Hale Observatories/Photo Researchers, Inc.; **B156,** Fred Espenak/Science Photo Library/Photo Researchers, Inc. **B157 (t),** Royal Observatory, Edinburgh/Science Photo Library/Photo Researchers, Inc., **(b),** Space Telescope Science Institute/NASA/Science Photo Library/Photo Researchers, Inc.; **B160,** ©Matt Meadows; **B165 (t),** Michael J. Howell from Rainbow, **(c),** Malcolm S. Kirk/Peter Arnold, Inc., **(b),** ©Dewey Vanderhoff; **B166 (t),** Peter Bassett/Science Photo Library/Photo Researchers, Inc., **(b),** NASA/Science Photo Library/Photo Researchers, Inc.; **B167,** Corbis/Bettmann; **B168,** Corbis/AFP; **B170, B171,** ©Matt Meadows; **B175,** ©KS Studios; **C2-C3,** JISAS/Lockheed/Science Photo Library/Photo Researchers, Inc.; **C5,** Inner Light/The Image Bank; **C7,** Dr. R. Clark & M. Goff/Science Photo Library/Photo Researchers, Inc.; **C12, C13,** ©KS Studios; **C15,** ©Matt Meadows; **C16,** Platinum Studios; **C18,** Phillip Hayson/Photo Researchers, Inc.; **C21,** ©KS Studios; **C25,** Alfred Pasieka/Peter Arnold, Inc.; **C27 (t),** David Parker/Science Photo Library/Photo Researchers, Inc., **(b),** ©KS Studios; **C29,** Tom Lang/The Stock Market; **C30 (tl),** Tom & Pat Leeson/Photo Researchers, Inc., **(tr),** R.V. Fuschetto/Photo Researchers, Inc., **(bl),** St. Meyers/Okapia/Photo Researchers, Inc., **(br),** Visuals Unlimited/©Inga Spence; **C31 (t),** Calvin Larsen/Photo Researchers, Inc., **(b),** Lowell Georgia/Photo Researchers, Inc.; **C32 (t),** Vandystadt/Photo Researchers, Inc., **(b),** Eunice Harris/Photo Researchers, Inc.; **C33,** Jeff Greenberg/Peter Arnold, Inc.; **C34,** Scottish Hydroelectric Plant; **C35,** John Cancalosi/Peter Arnold, Inc.; **C36 (t),** Helga Lade/Peter Arnold, Inc., **(c),** Visuals Unlimited/©Kevin and Betty Collins, **(b),** Stephen J. Krasemann/Peter Arnold, Inc.; **C37,** Hank Morgan/Photo Researchers, Inc.; **C38, C39,** ©KS Studios; **C42-C43,** Alfred Pasieka/Science Photo Library/Photo Researchers, Inc.; **C45,** Adam Hart-David/Science Photo Library/Photo Researchers, Inc.; **C46 (t),** Gabor Demjen/Stock Boston, **(b),** ©Matt Meadows; **C47,** Jerry Schad/Photo Researchers, Inc.; **C48,** ©Matt Meadows; **C49 (t),** Michael Newman/PhotoEdit, **(b),** ©KS Studios; **C50,** ©David Young-Wolff/PhotoEdit; **C51,** Jeff Greenberg/PhotoEdit; **C52, C53,** Studiohio; **C56 (t),** First Image, **(bl),** Richard Choy/Peter Arnold, Inc., **(br),** Ray Pfortner/Peter Arnold, Inc.; **C58,** Corbis/Richard Hamilton Smith; **C61,** ©KS Studios; **C62,** Brent Turner/BLT Productions; **C65,** Visuals/Unlimited/©John Sohlden; **C66,** S.D. Halperin/Earth Scenes; **C67,** Visuals Unlimited/©Inga Spence; **C70,** Visuals Unlimited/©W.A. Banaszewski; **C72,** Studiohio; **C76-C77,** ©KS Studios; **C79,** Stephen Saks/Photo Researchers, Inc.; **C80 (tl),** Michael Newman/PhotoEdit, **(tr),** Tony Freeman/PhotoEdit, **(c),** First Image, **(b),** Mark M. Lawrence/The Stock Market; **C81,** Charles D. Winters/Photo Researchers, Inc.; **C85,** Fermilab/Peter Arnold, Inc.; **C89 (t),** Neal & Mary Mishler/Tony Stone Images, **(b),** ©Matt Meadows; **C93 (t),** Barry L. Runk from Grant Heilman, **(b),** First Image; **C96, C97,** Studiohio; **C99,** ©KS Studios; **C100,** ©David Young-Wolff/PhotoEdit **C101 (l),** Clyde H. Smith/Peter Arnold, Inc., **(r),** Rosenfeld Images LTD/Science Photo Library/Photo Researchers, Inc.; **C103,** Photography by Rannels from Grant Heilman; **C104 (l),** ©David Young-Wolff/PhotoEdit, **(r),** Richard Gross/The Stock Market; **C105 (l),** Richard Hutchings/PhotoEdit, **(r),** Frank Siteman/Stock Boston; **C106, C107, C111,** ©KS Studios; **D2-D3,** Richard Hutchings/PhotoEdit; **D5,** ©David Young-Wolff/PhotoEdit; **D9,** Tom Prettman/PhotoEdit; **D10,** Michael Newman/PhotoEdit; **D12, D13,** ©Matt Meadows; **D15,** Alfred Pasieka/Science Photo Library/Photo Researchers, Inc.; **D18,** ©KS Studios; **D19,** ©David Young-Wolff/PhotoEdit; **D20,** Corbis/Kevin R. Morris; **D21,** Myrleen Cate/PhotoEdit; **D22, D23,** ©Matt Meadows; **D26-D27,** Ken Straiton/The Stock Market; **D29,** Jeffry Myers/Stock Boston; **D30,** Matt Meadows/Peter Arnold, Inc.; **D36,** ©KS Studios; **D37,** ©M. Wurtz/Biozentrum, University of Basel/Science Photo Library/Photo Researchers, Inc.; **D39,** Richard Brooks/Photo Researchers, Inc.; **D40,** Calvin Larsen/Photo Researchers, Inc.; **D41,** Tom McHugh/Photo Researchers, Inc.; **D42,** Corbis/Leif Skoogfors; **D43,** Ray Pfortner/Peter Arnold, Inc.; **D44,** Jeff Greenberg/PhotoEdit; **D45,** Skjoil/PhotoEdit; **D46, D47,** ©KS Studios; **D49 (t),** Matt Meadows/Peter Arnold, Inc., **(b),** Jeff Greenberg/PhotoEdit; **D50,** Corbis/Joseph Sohm/ChromoSohm, Inc.; **D51,** Corbis/Richard Ellis/Cordai Photo Library Ltd.; **D52,** Patrick Robert/SYGMA; **D53,** Michael Newman/PhotoEdit; **D54,** Zeva Oelbaum/Peter Arnold, Inc; **D55,** ©NASA/Science Photo Library/Photo Researchers, Inc.; **D56,** ©Matt Meadows; **D60-D61,** Michael Newman/PhotoEdit; **D64, D67, D68,** ©KS Studios; **D69,** First Image; **D70,** ©Matt Meadows; **D74,** David Madison; **D76,** Ed Bock/The Stock Market; **D78,** Roda Sidney/PhotoEdit; **D79,** BioPhoto Associates/Photo Researchers, Inc.; **D80, D81,** ©Matt Meadows; **D83,** Roland Birke/Peter Arnold, Inc.; **D85,** Jerry Irwin/Photo Researchers, Inc.; **D86,** John Kieffer/Peter Arnold, Inc.; **D88,** Arthur C. Smith III from Grant Heilman Photography; **D90, D91,** ©Matt Meadows; **D95,** ©KS Studios; **R4 (t),** IFA/Peter Arnold, Inc., **(cl),** Elisabeth Weiland/Photo Researchers, Inc., **(cr),** Holt Studios International/Photo Researchers, Inc., **(b),** Chuck Dresner/DRK Photo; **R5 (tl),** Tom McHugh/Photo Researchers, Inc., **(tr),** Tom & Pat Leeson/DRK Photo, **(tcr),** Tom Brakefield/DRK Photo, **(btl),** Doug Cheeseman/Peter Arnold, Inc, **(bl),** John Cancalosi/DRK Photo, **(bc),** James P. Rowan/DRK Photo, **(br),** Stephen J. Krasemann/DRK Photo; **R7 (cow),** Clyde H. Smith/Peter Arnold, Inc., **(eggs),** ©KS Studios, **(oranges),** Doug Martin, **(pig),** Nigel Cattlin/Holt Studios International/Photo Researchers, Inc, **(tc),** ©David Young-Wolff/PhotoEdit, **(tl),** David Schleser/Photo Researchers, Inc., **(tr),** Stephen J. Krasemann/DRK Photo; **R10 (t),** Alexander Tsiaras/Photo Researchers, Inc., **(b),** OMIKRON/Photo Researchers, Inc.

Art Credits

A7 A19 A26 A73 A75 A76 A77 A78 A79 Precision Graphics; **B21** SRA; **B92** Ortelius Design; **B93 B143** Rolin Graphics Inc.; **C5 C6 C8 C9** Precision Graphics; **C18 C23** Chris Higgins/PP/FA; **C67 C84 C90** Precision Graphics; **D5 D6 D7 D8 D11 D15 D16 D17 D30** Rolin Graphics Inc.; **D31** Precision Graphics; **D32 D33 D34 D73 D74 D75 D76 D77 D84** Rolin Graphics Inc.